Susanne Knaller (ed.)
Writing Facts

**Lettre**

**Susanne Knaller** (Prof. Dr.) teaches cultural studies and general and comparative literature at the Karl-Franzens-Universität Graz. In 2002, she received her habilitation at Johann Wolfgang Goethe-Universität Frankfurt am Main. In 2009, she founded the research department General and Comparative Literature (AVL) in Graz. Since 2013, she has been the director of the Centre for Cultural Studies. Her research focuses on aesthetic theories 18th to 21st century, theory of authenticity, concepts of reality in modernity, emotion theories, writing as practice.

Susanne Knaller (ed.)
# Writing Facts
Interdisciplinary Discussions of a Key Concept in Modernity

[transcript]

**Bibliographic information published by the Deutsche Nationalbibliothek**
The Deutsche Nationalbibliothek lists this publication in the Deutsche Nationalbibliografie; detailed bibliographic data are available in the Internet at http://dnb.d-nb.de

This work is licensed under the Creative Commons Attribution 4.0 (BY) license, which means that the text may be remixed, transformed and built upon and be copied and redistributed in any medium or format even commercially, provided credit is given to the author.
Creative Commons license terms for re-use do not apply to any content (such as graphs, figures, photos, excerpts, etc.) not original to the Open Access publication and further permission may be required from the rights holder. The obligation to research and clear permission lies solely with the party re-using the material.

First published in 2023 by transcript Verlag, Bielefeld

© Susanne Knaller (ed.)

Cover layout: Kordula Röckenhaus, Bielefeld
Copy-editing: Gero von Roedern, Riccardo Schöfberger
Proofread: Gero von Roedern, Riccardo Schöfberger
Printed by: Majuskel Medienproduktion GmbH, Wetzlar
https://doi.org/10.14361/9783839462713
Print-ISBN 978-3-8376-6271-9
PDF-ISBN 978-3-8394-6271-3
ISSN of series: 2703-013X
eISSN of series: 2703-0148

Printed on permanent acid-free text paper.

# Contents

**Writing Facts**
A Short Introduction
*Susanne Knaller (University of Graz)* .............................................. 9

## THEORY AND HISTORY

**Facts in Modernity**
A Multifarious History of Meanings, Forms, and Purposes
*Susanne Knaller (University of Graz)* .............................................. 29

**Writing as a Cultural Way of Fact-Making**
Modest Reflections on the Genesis, Role, and Status of Facts
*Ansgar Nünning (University of Giessen)* .......................................... 53

**Facts**
What We Know about Them in the Postmodern Era
*Philipp Sarasin (University of Zurich)* ............................................ 85

## WRITING SOCIETY, POLITICS, AND LAW

**Writing Social Facts**
Some Observations on Max Weber's Concept of Modern Politics
*Harro Müller (Columbia University in the City of New York)* ........................ 93

**Writing 'Volksgemeinschaft' into 'Fact'**
Letters from the National Socialist Labor Service (RAD)
*Gero von Roedern (University of Graz)* ............................................ 107

**Manufacturing Legal Facts**
Kristin Y. Albrecht (University of Salzburg); Sebastian Ibing (Prosecutor Office in Germany) .................................................................. 125

## LITERATURE AND ARTS

**Towards a Poetics of Fact**
Subjugated Knowledges, Historiographic Metafiction, and the 'Terrible Truth' behind Words in Early Nineteenth-Century American Literature
Stefan L. Brandt (University of Graz).............................................. 143

**'Writing Facts' and 19th-Century English Realist Fiction**
Theoretical Reflections and the Complexity of the Relationship in Charles Dickens' *Hard Times*, and George Eliots *Adam Bede*
Werner Wolf (University of Graz) ................................................. 163

**A 'Real' Novel?**
Narrating Facts in *El hombre que amaba a los perros*
Iyari Martínez Márquez (Universidade Católica Portuguesa) ....................... 191

**Rewriting Gender?**
(De)constructions of Masculinities between Scientific Discourse and Literary Practice
Riccardo Schöfberger (University of Graz).......................................... 205

**The Loss of Biodiversity in the Anthropocene and Its Representations in Literature and the Arts (Late 20th and Early 21st Century)**
Annette Simonis (University of Giessen)............................................221

**"One + One is one two. Two is one two"**
(De-)Construction of Facts and Documentarism in Hanne Darboven's *Schreibzeit* (1975-1999)
Monika Voithofer (University of Vienna) ........................................ 239

# MEDIA AND WRITING PRACTICE

### An Iterative Poetics of Writing Facts
Louis de Cahusac's *La Danse Ancienne et Moderne ou Traité Historique de la Danse* (1754)
*Rita Rieger (University of Graz)* ............................................. 255

### Snapshot and Wage Table
The Importance of Facts in the Reports of Hugo von Kupffer (1853-1928) and Max Winter (1870-1937)
*Mario Huber (University of Graz)* ............................................. 273

### (Body) Positivity in Social Media
Mise-en-scène and Performing Digital Facticity
*Elke Höfler (University of Graz)* ............................................. 291

### 'Patchwriting' as Unintentional Fact Writing
*Doris Pany-Habsa (University of Graz)* ............................................. 311

# Writing Facts
## A Short Introduction

*Susanne Knaller (University of Graz)*

Everybody is talking about facts. They are not only a fixture in research and in law. Facts are increasingly becoming a major topic in politics, the (social) media, and everyday life. This produces certain linguistic formations that often contradict established meanings of the notion. The embarrassing creation of "alternative facts"[1] is just one example of such paradoxical constructions targeting at open replacements of the understanding of truth. It is opinions and affects, hearsay, algorithms, and outright lies expressed by populist leaders and self-marketing influencers that can stand for truth. Since the Trump era, the Brexit narratives and, of course, the Corona pandemic a blunt blurring of borders between lies, fiction, and facts is well underway in new forms. As a reaction, critical voices in research, journalism, and the arts often reinvigorate old dichotomies and antagonisms such as fact in the sense of truth or reality as an opposition to fake, lies, and fiction.[2] This often leads to initiatives

---

1   Kellyanne Conway, senior advisor of President Donald Trump, in an interview with NBC on January 21, 2017. Cf. https://www.nbcnews.com/meet-the-press/video/conway-press-secretary-gave-alternative-facts-860142147643 (02.03.2022). In Austria and Germany, "alternative Fakten" was elected as the "Unwort des Jahres" (non-word of the year). In 2016, *The Oxford Dictionary* chose "post-truth" for the international word of the year while the Gesellschaft für Deutsche Sprache opted for "post-faktisch." (Cf. van Dyk 2017: 348)

2   Philipp Sarasin defines the lie as a tool of power and as a prerogative of interpretation. (Cf. Sarasin in this volume and 2016) Silke van Dyk explains the new situation by pointing to the need of new critical perspectives able to deal adequately with today's situation of post-truth and the idea of an alternative reality aimed against the values of morality and education, critique, and research. (Cf. van Dyk 2017: 353) Both Sarasin and van Dyk reject the interpretation that the era of post-truth would be the result of postmodernism and poststructuralism. Instead of turning back to a positivist realism, sociologists, and historians like van Dyk or Sarasin stress the multidimensionality of

of fact checking in articles, accounts, interviews, research, and predictions and serves as a procedure of falsifications mostly targeted at misinformation and deception. The prestigious Parisian university Science Po for instance launched an initiative called *De Facto*[3], and nearly all serious newspapers have installed a fact checking section, while internet platforms and blogs are concerned with finding the truth (for instance, https://www.politifact.com). To strengthen their concerns and objectives, both the populist discourses and the initiatives of critique stress a reference to and concern about facts. The critical voices do so because of the relevance of the question of fact and nonfact today, while populist discourses wish to construct a system of post-truth and post-factual.[4]

It is the task of the present volume to take up current discussions and controversies while bearing in mind that the notion of fact never did have a fixed meaning or allowed just one approach. Since its modern beginnings in the 17$^{th}$ century, 'fact' is a highly complex notion that touches many of the most challenging questions in modernity. It concerns the systems of knowledge and arts as well as social, legal, and political institutions. As such, fact depends on everchanging epistemological discourses, multifaceted institutional functions, and interests while also encompassing questions of authentication and authority, individual standpoints as well as political and social dimensions. 'Fact' is further based on diverse and manifold formats, tools, and media. This collection of essays approaches the complex of 'fact' by taking into consideration its multidimensional applications, forms, and functions. An encompassing and constitutive feature of the concept was chosen by addressing the practices and formats of writing. Such a focus allows to lay bare and analyze the fact's dependence of practices of media, tools, instruments, formats, and specific modes of handling. As a notion that partakes in epistemological questions, in paradigms and models of the sciences and philosophy, of law, history and the arts, 'fact' underlies multiple practices that are supposed to translate and transform data, situations, events, things, objects, or human beings into what, from specific points of view and within

---

facts by emphasizing the ethical component of such an approach. With reference to Foucault, Silke van Dyk observes the invention of a new "Wahrheitsspiel" today. (Ibid.: 355) Sarasin for his part demands for "Redlichkeit" (integrity) which he sees realized when proper standpoints, theories, and sources are laid bare. See also Gess 2021.

3 Cf. https ://www.sciencespo.fr/fr/actualites/actualit%c3%a9s/decouvrez-de-facto -un-outil-inedit-au-service-d-une-information-de-qualite/6996 (03.03.2022).

4 Cf. van Dyk 2017: 348.

specific discourses, is called a fact. Numbers, diagrams, geometric figures, mathematical formulas, language, visual and auditive instruments are some of the applied tools and media. Often overlooked in this context is the relevance and effectivity of the practice of writing in different fields. Therefore, a major task of this volume is to look at the practice of writing in various discursive and institutional settings by also considering the formats accompanying it. It is not intended, however, to come up with a final definition or an all-over valid description of 'fact.' Even if a realist approach is most popular in common dictionaries, this volume does not favor a particular standpoint but rather confronts the notion in its complexity and multidimensionality. Of course, a realist point of view allows for a certain obviousness concerning the notion's constituents. An example: "A thing that has really occurred or is actually the case; a thing certainly known to be a real occurrence or to represent the truth. Hence a particular truth known by actual observation or authentic testimony, as opposed to an inference, a conjecture, or a fiction; a datum of experience, as distinguished from conclusions that may be based on it."[5] The *Oxford English Dictionary* further proclaims facts as "[t]hat which is known (or firmly believed) to be real or true; what has actually happened or is the case; truth attested by direct observation or authentic testimony; reality."[6] The *Online Etymology Dictionary* states that the understanding of 'fact' as a "real state of things (as distinguished from a statement or belief)"[7] is from the 1630s. A second look discloses a couple of challenging aspects. Neither of the described components such as reality, truth, and objectivity, nor referents like events, people and executed works are universally agreeable. Since the beginning of the modern fact in the 16th and 17th centuries, the question why and by whom and in which mode something is considered a fact, provokes many different answers and ever new questions alike. As such, the question of fact allows a view to modernity that embraces its institutions, discourses, artifacts, tools, instruments, media, and practices alike. It also highlights specific focuses in scientific disciplines and further helps us to understand theoretical and methodological models of philosophy concerning the interrelation of individuals, things, and media. Finally, the observation of different uses and

---

5   "fact", in: *OED Online*, https://www.oed.com/view/Entry/67478?rskey=zH7ZgP&result=1 (21.03.2022).
6   Ibid.
7   "fact", in: *Online Etymology Dictionary*, https://www.etymonline.com/search?q=fact#etymonline_v_1064 (11.03.2022).

functions of 'facts' opens up a comparative view on systems and discourses of the sciences, the arts, politics, society, and everyday life. In the following, I will outline a couple of historically and systematically interesting aspects of 'fact' together with some of the theoretical and methodological challenges accompanying it.

## Some Historical and Systematic Observations

No doubt, the idea of 'fact' is one of the most influential and crucial inventions of modern times. It regulates the laws of private action and communication as well as rules for public performances and patterns of behavior. Thus, the idea of fact concerns moral and ethical codes. As such, it takes part in semantic fields like truth, honor, decency, and correctness. Not to lie and to be honest is one of the oldest moral and religious precepts of Western culture. Current discussions show that such moral components are still at issue today. This is not only the case in critical discourses against the post-factual but also common within the new regimes of post-truth where 'facts' are the result of open lies. A look at the conceptual history and etymological aspects of fact provides an initial clue as to when the modern notion came into the picture and why it involves relevant questions concerning epistemology and knowledge that are still valid today.

There is consensus that with the wave of modern secularization in the 17$^{th}$ and 18$^{th}$ centuries, which went hand in hand with the rise of the idea of a subject dependent of a standpoint and that of a given real world in tension between objectivity and contingency, the question of fact became fundamental for systems of knowledge, epistemology, and modern law. However, to write a history of the notion of fact is no easy task. Jocelyn Holland states that it is quite impossible "to follow the manifold branches of the fact's genealogy, or to narrate even one of its many histories."[8] Nevertheless, we can observe that the English word 'fact' as well as the German use of the Latin 'factum' and its later equivalent 'Tatsache' have a strong legal basis going back to the Early Modern Age. The *Centre national de Ressources Textuelle et Lexicales* defines "fact" as a material act of a person and an event with juridical effects.[9] In *Das*

---

8 Holland 2016 : 34.
9 "Tout acte matériel d'une personne, tout événement extérieur pouvant avoir un effet juridique." A fact is also an infraction, a crime, and the result of an effective act ("In-

*Etymologische Wörterbuch des Deutschen* one learns that during the 16<sup>th</sup> century "Faktum" and "Tatsache, beglaubigtes Ereignis" were integrated into the legal discourse (also in the sense of crime), during the 18<sup>th</sup> century as an authenticated event, while in the 19<sup>th</sup> century, "faktisch" – probably coming from the English word "fact" – meant "being real, in reality."[10] The German language, just like legal discourses, generally differentiates between a real event and a legally relevant fact, i.e., "*de facto* 'tatsächlich, in Wirklichkeit' as opposed to *de iure* 'dem Recht entsprechend.'"[11]

However, there is also a theological and philosophical content in "factum," "fact," "fait" and "Tatsache" referring to *res facti*. As for instance, it is discussed as to whether "Tatsachen" (based on the English equivalent "matter of fact") – in the sense of real events – can form the basis for theological questions.[12] Until the 18<sup>th</sup> century, the Latin notion of "factum" was widely distributed in French and most prevalent in German.[13] In the *Deutsches Wörterbuch*, the Grimm brothers quote Lessing, Fichte, Wieland, Kant, Pestalozzi, Goethe among others by stating that "Thatsache" is still rare and quite unknown in its meaning but already allover and steadily used.[14] By this time

---

fraction, délit, crime résultant d'un acte effectif positif"). Cf. "fait", in : *Centre national de Ressources Textuelle et Lexicales*, https ://cnrtl.fr/definition/fait (04.03.2022). The *Online Etymology Dictionary* observes that "fact" is a crime, an occurrence, a deed, a condition, a thing done and in the more modern sense of a thing known to be true (around 1630). Cf. "fact", in: *Online Etymology Dictionary*, https://www.etymonline.com/search?q=fact (11.03.2022).

10   Pfeifer 1995: 319.
11   Ibid. in German: "Im 16. Jh. wird lat. factum 'Tat, Handlung' in die dt. Rechtssprache übernommen (auch in der Bedeutung 'Delikt') und seit dem 18. Jh. als 'Tatsache, beglaubigtes Ereignis' allgemein geläufig. Fakt m. gleichbed. mit Faktum, im 19. Jh. üblich; Einfluß von engl. fact ist möglich. faktisch Adj. 'tatsächlich, wirklich' (Ende 18. Jh.), meist adverbial gebraucht und schon im 19. Jh. häufig nur verstärkend. de facto 'tatsächlich, in Wirklichkeit', Übernahme des 16. Jhs. aus der lat. Juristensprache (Gegensatz zu de iure 'dem Recht entsprechend')."
12   Cf. Gabriel 2004 : 209.
13   Cf. "factum", in : *Trésor de la langue française*, http ://atilf.atilf.fr/tlf.htm (03.03.2022).
14   Cf. "Thatsache", in: *Deutsches Wörterbuch von Jacob Grimm und Wilhelm Grimm. Digital Version of the Trier Center for Digital Humanities* 01/21, https://www.woerterbuchnetz.de/DWB?lemid=T02891 (23.02.2022): "'Das wörtlein thatsache ist noch so jung. ich weisz mich der zeit ganz wohl zu erinnern, da es noch in niemands munde war. aber aus wessen munde oder feder es zuerst gekommen, das weisz ich nicht (nach HEYNATZ 2, 467 hat zuerst J. J. SPALDING in der übersetzung eines Buttlerschen werkes vom j. 1756 das wort thatsache für res facti, nicht gerade für factum gebraucht). noch weniger weisz ich, wie

dominant is the meaning of a real event, an objectively given or a thing or idea or content confirmed by ratio or perception.[15] The article in Zedler's encyclopedia at the beginning of the 18$^{th}$ century still favors "factum" in all its combinations. However, just a couple of years later the more broadly used "Tatsache" superseded "factum."[16] During the 18$^{th}$ century, a modern notion of fact became predominant. It was Kant who initiated what analytical philosophy and logic would later maintain, namely that "Tatsache" not only had the quality of a real event but also that of the knowledgeable ("Wißbares").[17] As a result, during the 18$^{th}$ and 19$^{th}$ centuries, science, philosophy and the arts alike were ridden by the question as to whether facts should be handled as part of a given reality/nature, or if they were only given when perceived and represented through the creative process of a subject.[18] Both positions are equally present in the sciences as well as in the arts, but both approaches also lead to ever greater abstractions. This is the case in the scientific and epistemological

---

es gekommen sein mag, dasz dieses neue wörtlein ganz wider das gewöhnliche schicksal neuer wörter in kurzer zeit ein so gewaltiges glück gemacht hat; noch, wodurch es eine so allgemeine aufnahme verdient hat, da man in gewissen schriften kein blatt umschlagen kann, ohne auf eine thatsache zu stoszen' LESSING 11, 645." In English: "'The word fact is still so young. I can remember the time quite well when it was not yet on anyone's lips. But from whose mouth or pen it came first, I don't know (according to HEYNATZ 2, 467, J. J. SPALDING first used the word fact for res facti, not exactly for factum, in the translation of a work by Buttler from 1756). I know even less how it came about that this new little word, completely contrary to the usual fate of new words, has made such a tremendous fortune in a short time; nor, through which it has earned such a general reception, since one cannot turn a page in certain writings without encountering a fact.' 11, 645." (Transl. S.K.)

15   Cf. ibid.: "[...] eine vorgefallene, wirklich geschehene sache, etwas feststehendes, das nicht bezweifelt werden kann: ein aufrichtiger wahrheitsforscher von thatsachen. STURZ 1, 140 (vom j. 1768) [...] gegenstände für begriffe, deren objective realität es sei durch reine vernunft oder durch erfahrung bewiesen werden kann, sind thatsachen (z. b. die mathematischen eigenschaften der gröszen). KANT 7, 356 und anm. (vom j. 1790)." In English: "[...] a thing that has really happened, something established that cannot be doubted: a sincere truth seeker of facts. STURZ 1, 140 (dated 1768) [...] objects for concepts whose objective reality can be proved through pure reason or through experience are facts (e.g., the mathematical properties of quantities). Kant 7, 356 and note (dated 1790)." (Transl. S.K.)
16   Cf. "factum", in: Zedler 1735.
17   Cf. Gabriel 2004: 209.
18   Cf. Lehleitner 2016b: 11.

model of positivism, in the format of proposition and mathematical formulas in logic and rational statistics. By the end of the 19$^{th}$ and beginning of the 20$^{th}$ century, 'fact' could not only mean a real event/state/object but more and more denominate the result of a process of logic and media that had to be formatted in abstraction. As such, 'fact' represented a concept in the sense of truth. Frege and others have stressed the abstraction of fact to "ein Gedanke, der wahr ist."[19] Up to now, the question of fact was discussed in those terms of truth: "A fact is, traditionally, the worldly correlate of a true proposition, a state of affairs whose obtaining makes that proposition true."[20] It is also proposed in linguistic terms of communication and true information.[21]

Of relevance for the German situation is that "Tatsache" or "Sachverhalt" remained a legal term, while the foreign word "Fakt" became the dominant notion in the sciences and in current popular discourses.[22] The *Centre national de Ressources Textuelle et Lexicales* quotes "fact" in the context of the sciences as something given and as the result of observation and experience – "Toute donnée de l'expérience, observée ou observable, directement ou indirectement (p. oppos. aux hypothèses, aux théories)."[23] The issue here concerns a popular dichotomy from the 19$^{th}$ century, namely fact vs. theory. Such a "fact" can be augmented into "fait brut" which is the result of a direct observation. A "fait scientifique" would be an objectivated phenomenon interpreted by cognition/*esprit* and introduced into a general law: "Phénomène objectivé (car

---

19   Gabriel 2004: 209–210.
20   Lowe 2005: 267; also quoted in Ryan 2020: 79. See also the article "fact" in the *Stanford Encyclopedia of Philosophy* which gives a proper insight into such formats and approaches. (Cf. Mulligan/Correia 2021)
21   Fludernik/Ryan 2020b : 2–4.
22   Cf. Pfeifer 1995 : 316.
23   "fait", in : *Centre national de Ressources Textuelle et Lexicales*, https ://cnrtl.fr/definition/fait (04.03.2022). Cf. in ibid. an example from the 19$^{th}$ century: "Ce quelque chose, qui constitue l'essence même de la recherche expérimentale, c'est le fait. Établir une expérience, c'est déterminer un ou plusieurs faits, rien de plus. La science a été sur la voie de sa prospérité du jour où les savants ont eu le culte, la passion exclusive du fait et rien que du fait. BOURGET, Essais psychol. contemp., 1883, p. 169." In English: "That which constitutes the very essence of experimental research, is the fact. To establish an experiment is to determine one or more facts, nothing more. Science has been on the way to its prosperity from the day when scholars had the cult, the exclusive passion for the fact and nothing but the fact." (Transl. S.K.)

apparaissant régulièrement dans certaines conditions), interprété par l'esprit et rapporté à une loi générale."[24]

The latter example and the legal semantics around 'fact' in general show that the notion contains the semantic aspect of a process underlying a doing and proceeding. This goes back to the Latin roots of *facere* in the sense of "doing" and "making." Like the English "fact," definitions of the German "factum" and "Tatsache" embrace doing or making, which is still the case also in English ("action, deed, process of making"), French ("action"), and Italian ("atto, opera, azione, operazione").[25] At the same time, facts are the *result* of such a process and making.[26] This leads to the question of the relation between the process of finding and constructing facts and that of the status and function of the result, and further, the question of the kind of procedures as well as the ontological status and moral/institutional value/function of 'fact.'

Based on these considerations and the etymology of 'fact,' the notion in its current understandings is the result of at least four major discourses of modernity:

1) modern law with its norms and institutional settings (judges, advocates, case-finding, court rulings etc.), which follows the task to create data into legal facts (since the 15th century),
2) modern epistemology with its new concepts of reality based on the invention of a modern subject that perceives and observes (starting in the 17th century),
3) modern science with its models of objectivity and secular universal truth (19th century). Only the latter provoke the whole meanings of fact that are in use today. The basis of such facts are entities or data that have very concrete contours (things, events, actions, deeds, persons, etc.), while for their part they result from the processing of such data via actions and procedures like abstractions, processes of authentications, formats, and practices. Nevertheless, an event only becomes a fact if someone declares it as such.
4) Hence, and this has been an issue since the late 19th century, facts are understood as dependent on media, formats, and practices, changing epistemologies and concepts of reality. In that respect, Nietzsche

---

24 Ibid.
25 Cf. *The Oxford English Dictionary*; *Le Grand Robert*; "fatto", in: Battaglia 1972: 727–734.
26 Cf. Knaller 2010: 188.

mainly comes to mind, but Ludwik Fleck's *Entstehung und Entwicklung einer wissenschaftlichen Tatsache* (1935) could also serve as an example.[27] Consequently, from then on, the process of making facts could be thought of as exposed to constant changes and everchanging results.

## Possible Approaches Today

Departing from the described interrelations of 'fact' (empirical realities and assertions based on media, formats, and practices) laid out in the term, I would like to outline five approaches that are possible today:

1) The first is the understanding of fact as a correlate to true propositions, meaning a fact is true because of a cognitive and medial act based on language or formulae. This is a task pursued by analytical philosophy and logic.[28]

2) Another approach to fact departs from a metalevel to view the disciplinary challenges and institutional interrelations concerning fact. The relationships between the systems of knowledge and the arts are often at the center of interest. Discussing 'fact' allows to understand the tasks and challenges of both the sciences and the arts, as Christine Lehleitner shows in her collection of essays *Fact and Fiction. Literary and Scientific cultures in Germany and Britain*[29], where authors discuss different positions of literature in relation to the sciences and academic disciplines. The publication by Daniel Fulda and Thomas Prüfer, *Faktenglauben und fiktionales Wissen*, is another example.[30] Closely related to such approaches are publications that consider specific contents and formats in the context of fact and literature. Monika Fludernik and Marie-Laure Ryan, for example, give a profound insight into narrative modes in the context of facts in different fields and disciplines.[31]

---

27 Cf. Nietzsche 1999 [1873]; Fleck 1980 [1935].
28 Cf. Mulligan/Correia 2021; Lowe 2005: 267; Goodman 1965.
29 Lehleitner 2016a.
30 Fulda/Prüfer 1996.
31 Fludernik/Ryan 2020a; also: Holland 2016; Lavocat 2016; Fludernik/Falkenhayner/Steiner 2015; Skalin 2005; Lounsberry 1990; Genette 1990.

3) A third possibility would be to approach 'fact' from a historical point of view by stressing epistemological questions as well as those concerning the history of philosophy and science. Lorraine Daston's works are highlights in that regard. A recent study by Mary Poovey deals with institutional models and formats besides epistemological questions.[32]

4) A fourth one would be to understand both as real and material, i.e., the empirical event or matter to be proven, as well as the medial act and its outcomes. That would mean, for instance, that the event of Napoleon's defeat at Waterloo is a fact just as the act of writing about it has the quality of fact, together with all its related processes and institutions involved (archives, writing processes etc.) and the produced texts (e.g., narration, chronicle). As soon as a scientist, philosopher or author starts writing about an event, they also produce events/facts within a fact-finding process.[33] As such, facts constitute several levels of data and dimensions of reality. Science studies and network theories pursue that path when considering science and knowledge as the result of a doing and saying. Facts build a conglomerate of theories, methods as well as processes of authentication and practices.[34] The etymological observations above show that such an approach is implied in the term itself.

5) The latter approach leads to the fifth one, which primarily considers the multidimensional profile of facts by pointing to the everchanging constituents and discourses of facts. This sparks a discussion on the challenges of 'fact' today as described at the beginning. The discussions of Philipp Sarasin, Silke van Dyk and Nicola Gess[35] are examples of a critical discussion on current confrontations between realist objectivists, critical-Foucauldian and populist-manipulating discourses in the context of fact or non-fact. Taking into account the above-mentioned approaches, the volume addresses the question of fact by considering this multidimensionality and historicity, which allows a closer look at modernity and its systems of knowledge and the arts with its institutions, tools, and practices.

---

32 Daston/Galison 2007; Daston 1998; Poovey 1998.
33 Cf. Knaller 2010: 188.
34 Cf. Stern 2020: 399.
35 Gess 2021; van Dyk 2017; Sarasin 2016.

## Writing Facts/Writing *Facts*

The described interrelations of fact (empirical realities and assertions based on media, formats, and practices) allow me to come back to the topic of writing, which touches pragmatic, semantic, and conceptual dimensions, preparatory procedures as well as formal choices, models of argumentation and narrative patterns, and, of course, the result – texts/writings. Thus, the present volume considers both perspectives in this context – the *writing* of facts as well as the writing of *facts*. A look at writing as part of the fact-finding procedure as well as of dealing with what is considered facts, shows that the concept is the outcome of institutional and lifeworld practices and subject to formal and modal strategies. Questions of writing[36] concern the entire process, and thus, that which remains inseparable from productive (real-life) actions and practices.[37] They also consider the formats and styles of certain approaches and groups. In the context of writing as practice, Roland Barthes is a useful point of reference.[38] He addresses the physical, corporeal elements of writing and of using writing utensils, thus setting himself apart from a purely metaphorical notion of writing (in the sense of style or a particular kind of form and work). Particularly Barthes's concept of "*écriture*"[39] has become prevalent in the study of writing processes.[40] Rüdiger Campe's "Schreibszene" model (1991), which he developed for literary studies, builds on the notion of Barthes's *écriture*.[41] In his study on writing processes, Martin Stingelin for his part takes up this notion and differentiates between

---

36 Besides Barthes's *écriture*, Kittler's 'Aufschreibesysteme' (cf. Kittler 1985) can be quoted as a precursor; regarding the notion of 'process,' the *critique généalogique* (Grésillon 2012, 1999; Hay 1984) has brought forth some findings. The researchers involved in Martin Stingelin's project "Zur Genealogie des Schreibens" ("On the Genealogy of Writing"), however, put an even stronger focus on the nexus between writing and life (or writing as life) than the other models. Besides the text itself, this processual element also incorporates the (biographical, institutional, technical/material and poetological) conditions under which a text is produced. (Cf. Zanetti 2012a, 2012b; Stingelin 2012, 2004)
37 Cf. Giuriato/Stingelin/Zanetti 2004.
38 Cf. Barthes 1984b.
39 Cf. Barthes 1984b: 344–345; also: Barthes 1984a.
40 Cf. Knaller 2017; Stingelin 2004: 13; Campe 1991: 759; also: Brink/Sollte-Gresser 2004: 18–19.
41 Cf. Campe 1991: 759.

"Schreibszene" and "Schreib-Szene." The latter thematizes and problematizes, within the text, the ensemble of the 'Schreibszene' by revealing its heterogeneity and non-stability.[42] As for Stingelin, the ensemble of the "Schreibszene" consists of language (semantics of writing), instrumentality (technology of writing), gesture (physical dimension), frames, the distribution of roles, and directing. Gesture/physical dimension, the distribution of roles, and directing can be linked to emotion paradigms, i.e., those discursive and psychophysical traces left at the very moment of productive and receptive activity.

A look at writing as a practice allows to extend 'fact' beyond a theoretical and abstract concept and to understand it as part of a practice on several levels: As a psychophysical process, writing relates to self- and other-experiences, emotions, judgments, evaluations, understanding, and perception; as a cultural practice, it is tied to respective media, techniques, modes, rules of the field and societal norms; as an aesthetic practice, it is determined by respective models and its own aesthetic/creative impulses; finally, as a lifeworld practice, writing ultimately depends on environmental and economic conditions as well as on communication models.[43] "Writing facts" must therefore be perceived not only as a concrete process linked to verbal and textual media but also as a process that allows us to observe the epistemological, theoretical, and practical impact of dealing with and naming facts in systems, discourses, and everyday life.

## Sections of the Volume

This volume is based on a symposium held at the Centre for Cultural Studies at the University of Graz in November 2021. The event was the result of a cooperation between the European PhDnet "Literary and Cultural Studies," the University of Giessen and the doctoral program "Culture-Text-(Act)ion" coordinated at the Centre for Cultural Studies. Scholars from different disciplines participated in the conference with lectures and discussions on writing facts. The proposed interdisciplinary approach of the symposium also forms the foundation for the present collection of essays. As such, the volume considers the multidimensional applications, forms, and functions of the notion of 'fact'

---

42  Cf. Stingelin 2004: 15.
43  Cf. Knaller 2022: 91–102.

and is therefore divided into several sections that touch on multiple themes, thereby allowing plural disciplinary and discursive perspectives on 'fact.' The first section "Theory and History" includes a historical overview of the notion and a theoretical/methodological proposal of how to deal with questions of fact today (Knaller), further a profound discussion of the role of writing as one of the most powerful ways of cultural fact- and worldmaking (Nünning) and finally, the questioning of discourses of fact and its challenges to current political, epistemological, and public constellations. (Sarasin) The contributions of the second section "Writing Society, Politics, and Law" present possible confrontations of 'fact' within these contexts and discourses. They consider the importance of the notion for modern concepts in the social and political sciences (Müller), the function of the act of writing for fascist and authoritarian concepts (von Roedern) and the specific role and constitution of legal and non-legal facts within the law and its norms (Albrecht/Ibing). A third section ("Literature and Art") deals with questions of the factual in their importance for literature and art during the $18^{th}$ and $19^{th}$ centuries by confronting colonial concepts with an early postcolonial fact-writing (Brandt) and by investigating some $19^{th}$ century realist approaches (Wolf). Fact-writing during the $20^{th}$ and $21^{st}$ centuries is exemplified through discussions on writing gender/masculinity in literature and popular essays in Germany and Italy (Schöfberger). Furthermore, through an analysis of writing the tragedy of the extinction of animals in the era of the Anthropocene (Simonis) and by engaging with new documentarist and literary approaches that question traditional concepts of history (writing) (Voithofer, Martínez). Since dealing with fictive and fictional writings and text formations, the relation between fact/reality/history and fiction/fictional is a persistent topic in these essays. At the same time, it is questioned and brought up for discussion as to whether such a confrontation necessarily leads to dichotomies and oppositions. The last section ("Media and Writing Practice") analyzes the way in which medial aspects play a role within discourses and practices around 'fact.' This includes an insight into specific formats of representing and conceptualizing dance, i.e., bodily and emotional movements into writing (Rieger), an analysis of approaches of early modern journalism and its writing practices at the beginning of the $20^{th}$ century (Huber) and of how social media and the internet produce 'digital facts,' also considering their particular impact on young adults (Höfler). The last contribution turns to the important aspect of writing practices and discusses ways of creating facts through writing in an academic context by looking at the questions coming with it for early stage students and instructors alike (Pany-Habsa).

The publication of this volume would not have been possible without great help from my colleagues. I would therefore like to thank Marie-Therese Pachner for her considerate and careful proofreading of the papers collected here. Moreover, Gero von Roedern and Riccardo Schöfberger contributed significantly to the realization of this book by taking care of the layout and the whole editing process.

## Bibliography

Barthes, Roland (1984a): "Écrire, verbe intransitif?", in: id.: *Le bruissement de la langue. Essais critiques*. vol. 4, Paris, 21–32.
— (1984b): "Longtemps, je me suis couché de bonne heure", in: id.: *Le bruissement de la langue. Essais critiques*. vol. 4, Paris, 333–346.
Battaglia, Salvatore (1972): "fatto", in: *Grande dizionario della lingua italiana*. vol. 5. E-Fin, Turin, 727–734.
Brink, Margot/Solte-Gresser, Christiane (2004): "Grenzen und Entgrenzungen. Zum Verhältnis von Literatur und Philosophie", in: id. (eds.): *Écritures. Denk- und Schreibweisen jenseits der Grenzen von Literatur und Philosophie*, Tübingen, 9–29.
Campe, Rüdiger (1991): "Die Schreibszene, Schreiben", in: Gumbrecht, Hans Ulrich/Pfeiffer, K. Ludwig (eds.): *Paradoxien, Dissonanzen, Zusammenbrüche. Situationen offener Epistemologie*, Frankfurt am Main, 759–772.
Daston, Lorraine (1998): "Fear and Loathing of the Imagination in Science", in: *Daedalus* 127, 73–95.
Daston, Lorraine/Galison, Peter (2007): *Objectivity*, New York.
"fact", in: *Online Etymology Dictionary*, https://www.etymonline.com/kword/fact#etymonline_v_1064 (04.03.2022).
"fact", in: *OED Online*, https://www.oed.com/view/Entry/67478?rskey=zH7ZgP&result=1 (21.03.2022).
"factum", in: *Trésor de la langue française*, http://atilf.atilf.fr/tlf.htm (03.03.2022).
"factum", in: *Centre national de Ressources Textuelle et Lexicales*, https://cnrtl.fr/definition/factum (04.03.2022).

"fait", in: *Centre national de Ressources Textuelle et Lexicales*, https://cnrtl.fr/definition/fait (04.03.2022).

"fait", in: *Le Grand Robert de la langue française*, https://grandrobert.lerobert.com/robert.asp (04.03.2022).

Fleck, Ludwik (1980) [1935]: *Entstehung und Entwicklung einer wissenschaftlichen Tatsache. Einführung in die Lehre vom Denkstil und Denkkollektiv*, Frankfurt am Main.

Fludernik, Monika/Falkenhayner, Nicole/Steiner, Julia (eds.) (2015): *Faktuales und fiktionales Erzählen. Interdisziplinäre Perspektiven*, Würzburg.

Fludernik, Monika/Ryan, Marie-Laure (eds.) (2020a): *Narrative Factuality. A Handbook*, Berlin/New York.

— (2020b): "Factual Narrative. An Introduction", in: id. (eds.), *Narrative Factuality. A Handbook*, 2–18.

Fulda, Daniel/Prüfer, Thomas (1996): *Faktenglaube und fiktionales Wissen. Zum Verhältnis von Wissenschaft und Kunst in der Moderne*, Frankfurt am Main.

Gabriel, Gottfried (2004): "Tatsache", in: Mittelstraß, Jürgen (ed.): *Enzyklopädie Philosophie und Wissenschaftstheorie*. vol. 4, Sp-Z, Stuttgart/Weimar.

Genette, Gérard (1990): "Fictional Narrative, Factual Narrative", in: *Poetics Today* 11/4, 755–774.

Gess, Nicola (2021): *Halbwahrheiten. Zur Manipulation von Wirklichkeit*, Berlin.

Giuriato, Davide/Stingelin, Martin/Zanetti, Sandro (eds.) (2004): *"Mir ekelt vor diesem tintenklecksenden Säkulum." Schreibszenen im Zeitalter der Manuskripte*, München.

Goodman, Nelson (1965): *Fact, Fiction, and Forecast*, Indianapolis/New York/Kansas City.

Grésillon, Almuth (2012): "Die allmähliche Verfertigung von Texten beim Schreiben", in: Zanetti (ed.), *Schreiben als Kulturtechnik. Grundlagentexte*, 152–186.

— (1999): *Literarische Handschriften. Einführung in die "critique génétique"*, Bern.

Hay, Louis (1984): "Die dritte Dimension der Literatur. Notizen zu einer critique génétique", in: *Poetica* 16/3 (4), 307–323.

Holland, Jocelyn (2016): "Facts are What one Makes of Them: Constructing the Faktum in the Enlightenment and Early German Romanticism", in: Lehleitner (ed.), *Fact and Fiction. Literary and Scientific Cultures in Germany and Britain*, 33–49.

Kittler, Friedrich (1985): *Aufschreibesysteme. 1800-1900*, München.

Knaller, Susanne (2022): *Mit Texten umgehen. Ein theoretisch-methodologisches Modell*, Bielefeld.

— (2017): "Emotions and the Process of Writing", in: Jandl, Ingeborg et al. (eds.): *Writing Emotions. Theoretical Concepts and Selected Case Studies in Literature*, Bielefeld, 17–28.

— (2010): "Realismus und Dokumentarismus. Überlegungen zu einer aktuellen Realismustheorie", in: Linck, Dirk et al. (eds.): *Realismus in den Künsten der Gegenwart*, Zürich, 175–189.

Lavocat, Françoise (2016): *Fait et fiction*, Paris.

Lehleitner, Christine (ed.) (2016a): *Fact and Fiction. Literary and Scientific Cultures in Germany and Britain*, Toronto.

— (2016b): "Introduction. Fact and Fiction: Literary and Scientific Cultures in Germany and Britain – Thoughts on a Contentious Relationship", in: id. (ed.), *Fact and Fiction. Literary and Scientific Cultures in Germany and Britain*, 1–30.

Lounsberry, Barbara (1990): *The Art of Fact. Contemporary Artists of Nonfiction*, New York.

Lowe, E. J. (2005): "Fact", in: Honderich, Ted (ed.): *The Oxford Companion to Philosophy*, New York, 267.

Mulligan, Kevin/Correia, Fabrice (2021): "Facts", in: Zalta, Edward N. (ed.): *The Stanford Encyclopedia of Philosophy*, https://plato.stanford.edu/archives/win 2021/entries/facts.

Nietzsche, Friedrich (1999) [1873]: "Ueber Wahrheit und Lüge im aussermoralischen Sinne", in: Colli, Giorgio/Montinari, Mazzino (eds.): *Sämtliche Werke. Kritische Studienausgabe in 15 Bänden. Die Geburt der Tragödie. Unzeitgemäße Betrachtungen I-IV. Nachgelassene Schriften 1870-1873*. vol. 1, München, 875–890.

Pfeifer, Wolfgang (ed.) (1995): "factum", in: *Etymologisches Wörterbuch des Deutschen*, München, 319.

Poovey, Mary (1998): *A History of the Modern Fact. Problems of Knowledge in the Sciences of Wealth and Society*, Chicago.

Ryan, Marie-Laure (ed.) (2020): "Fact, Fiction and Media", in: Fludernik/id. (eds.), *Narrative Factuality. A Handbook*, 75–94.

Sarasin, Philipp (2016): "#Fakten. Was wir in der Postmoderne über sie wissen können", in: https://geschichtedergegenwart.ch/fakten-was-wir-in-der-p ostmoderne-ueber-sie-wissen-koennen/) (04.03.2022).

Skalin, Lars-Åke (2005): *Fact and Fiction in Narrative*, Örebro.

Stern, Simon (2020): "Factuality, Evidence and Truth in Factual Narratives in the Law", in: Fludernik/Ryan (eds.), *Narrative Factuality. A Handbook*, 391–400.

Stingelin, Martin (2012): "'Unser Schreibzeug arbeitet mit an unseren Gedanken'. Die poetologische Reflexion der Schreibwerkzeuge bei Georg Christoph Lichtenberg und Friedrich Nietzsche", in: Zanetti (ed.): *Schreiben als Kulturtechnik. Grundlagentexte*, 283–304.

— (2004): "'Schreiben'. Einleitung", in: Giuriato/id./Zanetti (eds.), *"Mir ekelt vor diesem tintenklecksenden Säkulum." Schreibszenen im Zeitalter der Manuskripte*, 7–21.

"Thatsache", in: *Deutsches Wörterbuch von Jacob Grimm und Wilhelm Grimm. Digital Version of the Trier Center for Digital Humanities* 01/21, https://www.woerterbuchnetz.de/DWB?lemid=T02891 (23.02.2022).

Van Dyk, Silke (2017): "Krise der Faktizität? Über Wahrheit und Lüge in der Politik und die Aufgabe der Kritik", in: *PROKLA* 47, 347–367.

Zanetti, Sandro (ed.) (2012a): *Schreiben als Kulturtechnik. Grundlagentexte*, Berlin.

— (2012b): "Einleitung", in: id. (ed.), *Schreiben als Kulturtechnik. Grundlagentexte*, 7–34.

Zedler, Johann Heinrich (1735): "factum", in: *Großes vollständiges Universal-Lexicon aller Wissenschafften und Künste*. vol. 9, Halle, 65–67.

# THEORY AND HISTORY

# Facts in Modernity
## A Multifarious History of Meanings, Forms, and Purposes

Susanne Knaller (University of Graz)

## 1.

In December 2020, the cover of the fashion journal *Vogue* featured singer-songwriter Harry Styles as the first male person dressed in a gown. The headline read, "Harry makes his own style". This widely received event provoked the actor Billy Porter, famous for his political engagement and lush outfits to the following statement: "I changed the whole game. [...] I. Personally. Changed. The. Whole. Game. And that is not ego, that is just fact. I was the first one doing it and now everybody is doing it."[1] Porter argued that it should have been him to be on the cover, not Styles.

Of course, ignoring conventional gender rules concerning outfits at public events is *not* an invention of Billy Porter (or Harry Styles or *Vogue*). Marlene Dietrich in her elegant swallowtail in the 1930s or more recently Conchita in a Jean-Paul Gaultier evening gown at the Vienna Life Ball (2014) are two worldwide famous examples preceding Porter's glamourous performances. All this could lead to the conclusion that something does not become a fact only because someone declares it as such, has photographs taken or gives interviews in journals. But things are more complex than that. Although there is evidence that Porter was mistaken, some might consider it a fact that he was the first one to infringe gender conventions in public dressing: Porter himself for the reason of his popular political agenda,[2] others, because it is

---

1   Grady 2021: 39.
2   Porter claims in the interview: "I feel like the fashion industry has accepted me because they have to. I'm not necessarily convinced and here is why. I created the conversation [about non-binary fashion] and yet *Vogue* still put Harry Styles, a straight white man,

a statement by a famous actor or a post on a trusted social media platform. For some, because of the gender issues coming with it, for others because of not doing further research[3] or simply because of the will to have it like that by insisting on the right of opinion. Who or what could, and ultimately would have the right to declare something a fact? Alternatively, who or what could declare something a misunderstanding, a false belief, a lie, an illusion, or an ignorance instead of a fact? In the following, I would like to approach those questions by stressing the epistemological contours of fact in the context of the sciences, philosophy, and the arts.[4]

## 2.

As the example shows, the question of fact or non-fact is a fundamental issue. It is part of our everyday life, the systems of knowledge, the media, and the arts. Moreover, it is a fixture within political, social, scientific, and legal models and subject to norms, rules, and functions. As such, the attribution of fact is dependent on epistemological, institutional, and individual interests, while also underlying processes of authentication and authorization. A

---

in a dress on their cover for the first time." [...] "[...] He doesn't care, he's just doing it because it's the thing to do. This is politics for me. This is *my life*. I had to fight my entire life to get to the place where I could wear a dress to the Oscars and not be gunned now. All he has to do is be white and straight." (Ibid.) Porter later apologized to Styles for his comments.

3   The magazine *People* like the *Frankfurter Allgemeine Zeitung* (and others) stated that Styles became the first man solo on a *Vogue* cover. (Flanagan 2020; Kaiser 2020) This is not correct. Zayn Malik was the first man to front a digital edition. Helmut Berger became the first man to appear on the cover of *Vogue* when he co-starred with Marisa Berenson on the July 1970 issue, photographed by David Bailey. Since then, men including Elton John and a naked Robbie Williams have followed Berger's lead. What is true is that Harry Styles was the first man in a gown solo on a *Vogue* cover. Couples like Gigi Hadid and Zayn Malik already blurred gender roles. (Singer 2017)

4   With the Trump presidency, the Brexit campaign, and the Corona pandemic the notion of fact is a constant topic in the media, in research and certain fields like politics, sociology, and cultural studies. For an insight into the social and political impacts of this discussion see e.g., Gess 2021, van Dyk 2017, Sarasin 2016, and Rabin-Havt 2016. For some notes on the disputes around 'fact' and 'truth,' see the chapter "Introduction" in this volume.

glimpse at the etymological contours of the notion and the everchanging discourses and practices coming with 'fact' already reveals a multitude of possible definitions, applications, and functions. Even the most popular definitions of 'fact' as a given, an occurred event, a work or a provable and authenticated result or truth depend on the question of who in which manner deals with fact and its determinants like chosen data, discourses to consider, institutional norms, available formats, and necessary practices. 'Fact' in its secular and modern versions is a highly heterogenous and multileveled notion.

A productive approach to the understanding of the complex of 'fact' is to regard it as an invention of modernity with which it shares epistemological disputes and institutional conflicts. Moreover, 'fact' can be considered a battleground of modern antagonisms. Since the $16^{th}$ and $17^{th}$ centuries, questions of fact are at the heart of epistemological and institutional disputes in the sciences and the arts and contribute to building modern dichotomies such as imagination vs. ratio, subjectivity vs. objectivity, fiction vs. reality, spirit vs. body, real vs. possible, or contingent vs. necessary.[5] However, the various debates and conflicts contain a highly prolific side, since both fact and modernity have underlying conflicts, institutional divergences and epistemological plurality. Moreover, the multifaceted fact is a decisive constituent of modernity. This is also the position of Reinhart Koselleck who, observing a close interrelation of partisanship, standpoints, and objectivity at the base of historiography, concludes that only with the knowledge of ever-changing perspectives can the historian make true (objective) assertions on historical facts. To that one could add: or even create ever new and diverse historical facts. For Koselleck, the contingencies of fact helped to build the fundament of the idea of a historical world itself.[6]

These challenges of fact and modernity are – and this is a main argument of this paper – the result of ever-changing modern concepts of reality which

---

5   Early applications of "fact" (often also "factum") can be found in English ("fact"), Italian ("fatto") and French ("fait") in the sense of action, work, venture, crime, etc. Cf. Battaglia 1972, *Trésor de la langue française*, *Dictionnaire de l'Académie française*, Rey 1993, *The Oxford English Dictionary*, *Merriam Webster*, *Le Grand Robert*, Zedler 1735. In German as in other languages, the modern origins dating back to the $16^{th}$ and $17^{th}$ centuries are rooted in law. (Cf. Holland 2016: 35–36) During the $18^{th}$ century, the traditional term "factum" becomes more and more obsolete and is translated into the common "Thatsache" or "beglaubigtes Ereignis" (already applicated in law). (Pfeifer 1995: 319; also: Kluge 1948/2020: 613; Gabriel 2004: 204–205)

6   Koselleck 1977: 19.

define and shape discourses and institutional practices and norms. As dependent of epistemological and institutional models with their practices and functions, 'facts' are determined by such concepts of reality while also actively taking part in building them. This is not only the case when it comes to the epistemological dimension of fact but is also valid concerning functions, specific deployments, and practices. Modern concepts of reality allowed modern concepts of fact to emerge. Only since the wave of secularization and modern law, the process of differentiation of the systems of knowledge including the arts and the rise of the idea of a modern perceiving and rational subject, bringing with it the conflict between reality as an objectively given or a subjectively and/or experimentally perceived, did the question of fact or non-fact become fundamental for systems of knowledge and science.

As one can easily see, notions of reality are plural. Even if until the $19^{th}$ century an all-encompassing and metaphysically marked idea of nature is a constant, the question of how to approach, to describe, to understand and to represent it is open to numerous and conflicting solutions. And even if in the second half of the $19^{th}$ century the sciences reached a point of full self-confidence and believed to have found the basis for ever true results and hard facts, things got out of control so that by the end of the $19^{th}$ century, the sciences were forced to engage with even more new conflicts.[7] The modern fact could be certified through objectivity or subjectivity, verified by a subject and/or a theory, conceived via perception or abstraction or expressed in numerous formats (numbers, language, diagrams, images, geometric figures, audio and video, etc.).

Below, I will clarify other consequences of such pluralities by providing short examples from law, philosophy, and literature. This will include a methodological proposal for an open systematization of concepts of reality which allows to discuss various conflicting theories and discourses as well as the formats accompanying them. For now, I would like to emphasize the multifarious and formative role of facts within the modern sciences and their strong presence in arts and philosophy. As such, 'fact' allows us to understand the aspects of modernity and its changing concepts of reality. Moreover, the question of fact provokes a closer look at practices in the systems of knowledge and the arts. The writing of facts is one of them.

---

7   Cf. Daston/Galison 2007; Daston 1998: 73–95; Fulda/Prüfer 1996: 7–8.

## 3.

As seen in the example of Porter and Styles, the declaring of 'fact' not only requires a medium and a media practice but also an authenticator and/or a process of authentication. As such, facts are the result of research, norms and knowledge and the outcome of practices and strategies of description, argumentation, and narration. Thus, from a current point of view and considering the historical basis, 'fact' must be understood as a complex of several dimensions of reality and the result of many processes and acts in their respective formats and modes. An example of these constellations is the construction of legal cases in law. As early as the beginnings of modern law in the $16^{th}$ and $17^{th}$ centuries,[8] to close a case or to decide what in the end were matters of fact ("Sachverhalt/Tatbestand" in German and "fait" in French), one had to refer to objects, things, situations, actions, and individuals which, in turn, were part of private and institutional settings, linked to social and cultural paradigms, and – of course – to legal norms. During legal processes, these dimensions are considered in their interrelations and in their relevance for the legal question to be resolved. Only then, and after being put into a legally evident and proper narration, can a case be built and further processed.[9] What might be a fact in real life could be irrelevant for the legal case, and therefore only void data.[10]

The example of legal fact- and case-finding demonstrates that facts are the result of discourses (what can and should be said, what is where, how, and why regulated by which institutions, legitimated authenticators, systems of knowledge, properly designed spaces, and codes regarding the representation of self and other) *and* cultural practices (the doing, acting, and saying in such environments, its tools, and instruments). Data only becomes fact when legitimated, recognized, represented, authenticated, and authorized as such by doing.

---

8   Cf. Holland 2016: 35–36.
9   Cf. Stern 2020.
10  An example of the legal dimensions of fact can be found in French: In a general sense, fact among others has the meaning of what exists in reality – "[c]e qui existe, ce qui constitue la réalité." Thus, "in fact" is opposed to "valid in law" or "in a legal sense" ("p. oppos. au droit, à ce qui est voulu ou reconnu par la loi.") and means "in reality/without reference to law" : "Sur le plan de la réalité" (sans référence à la loi). ("fait", in : *Centre National de Ressources Textuelle et Lexicales*, https ://cnrtl.fr/definition/fait) (04.03.2022)

'Writing' within this complex is a productive practice. It has always allowed to obtain, to realize, to recognize, to archive, and to define what can be considered a fact. The act of 'writing facts' concerns not only a final text in its pragmatic, semantic, and conceptual dimensions but also preparatory procedures as well as formal choices, models of argumentation and narrative patterns. As such, a look at writing as part of procedures of fact-finding reveals that facts are also the outcome of institutional and lifeworld practices and are subject to formal and modal strategies. In the context of writing as a practice, Roland Barthes is a useful point of reference.[11] He thereby addresses the physical, corporeal elements of writing and of using writing utensils, thus setting himself apart from a purely metaphorical notion of writing (in the sense of style or a particular kind of form and work). Particularly Barthes's concept of *écriture* has become prevalent in the study of writing processes.[12] It allows us to discern and define the following aspects (I limit my observations on what is of relevance in the context of facts): 1) The level of explicitness of writing (as traces in the text, as an element of content or as program) which often leads to the crossing of genre boundaries. 2) Life as the surrounds of the writing process. 3) Writing encompasses and points to the entire process in all its dimensions. 4) Dealing with writing shows the relevance of texts concerned with writing (notebooks, diaries, and essays, etc.).[13]

Based on her example of double-entry bookkeeping, Mary Poovey shows that processes of writing form a fundamental practice for the modern fact. While concentrating her research on fact in the 18$^{th}$ and 19$^{th}$ centuries and on numbers as a format, she also observes the impact and function of writing processes during early modern economical managements, defining them as decisive for further developments in "high and low culture": "[T]he availability of a prototype of the modern fact in a familiar (but socially devalued) cultural practice like commerce enabled natural philosophers to explain what kind of knowledge they wanted to produce."[14] The accuracy of the books, their dealing with abstract notions like money and the implicitly represented ideal of honesty are a perfect example of establishing new systematic knowledge while still obeying to a reality concept based on the design of God's harmonious

---

11  Cf. Barthes 1984.
12  Cf. Stingelin 2004: 13; Brink/Solte-Gresser 2004: 18–19; Campe 1991: 759. Barthes uses the term repeatedly, e.g., in Barthes 1984a, 1984b.
13  Cf. Barthes 1984b: 344–345.
14  Poovey 1998: 11.

nature in the early modern world. Such an epistemology of reality is increasingly disputed, as Poovey's examples of the 17$^{th}$ and 18$^{th}$ centuries show.[15] Theologically oriented concepts of reality (or 'nature') clashed with innovative approaches like those of Hume who refused to accept any kind of explanation not based on empirically observed particulars. With philosophers like Hume (and Bacon), 'fact' indeed became a philosophical problem openly linked to knowledge, acts of perception and explanations of nature/reality.[16]

Another example for the relevance of writing processes concerning the constitution of the modern fact is (again) law. As Simon Stern demonstrates, the invention of fact formed the basis of modern law.[17] A legally valid fact is the result of many speech acts and practices dependent on environments, rituals, rules, and norms of authentication. But up to now, it is the writing that in the end constitutes the facts and builds a case, obeying the normative requirements of the law:

> If the judge must find the facts, the final result will be a written judgment that begins by summarizing the facts, and then moves on to the law. [...] [Like detective stories] [l]egal decisions also combine two stories: the narrative of a conflict that has blossomed into a lawsuit (which may, indeed, be a criminal prosecution) and the narrative of its legal resolution. Judicial writing, however, does not present these stories as two alternative versions of the same narrative. [...] The analyst's tools are directed not at discovering the true state of affairs leading up to the dispute, but at producing a satisfying legal assessment of the events.[18]

Legal fact- and case-findings have a great appeal to literature which understands that juridical processes are always embedded within a narrative framework in the broader sense.[19] This holds true for the verdict, the decision, and the grounds for judgment. In contrast to the legal narrations, it is the facts left out and the process of fact-finding itself that are interesting for the writing of

---

15   Cf. ibid.
16   Cf. ibid.: 14.
17   One can add that the relationship is reciprocal since the concept of the modern fact has a strong legal basis. (Cf. Holland 2016: 35–36) Fact and the constitution of modern systems of knowledge often go hand in hand as Koselleck's example of historiography shows.
18   Stern 2020: 397.
19   Cf. Olson 2014.

literary case narrations. A legal decision[20] always means a caesura, such as interrupting the chains of evidence and data and conducting interpretations in support of creating legal facts and a judgment. Literature, for its part, transforms into writing what has been left out, what could not have been told, or what did not hold as legal evidence. This explains why literary case narratives, unlike legal ones, are often multi-perspectival, full of narrative gaps and unexpected turns by also pointing out the struggle of finding a conclusion and coming to a full story and facts.[21] Facts are openly contingent. It is because of this contingency that the texts pursue a moral and social mandate of truth finding by discovering gaps, manipulations, and political strategies when it comes to legal cases. Literary case studies often have spectacular and widely received criminal events full of open questions, politically explosive force, and moral ambiguities at their base. A famous example is Truman Capote's *In cold blood*. (1966) One could also mention Alfred Döblin's *Die beiden Freundinnen und ihr Giftmord* (1924) and more recently, Emmanuel Carrère's *L'Adversaire* (2000) and Ivan Jablonka's *Laëtitia* (2016).

What has been said so far shows that dealing with facts also means dealing with discourses and practices characterizing modernity. It allows glimpses into the tasks of systems of knowledge, their practices, and their outputs of knowledge. In the following, I elaborate on the question of the impact of concepts of reality on 'fact' by outlining some important points regarding the epistemological side of reality and fact. A short look at the interrelations between the sciences, philosophy and literature will serve as an example of the modern fact in the context of writing.

## 4.

At the beginning of modern concepts of reality is the Cartesian model which had two major consequences for the Western episteme: a) knowledge is based on a division between cognitive subjects and objects independent of them, and b) since truth is based on cognition, the real is formed by *res extensa* (objects, matter) as well as by *res cogitans* (thought). As *res cogitans* provides the basis for truth and knowledge, *res extensa* is only real because of its being a

---

20 Cf. Niehaus 2006: 17–36.
21 Cf. Knaller 2021: 139. Cf. also Pethes 2016; Brière 2009: 157–170; Viart 2002: 30–46; Barthes 1964: 188–197.

representation or the content of *res cogitans*. Knowledge and truth are thus cognitive and conceptual. Only at this point does a modern concept of reality unfold: Reality as an ontological, philosophical concept is the other of the subject. To be true, it must be grasped by the subject rationally and abstracted into cognitive meaning.

This relation between the empirically given and a cognitive act implies a semiotic process that brings creativity and subjectivity into the picture. By disputing Descartes, Kant in his *Kritik der reinen Vernunft* (1781) takes further steps in this direction and establishes a system in which reality only becomes such if perceived.[22] Nevertheless, as opposed to the empirically given ("Wirklichkeit"), the true real ("Reale") itself is only conceivable but never recognizable in its matter, form, and idea.[23] Even before Kant, Denis Diderot had elaborated new ideas on the relation between nature and human beings as early as 1753. In his *Pensées sur l'interprétation de la nature*, he discusses experimental methods based on observation.[24] Absolute knowledge of nature is no aim for him. The truth lies in particulars and experiments.[25] As opposed to naturalist philosophers like Bacon and Hume, experimental scientists saw reality as the result of a performative act which at the same time had to be creative and individual. Nevertheless, Diderot, like Kant, still embraced a metaphysical idea of nature as the basis of their episteme. Kant's definition of the genius illustrates this: "*Genius* is the talent (or natural gift) which gives the rule to Art. Since talent, as the innate productive faculty of the artist, belongs itself to Nature, we may express the matter thus: *Genius* is the innate mental disposition (*ingenium*) *through which* Nature gives the rule to Art."[26] Such an encompassing concept of nature allowed 18th century philosophers to confront both sciences and aesthetics on similar terms of fact.[27] Aesthetic concepts of real-

---

22   Cf. Kant 1989: 301.
23   Kant distinguishes "Dasein" and "Realität." (Cf. Kant 1989: 150, 154–156, 218–219, 243–253, 304–305; see also Courtine 1992: 189–190 and Kible 1992: 197; for modern concepts of reality, cf. Knaller 2015)
24   Cf. Duflo 2005: 12.
25   Cf. Diderot 2005: 67–68.
26   Kant 2007: 112. In German: "G e n i e ist das Talent (Naturgabe), welches der Kunst die Regel gibt. Da das Talent, als angebornes produktives Vermögen des Künstlers, selbst zur Natur gehört, so könnte man sich auch so ausdrücken: G e n i e ist die angeborne Gemütsanlage (ingenium), d u r c h   w e l c h e die Natur der Kunst die Regel gibt." (Kant 1991: 235)
27   Cf. Daston 1998: 80.

ity and those of the natural philosophers and scientists were not necessarily seen in an antagonistic relationship as in the 19th century. Kant's ideas on the arts and the genius and Diderot's essays on theater and painting (apart from his own formidable literary works) are just two examples.[28] The notion of fact ("factum" or "Tatsache" in German) is a constant in these discourses. It was disputed in the writings of idealistic philosophy, in novels and essays of Early Romanticism, for example, by Fichte, Wieland, and Novalis.

At the same time, the arts and the sciences collided to an even greater extent when it came to their epistemological principles. By the end of the 18th century, the relationship was still close but full of conflict. One example is Schiller's sharp critique of Alexander von Humboldt, which equaled a rejection of an empirical rational concept of reality.[29] Instead of natural science, Schiller propagated the idealistic images of landscape painting.[30] In his *Ideen zu einer Physiognomik der Gewächse*, Humboldt, however, still postulated aesthetic modes as the basis for evidence and facts.[31] Later, he would ask for a strict separation between aesthetics and empirical natural sciences.[32]

The cards were again reshuffled in the 19th century. Because of a prolific interrelation between literature, art and sciences in realism and naturalism and a certain dominance of positivist concepts of reality, the scientific question of fact became a prominent issue within aesthetic discussions. The idealistic notion of reality proposed by Schiller was challenged by a new approach that stressed the empirical facticity and materiality of things and adopted objectivity as developed in the natural sciences as ideal. Émile Zola is a prominent example. In his manifesto *Roman éxperimental* he stresses the importance of objective facts for the new novel:

> Well! Returning to the novel, we can easily see that the novelist is equally an observer and an experimentalist. The observer in him gives the facts as he has observed them, sets the starting point, establishes the solid ground on which the characters will walk and the phenomena develop.[33]

---

28 For example: Diderot 1959; cf. Sauerwald 1975.
29 Cf. Schiller 1977: 112–113.
30 Cf. Knaller 2013 : 55–72 ; Robert 2008 : 35–43.
31 Humboldt 1987 : 175–297.
32 Cf. Robert 2008 : 52.
33 Transl. S.K. In French : "Eh bien ! En revenant au roman, nous voyons également que le romancier est fait d'un observateur et d'un expérimentateur. L'observateur chez lui donne les faits tels qu'il les a observés, pose le point de départ, établit le terrain so-

In the late 19th century, the institutional consolidation of the sciences and a differentiation of systems and disciplines shape institutions of knowledge and arts, while at the same time a productive fusion of the sciences and the arts was forming. Moreover, things were becoming even more complex. New models of perception accompanied by the creative forces of media such as photography and film, including new models of the constructiveness of language as elaborated in structuralism and analytic philosophy, started shaking the self-assurance of the 'old' Cartesian realist philosophy and positivist science as well as naturalist poetics. The arts and the sciences acknowledge the constructive force of visual and linguistic media and recognize the impact of individual modes of perception when it comes to the question of fact. Consequently, the 20th century found a fertile ground for fierce battles between rationalist and constructivist concepts of fact. Models of definition, description, representation, and explanation of reality were becoming even more pluralist, contradictory and complex. Highly popular were the new concepts of world, existence, and life with which abstract models are given up in favor of dynamic, psycho-physical, and social dimensions. A notion of human beings that included body, emotions, feelings, language, symbols, and acting replaced an abstract, ahistorical, rational, and/or idealistic subject. Nelson Goodman writes about this productive dilemma between facts, the empirical, symbols, and perception:

> Did the sun set a while ago or did the earth rise? Does the sun go around the earth or the earth go around the sun? Nowadays, we nonchalantly deal with what was once a life-and-death issue by saying that the answer depends on the framework. But here again, if we say that the geocentric and heliocentric systems are different versions of "the same facts", we must ask not what these facts are but rather how such phrases as "versions of the same facts" or "descriptions of the same world" are to be understood. This varies from case to case; here, the geocentric and the heliocentric versions, while speaking of the same particular objects – the sun, moon, and planets – attribute very different motions to these objects. Still, we may say the two versions deal with the same facts if we mean by this that they not only speak of the same objects but are also routinely translatable each into the other. As meanings

---

lide sur lequel vont marcher les personnages et se développer les phénomènes." (Zola 1903: 7)

vanish in favor of certain relationships among terms, so facts vanish in favor of certain relationships among versions.[34]

Now, with the new digital formats, their open borders between private and public areas, between fiction, virtuality, and reality, together with the overall mission for permanent self-performance of private as well as public persons, the arts and sciences are once again challenged when it comes to the question of fact or non-fact. The politically marked dispute around Porter and Styles is an expression of how the complex 'fact' is shaping our everyday culture and society.[35]

Drawing an interim conclusion, I can emphasize that the understanding of the various concepts of reality serves as a theoretical and methodological directive to understand 'fact' in modernity and in our present world. In return, a look at fact allows us to describe the impact of models of reality on the modern world. In the following, I would like to substantiate this argument by outlining a systematization of modern concepts of reality based on some of its epistemological key points including their formal translations/solutions. Literary examples of the early and late 20$^{th}$ century will provide further explanations regarding the interrelation between reality, fact, and practices of writing.

## 5.

Modern notions of reality contain concepts of knowledge, experience, perception, and cognition. They further encompass questions of materiality, semiosis, and formation but also depend on the conditions of the chosen media and formats and are subject to practices. As such, reality is based on the interrelation of a *model* (what does one mean by reality?) and a *mode* (how and up to which point can it be represented, understood, experienced, and perceived?).[36] In a first important phase of modern concepts of reality, we can observe *rational models* as designed in the 17$^{th}$ century where the subject has the role of an interface between the real and its order/sense. The subject is the point "from which the world can be logically deduced by a progressive

---

34   Goodman 1978: 93.
35   Cf. footnote 4 and the chapter "Introduction" in this volume.
36   Cf. Knaller 2015: 59–63; also: Knaller 2022: 35–39.

accumulation and combination of signs."[37] Form means to create order, visuality and form. The ideal mode is *representation*. To obtain an image of the being, the new sciences represent the rules of reality/nature in a numerical, rational system (calculus or geometry, for instance). Facts are the result of abstracting procedures, and as such evidence of a given and ultimately metaphysically legitimated truth. As already noted, it was Kant who first designed a comprehensive theory of cognition that could define the relation of subject/observer and object/the observed in a radically new way. For this *constructive model*, the ideal mode is *performative*. Reality becomes dependent of an act of performance. Diderot provides an example of this epistemological distance from the rational models of Descartes and Newton. For him, the basis of the new sciences included individual passion, a subjectively marked interest and a specific standpoint of an observer.[38] Knowledge and form are the results of a performative process, of individual perception and a creative practice. As such, facts do not prove an unchangeable given but are the evidence of a reality which has its consistency through reflection and formation.[39]

An example of the popularity of the discussion of facts during the 18th century, and with it the discussion of notions of reality and their conflicts between rational and constructive models, is provided by Christoph Wieland's novel *Die Geschichte des Philosophen Danischmende* (1775).[40] It narrates the story of Danischmende who invites a traveling mendicant named Kalender to discuss mankind but later rejects the quite negative opinions of the guest. As a reaction, Kalender points out that he only narrated things as they were and not what he wanted or dreamed or hoped them to be. In turn, Danischmende stresses his constructive (and performative) standpoint by emphasizing the dependence of facts of ever new points of view. For Danischmende, "[f]acts [facta] are what one makes of them," but for Kalender, real facts always show the same form and provide the same results.[41] Such a dispute between the idea of facts as dependent on perception and standpoint on the one hand, and that of facts as freed of theories and interpretation on the other, was

---

37 Crary 1990: 48.
38 Cf. Diderot 2005: 64.
39 Uwe Wirth writes that on the contrary to constative descriptions of conditions and situations, which can be false or true, performative expressions do not describe facts but create such – also social ones. (Cf. Wirth 2002: 10–11)
40 Wieland 1854. The novel is quoted as an example for the Romanticism's discussions of fact by Holland 2016: 33–34.
41 Wieland 1854: 60. Quoted in Holland 2016: 33.

already underway in the 17$^{th}$ century. Lorraine Daston describes this when she refers to Descartes and the Académie Royale des Sciences among others. Another good example is Hume:

> Morals and criticism are not so properly objects of the understanding as of taste and sentiment. Beauty, whether moral or natural, is felt, more properly than perceived. [...] If we take in our hand any volume; of divinity or school metaphysics, for instance; let us ask, *Does it contain any abstract reasoning concerning quantity or number?* No. *Does it contain any experimental reasoning concerning matter of fact and existence?* No. Commit it then to the flames: for it can contain nothing but sophistry and illusion.[42]

No doubt, during the 18$^{th}$ century 'fact' was becoming an antonym for fiction, dreams, and artifact. Nevertheless, Daston's statement that the modern notion of fact gets rid of its etymologic roots of "facere"/making is mostly true for the natural sciences but not fully valid for the new epistemological models of aesthetics and idealism as the example of Wieland demonstrates.[43] Johann Gottlieb Fichte, Novalis, and Friedrich Schlegel show that with the (early) Romanticist's discussions, notions of fact touch on questions of contingency and temporality (Danischmende speaks of hypotheses), of relations between the individual and reality. For them, facts are processual and part of a dynamic and creative complex of self- and other reflection.[44] Friedrich Schlegel writes, "A so-called investigation is a historical experiment. The object and the result thereof is a fact. What a fact should be has to have strict individuality, be at once a secret and an experiment, namely an experiment of formative nature."[45]

With the avant-garde movements and later the New Media, such a constructive/performative-constellation would be radicalized and produce *virtual models* by asking for a revised approach to the constellation of subject, objects,

---

42  Hume 1999: 210–211.
43  Daston 1998: 73–95. Cf. also Zedler's broad use of "factum," which, in the opinion of Holland, allows to encompass the double meaning of doing and making. (Holland 2016: 36)
44  Ibid.: 34.
45  Transl. S.K. In German: "Eine sogenannte Recherche ist ein historisches Experiment. Der Gegenstand und das Resultat desselben ist ein Faktum. Was ein Faktum seyn soll, muss strenge Individualität haben, zugleich ein Geheimnis und ein Experiment seyn, nämlich ein Experiment der bildenden Natur." (Schlegel, AugustWilhelm/Schlegel, Friedrich: *Athenaeum. Fragment 427*. vol. 1, 135; quoted in Holland 2016: 40)

and form. Theocentric and transcendental concepts of nature became obsolete, which is also an outcome of 19th century realism. However, as opposed to this rational radicalism, virtual models blur traditional demarcations between outer and inner realities, language and reality, fact, and fiction.[46] The ideal mode is an augmentation of the performative that could be called *experimental*, which means a constant intervention on dimensions of reality and self, together with a laying bare and discussion of the formation processes. Texts by André Breton and Marguerite Duras provide examples of such a virtual and experimental approach to the question of facts in the 20th century from the point of view of literature. They also provide an example of new interrelations between sciences and literature, and the functions of writing in the context of fact. At the core of both lies not only an aesthetic and epistemological motivation but also the task of a historically, politically, and socially relevant fact-finding.

Breton's poetics of *hasard*, open *écriture*, his refusal of linear narration and causal psychology results in a montage of provoked, and at the same time contingent situations. His seminal texts like *Amour fou* or *Nadja* present a world of coincidental constellations, of *objects trouvés* and passion as the basis of all writing.[47] It is the spirit of the discoverer that guides Breton and has him dissolve differences between real and imaginary, subjective and objective, fact, and fiction. The explorer is a writer openly performing his inner and outer experiences and observations while being on an ongoing adventure of fact-finding:

> It is only by making evident the intimate relation linking the two terms of *real* and *imaginary* that I hope to break down the distinction, which seems less and less well founded to me, that of the subjective and the objective. Only the contemplation of this relationship leads me to wonder if the idea of *causality* doesn't turn out quite haggard. Only by emphasizing the continuous and perfect coincidence of two series of facts considered – until further notice – as rigorously independent, I intend to justify and advocate more and more a *lyric behavior* such as it is indispensable to everyone, even if only for one hour of love and such as surrealism has tried to systematize it for all possible purposes of divination.[48]

---

46  Cf. Esposito 1998 : 269–296.
47  Breton 1937.
48  Breton 1988 : 53. In French : "C'est seulement par la mise en évidence du rapport étroit qui lie ces deux termes, le réel, l'imaginatif, que j'espère porter un coup nouveau à la

Surrealism discovers, writes, and authenticates such new facts. Breton propagates in *Amour fou*:

> Surrealism has always proposed that the relation [between subject and world] should be encountered. Not an incident can be omitted, no name altered without entering immediately the arbitrary. The revelation of the immediate, bewildering irrationality of certain events requires the most severe authentication of the human document recording them.[49]

An experimental approach to writing facts also characterizes many of the texts of Marguerite Duras. The collection of essays with the talking title *Écrire*, published as one of her last,[50] contains written transformations of interviews, notes, films, and talks guided by a personal and historiographical interest. Only through writing, has historical data become valid facts. This is apparent in the autobiographically marked story "La mort du jeune aviateur anglaise":

> It is emotions of this order, very subtle, very deep, very carnal, also essential, and completely unpredictable, which can brood entire lifetimes in the body. That's writing. It is the train of writing that passes through your body. Crosses it. This is where one starts talking about these emotions so difficult to say, so strange and which nevertheless, suddenly, take hold of you. [...] I write because of this chance to get involved in everything, with everything, this chance to be in this field of war, in this theater emptied of war.[51]

---

distinction, qui me paraît de plus en plus mal fondée, du subjectif et de l'objectif. C'est seulement de la méditation qu'on peut faire porter sur ce rapport que je demande si l'idée de *causalité* ne sort pas complètement hagarde. C'est seulement, enfin, par le soulignement de la coïncidence continue, parfaite, de deux séries de faits tenues, jusqu'à nouvel ordre, pour rigoureusement indépendantes, que j'entends justifier et préconiser, toujours plus électivement, le *comportement lyrique* tel qu'il s'impose à tout être, ne serait-ce qu'une heure durant dans l'amour et tel qu'a tenté de le systématiser, à toutes fins de divination possibles, le surréalisme." (Breton 1937 : 76–77)

49 Transl. S.K. In French : "C'est sur le modèle de l'observation médicale que le surréalisme a toujours proposé que la relation en fût entreprise. Pas un incident ne peut être omis, pas même un nom ne peut être modifié sans que rentre aussitôt l'arbitraire. La mise en évidence de l'irrationalité immédiate, confondante, de certains événements nécessite la stricte authenticité du document humain qui les enregistre." (Ibid. : 58–59)

50 Duras 1993.

51 Transl. S.K. In French : "Ce sont des émotions de cet ordre, très subtiles, très profondes, très charnelles, aussi essentielles, et complètement imprévisibles, qui peuvent couver des vies entières dans le corps. C'est ça l'écriture. C'est le train de l'écrit qui passe par votre corps. Le traverse. C'est de là qu'on part pour parler de ces émotions difficiles à

Duras' everlasting grief over her young brother killed in action is the starting point for the writer's engagement to uncover and narrate the forgotten story of a young British aviator killed by the Wehrmacht in France. Writing and discovering the facts allows to experiment and to express open and hidden interrelations between personal, political, and social life.[52]

## 6.

Of course, the model-modus-constellations outlined above only represent a selective typology of reality conceptions and modes in modernity. The history of the sciences, philosophy, and the arts shows that there is no linear progression of models and modes. Rational models can contain experimental modes (as in simulation formats), while virtual models often work with representative and performative modes (like computer games). Photographic and filmic images are an open field of all combinations. There are no fixed rules of combination between model and mode, but the model/modus-paradigm allows us to recognize and analyze the epistemological and practical reasons for the very different and often contradicting approaches to fact in modernity. The proposed ternary structure considers the epistemological sides as well as the formats. Such an approach goes beyond a discussion and comparison of single theories (rationalism vs. idealism, Kant vs. Descartes, etc.) or specific dichotomies (fact vs. fake, reality vs. fiction, objectivity vs. imagination/subjectivity, etc.). At the same time, it confronts and considers such aspects as well. The definitions enlisted by Mary Poovey show that up to now (or particularly today), the question of fact offers various approaches (and solutions). The implicit answers to the question of what facts could mean not only demonstrate the variety of notions of fact but also their dependence on concepts of reality with its formats:

> What are facts? Are they incontrovertible data that simply demonstrate what is true? [rational, representative] Or are they bits of evidence marshaled to persuade others of the theory one sets out with? [open model/modes-combinations] Do facts somehow exist in the world like

---

dire, si étrangères et qui néanmoins, tout à coup, s'emparent de vous. [...] ] J'écris à cause de cette chance que j'ai de me mêler de tout, à tout, cette chance d'être dans ce champ de la guerre, dans ce théâtre vidé de la guerre [...]." (Ibid. : 97–98)

52   Ibid. : 84.

pebbles, waiting to be picked up? [rational, representative] Or are they manufactured and thus informed by all the social and personal factors that go into every act of human creation? [constructivist or virtual/performative, virtual or representative] Are facts beyond interpretation? [rationalist, representative] Or are they the very stuff of interpretation, its symptomatic incarnation instead of the place where it begins? [virtual, experimental]⁵³

Moreover, a 'reality check' allows to consider the various functions and the epistemological impact of such modes and formats. It also considers that forms not only have a formal but also a practical, discursive, conceptual value and function. Particularly models stressing the act of *writing* facts emphasize a relationship between the arts and the sciences and the relevance of fact accompanying it. I would like to demonstrate this with the example of a historical novel where experimental *écriture* and fact-finding build an active factor promoting a virtual understanding of reality.

Marguerite Yourcenar's *Mémoires d'Hadrien*⁵⁴ is a masterpiece of historiographic literature. On the one hand, it consists of a long letter from Emperor Hadrian to his successor Marc Aurelius containing reflections on his political and personal achievements and failures at the end of his life. On the other hand, it narrates the story of Yourcenar's writing and constructing the novel based on her notes and research. These efforts of *écriture* were also documented by a published notebook. Yourcenar uses historiographic texts and (more or less) historically proven documents of the Empire. Her approach is scientific and poetic at the same time. In her *Carnets de notes* she describes the strategy as such: "Today the historical novel, or what we agree for convenience to call such, can only be immersed into a recovered time appropriated by an interior world."⁵⁵ The novel is a long commentary to the writing of history and literature alike. Always at stake is an (auto)biographical factor. Yourcenar notes:

> Take a known, completed life, fixed by History (as far as this is possible), so as to embrace the whole arch in a single stroke; further, chose the moment

---

53  Poovey 1998 : 1.
54  Yourcenar 1982b : 285–515.
55  Transl. S.K. In French : "De notre temps, le roman historique, ou ce que, par commodité, on consent à nommer tel, ne peut être que plongé dans un temps retrouvé, prise de possession d'un monde intérieur." (Yourcenar 1982a : 527)

where the man who lived this existence weighs and examines it, is for a moment capable to judge it. Manage that he is in front of his life in the same position as us.[56]

The historical person Hadrian and the fictional character Hadrian as well as the writer Hadrian and the author Yourcenar coexist as fact and fiction at the same time. The text elaborates a highly complex and precarious conglomerate of facts in their multiple dimensions. As such, it allows multiple perspectives on the participants, existing narrations, and different conclusions. In the meantime, many of the sources used by Yourcenar have proven to be false, or at least uncertain, and some historiographic results had to be revisited,[57] which just shows how politically and epistemologically precarious the contingency of facts and their appeal for writing them as literature really is.

## Bibliography

Barthes, Roland (1984a): "Écrire, verbe intransitif?", in: id.: *Le bruissement de la langue. Essais critiques*. vol. 4, Paris, 21–32.
— (1984b): "Longtemps, je me suis couché de bonne heure", in: id.: *Le bruissement de la langue. Essais critiques*. vol. 4, Paris, 333–346.
— (1964): "Structure du fait divers", in: *Essais critiques*, Paris: 188–197.
Battaglia, Salvatore (1972): "fatto", in: *Grande dizionario della lingua italiana*. vol. 5. E-Fin, Turin, 727–734.
Breton, André (1988): *Mad Love*, Lincoln/London.
— (1937): *L'Amour fou*, Paris.
Brière, Émile (2009): "Faits divers, faits littéraires. Le romancier contemporain devant les faits accomplis", in: *Études littéraires* 40, 157–170.
Brink, Margot/Solte-Gresser, Christiane (2004): "Grenzen und Entgrenzungen. Zum Verhältnis von Literatur und Philosophie", in: id. (eds.): *Écritures. Denk- und Schreibweisen jenseits der Grenzen von Literatur und Philosophie*, Tübingen, 9–29.

---

56   Transl. S.K. In French: "Prendre une vie connue, achevée, fixée (autant qu'elles peuvent jamais l'être) par l'Histoire, de façon à embrasser d'un seul coup la courbe tout entière; bien plus, choisir le moment où l'homme qui vécut cette existence la soupèse, l'examine, soit pour un instant capable de la juger. Faire en sorte qu'il se trouve devant propre vie dans la même position que nous." (Ibid.: 520)
57   Cf. Geerts 2014: 51.

Campe, Rüdiger (1991): "Die Schreibszene, Schreiben", in: Gumbrecht, Hans Ulrich/Pfeiffer, Karl Ludwig (eds.): *Paradoxien, Dissonanzen, Zusammenbrüche. Situationen offener Epistemologie*, Frankfurt am Main, 759–772.

Courtine, Jean-François (1992): "Realität/Idealität", in: Ritter/Gründer (eds.), *Historisches Wörterbuch der Philosophie*. vol. 8, 185–193.

Crary, Jonathan (1990): *Techniques of the Observer. On Vision and Modernity in the Nineteenth Century*, Cambridge/London.

Daston, Lorraine (1998): "Fear and Loathing of the Imagination in Science", in: *Daedalus* 127, 73–95.

Daston, Lorraine/Galison, Peter (2007): *Objectivity*, New York.

Diderot, Denis (2005): *Pensées sur l'interprétation de la nature*, ed. Colas Duflo, Paris.

— (1959): *Œuvres esthétiques*, ed. Paul Vernière, Paris.

Duflo, Colas (ed.) (2005): "Introduction", in: Diderot, *Pensées sur l'interprétation de la nature*, 9–54.

Duras, Marguerite (1993): *Écrire*, Paris.

Esposito, Elena (1998): "Fiktion und Virtualität", in: Krämer, Sybille (ed.): *Medien, Computer, Realität. Wirklichkeitsvorstellungen und Neue Medien*, Frankfurt am Main, 269–296.

"fact", in: *Merriam-Webster Dictionary*, https://www.merriam-webster.com/dictionary/fact (04.03.2022).

"fact", in: *OED Online*, https://www.oed.com/view/Entry/67478?rskey=zH7ZgP&result=1 (21.03.2022).

"factum", in: *Centre national de Ressources Textuelle et Lexicales*, https://cnrtl.fr/definition/factum (04.03.2022).

"fait", in: *Anglo-Norman Dictionary Online Edition*, http://anglo-norman.net/entry/fait_1 (04.03.2022).

"fait", in: *Centre national de Ressources Textuelle et Lexicales*, https://cnrtl.fr/definition/fait (04.03.2022).

"fait", in: *Dictionnaire de l'Académie française*, https://www.dictionnaire-academie.fr/ article/A9F0130 (04.03.2022).

"fait", in: *Le Grand Robert de la langue française*, https://grandrobert.lerobert.com/robert.asp (04.03.2022).

"fait", in: *Trésor de la langue francaise*, http://stella.atilf.fr/Dendien/scripts/tlfiv5/visusel.exe?12;s=2456632005;r=1;nat=;sol=1; (03.03.2022).

Flanagan, Hanna (2020): "Harry Styles Models a Gucci Gown as He Becomes the First Man to Land a Solo Cover of *Vogue*", in: *People Magazine* (13.11.2020).

Fulda, Daniel/Prüfer, Thomas (1996): "Das Wissen der Moderne. Stichworte zum Verhältnis von wissenschaftlicher und literarischer Weltdeutung und -darstellung seit dem späten 18. Jahrhundert", in: id. (eds.): *Faktenglaube und fiktionales Wissen. Zum Verhältnis von Wissenschaft und Kunst in der Moderne*, Frankfurt am Main, 1–22.

Gabriel, Gottfried (2004): "Tatsache", in: Mittelstraß, Jürgen (ed.): *Enzyklopädie Philosophie und Wissenschaftstheorie*. vol. 4. Sp-Z, Stuttgart/Weimar.

Geerts, Walter (2014): "L'Embarras du choix. Marguerite Yourcenar et ses lectures historiographiques préparant Mémoires d'Hadrien", in: Poignault, Rémy/Torres, Vincente (eds.): *Les Miroirs de l'altérité dans l'œuvre de Yourcenar*, Clermont-Ferrand, 49–68.

Gess, Nicola (2021): *Halbwahrheiten. Zur Manipulation von Wirklichkeit*, Berlin.

Goodman, Nelson (1978): *Ways of Worldmaking*, Indianapolis.

Grady, Oliver (2021): "Did I ever think I'd be this successful? No, because I'm gay", in: *Sunday Times Style Magazine* (17.10.2021), 36–39.

Holland, Jocelyn (2016): "Facts are What one Makes of Them: Constructing the Faktum in the Enlightenment and Early German Romanticism", in: Lehleitner, Christine (ed.): *Fact and Fiction. Literary and Scientific Cultures in Germany and Britain*, Toronto, 33–49.

Humboldt, Alexander von (1987): "Ideen zu einer Physiognomik der Gewächse", in: id.: *Ansichten der Natur. Erster und Zweiter Band*, ed. Hanno Beck, Darmstadt, 175–297.

Hume, David (1999): *An Enquiry concerning Human Understanding*, ed. Tom L. Beauchamp, Oxford/New York.

Kaiser, Alfons (2020): "Harry Styles als erster Mann allein auf dem Cover der Vogue", in: *Frankfurter Allgemeine Zeitung* (15.11.2020).

Kant, Immanuel (2007): *Critique of Judgement*, New York.

— (1991): *Kritik der Urteilskraft*, ed. Gottfried Martin et al., Stuttgart.

— (1989): *Kritik der reinen Vernunft*, ed. Ingeborg Heidemann, Stuttgart.

Kible, Brigitte (1992): "Realität, formale/objektive", in: Ritter/Gründer (eds.), *Historisches Wörterbuch der Philosophie*. vol. 8, 193–199.

Kluge, Friedrich (1948/2020): "Tatsache", in: id./Götze, Alfred (eds.): *Etymologisches Wörterbuch der deutschen Sprache*, Berlin, 613.

Knaller, Susanne (2022): *Mit Texten umgehen. Ein theoretisch-methodologisches Modell*, Bielefeld.

— (2021): "When Law Meets Literature: The Emotional Value of Literary Texts", in: *REAL: Yearbook of Research in English and American Literature* 35, 131–146.

— (2015): *Die Realität der Kunst. Programme und Theorien zu Literatur, Kunst und Fotografie seit 1700*, Paderborn.

— (2013): "Verschiebungen im Kunstsystem. Zum Verhältnis von Sprachkunst und Bildkunst in ästhetischen Diskursen des 18. und 19. Jahrhunderts", in: *Komparatistik 2012. Jahrbuch der Deutschen Gesellschaft für Allgemeine und Vergleichende Literaturwissenschaft*, Heidelberg, 55–72.

Koselleck, Reinhart (1977): "Standortbindung und Zeitlichkeit. Ein Beitrag zur historiographischen Erschließung der geschichtlichen Welt", in id./Mommsen, Wolfgang J./Rüsen, Jörn (eds.): *Objektivität und Parteilichkeit in der Geschichtswissenschaft*, München, 17–46.

Niehaus, Michael (2006): "Die Entscheidung vorbereiten", in: Vismann, Cornelia/Weitin, Thomas (eds.): *Urteilen, Entscheiden*, München, 17–36.

Olson, Greta (2014): "Narration and Narrative in Legal Discourse", in: Hühn, Peter et al. (eds.): *Living Handbook of Narratology*, Hamburg.

Pethes, Nicolas (2016): *Literarische Fallgeschichte. Zur Poetik einer epistemischen Schreibweise*, Konstanz.

Pfeifer, Wolfgang (ed.) (1995): "factum", in: *Etymologisches Wörterbuch des Deutschen*, München, 319.

Poovey, Mary (1998): *A History of the Modern Fact. Problems of Knowledge in the Sciences of Wealth and Society*, Chicago.

Rabin-Havt, Ari (2016), *Lies Incorporated. The World of Post-Truth Politics*, New York.

Rey, Alain (1993): "fait", in: *Dictionnaire Le Robert. Dictionnaire historique de la langue francaise*. vol. 1. A-L, Paris, 3708–3709.

Ritter, Joachim/Gründer, Karlfried (eds.) (1992): *Historisches Wörterbuch der Philosophie*. vol. 8, Darmstadt, 193–199.

Robert, Jörg (2008): "Weltgemälde und Totalansicht. Ästhetische Naturerkenntnis und Poetik der Landschaft bei Schiller und Alexander von Humboldt", in: Feger, Hans/Brittnacher, Hans (eds.): *Die Realität der Idealisten. Friedrich Schiller, Willhelm von Humboldt, Alexander von Humboldt*, Köln/Weimar/Wien, 35–52.

Sarasin, Philipp (2016): "#Fakten. Was wir in der Postmoderne über sie wissen können", in: https://geschichtedergegenwart.ch/fakten-was-wir-in-der-p ostmoderne-ueber-sie-wissen-koennen/) (04.03.2022).

Sauerwald, Gregor (1975): *Die Aporie der Diderot'schen Ästhetik (1745–1781). Ein Beitrag zur Untersuchung des Natur- und Kunstschönen als ein Beitrag zur Analyse des neuzeitlichen Wirklichkeitsbegriffs*, Frankfurt am Main.

Schiller, Friedrich (1977): "An Körner, Jena, 06.08.1797", in: Oellers, Norbert/ Stock, Frithjof (eds.): *Schillers Werke. Briefwechsel. Schillers Briefe 01.11.1796-31. 10.1798.* vol. 29, Weimar, 111–113.

Singer, Maya (2017): "Gigi Hadid and Zayn Malik Are Part of a New Generation Who Don't See Fashion as Gendered", in: *Vogue Magazine* (13.07.2017).

Stern, Simon (2020): "Factuality, Evidence and Truth in Factual Narratives in the Law", in: Fludernik, Monika/Ryan, Marie-Laure (eds.): *Narrative Factuality. A Handbook*, Berlin/New York, 391–400.

Stingelin, Martin (2004): "'Schreiben'. Einleitung", in: id./Giuriato, Davide/ Zanetti, Sandro (eds.):*"Mir ekelt vor diesem tintenklecksenden Säkulum." Schreibszenen im Zeitalter der Manuskripte*, München, 7–21.

Van Dyk, Silke (2017): "Krise der Faktizität? Über Wahrheit und Lüge in der Politik und die Aufgabe der Kritik", in: *PROKLA* 47, 347–367.

Viart, Dominique (2002): "Les 'Fictions critiques' dans la littérature contemporaine", in: Majorano, Matteo (ed.): *Le gout du roman*, Bari, 30–46.

Wieland, C. M. (1854): *Sämmtliche Werke.* vol. 9. Leipzig.

Wirth, Uwe (2002): "Der Performanzbegriff im Spannungsfeld von Illokution, Iteration und Indexikalität", in: id. (ed.): *Performanz. Zwischen Sprachphilosophie und Kulturwissenschaften*, Frankfurt am Main, 9–60.

Yourcenar, Marguerite (1982a): "Carnet de notes de *Mémoires d'Hadrien*", in: id.: *Œuvres romanesques*, ed. Yvon Bernier, Paris, 519–541.

— (1982b): "Mémoires d'Hadrien", in: id. : *Œuvres romanesques*, ed. Yvon Bernier, Paris, 285–515.

Zedler, Johann Heinrich (1735): "factum", in: *Großes vollständiges Universal-Lexicon aller Wissenschafften und Künste.* vol. 9, Halle, 65–67.

Zola, Émile (1903): *Le roman expérimental*, Paris.

# Writing as a Cultural Way of Fact-Making
## Modest Reflections on the Genesis, Role, and Status of Facts

*Ansgar Nünning (University of Giessen)*

## 1. Introducing Writing as a Way of Fact- and Worldmaking: Reframing the Ontology of Institutional and Social Facts

One might as well begin with the observation that everybody seems to know what facts are although relatively few scholars in the humanities or social sciences have volunteered to define this notoriously slippery concept in print. There are, of course, plenty of definitions of the term in standard dictionaries which sound straightforward enough and in accordance with common sense. According to the *O.E.D.*, for instance, a fact is something "that has really occurred or is actually the case." Similarly, according to *Merriam-Webster*, the noun 'fact' refers to "something that has actual existence," i.e., an "actual occurrence," or a "piece of information presented as having objective reality." Facts are, furthermore, often simply defined as "something known to be true or accepted as true" (*Oxford Advanced Learner's Dictionary of Current English*) or "a true piece of information" (*Britannica Dictionary*). The *Cambridge Dictionary* informs the reader that a fact is "something that is known to have happened or to exist, especially something for which proof exists, or about which there is information." One does not need to be a philosopher to be able to realize that such definitions provide less clarity and enlightenment about what facts are than one might assume at first sight. Instead, they shift the definitional burden onto such notoriously contested terms as 'actuality,' 'reality,' 'truth,' or 'verifiability,' thereby raising a series of complex epistemological and ontological issues which have been hotly debated for centuries.

As far as the title and topic of the present volume *Writing Facts* is concerned, it is interesting to note that, although none of the definitions quoted above refers to the concept of 'writing' as such, at least the definition in the *Cambridge Dictionary* indicates that for something to be accepted as a fact hinges upon the existence of verifiable information or proof. If a fact is indeed "something for which proof exists, or about which there is information," then writing seems to play a key role as a means of providing such proof. Written texts are thus important for verifying facts and testing the truth-value of statements. Standard reference works and academic publications, for instance, are often used to check whether something can pass the test of factuality. Moreover, in the day and age of 'alternative facts,' 'fake news,' and 'post-truth,' fact-checkers have become more important than ever before, while facts, reality, and truth seem to have become more elusive. Additionally, fact-checking often relies on the written word in order to determine whether a piece of information can be regarded as being true or having objective reality. Although facts and writing thus seem to be much more closely intertwined than one might have assumed, their complex relations have not yet been properly gauged.

This contribution presents some modest reflections on the question of whether writing generally provides objective representations of occurrences that have actually happened in the real world and of phenomena that are accepted as true, or whether writing should rather be seen as one of the most powerful ways of cultural fact- and worldmaking. As the title already indicates, this article argues that writing can indeed be conceptualized as the latter, because it is a performative act that constructs and establishes the very facts that texts seem to merely represent. The main reason for this is that putting things in writing not only provides documentation, evidence, and proof of a particular version or view of the world, but writing can also exert performative power by constituting the very reality that it purports merely to represent. This performative force stems from the reality-constituting, identity-, sense-, and indeed, worldmaking qualities that characterize writing in general.

Such a constructivist view of writing as a way of fact-making is, of course, indebted to the concept of 'ways of worldmaking,' a felicitous term coined by the philosopher Nelson Goodman. One of his main claims is that the world we know is always already made "from other worlds."[1] According to Goodman, there is no such thing as a 'given world' – the only thing we can ever have access to are culturally shaped world models or versions. Goodman managed to

---

1   Goodman 1992: 6.

shed a great deal of light on the question of how worlds are made by identifying and discussing five basic procedures for constructing worlds, viz. composition and decomposition, weighting (i.e., emphasis or ratings of relevance), (re)ordering, deletion and supplementation, and deformation.[2]

As anyone familiar with his seminal monograph *Ways of Worldmaking* will know, Goodman was neither particularly concerned with facts nor with the role of writing as a means of representing or constructing facts. As an analytical philosopher, he was also not interested in narratives as a way of worldmaking. As Herman has rightly pointed out, "there is nothing distinctively story-like about the worlds over which Goodman's account ranges, though there is nothing about the analysis that excludes storyworlds, either."[3] Recent years have seen an increasing interest across a broad range of disciplines in the question of exactly how worlds are made and how the relation between worldmaking and orders of knowledge can be described.[4]

As its title already indicates, this essay argues that ever since its invention, writing has been, and continues to be, one of the most powerful cultural ways of fact-making, playing a crucial role in prevalent "ways of worldmaking." While the word 'facts' is omnipresent in today's media, it is usually used without exploring the question of how mere occurrences and incidents become facts in the first place. In a constructivist framework, 'facts' should not be misunderstood as real occurrences but rather conceived of as results of performative cultural practices or techniques such as storytelling, visualization, and writing. By drawing on concepts from both the theory of historiography and literary narratology, the overall aim of this article is to shed light on the processes by which an event becomes a fact in the first place, i.e., the processes involved in the making of facts through writing.

Taking its cue from the basic procedures for constructing worlds identified by Goodman, this article pursues three main aims: Firstly, it attempts to explore the formal choices, narrative patterns, and cultural ways in which writing has been involved in the genesis or production of facts. Secondly, it tries to reframe the problem of narrative factuality in terms of the 'fabrication' or *Manufacture of Knowledge*.[5] Thirdly, a brief attempt will be made to look at

---

2   Cf. ibid.: 7–17; for an excellent brief summary, cf. Herman 2009: 77–78.
3   Herman 2009: 78.
4   Cf. ibid.; Sommer 2009, and the articles in Nünning/Nünning/Neumann 2010.
5   Knorr-Cetina 1981.

the role of digital technology and social media in the construction and dissemination of 'facts' (of all sorts, including 'alternative facts') and to address the question of why some 'facts' have more impact and become much more powerful than others. Using various examples, ranging from the so-called 'war on terror' based on alleged 'weapons of mass destruction' to the pseudo-facts used as a legitimization of Brexit, this contribution will try to show that writing can turn even 'fake news' and obvious 'untruths' into widely accepted (pseudo-)facts, while many 'inconvenient truths' are either not acknowledged as 'facts' or go largely unnoticed. By doing so, I also hope to offer some hypotheses and modest reflections on the ways in which words like 'post-factual,' 'post-truth,' or 'alternative facts' have gained such currency and traction in the present era, that one finds entries for them in renowned dictionaries.

## 2. Writing and Storytelling as Cultural Ways of Fact- and Worldmaking: Hypotheses about the Performative Power of Writing for Constructing Facts and Knowledge[6]

While the role of writing for the construction and dissemination of facts has not yet received the attention it arguably deserves, any attempt to come to terms with the topic of 'writing facts' can fruitfully draw on both Goodman's pioneering work and relatively recent narratological attempts to explore "Narrative Ways of Worldmaking", to quote the title of a ground-breaking article by David Herman, who proceeds from the same point of departure. "Narrative worldmaking," Herman argues, "involves specific, identifiable procedures set off against a larger set of background conditions for world-creation – irrespective of the medium in which the narrative practices are being conducted."[7] Whereas Herman is mainly concerned with "the cognitive processes underlying narrative ways of worldmaking,"[8] i.e. with the question of how

---

6   The second and third sections of this article are largely based on an argument developed in an earlier article on the topic of "Narrative Worldmaking" (Nünning 2010), which I have adapted to the theme of the present volume. The examples referring to the stories about 'weapons of mass destruction' are adapted from Nünning/ Nünning 2017. I should like to thank my wonderful assistants Louise Louw and Anna Tabouratzidis for their careful proofreading and formatting of this contribution and for suggesting a few stylistic improvements.
7   Herman 2009: 71.
8   Ibid.

textual cues encourage the reader or viewer to build up a "mentally configured storyworld"[9] or representations of the worlds evoked by stories, this essay will focus more on writing as a cultural way of fact- and worldmaking from a classical narratological rather than cognitive point of view. Though I agree with Herman that "classical, structuralist narratologists failed to come to terms with the referential or world-creating properties of narrative,"[10] I will argue that the analytical toolkit developed by said narratologists can shed quite a bit of light on the actual procedures that go into and shape the construction of worlds in narrative contexts. Since narratology has provided a range of useful concepts for exploring this question, the focus of this essay is on the questions of how events, facts, and storyworlds are made, as well as how narratological categories can serve to illuminate the fact- and worldmaking power of writing in general and of storytelling in particular.

Although the fact- and worldmaking capacity of writing and of storytelling has not received the degree of attention that it arguably deserves, most people would probably agree that narratives are of fundamental importance for the ways in which we make sense of our experiences and of the world at large. In his pioneering account of the creation of an autobiographical self, felicitously titled *How Our Lives Become Stories: Making Selves*, Paul John Eakin has shown that narratives are at work in processes such as identity formation, ordering of experiences, and remembering and negotiating values. In a similar vein, I will argue that stories, and storytelling, are not only the most important means of making autobiographical selves but also an equally important means of fact- and worldmaking. This contribution is particularly concerned with the building-blocks of fact- and worldmaking, i.e., with the so-called 'event' as the elementary unit of both facts and narratives, with the notion of emplotment, and with the role of point of view. It does not pretend to offer a comprehensive, let alone exhaustive, account of writing as a cultural way of fact- and worldmaking at large but is rather intended to complement other recent attempts to come to terms with narrative as an important way of worldmaking.

This article takes as its point of departure the somewhat astounding observation that whilst such terms as 'events' and 'facts' are indeed omnipresent in both historiography and the media, they are generally used "without ever systematically following up on the question of what events actually are, and

---

9   Ibid.
10  Ibid.

how occurrences and incidents become events."[11] What Nelson Goodman said about the modes of organization and worldmaking that he was particularly interested in applies equally well to the notions of events and facts: "they are not 'found in the world' but *built into a world*."[12] The same holds true for facts: they are made rather than just found out there in the real world, and writing is one of the most powerful ways of making sure that something is accepted as a fact.

By drawing on concepts from the theory of history and from narratology, the aim of this article is, on the one hand, to illuminate the processes and discourse-strategies by which writing turns something that happens into an event and an established fact in the first place. On the other hand, it tries to illustrate, and comment on, some of the processes that go into cultural ways of fact- and worldmaking. Without aiming to cast doubt on the existence of facts, the goal is to show that what we call historical or political facts, or media events, are not only the result of selection, abstraction, ordering, and prioritization but are also perspective-dependent, culturally specific, and historically variable, contingent constructs which are produced by discourses, writing, and other media. Lots of things happen every day, but only very few of them become events or facts, let alone what posterity will regard as 'important facts' or 'great historical events.' Though it is generally agreed that the constitution of a fact or a media event is a product of the modes of representation and mediation as well as of social communication, this hypothesis does not really provide much enlightenment on how events and facts are constructed. Therefore, it might be worthwhile to examine some ways of fact- and worldmaking as well as the performative power of writing in greater detail.

Let us, first of all, take a brief look at some examples in order to illustrate how writing can exert performative power and serve to make facts. Since news is ubiquitous in the contemporary media world, any newspaper could serve as an example of how writing can be seen as a cultural way of fact- and worldmaking. We might, therefore, just as well begin with the news before moving on to the more individual examples of George W. Bush and the contemporary American novelist Paul Auster, strange bedfellows though the latter two are, both are very powerful makers of political facts and fictional story-worlds respectively.

---

11   Rathmann 2003: 4.
12   Goodman 1992: 14, original emphasis.

For anyone interested in the role of writing as a way of fact- and world-making, what has come to be known as 'The News' offers a paradigm example. Although anyone reading a newspaper or watching 'The News' on TV will quite rightly assume that what is presented are events that actually happened and thus 'facts' to all intents and purposes, the news, on closer inspection, tends rather to present news-stories that are made by the media than to merely depict brute facts. In his highly readable book on the topic, Alain de Botton shrewdly observes: "The news [...] fails to disclose that it does not merely *report* on the world, but is instead constantly at work crafting a new planet in our minds in line with its own often highly distinctive priorities."[13] Instead of merely providing factual information about actual events, the news is shaped by such categories as novelty, and breaches of normalcy, with an emphasis on catastrophes, crises and disasters, all of which are regarded as being especially eventful and newsworthy. Moreover, while many items in the news are not "reports of events but speculations about the future," such items are, amazingly, nonetheless "quickly absorbed as fact."[14] The central hypothesis of the present contribution, that writing should be seen as a cultural way of fact-making, thus also promises to shed light on the processes involved in the making of news-stories and what the 'distinctive priorities' of these might be. Emphasizing "the extraordinary capacity of news outlets to influence our sense of reality," de Botton goes so far as to call them "the prime creator of political and social reality."[15] In other words, an analysis of the news shows that journalistic writing does not record or transcribe facts, but rather turns them into news and "selectively *fashions* reality."[16] Crises and catastrophes in various media should thus not be seen as brute facts that are simply given but rather as something that is made by particular types of news-stories that are, within themselves, shaped by the choice of metaphors and narratives.[17]

There are additional reasons, however, why writing should be conceptualized as a way of fact-making rather than as a neutral medium that merely documents facts or represents events. As Hans Rosling forcefully argues in his book *Factfulness*, there are many biases, misconceptions, and other ways of getting 'facts' out of proportion that we need to consider if we want to come

---

13 De Botton 2014: 11, original emphasis.
14 Heffernan 2021: 39, 40.
15 De Botton 2014: 12.
16 Ibid.: 42, original emphasis.
17 Cf. Nünning 2012.

to terms with the relationship between writing and facts. Such (negativity) biases and misconceptions include, for instance, the selection of 'facts' that are considered to be breaches of normalcy and, thus, 'newsworthy' and the filtering out of what are not. One of Rosling's examples of how we often blow alleged facts out of proportion concerns the highly exaggerated view the news provides about the number of deaths caused by fatal attacks by wild animals such as bears, crocodiles, and sharks, all of which are generally considered to be highly newsworthy, while the much higher number of deaths related to domestic murders and racist violence remains under-reported at best.[18]

On a larger, and politically even more important scale, many of the 'alternative facts' and stories generated and disseminated by the Bush administration since 9/11, especially those about the alleged production of weapons of mass destruction in Iraq, underline the central hypothesis that writing is a very powerful, and potentially dangerous, way of fact- and worldmaking. Though we now know that the narratives revolving around weapons of mass destruction failed to correspond to either reality or truth, at the time they had the capacity to create political and military facts, and to change the course of history. The fact-making and reality-changing potential of these stories also depended on their correspondence to the culturally available schemata, metaphors, and plots that the contemporary American society lives by, i.e., whether they appear sufficiently plausible to the majority of people. This example also serves to show that writing powerful narratives can, within itself, be seen as generating weapons of mass destruction. The same holds true for other stories created by the Bush administration, the 'war on terror' being the most destructive case in point.

The performative and indeed fact-making power that writing can exert is highlighted in Paul Auster's somber post 9/11-novel *Man in the Dark* (2008), in which he conjures up a metafictional scenario that can be read as a satiric commentary on how the stories about alleged weapons of mass destruction led to the 'war on terror.' When sleep refuses to come to the eponymous seventy-two-year-old August Brill, the narrator-protagonist tells himself stories to try to keep recent traumatic events, including his wife's death, the murder of his granddaughter's boyfriend, 9/11, and the war in Iraq, at bay. In the embedded narrative that he creates while suffering from insomnia, the protagonist finds himself in an alternative world: An America not fighting a war in Iraq but rather an America ravaged by a terrible civil war that has been going

---

18   Cf. Rosling 2018: 133; cf. V. Nünning 2020: 72–79.

on for four years. Here, mysterious men tell him that he has been picked for what is referred to as "the big job" of becoming an assassin, the assignment being to kill someone who is said to deserve death because he purportedly invented a war by writing down a particular story. The dialogue between the mysterious men and the highly reluctant assassin-to-be deserves to be quoted at some length due to the light it can shed on the topic at hand:

> Because he owns the war. He invented it, and everything that happens or is about to happen is in his head. Eliminate that head, and the war stops. It's that simple.
> Simple? You make him sound like God.
> Not God, Corporal, just a man. He sits in a room all day writing it down, and whatever he writes comes true.[19]

What, then, do these random examples tell us about the ways in which writing plays an important role as a medium of fact- and worldmaking? They all show that writing is by no means an innocent or neutral way of merely describing events or facts. Instead writing is, within itself, capable of exerting a great deal of performative power in that it can create the very facts that it purports merely to document or record. Blowing reality widely out of proportion in the news or perceiving imaginary weapons of mass destruction as facts consists in producing not only weapons in the mind but also stories that can change reality and have far-reaching consequences for a potentially great number of people. Recognizing a crisis in Iraq, or any other country, for that matter, can be very much a matter of creating, inventing, and shaping it: Once the diagnosis is formulated in writing that there 'is' a crisis, it comes to be regarded as a political fact or economic reality. Culturally available crises-plots are then activated, assigning not only roles to the participants involved but also a particular meaning to the event thus designated.[20] In short, the activity of cultural fact- and worldmaking, including the choice of a particular kind of metaphor and story, is not so much a matter of recognizing crises or historical changes 'out there' but of imposing order and meaning on a mere sequence of happenings. All of this should give anyone interested in the ways in which facts are made through processes of writing, or political speeches, reason to pause and to take a fresh look at the ways in which events are created and stories are made.

---

19  Auster 2008: 10.
20  Cf. Nünning 2008.

## 3. Writing Facts, Constructing Events, Making Stories: Axes and Dimensions of Writing as a Cultural Way of Fact- and Worldmaking from a Narratological Point of View

Using these random examples from literature and recent history as a point of departure, let us now turn our attention to the processes that go into writing as a cultural way of fact- and worldmaking. How can concepts of literary studies and narratology, in particular, shed light on the ways in which writing can turn happenings, phenomena or states of affairs into facts, events, and even news-stories? The question already implies that from the point of view of literary and cultural theory, an event, a fact, or a story is not understood as something given or natural but rather as something made or constructed. What Brian McHale said about literary-historical objects is equally true of events and facts: "If literary-historical 'objects' [...] are constructed, not given or found, then the issue of *how* such objects are constructed, in particular the genre of discourse *in which* they are constructed, becomes crucial."[21]

Thus, the interest is shifted away from the completed product called the 'event' or 'fact' towards the construction process, to the question of how events, facts, and stories are produced, as well as the procedures through which they are constructed. If we want to gain a better understanding of what I have been calling 'writing as a cultural way of fact- and worldmaking,' we need to explore the processes of selection, configuration, and textual representation that it involves. Although the following description of these processes is merely a sketch and does not pretend to make any claim to completeness, it may nonetheless serve the purpose of pointing out that the terminological and analytical instruments of narratology provide a number of useful categories for developing a descriptive model for coming to terms with writing as a way of fact- and worldmaking. The latter is a complex process that arguably consists of at least five procedures which can be found across the different forms of writing in various genres, text-types, and media.

Let's call these procedures fact- and worldmaking acts I, II, III, IV, and V. Writing as a cultural way of fact- and worldmaking usually begins with act I: the selection and prioritization of certain events. Selection inevitably involves a concomitant deletion and obfuscation of everything else that is not mentioned in a given piece of writing. In other words, writing not only makes certain facts, it also entails a dismissal and editing out of whatever is not

---

21   McHale 1992: 3.

mentioned or recorded in a text. For any attempt to come to terms with the question of how acts of writing make facts and shape worlds, the concept of the event seems to be helpful, since events are generally agreed to be paradigmatic facts, while also being among the constitutive properties that make up narratives. At first sight, the meaning of the key term 'event,' just like that of 'facts,' seems to be self-evident. Intuitively, everybody knows what an event and a fact is or is supposed to be. At the same time, however, there are few concepts which are more pre-conditioned than those of the event and of facts, terms which are anything but self-explanatory or indeed well-defined. Since events and facts are the stuff that narratives and histories are made of, outlining some criteria for the definition of the terms 'event' and 'happening' as well as for the gradation of 'eventfulness' can shed some light on the ways in which writing makes facts.

In the light of the importance of facts and events in historiography, it is, at first glance, astonishing to see that these terms are usually taken for granted, having hardly ever been the subject of definitions or theoretical reflections. Definitions of the key term 'event,' for instance, are rare, and this fundamental concept cannot even be found in most of the salient historical reference works. Paul Ricœur once laconically noted that "most historians have a poor concept of 'event,'"[22] and of 'facts,' one might well add. However, in *Time and Narrative* Ricœur himself had comparatively little to say about the event, which supposedly comprises the fundamental constituents of narratives. In his useful *Dictionary of Narratology*, Gerald Prince defines an 'event' as a "change of state manifested in discourse by a process statement in the mode of *Do* or *Happen*."[23] While any change of state can be regarded as an event in general, only particular kinds of happenings will qualify as an event or fact or will ever be mentioned in the news.

That is to say that from a narratological perspective, events and facts are neither givens nor anything natural but should rather be conceived of as the results of choices or procedures manifested in writing, including selection, deletion, abstraction, and prioritization or 'weighting.'[24] Narratology provides criteria to define the term 'event' which can be helpful in understanding the selection process involved in the making of facts. For one, the narratological concept of the event is defined against the term 'happening.' In addition to

22 Ricœur 1984 [1983]: 171.
23 Prince 1987: 28, original emphasis.
24 Goodman 1992: 10–12.

this, narratologists have proposed to distinguish different degrees of 'eventfulness.' Tying in with the everyday meaning of 'event' as a 'significant incident' or a 'significant occurrence,' narrative theory first of all makes a distinction between all the chaotic and contingent things that happen (the totality of all occurrences) and the event as an especially relevant and significant part of it. The constitution of an event is, thus, based upon its being singled out from the continuous flow of occurrences and thereby being qualified as something especially important or surprising.

Following such an understanding of events, one can argue that the making of facts through writing is also based on selection, deletion, and weighting by an observer. In the last chapter of his critical book *La Pensée sauvage* (1962), i.e. *The Savage Mind* (1966) or *Das wilde Denken* (1973), Claude Lévi-Strauss clearly describes the way in which there is always a high degree of abstraction involved in determining a historical fact:

> For, *ex hypothesi*, a historical fact is what really took place, but where did anything take place? Each episode in a revolution or a war resolves itself into a multitude of individual psychic movements [...]. Consequently, historical facts are no more *given* than any other. It is the historian, or the agent of history, who constitutes them by abstraction and as though under the threat of an infinite regress.[25]

Writing can thus be seen as a way of making facts and constructing events by way of selection and deletion, these events are then further constituted by a high degree of abstraction. Subsumed under a generic term, historical events and so-called 'facts' are abstractions in that they consist of a multitude of actions, condition changes, and movements. The designation of historical events and facts that are regarded as media events provides cases in point, with terms like 'Brexit' or indeed the abbreviated mega-event of '9/11' being typical examples. Such abstractions refer to a heterogeneous multitude of actions, events, political decisions, deliberations, and any number of other, allegedly minor, facts.

Hence, the constitution of an event is itself a paradigm example of how writing makes facts in that it is the result of a complex set of procedures involving selection, deletion, and, even more so, the kind of privileging Goodman called 'weighting.' The latter term designates such processes as "ratings

---

25 Lévi-Strauss 1972: 257, original emphasis.

of relevance, importance, utility, value,"[26] through which what is regarded as substantial is highlighted while the irrelevant elements are disregarded and edited out. Such procedures of fact- and worldmaking reflect but arguably also generate and shape cultural hierarchies of norms and values.[27] The fact that these distinctions and hierarchies are neither given nor found but rather a matter of attribution, valuation, and assigning meaning, becomes even clearer in the case of especially important historical events which are considered as 'great' or 'epoch-making.' This was already stressed by Nietzsche at the beginning of the fourth installment of *Untimely Meditations* of 1875: "In itself no event is great; even if whole constellations disappear, nations collapse, powerful states are founded, and incredibly violent and destructive wars are waged, the breath of history may scatter them like down. [...] History seldom remembers such nonevents."[28]

If we want to come to terms with how writing constitutes and generates facts, we need additional criteria by means of which we can agree on when happenings or mere occurrences are perceived as a fact or as a 'great event.' An important condition for qualification is, at first, that it transgresses the norms and routine of everyday experience. There must be a certain degree of novelty or surprise for something that happens to qualify as a 'fact' that is considered to be newsworthy. In his insightful essay on "The Narrative Construction of Reality", the psychologist Jerome Bruner already drew attention to some of the key dimensions of eventfulness, especially to the important role of norms as a point of reference and the deviation thereof. He uses the felicitous concepts of "canonicity and breach"[29] to describe how an event usually results from a deviation from the canonical, i.e., from what is regarded as normal, pointing out that any break with expectations always involves norms.[30] Decisions about what constitutes an important fact thus always partake in the culture's ways of worldmaking, including its hierarchies of norms and values.

---

26  Goodman 1992: 12.
27  Cf. the introduction and articles in Erll/Grabes/Nünning 2008.
28  Nietzsche 1990: 253. The German original reads as follows: "An sich hat kein Ereignis Größe, und wenn schon ganze Sternbilder verschwinden, Völker zugrunde gehen, ausgedehnte Staaten gegründet und Kriege mit ungeheuren Kräften und Verlusten geführt werden: über vieles bläst der Hauch der Geschichte hinweg, als handele es sich um Flocken. [...] Die Geschichte weiß auch von solchen gleichsam abgestumpften Ereignissen beinahe nichts zu melden." Nietzsche 1954 [1875]: 367.
29  Bruner 1991: 11–13.
30  Cf. ibid.: 15–16.

The criteria proposed by narratologists for defining the term 'event,' and for distinguishing varying degrees of eventfulness, shed additional light on the ways in which writing can be seen as a way of fact-making. Working within a structuralist narratological framework, Wolf Schmid defines the event as 'a change of condition, which meets with certain requirements.'[31] To my knowledge, Schmid was the first narratologist to compile a systematic list of criteria or fundamental requirements which a condition-change must fulfill to be recognized and distinguished as an 'event.' According to Schmid, events are to be defined as changes of state or condition which initially need to meet two stipulations, namely 'facticity' (or reality) and 'resultivity.' The criterion of facticity distinguishes events from mere subjective desires, dreams, or imaginations, i.e., from what Marie-Laure Ryan and other representatives of Possible-Worlds Theory call 'possible worlds.' Resultivity simply means that events are not only begun but also brought to a close.

Since fact-making usually implies ratings of relevance, the five properties that a change of state must display to qualify as an event and to be attributed a high degree of eventfulness are useful for coming to terms with writing as a way of fact-making. According to the model proposed by Schmid, and applied and refined by other narratologists, changes can be "more or less eventful depending on the extent to which these five properties are present."[32] The approximate degree of eventfulness can thus be measured by means of the following five characteristics:[33]

1) Relevance of the change and/or its significance: The eventfulness increases at the rate at which the change of condition in the respective narrative world is felt.
2) Unpredictability and/or unexpectedness: The eventfulness increases at the rate of the variation from the narrative 'doxa,' i.e., the general expectance of the respective world. An event can also consist in the break with an expectation.
3) Consecutivity and/or potential consequences of the change: The eventfulness of a change of condition increases at the rate at which a change in the frame of the narrated world has consequences for the thinking and the acting of the affected subject.

---

31  Cf. Schmid 2005: 20.
32  Hühn 2009: 89.
33  Cf. Schmid 2005: 22–26.

4) Irreversibility: The eventfulness increases through the improbability of revoking the achieved state.
5) Non-iterativity and/or non-repeatability: Changes, which are repeated, only constitute a remote eventfulness at most, even if they are relevant and unpredictable.

These narratological characteristics that define eventfulness can fruitfully be applied to the domain of cultural fact- and worldmaking in the real world, in that they offer useful starting points for the issues involved in 'writing facts.' First, they provide precise criteria for the selection and qualification of especially 'eventful' occurrences that are likely to be accepted as facts. Secondly, they raise the awareness of the preconditions that have to be fulfilled in order for things that happen to ever become a cultural fact or historical event. Moreover, these criteria emphasize the hypothesis that events and facts are not something that is objectively given but rather the result of selection, abstraction, prioritization, weighting, and hierarchies of values.

The second act involved in writing as a cultural way of fact- and worldmaking consists of the transformation of mere happenings into events, stories, and textual representations. The above-mentioned distinction between happenings and events provides the basis for further illustrating the processes of transformation that are involved in fact- and worldmaking. For this purpose, one can resort to the terminological triad 'happenings, story, and textual representation of the story or narrative,' which goes back to a seminal article by Karlheinz Stierle, and which Schmid developed into a four-stage model. These models can be profitably adapted in order to answer the question of how happenings in the real world are turned into facts, events, stories, and texts through writing. Stierle and Schmid understand the term 'happening' to mean the totality of all situations, occurrences, and actions. A happening is a continuum without beginning or end and without meaning. For something that happens to become a fact, an event, and a story, a certain temporal section must be singled out and – not least through such ways of fact- and worldmaking as selection, ordering, and weighting – be given meaning, and it is thereby already interpreted in a certain way. Accordingly, the respective facts and story told are the result of a selection of certain moments and qualities from the happening, whose amorphous endlessness writing then transforms into a limited, structured form which is enriched with meaning. The story contains the selected facts in their chronological order, however, without already transferring them into a plot. The latter does not happen until the story is transformed into a particular narrative through writing, which involves shaping and arrangement. Whereas the levels of story and narrative can, in the sense of Stierle, be considered as deep structures which can only be identified through abstraction, the level of the text of the story or the actual piece of writing, i.e., the textual representation of the narrative, is the only level which can be observed directly. One might thus even go so far as to maintain that without writing there would not be any facts that would be generally accepted or that can be publicly debated.

The immediate relevance of these narratological considerations for the question of cultural fact- and worldmaking is based on the insight that the chaotic events of a crisis like the COVID-19 pandemic or a war, for example, can only be made accessible and communicated in society after such chaotic happenings have been transferred into writing and comprehensible stories. This, again, requires narratives and rhetorical strategies, which are by no means inherent to the events or facts as such but are imposed on them by the forms of the narrative discourse which functions as a shaping pattern. Facts and stories are not only the result of a selection from the manifold happenings but also the result of a multitude of forms of arrangement, ordering, and (linguistic, narrative, literary, etc.) composition on the level of writing. As a result, there is always a range of stories and texts that can be generated about any event or fact. Moreover, since different meanings can be assigned to the same fact by different observers, the choice of a point of view also has to be taken into consideration in any account of cultural ways of fact- and worldmaking. Stories and narratives as the means of representing facts in writing are characterized by the methods of configuration and perspectivization which are described below as acts III and IV.

The third act of cultural fact- and worldmaking through writing can therefore be conceptualized in terms of configuration and emplotment. The configuration of facts and emplotment of events in the form of a narrative of a particular kind do not only serve as modes of textual organization, but they are also important for the construction of meaning through writing facts. It is not just the selection and weighting of certain things and the deletion of others which is important for the analysis of how facts and events are made or constructed, but the arrangement of the selected material into a certain order plays an equally important role. The significance of what Goodman calls "ordering," refers to the structuring of events through narrative procedures and the establishment of a relationship between the selected facts: "First, the configurational arrangement transforms the succession of events into one meaningful whole [...]. Second, the configuration of the plot imposes the 'sense of an ending' [...] on the indefinite succession of incidents."[34] The configuration of the selected events, facts, and persons consists in establishing connections, interrelations, and patterns between them, turning them into a particular kind of story.

In his seminal works, the metahistorian Hayden White managed to demonstrate that facts do not speak for themselves but are endowed with meaning through the narrative forms, genres, and techniques through which they are narrativized. His insights about "The Value of Narrativity in the Representation of Reality", to quote the telling title of one of his seminal articles, also pertain to writing as a way of fact-making. By coining the term emplotment, White called attention to the ways in which historical facts and events are always embedded in a superordinate textual context. Adopting certain frames of reference, emplotment-strategies serve the purpose of overcoming the contingency of historical occurrences, narratively structuring the selected events, and shaping them into a particular story: "Emplotment is the way by which a sequence of events fashioned into a story is gradually revealed to be a story of a particular kind." The contextual meaning is not inherent in an occurrence or facts as such but is primarily created through the choice of a certain genre and mode, thus turning the facts into a particular plot. Through processes of narrativization and writing, events and facts are given not only a certain structural and narrative pattern but also sense and meaning.

Writing is thus not a transparent medium by means of which historic events and facts can be presented neutrally. According to White, it is the narrative discourse which initially integrates facts into a narrative context and framework by means of emplotment-strategies. Narrative configuration and emplotment are thus also always modes of fact-, sense-, and worldmaking. In her book on Possible Worlds, Andrea Gutenberg elaborated several dimensions of the constitution of meaning through the methods of emplotment. Firstly, the selection and emphasis of the chosen elements leads to a 'hierarchization of meanings' on the paradigmatic axis, representing one of the procedures of what Goodman called 'weighting.' Secondly, the methods of plot configuration on the syntagmatic axis, which encompasses arrangement, combination, and causal and logical interconnections, are crucial for the processes of narrative fact- and meaning-making. Thirdly, the discursive

---

34  Ricœur 1984 [1983]: 67.

axis plays a pivotal role in cultural fact- and worldmaking because the explicit and implicit constitution of meaning also greatly depends on the structure of narrative mediation and choice of perspectives. Perspective, or point of view, deserves special attention as another act or procedure of fact- and worldmaking in its own right because it influences all of the processes involved in the making of events, plots, and storyworlds discussed above.

In addition to the making of facts through writing as a means of textual representation, cultural fact- and worldmaking also involves a fourth important aspect or dimension: perspectivity or point of view which is arguably at least as important as emplotment in writing. Writing facts inevitably involves what I propose to be act IV: the choice of a point of view as well as perspective-dependent attributions of meaning and significance. Different dimensions of perspective or point of view, viz. perceptional, spatial, temporal, and ideological perspective, impinge on all the processes that are involved in the transformation of mere happenings or occurrences into facts, stories of a particular kind, and textual representations of narratives. Not only does the observer's spatial and temporal perspective of perception already play a decisive role in the choice of certain elements of the event, but his or her ideological perspective, i.e., his or her values and norms, is equally important. The same is true for the processes of composition through which a story becomes a narrative of a particular kind, as well as for the verbalization which creates the text or the representation of the story. While key narratological concepts like focalization, unreliable narration, and narrative perspective have proved to be very good descriptive and analytical tools, they have rarely been deployed to capture the procedures of fact- and worldmaking through writing. Narrative theory emphasizes that the choice of point of view and methods of perspectivization always play a crucial role in narrative worldmaking. Whether or not any given event or story is attributed a high degree of significance and the kind of meaning assigned to it, largely depends on the point of view from which facts and stories are focalized or told.

Written representations of wars offer a case in point that serves to illustrate that what passes as 'facts' can be highly contested, and that the events and stories projected by a piece of writing largely depend on the point of view from which they are presented. In the case of news coverage of war, the extensive importance which the chosen perspective has for the acceptance of the events as facts is immediately evident. The various dimensions of perspectivity, i.e., the spatial, temporal, perceptional, and ideological dimension, each serves to color the narratives and stories that are disseminated about military conflicts. As Goodman observes, "some changes are reshapings or deformations that may according to point of view be considered either corrections or distortions." Written representations of the contested facts of wars, for instance, are always colored by perspective and point of view, regardless of their form of manifestation (e.g., literary, historiographic, or journalistic writings, in photography or other visual media). However, not only do the perspectives of witnesses, authors of press reportage, or photographers need to be considered, but so do the cultural frames of reference and culturally available plots, genres and media used and their respective conventions of representation.

The fifth act or dimension of cultural fact- and worldmaking through writing revolves around the insight that events, facts, and stories are not only discursively created and medially represented but also culturally specific and historically mutable constructs. One does not need to be a constructivist or historian, to want to add further characteristics to the criteria of eventfulness and the procedures of fact- and worldmaking which have been formulated so far: What immediately comes to mind here, is the constructivity, performativity, discursivity, and mediality of events, facts, and news stories. A happening only becomes an event through being reflected, or rather (re)constructed, in discourses and writing and by being represented or staged by media productions. The constructedness of facts and their dependence on writing and other media are based on the fact that events and facts are never simply given or found 'out there' but are made by the people and media outlets who provide accounts of them in writing or visual form: As analyses of the representations of great historical events like 9/11 or the wars in Iraq have amply demonstrated, the writings and images disseminated by the media have a performative function insofar that medial representations construct the events and facts as opposed to merely describing or reporting on them. In that sense, just as 'The Medium is the Witness', writing is as much the maker of facts and events as it is a medium for documenting and recording them.

## 4. Reframing Narrative Factuality in Terms of the Fabrication of 'Knowledge', or: Writing as a Cultural Way of Making Facts, Conflicts and Crises, and Limiting the Horizon of Possibility

What are the consequences of the argument delineated above, stating that writing does not necessarily describe facts or provide objective representations of occurrences that actually happened in the real world but should rather be seen as a cultural way of fact- and worldmaking? If we accept such a constructivist view, it seems apposite to reframe the problem of "narrative factuality"[35] in terms of the 'fabrication' or "manufacture of knowledge." Although Karin Knorr-Cetina's pioneering monograph *The Manufacture of Knowledge* is not primarily concerned with writing, her *Essay on the Constructivist and Contextual Nature of Science* can serve as a timely reminder that facts – just like scientific knowledge at large – are constructed or made rather than found.[36] Knorr-Cetina did a brilliant job in demonstrating why Dorothy L. Sayers' comparison of facts with cows, which she uses as the perfect epigraph in her first chapter ("My lord, facts are like cows. If you look them in the face hard enough, they generally run away."[37]), is much more than just a witty aphorism or famous quote. Instead of accepting the common-sense view underlying standard dictionary definitions according to which the term 'facts' refers to phenomena that are accepted as true, Knorr-Cetina reformulates the problem of factuality in terms of the fabrication of knowledge. She sheds a great deal of light on the procedures and processes involved in generating scientific facts in the laboratory, demonstrating that even science can be conceived of as a methodological way of *Making Truth*.[38]

The constructivist and contextual nature of the production of facts in the natural sciences delineated by Knorr-Cetina holds equally true for facts in other domains, especially in the humanities, social sciences, journalism, and in our everyday life-worlds. As the philosopher John R. Searle has shown in his book *The Construction of Social Reality*, such a view has far-reaching consequences for our understanding of the ontology of social facts.[39] Instead of accepting the naïve view that facts can be understood as something that has really occurred or is actually the case, Searle analyses in detail what he calls "the building blocks of social reality"[40] and the processes that underlie the creation of institutional and social facts. According to his "General Theory of Institutional Facts,"[41] social facts are created by such processes as iteration,

---

35  Cf. the recent handbook edited by Fludernik/Ryan 2020.
36  Knorr-Cetina 1981.
37  Sayers as cited in Knorr-Cetina 1981: 1.
38  Cf. the title of Brown 2003.
39  Cf. Searle 1995.
40  Ibid.: 1.
41  Ibid.: 79, 113.

interaction, and performative speech acts. Although important social phenomena like "money, property, government and marriages" no doubt really exist and are generally accepted as objective facts, they "are only facts by human agreement."[42] Distinguishing between such social facts and "brute facts" about the natural world, Searle proposes to designate the former as 'institutional facts': "Institutional facts are so called because they require human institutions for their existence."[43] Although Searle's book demonstrates the degree to which the creation and structure of institutional and social facts depend upon language, he focuses mainly on the role of speech acts rather than on writing as a way of fact-making.

Let us therefore turn our attention to the role of writing in the creation of institutional and social facts and look at a couple of examples that illustrate how writing can be used as a powerful way of fact- and worldmaking. For anyone working in academia, it will not come as a big surprise that universities, albeit probably unwittingly so, provide particularly rich examples of the importance of writing for the construction of institutional facts. The technocratic text-types known as five- or ten-year 'development plans,' 'masterplans,' and 'grant proposals' (e.g., in the context of the German 'Excellence Initiatives' and 'Excellence Strategy') are cases in point in that they do not so much represent the actual state of affairs at a given university but rather serve to create new institutional facts through writing. Although terminology differs from one university to the next, the act of designating particular research areas or disciplines as 'fields of focus,' 'centers of gravity' (i.e., '*Schwerpunktbereiche*'), or 'areas of potential' can be understood as a way of making institutional facts through writing. Such designations are not just a result of the ways of fact-making outlined above in that they involve processes of selection (and deletion) as well as hierarchization and prioritization, but they also serve to construct the institutional facts they purport merely to describe or reflect.

Representing a mode of governance, text-types like development plans and grant proposals not only provide paradigm examples of how writing serves to create institutional and social facts, they also unintentionally reveal that such institutional fact-making, despite its contingency and even arbitrariness, is both deterministic and prescriptive rather than descriptive, and has far-reaching consequences for the development of an institution and

---

42   Ibid.: 1.
43   Ibid.: 2.

the shaping future behavior. Being based on "intentional selection between possibilities,"[44] texts like development plans arguably foster a fixed and rigid mindset and inhibit creativity and fresh thinking. By prescribing the future form of an institution in a deterministic way, they limit "the scope of our ability to identify our choices"[45] as academics and reduce the range of institutional possibilities. Writing is thus not only a way of institutional fact-making but also an exercise of administrative power based on the implementation of a "selection and enforcement of one possibility among many."[46] Development plans can thus be understood as a form of inscribing in the present probable futures, while pre-empting other possible future trajectories. In that light, such forms of institutional writing represent "a regime of visibility and invisibility: the exclusion of different possible concatenations from the space of visibility."[47] Anything that is not delineated in strategic writing issued from the higher echelons of what can in many cases only be dubbed Kafkaesque administrations or bureaucracies (or in short: 'adminbureaucrazy'), ceases to be an institutional fact and does not really exist. Moreover, they also illustrate another form that power takes in today's corporate university in that texts that delineate an institution's 'strategy' can be seen as an "inscription of automated patterns of language and interaction."[48] Such plans and patterns shape future behavior, foster conformity as well as linear thinking, and inhibit the capacity to respond creatively to emerging concerns and challenges.

In view of the "Authoritarian Turn in Universities,"[49] we should be wary whenever authoritarian organizations and regimes attempt to make institutional facts through writing, define research fields that are deemed to be especially important, and tell us what to do. Relying on such authoritarian "systems means that we trade judgement for efficiency, reflection for obedience, inquiry for conformity and independence for constraint."[50] As Margaret Heffernan poignantly observes in her monograph *Uncharted*, "the danger in making science efficient is the risk of inhibiting innovation, marginalising un-

---

44   Berardi 2019: 16, to whose inspiring book these paragraphs are indebted.
45   Heffernan 2021: 61.
46   Berardi 2019: 103.
47   Ibid.
48   Ibid.: 107.
49   Fleming 2021.
50   Heffernan 2021: 81.

derrepresented ideas and discouraging new and multi-disciplinary fields."[51] Addressing the complex relations between writing and the making of institutional facts can thus serve as a timely reminder that academics familiar with critical theory should keep their minds "open to the possibilities that power attempts to reduce to a single one."[52] By making institutional facts and reducing the horizon of possibility, development plans often constrain "the dynamics of invention and innovation within the limits of a system"[53] rather than fostering creativity and the ability to think outside of the technocratic boxes defined from above. Moreover, we should always remember what the Italian activist and cultural theorist Franco 'Bifo' Berardi has dubbed "futurability," i.e., "the multiplicity of immanent possible futures," and fight against "the reduction of the range of possibilities inscribed in the present to a pattern that acts as a formatting gestalt."[54]

The ideologically charged story that the Bush administration disseminated about the alleged existence of weapons of mass destruction provides another pertinent example of how writing can exert performative power, make political facts, albeit 'alternative facts,' and shape future development in a particularly ill-fated manner. As we have shown in an earlier article,[55] the stories generated by the Bush administration turned out to be 'alternative facts' rather than true accounts of the actual state of affairs, resulting in propagandistic mass deception intended to justify aggressive military interventions. Here, political speeches and writing served to construct fake facts that provided the rhetorical justification for the ill-conceived and even more poorly executed so-called 'war on terror.' Such writings that intentionally disseminate misinformation and manipulate public opinion can even be seen as weapons of mass destruction in their own right in that many soldiers and civilians lost their lives as a result of propagandistic 'fact'-making. The rationale behind the Bush administration's preference for focusing on what Al Gore has aptly called "convenient untruths"[56] is perfectly obvious with the benefit of hindsight, since the idea "that a 'mushroom cloud' might threaten American cities

---

51   Ibid.: 84.
52   Berardi 2019: 65.
53   Ibid.: 195.
54   Ibid.: 13, 15.
55   For a detailed examination of this story as a paradigm example of conflict-, fact-, and worldmaking, cf. Nünning/Nünning 2017.
56   Gore 2008: 104.

unless we invaded Iraq to prevent Saddam Hussein from giving a nuclear weapon to the same terrorist group that had already attacked us with deadly consequences."[57]

The final example serves to demonstrate that writing can be much more than just a way of making political and social facts. Instead, it can even be seen as a form of world- and conflict-making that can function as "a very powerful – maybe even the most powerful – symbolic 'weapon' in structuring a world that is always, in the end, a cultural one."[58] Anyone who has followed the news in recent years will easily be able to cite any number of additional examples that underscore the key hypothesis of this essay, viz. that writing should be seen as a powerful way of fact-, conflict-, and worldmaking. Cases in point include the conflict between the reductive slogans issued by the Remain- and Leave-Campaigns that led to the 2016 Referendum and, ultimately, to Brexit, the remarkable series of 'convenient untruths' that the clownish British Prime Minister came up with to cover up his embarrassing blunders and misdeeds, and the more recent speeches and writings by the Russian dictator that also attempt to factualize lies and legitimize an aggressive invasion of and war against Ukraine. In all these cases, writing not only serves as an attempt to pass off bullshit, fake news, and lies as 'facts.' It is also a means of erasing the distinctions between facts and fictions and between truth and untruth.

In that respect, the former star of the reality TV show *The Apprentice*, who, unfortunately, also acted in the role of American President between 2016 and 2020, arguably takes the biscuit in that his writing is probably unsurpassed as a means of making alternative facts and perpetuating the erosion of truth. The speeches, tweets and other, well, pieces of writing that the former POTUS and uncrowned king of the tribe of the Twitterati bombarded the world-wide audience with show that accuracy or factuality are obviously no longer the default or norm for what passes as political communication. In his brilliant book *The Attention Merchants*, Tim Wu devotes a chapter tellingly entitled "An Absorbing Spectacle: The Attention Merchant Turned President" to how that notorious celebrity brander replaced factual forms of political communication with "techniques borrowed from entertainment and media industries, and especially reality TV and social media."[59] Although he often asserts (pseudo-)facts as truths, his notorious and erratic tweets are paradigm examples of what

---

57 Ibid.: 104–105.
58 Müller-Funk 2012: viii.
59 Wu 2017: 344.

happens to writing as a means of fact-making when the traditional yardsticks by which factuality can be measured are wantonly abandoned:

> Trump has rigorously elevated the exciting and outlandish at the expense of accuracy or consistency. Hence the importance of alternative facts and fake news, along with a constant barrage of presidential commentary, much delivered using Twitter – a form of attention carpet-bombing. Implicit is that values like consistency or truth would become subservient to the story being told. Trump, importantly, also never admits to being wrong but instead always reinforces his version of the truth.[60]

Once accuracy, consistency, and truth are abandoned, however, people will find it increasingly difficult to gauge whether they are dealing with facts or fictions. As far as the former POTUS or the former clown in Clowning Street are concerned, they probably could not have cared less, but for the world at large it will continue to be very important to agree on what is really the case. Just like the attention merchants examined in Wu's book, the "merchants of doubt" who willfully obscured truth on crucial issues are more interested in calling even well-established scientific facts about, e.g., the harmful effects of smoking and the existence and disastrous consequences of global warming, into question.[61] Since digitalization and the boom of 'social media' have served as catalysts for the erosion of scientific consensus and truth, let us briefly look at what happens to writing as means of fact-making in the twenty-first century that has seen an unprecedented proliferation of 'alternative facts' and 'fake news.'

## 5. Modest Reflections on the Performative Power of Writing as a Cultural Way of Fact- and Fiction-Making in the Age of "Post-Truth"

One of the conclusions which can be drawn from this account of writing as an important method of fact-making is that historical facts and events do not emerge 'naturally' but should rather be understood as the result of a series of complex procedures and processes of selection, deletion, abstraction, ordering, compression, and emplotment that go into fact- and worldmaking. By

---

60 Ibid.: 345.
61 Cf. Oreskes/Conway 2012.

recording things that happen (or perhaps never occurred) in writing, media and other means of written communication create facts and construct events, shape them in a certain way, and endow them with meaning. What I also hope to have shown is how pre-conditioned the notions of facts and events are, and how complex the processes of cultural fact- and worldmaking through which mere happenings and occurrences are gradually transformed into facts, events, and stories of a particular kind, are. The procedures which go into fact- and worldmaking include selection, deletion, abstraction, weighting and ratings of relevance, configuration, ordering, and emplotment, and, last but not least, the choice of point of view and the arrangement of perspectives. The range of fact- and worldmaking procedures discussed above suggests that Goodman's discussion of ways of worldmaking needs to be supplemented by additional categories if we are to fathom the complex dynamics of cultural fact- and worldmaking and the ways in which writing partakes in these processes. Goodman, however, struck the right sort of balance between, on the one hand, recognizing the usefulness of surveying the processes of worldmaking and, on the other hand, acknowledging the incompleteness and provisional nature that any attempt at systematizing ways of worldmaking necessarily entails: "All I have tried to do is to suggest something of the variety of processes in constant use. While a tighter systematization could surely be developed, none can be ultimate[...]."[62]

In the final section, I should like to offer some preliminary hypotheses and modest reflections on the ways in which the genesis, role, and status of 'facts' have changed in the transition from a more innocent period, in which the distinction between facts and fictions and between truth and lies seemed to be relatively straightforward, to the current digital era, in which words like 'alternative facts,' 'post-factual,' or 'post-truth' have gained such currency and traction that one finds entries for them in renowned dictionaries. Although I am more than just a bit skeptical about such sweeping period designations as the 'digital age,' the "Age of Sharing,"[63] or, more ominously, the "New Dark Age,"[64] there can be little doubt that in the wake of the ongoing digitalization of our life-worlds it has become more difficult than ever before to distinguish facts from fictions.

---

62   Goodman 1992: 17.
63   John 2017.
64   Bridle 2019.

As the editors and contributors to a recent volume on "postfactual storytelling" have shown, for the last two decades or so we have been witnessing a proliferation of alternative facts, fake news, and other forms of misinformation, and a concomitant erosion of truth.[65] The choice of the term 'post-truth' as the 'Word of the Year' by the O.E.D. in 2016 is certainly indicative of a widespread concern about public disputes revolving around what is generally accepted as true. The "2016 Masterclass on Truth-Bending"[66] and the ways in which the former POTUS shamelessly spread lies, show the degree to which postfactual forms of storytelling that disseminate alternative facts and fake news have become the new normal rather than the exception to the rules defined by the norms of factuality. The heated political debates in pre- and post-Brexit Britain also show that objective facts have become less influential in shaping public opinion than fake news, rumors, appeals to emotion, and personal beliefs. In her balanced account of the "Affordances and Limitations of the Post-Factual as an Explanatory Frame," Janine Hauthal rightly observes that "from the very beginning of the public debate 'Brexit' and 'post-factual' were linked."[67]

It stands to reason that such dangerous and daunting developments as the blurring of the boundaries between facts and fiction, as well as between truth and lies, necessitate a reassessment of the relations between writing and facts. I should like to conclude this contribution by suggesting that the argument delineated above, and the hypotheses about writing as a means of fact-making pertain just as much to fictions as they do to established facts. In his best-selling book *Homo Deus*, the historian Yuval Noah Harari observes that in "the twenty-first century fiction might therefore become the most potent force on earth, surpassing even wayward asteroids and natural selection. Hence, if we want to understand our future, cracking genomes and crunching numbers is hardly enough. We must also decipher the fictions that give meaning to the world."[68] Taking my cue from Harari and heeding his clarion-call, I should like to conclude by suggesting that it is high time that we begin to put the examination of fictions that cultures live by on the research agendas of literary and cultural studies. Probably even more so than established facts,

---

65 Cf. the articles in Weixler et. al 2021.
66 Sommer 2021.
67 Hauthal 2021: 299, 298.
68 Harari 2016: 151.

fictions not only serve as important ways of meaning-, sense-, and worldmaking, they are also among the most powerful cultural resources of resilience. Whether the "Vote Leave"-Campaign in Britain, or Putin's metaphysical view of Russian history and his propaganda, for that matter, correspond to actual historical facts is arguably less important than understanding how political speeches and writings fashion a particular view of the world and foster a sense of belonging to an imagined or a narrative community.

Moreover, in the twenty-first century, digital media and writing in the form of text-types like those offered by Twitter have arguably done more than any other cultural force to undermine the factuality of facts, to boost the proliferation of fictions, and to erase the distinction between what is real or true and what is fake. Although the role of writing in digital media has not yet received the amount of scholarly attention that it arguably deserves, one can venture the hypothesis that writing in so-called 'social media' has served as a catalyst for the corrosion of facts and the erosion of truth as a yardstick for gauging the difference between facts and fictions. In his brilliant manifesto *Ten Arguments for Deleting Your Social Media Accounts Right Now*, the Silicon Valley pioneer and scientist Jaron Lanier sums it up concisely in his Argument Four: "Social Media Is Undermining Truth."[69] With regard to the topic of writing facts, it is anything but good news that the dominant forms of writing in the age of ever more digitalization tend to disseminate more bullshit, conspiracy theories, fictions, lies, and nonsense than established facts: "Media forms that promote truth are essential for survival, but the dominant media of our age do no such thing," Lanier drily observes.[70]

In an age in which the so-called 'social media' provide platforms on which anyone can easily turn 'convenient untruths' into 'alternative facts,' and pass them off as real facts by sharing them with thousands or millions of 'followers,' we as cultural studies scholars and critical theorists, would be well-advised to pay more attention to the various acts and procedures of narrative fact- and worldmaking that prevail in the digital realm. Any attempt at understanding why some 'facts' become more powerful and have much more impact on economic and political developments than others, requires taking the mechanisms that are involved in some memes and stories going viral, no matter how factual they really are, into consideration.[71]

---

69   Lanier 2018: 53.
70   Ibid.: 61.
71   Cf. Shiller 2019.

Notwithstanding whether we accept the term 'the age of post-truth' as an apt designation of the current era, we should at least acknowledge that writing has become one of the most powerful cultural ways not only of fact-making but also of disseminating alternative facts, fake news, and other fictions. It is also important to realize that inscribing facts, no matter whether they are true or fake, entails prescribing options, shaping the future, and limiting or enhancing the horizon of possibility: "The future is inscribed in the present as a tendency that we can imagine. [...] The future is written, willy-nilly, in the present."[72] When writing and 'social media' are used to spread populist slogans like "Make America Great Again!", "Let's take back control!" or "We want our country back!", the prescriptive and performative dimension of such speech acts and writings as powerful ways of worldmaking becomes obvious. Berardi poignantly captures how such a deterministic strategy radically reduces the multiplicity of latent developments and possible futures: "The determinist strategy aims to subjugate the future, to constrain tendency into a prescribed pre-emptive model, and automate future behavior."[73] Since writing has become so important for the dissemination of conspiracy theories, fake news, and other fictions in the twenty-first century, I should like to leave the last words to Harari, who reminds us that fictions may have been more powerful than written facts in shaping the world, and that we have lived in the age of post-truth for much longer than the recent coinage of that term might suggest:

> In fact, humans have always lived in the age of post-truth. Homo sapiens is a post-truth species, whose power depends on creating and believing fictions. Ever since the Stone Age, self-reinforcing myths have served to unite human collectives. Indeed, Homo sapiens conquered this planet thanks above all to the unique human ability to create and spread fictions. [...] As long as everybody believes in the same fictions, we all obey the same laws, and can thereby cooperate effectively.[74]

---

72   Berardi 2019: 13, 234.
73   Ibid.: 12.
74   Harari 2018: 233.

## Bibliography

Auster, Paul (2008): *Man in the Dark*, London.
Berardi, Franco 'Bifo' (2019): *Futurability. The Age of Impotence and the Horizon of Possibility*, London.
Botton, Alain de (2014): *The News. A User's Manual*, London.
Bridle, James (2018): *New Dark Age. Technology and the End of the Future*, London/ New York.
Brown, Theodore L. (2003): *Making Truth. Metaphor in Science*, Urbana/Chicago.
Bruner, Jerome (1991): "The Narrative Construction of Reality", in: *Critical Inquiry* 18, 1–21.
Eakin, Paul John (1999): *How Our Lives Become Stories. Making Selves*, Ithaca/ London.
Erll, Astrid/Grabes, Herbert/Nünning, Ansgar (eds.) (2008): *Ethics in Culture. The Dissemination of Values through Literature and Other Media*, Berlin/New York.
Fleming, Peter (2021): *Dark Academia. How Universities Die*, London.
Fludernik, Monika/Ryan, Marie-Laure (eds.) (2020): *Narrative Factualiy. A Handbook*. Berlin/New York.
Goodman, Nelson (1992) [1978]: *Ways of Worldmaking*, Indianapolis.
Gore, Al (2008): *The Assault on Reason*, London/New York.
Gutenberg, Andrea (2000): *Mögliche Welten. Plot und Sinnstiftung im englischen Frauenroman*, Heidelberg.
Harari, Yuval Noah (2018): *21 Lessons for the 21$^{st}$ Century*, London.
— (2016): *Homo Deus. A Brief History of Tomorrow*, London.
Hauthal, Janine (2021): "(Re-)Thinking the Nexus of Nation and Narration in Pre- and Post-Referendum British Fiction", in: Weixler et. al (eds.), *Postfaktisches Erzählen?*, 297–321.
Heffernan, Margaret (2021): *Uncharted. How Uncertainty Can Power Change*, London.
Herman, David (2009): "Narrative Ways of Worldmaking", in: Heinen, Sandra/Sommer, Roy (eds): *Narratology in the Age of Cross-Disciplinary Narrative Research*, Berlin/New York, 71–87.
Hühn, Peter (2009): "Event and Eventfulness", in: id. et. al. (eds.): *Handbook of Narratology*, Berlin/New York, 80–97.
Isekenmeier, Guido (2008): *'The Medium is the Witness'. Zur Ereignis-Darstellung in Medientexten. Entwurf einer Theorie des Medienereignisses und Analyse der Fernsehnachrichten vom Irak-Krieg*, Trier.

John, Nicholas A. (2017): *The Age of Sharing*. Cambridge/Malden, MA.
Knorr-Cetina, Karin (1991): *Die Fabrikation von Erkenntnis. Zur Anthropologie der Naturwissenschaft*, Frankfurt am Main.
— (1981): *The Manufacture of Knowledge. An Essay on the Constructivist and Contextual Nature of Science*, Oxford.
Lanier, Jaron (2018): *Ten Arguments for Deleting Your Social Media Accounts Right Now*, London.
Lévi-Strauss, Claude (1972) [1966]: *The Savage Mind*, ed. Julian Pitt-Rivers/Ernest Gellner, London.
McHale, Brian (1992): *Constructing Postmodernism*, London.
Müller-Funk, Wolfgang (2012): *The Architecture of Modern Culture. Towards a Narrative Cultural Theory*, Berlin/New York.
— (2008) [2002]: *Die Kultur und ihre Narrative. Eine Einführung*, Wien/New York.
Nietzsche, Friedrich (1990): *Unmodern Observations*, ed. William Arrowsmith, New Haven/London.
— (1954) [1875]: "Unzeitgemäße Betrachtungen", in: id.: *Werke in drei Bänden*. vol. 1, ed. Karl Schlechta, München, 135–434.
Nünning, Ansgar (2012): "Making Crises and Catastrophes. Metaphors and Narratives Shaping the Cultural Life of Crises and Catastrophes", in: Meiner, Carsten/Veel, Kristin (eds.): *The Cultural Life of Catastrophes and Crises. Facts, Forms, Fantasies*, Berlin/New York, 59–88.
— (2010): "Making Events – Making Stories – Making Worlds: Ways of Worldmaking from a Narratological Point of View", in: Nünning, Vera/Nünning, Ansgar/Neumann, Birgit (eds.): *Cultural Ways of Worldmaking. Media and Narratives*, Berlin/New York, 191–214.
— (2008): "Steps Towards a Metaphorology (and Narratology) of Crises. On the Functions of Metaphors as Figurative Knowledge and Mininarrations", in: Grabes, Herbert/Nünning, Ansgar/Baumbach, Sibylle (eds.): *Metaphors. Shaping Culture and Theory*, Tübingen, 229–262.
Nünning, Ansgar/Nünning, Vera (2017): "Stories as 'Weapons of Mass Destruction', or: George W. Bush's Narratives of Crisis as Paradigm Examples of Ways of World- and Conflict-Making (and Conflict-Solving?)", in: Müller-Funk, Wolfgang/Ruthner, Clemens (eds.): *Narrative in Conflict(s)*, Berlin/New York, 189–229.
Nünning, Vera (2020): "Cultural Ways of Worldmaking", in: id./Löffler, Philip/Peterfy, Margit (eds.): *Key Concepts for the Study of Culture. An Introduction*, Trier, 43–84.

Nünning, Vera/Nünning, Ansgar/Neumann, Birgit (eds.) (2010): *Cultural Ways of Worldmaking. Media and Narratives*, Berlin/New York.

Oreskes, Naomi/Conway, Erik M. (2012): *Merchants of Doubt. How a Handful of Scientists Obscured the Truth on Issues from Tobacco Smoke to Global Warming*, London.

Prince, Gerald (1987): *A Dictionary of Narratology*, Lincoln/London.

Rathmann, Thomas (2003): "Ereignisse Konstrukte Geschichten", in: id. (ed.): *Ereignis. Konzeptionen eines Begriffs in Geschichte, Kunst und Literatur*, Köln/Weimar/Wien, 1–19.

Ricœur, Paul (1984) [1983]: *Time and Narrative*. vol. 1, Chicago/London [orig.: (1983): *Temps et récit*, Paris].

— (1980): "Narrative Time", in: *Critical Inquiry* 7, 169–190.

Rosling, Hans (2018): *Factfulness. Ten Reasons Why We're Wrong About the World – and Why Things Are Better than You Think*, London.

Schmid, Wolf (2005): *Elemente der Narratologie*, Berlin/New York.

Searle, John R. (1995): *The Construction of Social Reality*, New York.

Shiller, Robert J. (2019): *Narrative Economics. How Stories Go Viral & Drive Major Economic Events*, Princeton, NJ/Oxford.

Sommer, Roy (2021): "Dolus Trump. Presidential Lies and the 2016 Masterclass on Truth-Bending", in: Weixler, Antonius et. al (eds.), *Postfaktisches Erzählen?*, 47–64.

— (2009): "Making Narrative Worlds. A Cross-Disciplinary Approach to Literary Storytelling", in: Heinen, Sandra/Sommer, Roy (eds.): *Narratology in the Age of Cross-Disciplinary Narrative Research*, Berlin/New York, 88–108.

Stierle, Karlheinz (1975): "Geschehen, Geschichte, Text der Geschichte", in: id.: *Text als Handlung*, München, 49–55.

Weixler, Antonius et. al. (eds.) (2021): *Postfaktisches Erzählen? Post-Truth – Fake News – Narration*, Berlin/Boston.

White, Hayden (1980): "The Value of Narrativity in the Representation of Reality", in: *Critical Inquiry* 7/1, 5–27.

— (1973): *Metahistory. The Historical Imagination in Nineteenth Century Europe*, Baltimore, Md/London.

Wu, Tim (2017): *The Attention Merchants. The Epic Struggle to Get Inside Our Heads*, London.

# Facts
## What We Know about Them in the Postmodern Era

*Philipp Sarasin (University of Zurich)*

In 2004, the American journalist Ralph Keyes in his book *The Post-Truth Era. Dishonesty and Deception in Contemporary Life* enumerated for his compatriots, in a retrospectively downright old-fashioned moral way, how often they use euphemisms, are dishonest, or just plain lie. While Keyes primarily aimed to pinpoint everyday white lies, he also put into focus the media and politicians as role models for lying. Today, doubts seem to have tainted all political discourses from the left to the right as to whether one can still rely on something like 'truth' or 'facts' in the political public sphere. A book from 2016 is a further example of this: In *Lies Incorporated. The World of Post-Truth Politics* by Ari Rabin-Havt, lies and fact-free speech no longer appear to be primarily a moral problem for average Americans but a preferred tool in the struggle for interpretive sovereignty and power.

## 1. Postmodern Arbitrariness?

Disinformation and propaganda are certainly nothing new (they were commonplace during the Cold War). What is new, however – as Donald Trump and other politicians demonstrated every day – is that the goal has shifted from making false claims *look* like facts, something that intelligence agencies often put a lot of effort into during the Cold War. Today, perpetrators often no longer even attempt to make a serious, 'truthful' reference to facts. On the occasion of the dramatic US election campaign in 2016, *Weltwoche* chief editor Roger Köppel announced with a dry eye that "in the case of Trump, even the lies sound more honest than the highfalutin pseudo-truths of his competitor Clinton."[1]

That was not meant as criticism: it is better to lie 'honestly' than to tell the truth 'highfalutinly' (what on earth is a 'pseudo-truth' supposed to be?). Köppel did not hesitate to say what he thought of the truth in politics and journalism. And he is not alone. It now seems increasingly acceptable to suggest that all facts are up for 'interpretation'; to the right of the political center, this has become policy: The justification offered to historians is that what matters is not evidence and sources but "juicy stories."[2] Completely normal scientific discussions, for example by climatologists, are considered as evidence that they, too, had nothing more to offer than mere "opinions"[3] even in the serious *Neue Zürcher Zeitung*. Finally, a politician for the party 'Alternative for Germany' (AfD) countered the objection that there were far fewer refugees in Germany than claimed by his party with the now common, yet highly astonishing assertion: "It's not purely about statistics, it's about how the citizen feels. That means feelings are also reality."[4]

What has happened here? Can one seriously contradict official statistics because one 'feels' differently? Are scientific findings just a matter of opinion? Is it even possible to 'lie honestly'? Rubbing your eyes in disbelief, you wonder how it is even possible that people have started thinking that way. Many critical and rightly concerned observers claim that this is the result of postmodernity (and social media), i.e., the result of an allegedly widespread attitude that *anything goes*, the cynical play with mere words, the frivolous assertion that 'everything' is just an arbitrary 'construction' and knowledge cannot possibly be distinguished from belief. That would no doubt be confusing. Are facts truly not what they used to be? Are they now truth or constructions, even mere inventions?

## 2. Ask Kant!

Asking such questions, one quickly comes into contact with the truly big problems in the history of Western philosophy: What are truth, reality, reason,

---

1 Köppel 2016. All quotations are translated into English by Ph.S.
2 Keller 2015.
3 Binswanger 2016.
4 Pazderski 2016.

knowledge? Modernity – in this case post-Kant – has provided an answer to these old questions in many variants of the thought that we recognize of reality what our reason "puts into it," as Kant said.[5] Kant saw in this contribution of human reason nothing less than the guarantee for scientific knowledge in general: Definitive statements about reality are *only* possible because human reason structures the world substantially and reliably through its "categories" (starting with space and time). In other words, the immutable categories of our reason create knowable facts out of the "chaotic manifold" of the external world. The "things-in-themselves," on the other hand, remain hidden from us forever, are inaccessible to our perception.

Throughout modernity, this idea has varied up to our postmodern present. Since then, 'modern' has been a society or an epoch in which the prevailing thought is that there can be no absolute – such as religious – truths, only relative truths, i.e. truths dependent on our cognitive abilities. Kant tried to rescue the certainty of (scientific) knowledge by positing the structures of human reason as absolutely certain and immutable. Without wanting to unravel the entire history of philosophy since Kant, it can be said that this certainty has gradually dissolved. For example, in Hegel and Marx, but also in so-called historicism, truths were *historically* relativized by being viewed as time-bound, only valid for a specific epoch.

Equally influential was the assumption that there could be no truth outside of *language*, which had been forming since the end of the 19th century. Since we cannot think and make statements about reality without language, it is assumed that language forms the insurmountable framework, indeed, the limit of our knowledge of the world. After all, language is constantly changing, it never 'fits' completely but always represents the never completely successful attempt to put things into words. Nietzsche and Wittgenstein are the most important informants for this concept which is commonly attributed to postmodernity, i.e., the late 20th century. What is true, however, is that only postmodern philosophy has consistently thought through the epistemological concepts of modernity as proposed since Kant and further developed by Nietzsche and Wittgenstein.

---

5   Cf. Kant 2019 [1781/1787].

## 3. Facts Are Not Arbitrary

Truths, and thus what we call 'facts,' are bound to human cognitive faculties, vary historically and do not move beyond what is possible with our language. From the philosophy of the natural sciences, the insight also developed that "scientific facts" come from a "thought collective" and are inevitably shaped by a certain "thought style," as Ludwick Fleck has put it,[6] and finally that they also depend on the apparatus and instruments with which nature is observed, measured and analyzed.

Taken together, all this means that facts cannot be thought outside of theories, concepts, models and experimental systems, because without them it is not possible to somehow interpret or understand the 'chaotic manifold' of the world. However, because models and theories become outdated, knowledge can become stale and what was previously believed to be true can become false. What is more, statements about facts are fundamentally exposed to the danger of remaining trapped in erroneous assumptions and fixed convictions, in routine thinking and ideologies. Does this mean that facts are indistinguishable from feelings, truths from lies, and science from beliefs? And if not – why not?

In today's dominant philosophy of science – in the natural sciences as well as in the social sciences and humanities – facts are considered 'constructions,' i.e., *made* – that is *factum* – and shaped by the conditions of their production as scientific facts. Conversely, this does not mean, however, that they are therefore arbitrary, mere inventions, opinions or even indistinguishable from lies. No postmodernist has ever claimed that. Today, however, the assurance of the – always only relative – reliability of scientific knowledge no longer lies in reason, as with Kant, but in a research process of the scientific community that is structured by reciprocal examination, review and criticism. Arguments and claims about reality must be comprehensible and verifiable, they must convince other participants in the discussion, and they must be able to connect to previous discussions and explanatory models.

Statements about the world must, in a word, 'make sense.' If they do not, there are really only two possibilities: they will either be deemed wrong by all standards or uninteresting (or both) – *or*, sooner or later, they will become the source of new truths, new insights, new facts. Since modernity, and explicitly in our postmodernity, facts have therefore been "contingent" as the sociologist

---

6    Cf. Fleck 1980 [1935].

Niklas Luhmann said: They cannot be "ultimately" and "necessarily" proven to be "absolutely" true, and they belong in the space of what is, or can be the case (from which we exclude, for example, UFOs).

One last point: As far as the social, but not the natural world, is concerned, since postmodernity, it has become clearer than ever that our world consists exclusively of contingent rules and of time-bound institutions, of communication and of interpretation – from political constitutions to football games. Thus, the postmodern era has clearly revealed the extent of our inability to experience our own social reality outside of our media and speech. However, that does not mean that reality is arbitrary: A red traffic light is a fully contingent rule; a simple code that needs to be interpreted. If you misinterpret it, you risk death.

## 4. A Matter of Integrity

Despite this rejection of an 'objectivity' that is understood as absolute, facts are still 'robust' – they are confirmed by a lot of evidence and appear to be the best information currently available to us. Referring to facts as 'non-absolute,' i.e. contingent, and being aware of this contingency therefore has an ethical dimension: it is a matter of integrity to always footnote our sources for facts in order to disclose which assumptions, sources and models prove a certain fact to be 'possible,' even 'true.' To the best of my knowledge and belief, so to speak.

This integrity is a protection in two ways: *On the one hand*, it protects us from being positivists, that is, from making us believe that facts are – quite independently of our cognitive activity – inherently there and true and just have to be brought to light. Whoever asserts such a conception of facts is acting more powerfully than humanly possible – a dogmatist, an ideologue in the guise of a realist. In light of such temptations, postmodern philosophy has repeatedly warned us not only about constructedness but also the *variety* of statements about reality that is always possible in this context. However, as I said, this does not mean that one can say *n'importe quoi*, that one can say anything about reality. Statements about the world must be justifiable and understandable for others. Otherwise, they are beliefs – or lies. There is no pink elephant in the garden, even if someone claims to 'feel' it.

*On the other hand*, this integrity also protects against the kind of cynicism currently observable on the (broad) right edge of the political spectrum: Because science, experts and explanations of the world, which tend to be complicated, are strangely perceived by large parts of the political public as 'leftist' or 'elitist,' postmodern epistemology is used in a rather brazen way to flatten the distinction between lies and truth. This has nothing to do with the postmodern era per se, rather it reveals how little these people think of science, argumentation, verifiability and rationality. That is nothing new in itself. Today, however, it seems that there is no longer a need for intelligence agencies to carry out complicated operations of black propaganda to give lies the appearance of truth. The New Right simply laughs at those who still believe in something as silly as truth.[7]

## Bibliography

Binswanger, Matthias (2016): "Was die Wissenschaft weiss und was sie glaubt", in: *Neue Zürcher Zeitung* (15.09.2016), https://www.nzz.ch/feuilleton/zeitgeschehen/wissenschaftskritik-was-die-wissenschaft-weiss-und-was-sie-glaubt-ld.116772?reduced=true (11.05.2022).

Fleck, Ludwik (1980) [1935]: *Entstehung und Entwicklung einer wissenschaftlichen Tatsache. Einführung in die Lehre vom Denkstil und Denkkollektiv*, Frankfurt am Main.

Kant, Immanuel (2019) [1781/1787]: *Kritik der reinen Vernunft*, Frankfurt am Main.

Keller, Peter (2015): "Wir haben die saftigeren Geschichten", in: *Tagesanzeiger* (24.02.2015), https://www.tagesanzeiger.ch/wissen/geschichte/wir-haben-die-saftigeren-geschichten/story/27555266 (11.05.2022).

Keyes, Ralph (2004): *The Post-Truth Era. Dishonesty and Deception in Contemporary Life*, New York.

Köppel, Roger (2016): "Editorial: Hat Amerika die Wahl zwischen Pest und Cholera?", in: *Die Weltwoche* (06.10.2016), http://www.weltwoche.ch/ausgaben/2016-40/artikel/trump-die-weltwoche-ausgabe-402016.html (01.06.2022).

Pazderski, Georg (2016): in: *hr-online.de* (the article is no longer available).

Rabin-Havt, Art (2016): *Lies Incorporated. The World of Post-Truth Politics*, New York.

---

7 The original German text was first published online at *Geschichte der Gegenwart* on October 9, 2016.

# WRITING SOCIETY, POLITICS, AND LAW

# Writing Social Facts
## Some Observations on Max Weber's Concept of Modern Politics

*Harro Müller (Columbia University in the City of New York)*

Since this article on Max Weber is an essay, I would like to start with some personal remarks. In the 1960s, I studied German Literature, History and Philosophy at the University of Kiel. If I remember correctly, Max Weber was no topic during my studies. Just once, on the occasion of an introduction to modern history, Weber was mentioned briefly because of his application of typological argumentation. Nevertheless, I decided to buy the Kröner-edition[1] (first published in 1956), read some texts, but for a long time this was the only text of Max Weber in my private library. In 1973, I started to work at the Faculty of Linguistics and Literary Studies of the University of Bielefeld which was equipped with a famous History Department where eminent professors like Hans-Ulrich Wehler, Reinhart Koselleck, and Jürgen Kocka were teaching. Hans-Ulrich Wehler often mentioned that his design of modern social history had two founding fathers ("Säulenheilige"): Karl Marx and Max Weber. Later in 1991, I started to teach at Columbia University, met Guenther Roth, talked with him several times about Max Weber and read some of his texts on Weber. Fairly soon, I offered a class called "Theories of Modernity" for graduate students of various departments and repeated this class with some changes in the syllabus quite often. One session had always been reserved for Max Weber and a discussion of his "Science as a Vocation." My teaching of Weber was always met with great interest by the students and was quite a success (as, somewhat surprisingly, also the teaching of Carl Schmitt), although many students did not know anything about Max Weber. I retired in 2018. The emeritus status has its advantages and disadvantages. One huge advantage is that

---

1   Weber 1956.

you have much more time for reading books you could not deal with before. So, at a certain point, I started going through the many volumes of the Georg-Simmel-edition[2] by Otthein Rammstedt and wrote an article on the German author.[3] After Simmel, I chose Max Weber and read him in an intensive way. Even if I did not finish all the 47 volumes of the new edition,[4] I got a much better insight into the importance of Weber for the understanding of modernity and the modern social sciences. His discussion of what to understand by facts builds a decisive point in modernity.

The focus of this essay is on the analysis of Weber's practice of writing which builds the basis for his theoretical and methodological choices. After some general observations on the problem of writing facts in its theoretical and methodological implications, I will discuss two texts: Weber's inauguration lecture from 1895 "The Nation State and Economic Policy"[5] and his late talk "The Profession and Vocation of Politics" (1919).[6] Of a certain importance is that the work of Max Weber is a torso. During his lifetime, he published two books (his dissertation and his habilitation) and a large number of articles which he often qualified as sketches ("Skizzen") or attempts ("Versuche"). More or less all of his writings are concerned with the three dimensions of scientific work: the *context of discovery* (how to formulate the problem?), the *context of justification* (how to legitimate the claims of truth?), and the *context of application* (what are the functions of the scientific findings concerning their different social relations?). In the following, I will discuss Weber's scientific project in its approach to these three contexts.

## 1.

Let me start with some introductory remarks on Max Weber's general project by stressing the problem of writing facts. It seems very helpful to locate his project within a semantic-pragmatic model which not only concentrates on the dimension of meaning and arguments (in our case concerning 'fact') but also on writing texts as doing. Weber himself did not use the term 'Faktum/

---

2   Simmel 2015 [1989].
3   Müller 2020.
4   Weber 2021.
5   Weber 1994a: 1–28.
6   Weber 1994b: 309–369.

Fakt,' he prefers the term 'Tatsache' which combines a practical side ('Tat') with an empirical dimension by including its referential implications ('Sache'). At the same time, he did not differentiate between the term 'fact/Tatsache' and 'data' – another term he sometimes uses – in a systematic way. Since for Weber reality is definitely indefinite, from a systematic perspective there is always so much data that in the end one has to reduce the information to facts. Now, the interesting point here is: Within the context of discovery, facts are always the effect of questions/problem formulations concerning the way of *how* you want to formulate your object field. Facts are never just given. Contrary to Adorno,[7] I want to stress that Weber was not a positivist in a strict sense who starts with facts and continues with the construction of inductive rules. Rather, for Weber a fact could also have a negative connotation. He despised "men of fact/Tatsachenmenschen"[8] who only follow seemingly given facts and are unable to produce their own responsible decisions which for Weber are necessary to live a life that deserves the predicate 'human.' But more interesting concerning facts is, that for Weber one cannot deal with *the* or *a* fact in singular. As a starting point, one always has to think of facts in plural inserted in a relational field with its inferential and referential dimensions. Such an approach has massive consequences. Talking about facts here is to locate them within a semantic-pragmatic model which in its results cannot be reduced to one single and conclusive fact. As a consequence, there is no Archimedean point to be found within the social sciences. If, as for Weber, your aim is to produce a science of reality ("Wirklichkeitswissenschaft"), you always need different forms of scientific perspectivism which can never be homogenized. Just to quote the Bible exemplarily, "In the beginning was the word, and the word was with God, and God was the word." For Weber, this is a form of prescientific or metascientific religious talk that can never be scientifically proved. No one can verify if this sentence is right or wrong. As opposed to this, within the context of discovery you have to start with questions and problem formulations by using words which are facts themselves and which are selected out of an infinite amount of data. Such selections are constructions with certain referential dimensions on the one hand, and a certain reliance on excluding or complementary relations to other word fields on the other. Thus, Weber is a nominalist *cum grano salis* when it comes to the

---

7   Adorno 2003: 133–136.
8   Mommsen 1974: 119.

construction of facts. At the same time, he is a realist concerning the referential dimension. Therefore, my argument is that his position is much more complex than often formulated in the "Weberei."[9]

## 2.

Weber's science of reality is, in a strict sense, a science of realities. His perspectivism does not relate to a *universum* but to a *pluriversum*. Concerning the context of discovery, the latter depends on paradigms that were different in the past and will be different in the future. As for the context of justification, within the social sciences the writing (of) facts obeys the rules of scientific discourse and therefore includes the clarity of concepts, internal logical consistency, empirical and argumentative consistency, evidence, and, last but not least, plausibility. Weber adds the value of neutrality because for him only neutrality allows for the value of objectivity within the social sciences. Thus, there are value relations in the context of discovery that can always be transformed within the social scientific discourse concerning facts. Consequently, facts can be described, interpreted, and explained without any form of foundational normative discourse. On the methodological level, Max Weber resolves such an approach of nearly unlimited possibilities of facts through a construction of ideal types for which he is famous and which he later called pure types or just types (e.g., modern capitalism, types of legitimation, etc.). These ideal types are constructions stressing important points of the questions at issue and neglecting unimportant points. At the same time, they are methodological tools located on the level of heuristic, historical and systematic procedures. It is these ideal types that allow a comparison of the gained scientific evidence with reality data. But where in these procedures is objectivity to be found?

In a neo-Kantian way, Max Weber always asks a transcendental question: What are the conditions that make science possible, especially the social sciences? His Kantian answer: a theory of concepts combined with a theory of causality. But his concepts are always historical/changing concepts, his form of causal argumentation is a pragmatic form of argumentation for which professional skills are needed to terminate the plurality of causal explanations.

---

9   Knöbl 2022: 89.

At the same time, there is no fixed methodological rule for this ending. Therefore, in a certain sense, Max Weber pleads for a restricted form of objectivity which is a form of objectivity beyond any value presuppositions. In retrospective, though, one might not accept Weber's assumption. Because concerning the context of discovery the Weberian value relations also implicate value judgements which, to a certain degree, always influence the context of justification.[10] On the other hand, concerning the context of application, Max Weber opts for an openly normative approach. As a teacher, he is engaged in a humanistic program with the telos to educate mature people who follow their own individual laws and make responsible and autonomous decisions concerning a life within the different value spheres of modern capitalistic society. A life that, on the political level, can only be organized in a liberal-democratic way. This at least was the perspective of the late Max Weber.

All three dimensions – *the context of discovery*, *the context of justification* and *the context of application* – constituting Weber's scientific project concerning the foundation of the social sciences can be described as an empirical-normative project applying semantic-pragmatic models. In fact, Weber's project is a strictly historical-systematic project which reflects its own historicity. Therefore, it negates all forms of teleological philosophy of history, of essentialism, of substantialism, of naturalistic or organic holism, including all forms of theodicy and of cosmodicy, by offering an ambivalent form of anthropodicy on the level of philosophy. In his scientific project with its empirical and normative implications, Weber is a social scientist, a philosopher and at the same time an educator.[11]

Concerning his writing choices, Max Weber was a strong member of the Gutenberg galaxy. His scientific texts are handwritten and then published in the form of printed articles or books. In his role as a German citizen and a public intellectual, he also published non-scientific texts, especially during and after the First World War. The best example of such a form of writing seems to be the political treatise "Parliament and Government in Germany under a New Political Order". It presents "a reworked and extended version of articles which appeared in the *Frankfurter Zeitung* in the summer of 1917."[12] In general, theoretical reflections and ways of practical writing do not build a homogenous field. There may be tensions, sometimes also contradictions. Let

---

10   Oakes 1990: 143.
11   Marty 2019: 37.
12   Weber 1994c: 130.

us see how Weber proceeds and approaches such tensions in the two chosen examples.

## 3.

In 1894, Max Weber moved from the University of Berlin to the University of Freiburg to accept a chair of Political Economy ("Nationalökonomie"). In the following year, he delivered his inaugural lecture "The Nation State and Economic Policy" on May $31^{st}$ which he published in a rewritten version as a brochure of 34 pages by the end of June. In German university tradition, the inaugural lecture is a specific genre with a specific function. The new colleague introduces him-/herself not only to the university public but also to the general public, with a lecture presenting the respective way of doing research and giving hints on how to proceed in the future concerning one's own discipline. Max Weber fulfilled these expectations in a superb and courageous way. He exemplified his empirical approach combined with a massive intervention regarding the present and future role of political economy within the political and economic spheres of the German state. How did he structure his lecture? The solution is twofold:

> What I intend is firstly to illustrate, just *one example*, the role played by physical and psychological racial differences between nationalities in the economic struggle of existence. I should then like to add some reflections on the situation of states which rest on national foundations – as ours does – in the framework of a consideration of economic policy.[13]

After a preface, he continues with the presentation of a series of dry and uncomfortable facts concerning the present economic, political, and cultural situation between German and Polish people in West Prussia. He discusses the economic quality of land, the social stratification of the population and especially the differences between German and Polish people when it comes to their economic, cultural, religious, and political status which he characterizes in a racist neo-Darwinian way. Weber's point is the following: Economic and cultural problems must be discussed in political terms, there being a massive contradiction between the economic class interests of the landed gentry and

---

13   Weber 1994a: 2.

the political interests of the nation in the Eastern provinces. At the time, Germany was a powerful national state which, in the opinion of Weber, played an important role within world politics. Therefore, he sees the necessity of accelerating German industrialization in order to be able to maintain its function as world power within a capitalistic society. Now, Weber was always interested in the history of the present as well as in a scientifically oriented diagnosis of the present political, economic, and cultural situation. He diagnoses in his lecture an eminent lack of political leadership: The landed aristocracy is an economically declining class that can no longer exercise any political role in a responsible way (21), the German bourgeois class lacks political maturity. Even if it had a political vocation, it would not follow the call, while, at the same time, the working class is even more immature than the bourgeois class. (25) Weber confesses: "I am a member of the bourgeois (*bürgerlich*) classes, and I have been brought up to share their views and ideals." (23) He notices a situation of crisis in political leadership at the end of his century. This is even more precarious, since for Weber power struggle and power conflicts are necessary qualities of politics within and especially between national states. The national state as a power state (like Germany) has to continue its power policy with the necessary ingredients of different forms of violence and has to do so in a responsible way. For there is a permanent competition in peaceful or non-peaceful ways between powerful national states, which meant that there is always the possibility of war for which the state has to be prepared. Therefore, for Weber anarchism, pacifism, socialism, utilitarianism, universal happiness, even universal human rights and forms of democracy as proposed by Rousseau are off limits. He describes the function of political economy within the present situation as follows: "The science of political economy is a *political* science. It is a servant of politics, not the day-to-day-politics of the persons and classes who happen to be ruling at any given time, but enduring power-political interests of the nation." (16) Thus, regarding the context of justification in political economy, Weber negates all values like, e.g., happiness. In his historical argumentation, he implicitly favors value neutrality combining empirical, interpretative, explanative and to a certain degree narrative sentences. Later he stresses such an approach in an explicit way. As one can see in retrospect, the Weberian plea for the national power state has massive normative implications, and attributions like 'power state' would need further empirically tested evidence.

In the context of application, the situation is quite different and the program explicitly normative. Weber states in his role as educator: "We do not want to breed well-being in people, but rather those characteristics which we think of as constituting the human greatness and nobility of our nature." (15) Here, he favors a form of bourgeois aristocratic individualism which underlies the code noble/rough and which in its exclusivity negates all forms or moral argumentation with an egalitarian approach. Weber's plea for human greatness implies different possibilities. One is heroism during wartime: to sacrifice your life. Or to put it bluntly: to be prepared to kill or to be killed in national wars. The other one concerns his own way of thinking which makes him run one *syntagma* that seems most interesting: the "magic of *freedom*." (8) During his whole career as an academic, Weber was totally fascinated by this "magic of *freedom*." Freedom in the sense that one has to live one's own responsible, autonomous life is for Weber a main normative assumption decisive for all three contexts.[14] It is the central motivation for his extremely ambitious scientific project aimed at reflecting the historic present and future dimensions. Concerning the present and concerning the future dimension, especially political economy can play an important intervening role when it comes to increasing freedom. Or in other words: For Max Weber, it is not the charm of equality, fraternity, or the pursuit of happiness, but the charm of freedom that offers a normative starting point.

This inaugural lecture was the highly ambivalent beginning of an astonishing scientific career. There are continuities between its beginning and its end: the massive nationalism and apology of the national state, politics as struggle, conflicts with its necessary ingredients rule, power, and violence, the problem of responsibility concerning history, aristocratic individualism, heroic forms of existence, and, last but not least, the magic of freedom. But for the later Weber, all forms of racism and Neo-Darwinism no longer had any cognitive power. He also changed his political role. He started as a staunch conservative with liberal connotations and ended as a liberal who favored parliamentary democracy.

**4.**

In retrospect, Max Weber qualified his inaugural lecture as immature but provocative. A mature discussion of the concept of politics with its scientific, sociological, philosophical, and pedagogical implications can be found in his

---

14   Marty 2019: 35.

talk "The Profession and Vocation of Politics" from 28th January 1919. In the summer of the same year, he published the talk in a massively rewritten form compared to the stenographic version of his oral talk (67 pages). Contrary to his inaugural lecture, this text has no footnotes, does not discuss the state of the art of research and shows some stylistic hints to its original oral presentation. He starts his texts with the question: "What do we understand by politics (*Politik*)?"[15] The answer is similar to his earlier texts: "In our terms, then, 'politics' would mean striving for a share of power, [...] whether it be between states or between the groups of people contained within a single state." (311) And further: "The state is a relationship of rule (*Herrschaft*) by human beings over human beings, and one that rests on the legitimate use of violence." (Ibid.) Weber introduces a threefold typology of forms as to how the state could be legitimated: traditional, charismatic, and legal. (311–312) He then continues with a well-informed genealogical reconstruction of tendencies in Europe and America leading to the modern state with its form of rational administration, its party system, its forms of parliamentarianism. Regarding types of politicians, he introduces two. Either one lives for politics (mainly valid for the 19th century) or one lives from politics (mainly valid for 20th century). (318) This genealogical reconstruction of the modern political system reveals Max Weber to be a historically oriented sociologist who with the help of his typological procedures produces superb overviews concerning midterm and long-term periods of history in relation to the present. As such, the typologies are extremely convincing, although Weber does not discuss certain omissions and the form of selection. Since too complicated typologies are often unsuccessful, Weber limits his typology of forms of legitimation to three and the typology of politicians to two possibilities. As for the political situation, he constructs another binary opposition: "But the only choice lies between a leadership democracy with a 'machine' and democracy without a leader, which means rule by the 'professional politician' who has no vocation, the type of man who lacks precisely those inner, charismatic qualities which make leaders." (351)

What are the presuppositions, then, for a politician's successful career? First of all, there must be a feeling of power. (352) But as a politician you have to do justice to this power. And this is not only a question of power but also a question of ethics. In the perspective of Max Weber, three qualities are decisive for a politician: "passion, a sense of responsibility, judgement. [...] The

---

15   Weber 1994b: 309.

passionate commitment to a 'cause'" (352–353) is one requirement, but even more important is a *"responsibility* for that cause. [...] This requires [...] *judgement*, the ability to maintain one's inner composure and calm while being receptive to realities, in other words, *distance* from things and people." (353) The enemy of all political personalities is vanity leading to a lack of objectivity and responsibility. (354) The result would be the mere power politician whose actions steer into absurdity. He does know "nothing of the tragedy, in which all action, particularly political action, is in truth enmeshed." (354–355) This sentence about the tragic quality of all actions is an empirical statement, but it is also a massive philosophical-anthropological statement which demonstrates how Weber combines an empirical with a philosophical approach by also including pedagogical implications. The following citation explains this "fundamental fact" in an interesting way: "It is certainly true, and it is a fundamental fact of history [...], that the eventual outcome of political action frequently, indeed regularly, stands in a quite inadequate, even paradoxical relation to its original, intended meaning and purpose (*Sinn*)." (355) Now in the perspective of Max Weber, it is most interesting that the nature of the causes a politician seeks to serve by striving for power is a question of faith. These causes are values that belong to different spheres: religious, political, cultural, aesthetic, erotic, etc. Although the theory of value spheres is not elaborated by Max Weber in a systematic way, the consequences of this presupposition are evident. There is no hierarchy between the different values, and their validity cannot be scientifically proved. They just have to be chosen and defended.[16] The relations between these values – and this is the tragedy and a fundamental fact in this world as irrational *pluriversum* – are antagonistic. This not only concerns the relationship between different value spheres but is also active within a single value sphere.

Regarding the ethic of politics, Weber discusses two alternatives: the ethic of conviction and the ethic of responsibility. The ethic of conviction presupposes a dominant value and does not care about the consequences. The ethic of responsibility reflects consequences and side effects and makes decisions based on such reflections. Even after having opted for a decision, you have to take responsibility for your choice and to reflect the amount of guilt following the decision, because the problem of guilt is a massive problem in the political sphere. It has a "diabolic dimension" because politics cannot do without its essentials power and violence.

---

16   Bruun 2017: 292.

Now, what are the relations between the ethic of conviction and the ethic of responsibility? They can be paradox or mutually exclusive in a strict sense. But in the perspective of Weber – and this is the much better way of treating the dilemma – a form of cooperation between the ethic of conviction and ethic of responsibility seems possible. For such a form of cooperation, a quick reference in the sense of Luther and Kierkegaard is necessary:

> On the other hand, it is immensely moving when a mature person (whether old or young) who feels with his whole soul the responsibility he bears for the real consequences of his actions, and who acts on the basis of an ethics of responsibility, says at some point, 'Here I stand, I can do no other.' This is something genuinely human and profoundly moving. For it must be *possible* for *each* of us to find ourselves in such a situation at some point if we are not inwardly dead. In this respect, the ethics of conviction and the ethics of responsibility are not absolute opposites. They are complementary to one another, and only in combination do they produce the true human being who is *capable* of having a 'vocation for politics.'[17]

Thus, even in the sphere of politics with its demonic dimensions, it is possible for mature people to lead a form of life which could reclaim the predicate of authenticity.

At this point, I want to come back to the question of facts. The beginning of the last paragraph of Weber's essay contains the most famous citation of "The Profession and Vocation of Politics": "Politics means slow, strong drilling through hard boards, with a combination of passion and a sense of judgement." (369) Not so famous are the following sentences which reclaim factual empirical knowledge:

> It is of course entirely correct, and a fact confirmed by all historical experience, that what is possible would never have been achieved if, in this world, people had not repeatedly reached for the impossible. But the person who can do this must be a leader, not only that, he must, in a very simple sense of the word, be a hero. (Ibid.)

Thus, at the beginning of his career as social scientist and in his inaugural lecture "The Nation State and Economic Policy" Weber starts with the apology of great men. At the end of his career as social scientist, philosopher, and educator, he ends with an apology for political heroism. Therefore, it seems

---

17   Weber 1994b: 367–368.

quite correct to locate Weber within the period of tragic modern heroism with its catchwords of nation, sovereignty, charisma, and sacrifice.

## Conclusion

My excursion into the concepts of Max Weber concerning his ideas on the discipline of Social Sciences and the possible ways to treat them within this paradigm on politics brings me to the following conclusion. It is the view of the question of writing facts that allows to locate Weber within a semantic-pragmatic model. The way he treated *the context of discovery*, *the context of justification* and *the context of application* in his role as social scientist, philosopher, and educator allowed him to formulate an empirical-normative theory which reflects its own historicity and fallibility.[18] When looking at this approach in retrospective, one can state that as far as the context of justification is concerned, Weber reclaims a form of restricted objectivity and a form of restricted value neutrality. This postulated form of restrictive objectivity treats facts produced from data with typological procedures, mixing an empirical-factual with a constructive approach in such a way that this form of typological argumentation presents massive pragmatic implications. Weber's postulated restricted form of value neutrality enables his main normative assumption of freedom to be not only constitutive for the context of discovery (how to formulate the problem?) and the context of application (how to relate to social dimensions of reality?) but also for the context of justification (how to legitimize the claims of truth?).

At the end of this essay, I allow myself one more personal remark. In "Profession and Vocation of Politics", Max Weber offers the following perspective concerning the immediate future after the end of World War I: "What lies immediately ahead of us is not the flowering of summer but a polar night of icy darkness and hardness."[19] From a metaphorical perspective, this image might work. From a factual, empirical perspective, it is not correct. Polar nights are cold but have a magic light darkness, extremely clear skies with sparkling stars, and moreover, there is always the possibility of polar lights.

---

18   Weber 2012: 138.
19   Weber 1994b: 368.

## Bibliography

Adorno, Theodor W. (2003): *Einleitung in die Soziologie*, Frankfurt am Main.
Bruun, Hans Hendrik (2017): "Politics and Ethics, and the Ethic of Politics", in: *The Oxford Handbook of Max Weber*, ed. Edith Hanke/Lawrence Scaff/Sam Whimster, Sam, Oxford, 294–309.
Knöbl, Wolfgang (2022): *Die Soziologie vor der Geschichte. Zur Kritik der Sozialtheorie*, Frankfurt am Main.
Marty, Christian (2019): *Max Weber. Ein Denker der Freiheit*, Weinheim.
Mommsen, Wolfgang (1974): *Max Weber. Gesellschaft, Politik und Geschichte*, Frankfurt am Main.
Müller, Harro (2020): "Schreibszene, Schreibfeld, zwei Kriegsreden und *Lebensanschauung*", in: Knaller, Susanne/Pany-Habsa, Doris/Scholger, Martina (eds.): *Schreibforschung interdisziplinär. Praxis – Prozess – Produkt*, Bielefeld, 157–174.
Oakes, Guy (1990): *Die Grenzen kulturwissenschaftlicher Begriffsbildung. Heidelberger Max Weber-Vorlesungen 1982*, Frankfurt am Main.
Simmel, Georg (2015) [1989]: *Georg Simmel*, ed. Otthein Rammstedt, Frankfurt am Main.
Weber, Max (2021): *Max-Weber-Gesamtausgabe*, ed. Horst Baier et al., Tübingen.
— (2012): "The 'objectivity' of knowledge in social sciences and social policy", in: *Max Weber. Collected methodological writings*, ed. Hans Henrik Bruuns/Sam Whimster, London, 100–138.
— (1994): *Weber. Political Writings*, ed. Peter Lassman/Ronald Speirs, Cambridge.
— (1994a): "The Nation State and Economic Policy", in: *Weber. Political Writings*, 1–28.
— (1994b): "The Profession and Vocation of Politics", in: *Weber. Political Writings*, 309–369.
— (1994c): "Parliament and Government in Germany under a New Political Order. Towards a political critique of officialdom and the party system", in: *Weber. Political Writings*, 130–271.
— (1956): *Soziologie, weltgeschichtliche Analysen, Politik*, ed. Johannes Winckelmann, Stuttgart.

# Writing 'Volksgemeinschaft' into 'Fact'
## Letters from the National Socialist Labor Service (RAD)

*Gero von Roedern (University of Graz)*

## 1. Introduction

"The hard, unrelenting service doesn't affect me too much, because I always did a lot of sports,"[1] Friedrich Pohl wrote to his parents on June 18, 1940, after only four days in the National Socialist Labor Service (RAD).[2] Initially just intrigued by the choice of words, I started my investigation into Friedrich Pohl's letters with the assumption that the young man simply replicated discursive formations he may have picked up in the Labor Service. My scope then expanded to the hypothesis that the young author's reference to and replication of impressions from the Labor Service can be understood as participation in the organization's project of creating the avant-garde for the 'Volksgemeinschaft.'[3] Konstantin Hierl, the man in charge of the RAD, asserted: "The Labor Service is the best tool to realize this national socialist demand for a people's community."[4] Basing my work on a collection of a young man's letters stemming from his time in the organization, I investigate the RAD's claim of realizing the 'people's community' on a micro-level. In doing so, this study discusses the writing of 'facts' by Friedrich Pohl while also reflecting on its own perspective. I approach the letters with a combination of qualitative content analysis with inductive category-building[5] and close reading.

---

1  Pohl 1940: June 18. All quotes from the diary are originally in German and translated into English by G.v.R. The same applies to translations from other primary sources or secondary literature in German.
2  *Reichsarbeitsdienst* or short: RAD.
3  The 'people's community.'
4  Hierl 1941: 201. Hierl, a former soldier and *völkisch*/national socialist functionary, since 1935 was officially the leader of the RAD [*Reichsarbeitsführer*].
5  Mayring 2015: 85–90.

Since the merit of operating with 'Volksgemeinschaft' as an analytical category has been debated by historical scholars for nearly two decades,[6] it is critical to point out that the study at hand focuses on the social vision of the concept. As such, following historians Martina Steber and Bernhard Gotto, it entailed "a guideline for the actions both of private individuals and political leaders"[7] and contained the promise of a social 'utopia' for those it included.[8] At the latest *Historikertag* in October 2021, it was precisely this power of appeals to the "we", that formed the basis for a panel discussion on the making of collectives.[9] For the purpose of this essay, I therefore define the concept of 'Volksgemeinschaft' as a place of ideal perfection and impractical scheme for social improvement as well as a vague guide on how to achieve this state. I argue that the analyzed letters not only picked up on such vague directives but on a micro- and meso-level actively participated in the attempts of creating a new social reality.

In developing the argument, my analysis identifies and works on and with five different facets of reality.[10] Firstly, (1) the layer of historiography, on which I operate and on which I unfold 'facts,' which are intersubjectively comprehensible and verifiable but nevertheless characterized by my subjective emphasis and methodical approach to the sources.[11] Secondly, there is the (2) material aspect of the investigated letters,[12] whose text is a linguistic 'fact.' This text, however, does not need to resemble the (3) historical state of things in the Labor Service and national socialist Germany, which I understand as a product of historical relations[13] that can only be approximated through research. Rather, the letters also reveal (4) references to as well as interpretations of

---

6   Janosch Steuwer composed a report on the debate, which still provides a helpful overview on the major positions. Since then, some rapprochement can be observed. (Cf. Steuwer 2013)
7   Steber/Gotto 2018: 3.
8   Or from a non-national socialist point of view rather: dystopia.
9   Historikertag 2021: *Das umstrittene Wir: Auf der Suche nach neuen Wegen zur historischen Erforschung von Kollektiven.*
10  My gratitude for the suggestion goes to Susanne Knaller, who outlines her considerations on "several levels of data and dimensions of reality" in the introduction of this volume.
11  For the historian's/narrator's "situatedness between factuality and fictionality" cf. Jaeger 2019: 336. What is critical in this analysis is that 'facts' in historiography are created in a dialogue between the object of research, the approach and its result.
12  Cf. Henzel 2020.
13  Cf. Daniel 2016: 385–387.

the reality encountered in the RAD.[14] Such (re)actions in the letters may or may not be truthful, but as they can be interpreted both as indications and as parts of negotiating experiences,[15] in this respect they can be considered reliable. As a fifth facet of reality, I discuss the question regarding (5) the effect of the letters as participation in the construction of a new social reality[16] through language.[17] Based on these five facets, I undertake a cultural reading of personal documents that is dedicated to the interface between textual and social reality. Therefore, I intend to contribute to the expansion of our understanding of the writing of 'fact' in history and historiography. My analysis can reveal how all five identified facets are in one form or another affected by the social vision of the 'Volksgemeinschaft' and the attempts of the RAD to realize it as social 'facts.'

## 2. The *RAD*-Letters

In today's academic research, several lines of inquiry into the many facets of the RAD can be identified, which all contribute to the conception of this essay. Important studies into the institutional history of the Labor Service have, for instance, provided valuable insight into the size, composition, and political relevance of the organization.[18] They allow for the creation of a general framework that contributes to the contextualization of Friedrich Pohl's letters. Relatively early research into the RAD was undertaken by the Educational

---

14  Cf. Susanne Knaller's contribution in this volume for the underlying constructive model, traced to Immanuel Kant's theory of cognition.
15  The primacy of discourse or experience is subject to major debate in historical analysis. For the central positions, cf. Scott 1999 and Canning 1994. My use of "experience" touches on the issue, but as my focus is on negotiations in the letters, I avoid the summary of a lengthy polarizing and quasi-ontological debate.
16  Cf. Berger/Luckmann 1972.
17  Cf. Marszolek 2013.
18  For an overview of the Labor Service for the male youth (*RADmJ*) cf. Patel 2005; for the Labor Service for the female youth (*RADwJ*), cf. Stephenson 1982. For practical purposes, in this paper I speak only of the RAD.

Sciences, which investigated educational practices[19] in the organization.[20] Furthermore, the research of cultural anthropologist Manfred Seifert[21] and historian and cultural scholar Heidrun Zettelbauer[22] contribute to my own approach.

The focus of my investigation is directed at the Labor Service's role as the setting for an ideological project, which meant to create the avant-garde for the national socialist 'Volksgemeinschaft.'[23] From June 1935 onwards, (initially) 200,000 young men had to undergo this process per year.[24] In the organization "work, after-work [activities], local history, state education, folk culture and the nationalist interpretation thereof"[25] as well as incessant drilling and monitoring by the leaders[26] were dedicated to the cultivation of "innate abilities," which "require[d] training, namely self-education."[27] Even after the outbreak of World War II there existed units of the Labor Service that were particularly drilled in representative purposes such as performing at the *Reichsparteitage*. Friedrich Pohl was selected for such tasks and physical labor or the war remained only side topics in his letters.[28] In contrast, drill and

---

19  Cf. Tenorth 1989: 277. Following Heinz-Elmar Tenorth, the term education is used impartially in this paper. Tenorth argues that holding educational practices of the national socialist regime to the standard of pedagogics would render their investigation pointless. See also Langewiesche/Tenorth 1989: 111–144.

20  A still indispensable overview on educational theories provides: Lingelbach 1987.

21  Seifert 2012; Seifert 1996.

22  Zettelbauer 2018.

23  It is to be made explicit, however, that this was just one facet of the organization. The *RAD* was, among other things, a tool for combating mass unemployment, a source of manpower, a place for pre- and para-military training and a link in the chain of national socialist organizations dedicated to capture the hearts and minds of the German youth.

24  *Reichsgesetzblatt* I/1935: 769–772. Up until the year 1939, the number steadily increased to a peak of 370,000 men. (Cf. Seifert 2012: 105)

25  Zettelbauer 2018: 556.

26  Cf. Patel 2013: 317. Kiran K. Patel emphasizes the arrangement of the barracks, whose doors could all be monitored from a single viewpoint.

27  Hierl 1942: 131. Hierl voiced these notions in 1929, by then still coined for the training of military leaders. He later directly applied these thoughts to the Labor Service. (Cf. Hierl 1941: 265)

28  Entirely different was the case for young men and women in *RAD* units that were charged with the construction of defenses, production of armaments or work in the agricultural sector. As many of their letters – which form part of the corpus of my dissertation – demonstrate, the economic necessity of their work, stationing, or the sub-

(self-)education were central themes in his impressions of life in different camps of the RAD and are of central importance for this essay.[29]

The analyzed corpus of communication covers the time span from June 16 to October 2, 1940. In total it consists of 49 pieces of writing. 41 of these were sent by Friedrich Pohl to his family and eight were addressed to him and written by his mother and father.[30] My work is primarily based on the digitized correspondence and some other documents which were temporarily entrusted to the NS-Documentation Center of the City of Cologne by a niece of the author in the year 2010. As the youngest of eight children, Friedrich Pohl was born in Cologne on January 26, 1920. He left junior high school in Cologne in 1936 with his intermediate degree and then started to work in an architectural firm in his home city. When he was drafted into the RAD on June 14, 1940, he had finished his apprenticeship and had been gathering practical experience on construction sites for nearly a year. After having been discharged from the RAD on September 28, 1940, the young man was drafted directly into the Wehrmacht, in which he served until he was killed on July 24, 1942 on the Eastern Front.

The better part of the young man's letters in one form or another contain requests for daily necessities. However, many of them emphasize the good provisions and Friedrich Pohl's overall well-being in the camp. His letters can be read somewhat analogous to the signs of life encountered in most letters from the front, usually meant to put the recipients at ease. Requests for food for "[...] the time between dinner and going to sleep [which] is so long that one gets hungry"[31] and multiple bouts of homesickness underline the likely soothing, and not necessarily straightforward side of his regular assurances. The biggest challenge to the young man's efforts to continue his social life as much as possible through letters may be identified in the lack of time for

---

ordination of RAD units under the command of the Wehrmacht could make a huge difference in the individual experience of the Labor Service.

29  As part of such an unusual unit, the *Nürnbergzüge*, Friedrich Pohl was transferred multiple times. He served in Immenhausen near the city of Kassel, then in Türkismühle, 50 km to the north of the city of Saarbrücken. Afterward he was sent to Hermeskeil, a small town 25 km to the West and later returned to Türkismühle. Eventually he was assigned to a construction detail in the village of Ehr, 30 km south of Koblenz.

30  The frequency of mail sent remained quite constant for the first ten weeks, in September it dropped significantly. On average, Friedrich Pohl's letters are about 1.5 pages of handwriting (approximately 200–300 words).

31  Pohl 1940: June 23.

writing. Hierl's demand "In the Labor Service not a single quarter hour may be 'idled away', every single one has to serve for purposeful labor or intended relaxation and recuperation"[32] clearly shows in nine of the analyzed letters: "There is no time left to write at all. I am so tired. I can barely stand. [...] On Saturday or Sunday, I'll write more. I'm simply finished. I'm done."[33] Rigorously repetitive daily schedules and the "time-hysterical" (Seifert) frenetic activism complemented physical isolation, control and functionalization of social relationships as well as the removal of spaces to withdraw to:[34] "I lie in my bed and write. there [sic!] is no other time. Although it is forbidden."[35] Despite the many challenges, Friedrich Pohl attempted to still participate in his family's life and also mentions communication with at least two other individuals outside his family. He demanded to stay in the loop and used the letters as substitute for everyday communication as well as on special occasions and often begged for information on life at home.

## 3. Negotiation and Integration

When investigating the negotiation and narration of experiences in the letters (4) at their interface with the program of the RAD, the analysis needs to consider the difficult situation for writing while serving in the Labor Service as well as some unique properties which make letters distinct from most other texts. Private letters are conceptualized to fit a common frame of reference[36] and anticipate a particular reception by the addressee. Assumptions about who may read a letter and knowledge of their convictions, fears and one's relationship to them influences the text often in at least as much as the individual desire to share certain aspects of life with them.[37] "How do you, as an old soldier, like my posture in the picture, where we line up."[38] Friedrich Pohl for

---

32  Hierl 1941: 245.
33  Pohl 1940: September 19.
34  Seifert 1996: 143–144.
35  Pohl 1940: June 16.
36  As this frame of reference is not necessarily shared by me as a historiographer, private or secrete implications in the letters can be overseen and time-specific meanings lost. Additionally, my account of (4) experience as the fourth facet of reality of the letters is subject to and filtered through (1) my own perspective, knowledge and background.
37  Cf. Dobson 2009: 57.
38  Pohl 1940: July 7.

example asked his father, who, a veteran, responded positively and jokingly: "[...] I'm going to have the entire column stand at attention when I come for a visit. [...] Well, a bit of fun is essential. Always keep your head up."[39] Possible censorship in the RAD is also to be considered. While the extent of it is all but certain, it is clear that in Friedrich Pohl's unit received mail was centralized and given out after the daily ceremony of saluting the flag:[40] "I'm waiting every evening. But mostly in vain."[41] Compared with other authors writing such letters, the young man's criticism of his experience is very moderate. Although there is no clear indication of external censorship having been carried out by RAD officials in the unit, one can hold for certain that some form of self-censoring[42] influenced the young man's writing. These considerations are compounded by the social, cultural, and individual limitations of being able to formulate something which restrict all forms of communication.[43]

Addressing his life in the RAD, Friedrich Pohl's letters reveal both homesickness and dauntless optimism to rise to the task at hand. Approaching the sources from the field of *Erfahrungsgeschichte*, one may state that the young man drew on a store of societal knowledge. Knowledge, he acquired through primary and secondary socialization which to a great extent became routinized and turned into a frame of reference for making sense of things. When he successfully negotiated new challenges while in the Labor Service with knowledge obtained during his previous socialization, he was able to make experiences.[44] This makes the letters, as a space in which home and camp could be mediated, all the more important. Through fervent repetition the education in the camp was meant to facilitate a deep internalization of "[...] a kind of National Socialist consciousness [...] as well as ideological patterns of thinking, reasoning and causal relations."[45] For Friedrich Pohl, writing his letters and negotiating in them seems to have been both part and emblematic of this process.

When relating selected events of his everyday life in the RAD, he sometimes appears to have invested particular effort in attempts at making existing

---

39  Ibid.: July 9.
40  At least when stationed in camps in Immenhausen and Türkismühle.
41  Pohl 1940: August 27.
42  Cf. Dobson 2009: 62.
43  Cf. Schuster 2020: 25.
44  Cf. Latzel 1997: 13–14.
45  Zettelbauer 2018: 555.

and newly acquired knowledge fit.[46] In doing so, his letters picked up on one of the central demands of the concept of 'Volksgemeinschaft'– to integrate. "I am the most senior cadet in the room [Stubenältester] of the first squad. Even though I'm one of the youngest. Well, the sports helped a lot. Because of it, the hard and fast service doesn't affect the legs as much."[47] The young man repeatedly connected the rigorous drills in the RAD to his past experience with sports. Frequently he displayed a sportsmanlike attitude towards the harsh living conditions, characterized by a strong disregard for individual needs or privacy, constant stress and arbitrary harassment. But the missing separation between work and spare time, privacy, and shared life[48] clearly also affected him when he wrote to his mother: "I often go into the great silent pine-forest and dream of home. Those are my best hours."[49] Sometimes in the letters he also displayed anger or frustration: "Because of the reluctance towards this whole operation I, in fact, do not know what to write."[50] Considering these effects of life in the Labor Service on his writing, a likely explanation for his usually positive characterization of "[…] locker check, stool construction,[51] bed-making, inspection of the boots and all the other [tasks] that make life difficult for us"[52] as sports challenges is that it helped the young man to make sense of the routine. Thereby, it would have on the one hand provided him with a mode of dealing with the harassment, on the other hand of presenting himself to the family members as up to the challenge. Through the analogy

---

46   As the RAD was only a link in the chain of national socialist institutions devoted to seizing the hearts and minds of the German youth, it isn't always possible to determine whether an ideological pattern of thinking was learned in the organization or already existed before the Service. This makes no difference for my argument, since the RAD and its education provided context and content for the letters, which makes its contribution to the internalization unequivocal.
47   Pohl 1940: June 23.
48   Cf. Seifert 1996: 170.
49   Pohl 1940: August 23.
50   Ibid.: September 11.
51   A peculiarity of the Labor Service, for the "stool-construction" [Schemelbau] "the young men had to take off their clothes and to arrange them on their stool according to a precisely defined scheme. […] The least bit of real or alleged deviation or disorder provided a pretext for harassment by the leader, especially in the form of the so called Budenzauber, which referred to unscheduled cleaning and scrubbing of the barracks as a form of punishment." (Patel 2005: 225)
52   Pohl 1940: September 4.

of sports, the narration of life in the Labor Service could be formed and formulated according to the expectations of those who had not lived through something similar. This way he could convey these things to others and make them and himself comprehend without burdening the readers too much. In the words of Pierre Bourdieu "in the service of a general intention, [Friedrich Pohl] selected significant events and created own connections between them to make them coherent."[53] Supposing that fitting in, performing well or, in short, integration formed at least part of Friedrich Pohl's 'general intention,' in his letters he (5) actively integrated the education in the Service in his own biography. In writing, the social vision, underlying the ideological project, was woven into the events experienced in the RAD (4) and simultaneously as text turned into (2) material 'fact' in the form of letters.

## 4. Writing 'Volksgemeinschaft' into 'Fact'?

Did letters like these also affect the German society at the time? Did they contribute to turning a social vision into 'fact'? Following the premises of sociologists Peter L. Berger and Thomas Luckman,[54] every act of corresponding with another person entails some reflection on oneself and a response to the world which one finds oneself living in and reacts to. Friedrich Pohl then was, on the one hand, a product of social contexts and conditions. On the other hand, as a 'bridge' home, Friedrich Pohl's letters did not just represent attempts to continue his social life. Rather, through living and writing in a certain way, he himself influenced the society he lived in.[55] From the RAD camps as laboratories for the 'Volksgemeinschaft,'[56] text flowed to Friedrich Pohl's family outside. I do not mean to disguise that the lack of sources makes it nearly impossible to quantify the effect of this or to even say much about the reaction of Friedrich Pohl's parents. Nevertheless, the letters, in another way, appear to have (5) participated in the attempt of constructing a new social reality.

To reiterate: The Labor Service was supposed to form young people into the avant-garde of the 'people's community,' to (contribute to) turn the na-

---

53   Bourdieu 1990: 76.
54   Cf. Berger/Luckmann 1972.
55   Traceable to a micro-level of engaging with his family and a meso-level of being a functioning part of an organization.
56   Cf. Patel 2013: 323.

tional socialist vision of the 'Volksgemeinschaft' into social reality. The organization based its education on a three-step-practice: "Demonstrating [Vorleben], experiencing [Erleben] and imitating [Nachleben]."[57] The focus lay on creating a practical experience, which not only created knowledge but equally trained body and character. Youths were to be made fit into the 'people's community' and to put individual needs aside.[58] The process attempted to achieve deindividuation and the deprivation of individuality in favor of the 'Volksgemeinschaft.'[59] To be successful, the organization required the young people to live through its program, to replicate it and to apply it to their life. Therefore, when Friedrich, in writing his letters, actively tried to fit into the community and reproduced the education in the Labor Service, I interpret it as participation in the making of the 'Volksgemeinschaft' – the construction of social reality through writing.

Considering that subordination and disciplining of the recruits "was the signature element of the Labor Service,"[60] Friedrich Pohl's preoccupation with the drills and his reactions to them are important. The combination of drill and physical exercise was meant to foster obedience and to instill qualities identified as essential for the 'people's community' and military service. The ability to take initiative and responsibility, to make decisions and to unwaveringly stick to them were regarded equally important to self-control and the willingness to self-sacrifice oneself for one's people.[61] The already discussed characterizations of the drills as sports challenges show that the young man concerned himself with the drills. In his writing he tried to make sense of them and, in doing so, made and replicated the experiences of the daily events. He tried to make them fit with existing knowledge, with himself – and simultaneously made himself fit better into the (3) community of the RAD. He did so according to the guidelines of the social vision, but in his unique way. The letters speak of his *Eigensinn* (Lüdtke),[62] his very own take on the events in the RAD, negotiating (4) the reality of his experience in his letters and giving it a particular twist. It is the transformative, even subversive

---

57   Cf. Seifert 1996: 180–181; Zettelbauer 2018: 555 speaks of "demonstration, practice, imitation."
58   Cf. Hierl 1942: 201, 219; cf. ibid. 1941: 274.
59   Cf. Hierl 1941: 297.
60   Patel 2005: 225.
61   Cf. Hierl 1941: 196, 205, 267–270.
62   Cf. Lüdtke 2015.

power of this twist which stands at the core of historian Alf Lüdtke's concept. Friedrich Pohl's interpretation of the drills (5) did change a fraction of the social reality but rather through integration and subordination in an organization in which no "[...] private sphere, no space which could escape the law of the community"[63] was meant to remain. His acts of subscribing to the RAD's rules in his letters can, for instance, be observed when they affirmed the "[...] principle of achievement [which was] fully affirmed by our [national socialist] worldview,"[64] as Hierl put it. When, e.g., planning his home leave, Friedrich Pohl judged: "No comrade gets leave on Sunday. It very much depends on the conduct.[65] [...] As goes the work, so goes the reward."[66] Thus, the young man characterized the particular decision, the underlying principle as well as the power of the leader to decide such matters as just.

The process of subordination becomes especially perceptible where it is aligned with self-education. "Whatever may come, I am strong enough to take everything upon myself. Only one [person] can be victorious and that's me. Ha Ha Ha!", Friedrich Pohl wrote in a letter, in which he also mentioned his homesickness: "Homesickness comes in an ever-recurring wave. Then one is good for nothing. Maybe tomorrow it passes again for a couple days."[67] The proximity of the expressed homesickness to the boundless optimism of the previous quote in the same letter make it seem likely that the process of writing helped him in reassuring and educating himself. Actions demanded by the RAD: "Without the willingness of every individual to respond to the educational influences and to work on himself, there is no educational success."[68] In replicating the behavior required and putting it into writing, the young man did his part to (5) fit into the envisioned new society in the making and thereby partook in trying to create it. This also becomes apparent in efforts of reevaluation and re-formation of experiences in retrospect. Even particularly negative events and phases are made compliant with the guidelines of the Labor Service and purpose is attributed in hindsight: "The service may be tough but by far not as tough as that in Immenhausen. I am glad now to have

---

63  Krüger 1937: 99. Quoted in Seifert 1996.
64  Hierl 1941: 273.
65  "*Führung*," which could also be translated as leadership.
66  Pohl 1940: July 27.
67  Ibid.: August 27.
68  Hierl 1941: 265.

been there."[69] While this statement can also be read as him being glad to have been 'hardened' before joining the new unit, the bottom-line is the same: The young man asserted to acknowledge the merits of his education and created a narration that appeared to make sense. Thereby, in the letters he assumed the role the RAD had intended for him in the 'people's community': "You can be pleased with your workingman [*Arbeitsmann*]."[70]

Other central elements of the RAD's ideological project were also reproduced throughout the letters. One statement in particular, connected to the topos of 'challenge' in Friedrich Pohl's letters, is noteworthy: "I always wished for the tough, unrelenting service. If you are healthy and strong, you can make it. Otherwise however, it is nearly impossible."[71] The quote conveys more than self-praise as it corresponds strongly to a cornerstone of the Labor Service's agenda: biological selection. Selection was exercised in a two-pronged approach in the RAD. On the one hand, access to the Labor Service was denied on "Social Darwinian, political, and racist" grounds. "Community aliens" [*Gemeinschaftsfremde*] such as "Non-Aryans" or people married to them, individuals with a criminal record and the mentally or physically unfit were excluded.[72] On the other hand, Hierl's organization strove to select future leaders for the community: "Selection, which in turbulent revolutionary times is implemented by battle, in quieter times must be carried out by [...] human management [...] in order to prevent mediocrity and mechanical thinking to gain the upper hand in the leadership of the community."[73] In this process, attitude and character were regarded as being more important than theoretical knowledge or technical ability.[74]

In the letters, Friedrich Pohl's competitiveness, his praise of toughness and relentlessness can be read as manifestation of this agenda of selection. However, it becomes most apparent when he decidedly distanced himself from a comrade: "'Friend' Rosgen has three days special detention. He fell asleep while on guard duty. He isn't mentally accountable. He is the camel of the unit. He is always just writing to his 'Billa'. He isn't in my room anymore.

---

69   Pohl 1940: August 18.
70   Ibid.: July 7.
71   Ibid.: July 9.
72   Cf. Patel 2005: 129–32. Quote on p. 129.
73   Hierl 1941: 274.
74   Cf. ibid.: 273.

He was too bad at his duties. He isn't on the pictures either."[75] Friedrich Pohl's comment on mental unfitness does not necessarily refer to Social Darwinian selection, but it certainly corresponds to the processes of selection within the organization. As the Labor Service counted on 'education' by the peers,[76] one may assume that in (3) historical reality the pressure on comrade Rösgen and the consequences for him would have gone beyond not being in a photograph. The letter reiterates the clear-cut distinction between those adjusting to the norms in the Service and those not fitting in. In doing so, it (5) reproduced and asserted the norms of the 'Volksgemeinschaft' in the making and contributed to increasing the pressure on those not meeting the standard. In contrast to the inappropriate behavior of his comrade, Friedrich Pohl displayed the appropriate determination in his letters: "Tomorrow we'll go to work with a hurray. Nothing can unsettle us."[77] This now definitely was in accordance with what Hierl desired: "[...] the Labor Service needs men of action."[78]

## 5. Conclusion

If there is one thing most historians who work with and on the concept of 'Volksgemeinschaft' seem to be able to agree to, it is that the 'people's community' never came to exist in the form the national socialists vaguely and opaquely promised. Nevertheless, the social vision managed to affect all five facets of reality discussed in this analysis.

This influence on (1) historical research and historiography is obvious. For roughly two decades, 'Volksgemeinschaft' – both as an object of research but mostly as an analytical category – has been fiercely debated. While already "in the Weimar Republic almost no party was willing to refrain from the term,"[79] it is chiefly the complex relationship of national socialist propaganda, the effects of 'Volksgemeinschaft' as or on the historical reality, and considerations of approaching the two which give historians pause. The term is used as a

---

75   Pohl 1940: July 16.
76   Cf. Hierl 1941: 264. This is precisely where creating 'Volksgemeinschaft' on the meso-level of an institution like the RAD comes into play.
77   Pohl 1940: July 14.
78   Hierl 1941: 273.
79   Wildt 2011: 104.

reference to changed power relations, for the depiction of inclusion and exclusion or, as in my analysis, for the investigation of "the mobilizing force of the vision of a better community."[80]

The results of my analysis underline the value of focusing on the social promise of the discourse of the 'Volksgemeinschaft,' since "[...] in the mobilization lay its political power."[81] Cultural historian Inge Marszolek argued that "the NS-Volksgemeinschaft in all its aspects is generated again and again through communication, or, spoken with Foucault, that processes of communitization [Vergemeinschaftung] [...] were parts of the microphysics of power."[82] Following this view, the specific effect of Friedrich's letters on his parents, which due to a lack of sources cannot be ascertained anyhow, does not need to be measured. Rather, it is the revealed integration of the *RAD* into (4) the young man's experiences, his narration of self and biography which points to processes of participation and deindividuation. His subordination under and reiteration of the norms of the service contributed (5) to the actualization of an incomplete version of the 'Volksgemeinschaft' through communication – to the making of a community in the making. Allowing to investigate mobilization through an ideological project without reverting to dichotomies can be a significant benefit of using the concept of 'Volksgemeinschaft' as a social vision. With this approach, the 'fact' that it is possible to observe the intricate relationship of vision and effects is quite the opposite of a dilemma.[83]

Of course, the (3) historical reality of life in the *RAD* and in the German Society under the rule of national socialism as a whole was dependent on many factors. Also, aspects other than the "new social practice which served to symbolically emphasize the ideologically propagated community of all 'Volksgenossen', while excluding those discriminated as community aliens or those politically distanced."[84] But it is exactly this new social practice which Friedrich Pohl's letters were part of. A practice which did not turn the national socialist vision into 'fact' but nonetheless had very real effects – not the least of which was the reproduction of itself as well as the vague shadow of a community. It is precisely the driving forces inherent to the

---

80  Cf. Kershaw 2011: 3–9. Quote on p. 3.
81  Wildt 2011: 103–104.
82  Marszolek 2013: 67.
83  As stated by: Gruner 2018: 75.
84  Schmiechen-Ackermann 2012: 14.

social vision which are reflected in the sources and condensed in my analysis. When separating the different facets of reality, the simultaneity of vision and impact becomes discernible and becomes downright fundamental for the mechanism of the ideological project Friedrich Pohl underwent in the Labor Service.[85]

Friedrich Pohl wrote the national socialist social vision of a 'people's community' as text of letters into (2) material 'fact.' He made it 'fact' in (4) narrating his experiences and took part in an ideological project that influenced the German society. Even when the effects of his letters cannot be ascertained, I reason that the concept of 'Volksgemeinschaft' (5) had an impact on the (3) historical reality in becoming communicative and therefore social practice. The best example of its impact is to observe the driving force this social vision developed in Friedrich Pohl's letters.

Considering historian Wolf Gruner's caveat not to dismiss possible ambivalences in the experience of communitization,[86] I do not claim that Friedrich Pohl subscribed unconditionally or entirely to the *RAD*'s attempt to realize the social vision. I offer no more and no less than a reading of his letters as negotiations of and participation in an organization he at other times wrote very disapproving of. As presented in this paper, it was not simply the mobilizing capacity inherent to the national socialist vision which affected the young author of the analyzed letters. Rather, his texts speak of the cumulative effect of social promise and rigorous discipline, drill and (mutual) supervision in an ideological project. The realities of life in a prototypical community aiming for deindividuation created a setting that urged not only to obedience but also to self-education. A setting that demonstrated the importance of becoming a valuable part of the 'Volksgemeinschaft.'

Since for Hierl "[...] the regard for the collective" had to "[...] outrank the regard for the individual"[87] it is somewhat ironic that it is precisely in the writing of an individual that the effects of this social vision become evident. In Friedrich Pohl's letters, composed under difficult circumstances, substituting for other forms of interaction and serving various functions, the education in the *RAD* showed its effects: In and through the young man's writing the

---

85   The *RAD* served as a catalyst for existing knowledge and/or made new experiences available. Whether in the case of some individual letters only one of the two applies makes no difference for my argument.
86   Gruner 2018: 78–79.
87   Hierl 1941: 274.

mobilizing potential became 'fact' – something the 'Volksgemeinschaft,' as envisioned by the national socialists, never achieved.

## Bibliography

Berger, Peter L./Luckmann, Thomas (1972): *The Social Construction of Reality. A Treatise in the Sociology of Knowledge*, Harmondsworth.

Bourdieu, Pierre (1990): "Die Biographische Illusion", in: *BIOS - Zeitschrift für Biographieforschung und Oral History* 7/1, 75–81.

Canning, Kathleen (1994): "Feminist History after the Linguistic Turn. Historicizing Discourse and Experience", in: *Signs* 19/2, 368–404.

Daniel, Ute (2016): *Kompendium Kulturgeschichte. Theorien, Praxis, Schlüsselwörter*, Frankfurt am Main.

Dobson, Miriam (2009): "Letters", in: id./Ziemann, Benjamin (eds.): *Reading Primary Sources: The Interpretation of Texts from Nineteenth- and Twentieth-Century History*, London/New York, 57–73.

Gruner, Wolf (2018): "Das Dogma der 'Volksgemeinschaft' und die Mikrogeschichte der NS-Gesellschaft", in: Schmiechen-Ackermann, Detlef et. al. (eds.): *Der Ort der "Volksgemeinschaft" in der deutschen Gesellschaftsgeschichte*, Paderborn, 71–90.

Henzel, Katrin (2020): "Materialität des Briefs", in: Strobel et. al (eds.), *Handbuch Brief. Von der Frühen Neuzeit bis zur Gegenwart*, 222–231.

Hierl, Konstantin (1942): *Ausgewählte Schriften und Reden*. vol. 1, ed. Herbert Freiherr von Stetten-Erb, München.

— (1941): *Ausgewählte Schriften und Reden*. vol. 2, ed. Herbert Freiherr von Stetten-Erb, München.

Jaeger, Stephan (2019): "Factuality in Historiography/Historical Study", in: Fludernik, Monika/Ryan, Marie-Lauren (eds.): *Narrative Factuality. A Handbook*, Berlin/Boston, 335–349.

Kershaw, Ian (2011): "'Volksgemeinschaft': Potenzial und Grenzen eines neuen Forschungskonzepts", in: *Vierteljahrshefte für Zeitgeschichte* 59/1, 1–17.

Krüger, Alfred (1937): "Arbeit und Gemeinschaft. Zur Entwicklung der Arbeitsdienstidee", in: *Deutschlands Erneuerung* 21, 96–100.

Langewiesche, Dieter/Tenorth, Heinz-Elmar (eds.) (1989): *Handbuch der deutschen Bildungsgeschichte, vol. 5: 1918-1945. Die Weimarer Republik und die nationalsozialistische Diktatur*, München.

Latzel, Klaus (1997): "Vom Kriegserlebnis zur Kriegserfahrung. Theoretische und methodische Überlegungen zur erfahrungsgeschichtlichen Untersuchung von Feldpostbriefen", in: *Militärgeschichtlichen Mitteilungen* 56/1, 1–30.

Lingelbach, Karl-Christoph (1987): *Erziehung und Erziehungstheorien im nationalsozialistischen Deutschland. Ursprünge und Wandlungen der 1933-1945 in Deutschland vorherrschenden erziehungstheoretischen Strömungen, ihre politische Funktion und ihr Verhältnis zur außerschulischen Erziehungspraxis des "Dritten Reiches"*, Frankfurt am Main.

Lüdtke, Alf (2015): *Eigen-Sinn. Fabrikalltag, Arbeitererfahrungen und Politik vom Kaiserreich bis in den Faschismus*, Münster.

Marszolek, Inge (2013): "Verhandlungssache. Die 'Volksgemeinschaft' – eine kommunikative Figuration", in: von Reeken, Dietmar/Thießen, Malte (eds.): *"Volksgemeinschaft" als soziale Praxis. Neue Forschungen zur NS-Gesellschaft vor Ort*, Paderborn, 65–77.

Mayring, Philipp (2015): *Qualitative Inhaltsanalyse. Grundlagen und Techniken*, Weinheim.

Patel, Kiran K. (2013): "Volksgenossen und Gemeinschaftsfremde. Über den Doppelcharakter der nationalsozialistischen Lager", in: Jahr, Christoph/Thiel, Jens (eds.): *Lager vor Auschwitz. Gewalt und Integration im 20. Jahrhundert*, Berlin, 311–334.

— (2005): *Soldiers of Labor. Labor Service in Nazi Germany and New Deal America, 1933-1945*, Cambridge.

Pohl, Friedrich (1940): *Briefwechsel*, NS-Documentation Centre of the City of Cologne, N 3126.

Reichsministerium des Inneren (1935): Reichsarbeitsdienstgesetz vom 26. Juni 1935 und Erlaß des Führers und Reichskanzlers über die Dauer der Dienstzeit und die Stärke des Reichsarbeitsdienstes vom 27. Juni 1935, in: *Reichsgesetzblatt* 1935/I, 769–772.

Schmiechen-Ackermann, Detlef (2012): "'Volksgemeinschaft'. Mythos der NS-Propaganda, wirkungsmächtige soziale Verheißung oder soziale Realität im 'Dritten Reich'? Einführung", in: id. (ed.): *"Volksgemeinschaft". Mythos, wirkungsmächtige soziale Verheißung oder soziale Realität im "Dritten Reich"? Zwischenbilanz einer kontroversen Debatte*, Paderborn, 13–53.

Schuster, Britt-Marie (2020) "Linguistik" in: Strobel et. al (eds.), *Handbuch Brief. Von der Frühen Neuzeit bis zur Gegenwart*, 19–39.

Scott, Joan W. (1999): "The Evidence of Experience", in: McDonald, Terrence J. (ed.): *The Historic Turn in the Human Sciences*, Ann Arbor, 379–406.

Seifert, Manfred (2012): "'Ehrendienst am deutschen Volke' und 'Schule der Volksgemeinschaft'. Der Reichsarbeitsdienst (RAD)", in: Becker, Stephanie/Studt, Christoph (eds.): *"Und sie werden nicht mehr frei sein ihr ganzes Leben": Funktion und Stellenwert der NSDAP, ihrer Gliederungen und angeschlossenen Verbände im "Dritten Reich"*, Berlin, 105–140.

— (1994): *Kulturarbeit im Reichsarbeitsdienst. Theorie und Praxis nationalsozialistischer Kulturpflege im Kontext historisch-politischer, organisatorischer und ideologischer Einflüsse*, Münster/New York.

Steber, Martina/Gotto, Bernhard (2018): "'Volksgemeinschaft'. Writing the Social History of the Nazi Regime", in: id. (eds.): *Visions of Community in Nazi Germany. Social Engineering and Private Lives*, Oxford, 1–25.

Stephenson, Jill (1982): "Women's Labor Service in Nazi Germany", in: *Central European History* 15/3, 241–265.

Steuwer, Janosch (2013): "Was meint und nützt das Sprechen von der 'Volksgemeinschaft'? Neuere Literatur zur Gesellschaftsgeschichte des Nationalsozialismus", in: *Archiv für Sozialgeschichte* 53, 487–534.

Strobel, Jochen et. al. (eds.) (2020): *Handbuch Brief. Von der Frühen Neuzeit bis zur Gegenwart*, Berlin/Boston.

Tenorth, Heinz-Elmar (1989): "Erziehung und Erziehungswissenschaft von 1930-1945. Über Kontroversen ihrer Analyse", in: *Zeitschrift für Pädagogik* 35/2, 261–280.

Wildt, Michael (2011): "'Volksgemeinschaft'. Eine Antwort auf Ian Kershaw", in: *Zeithistorische Forschungen* 8/1, 102–109.

Zettelbauer, Heidrun (2018): "Unwanted Desire and Processes of Self-Discipline. Autobiographical Representations of the *Reichsarbeitsdienst* Camps in the Diary of a Young Female National Socialist", in: *zeitgeschichte* 45/4, 537–574.

# Manufacturing Legal Facts

*Kristin Y. Albrecht (University of Salzburg); Sebastian Ibing (Prosecutor Office in Germany)*

## 1. Introduction

In any legal proceeding, there needs to be a set of facts on which to base a decision. It is often said that the facts of a case are found by the court. In the folllowing, we will outline how these legal facts are manufactured in different types of proceedings before the court, and that in many cases they – intentionally – do not live up to the claim that truth can be found. We will thus delineate how legal facts are produced in different types of litigation and that the truth claim at stake varies depending on the type of litigation. Finally, we argue that legal facts are neither found nor constructed but manufactured.

Several perspectives can be distinguished in the field of 'law and fact': Firstly, one can describe law or individual legal systems as facts (law as fact). Secondly, one can look at how law reacts to facts: For example, it prohibits racist statements or the denial of the Holocaust, and it protects the free expression of opinions in public discourse (legal protection of facts). Thirdly, law itself creates facts by influencing behavior through law or judgements (facts by law). Furthermore, law itself determines facts within the framework of legal processes on the basis of which judicial decisions are made (legal facts).

In the first case, law itself is a fact. This perspective also includes positions such as Eugen Ehrlich's sociology of law which holds the view that the validity of law depends on facts. In this case, one can speak of a normative legal-realistic concept of validity which makes validity, among other things, dependent on factual relations of recognition. The second and third perspectives refer to extra-legal facts to which the law pertains. For example, expressions of opinion which are fundamentally protected by law. In the last case, it is a question

*Figure 1*

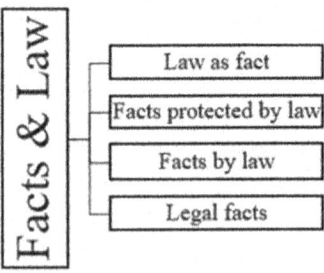

of how facts are recognized, established or (re)constructed as such according to the law. In law, there are basically two connecting factors. One is customary law. If a legal practice has existed for a long time and the conviction prevails that this is legal (*opinio iuris*), then one can speak of (legally binding) customary law. On the other hand, in the context of court proceedings, facts that are relevant for the proceedings are determined; in this respect, one can also speak of 'legal facts.' Our paper will focus on what it means when law itself establishes facts in the context of legal proceedings, especially civil and criminal proceedings. In doing so, we will draw on the legal situation in Germany.

## 2. Where Legal Facts Arise: A Very Brief Introduction

Before we talk about the rules of origin for legal facts, we must look at when they came into being. They arose in the context of legal proceedings. In national law, there are three types of legal proceedings in which facts are established: civil, administrative, and criminal proceedings.

In addition, there are other procedures such as lawsuits under constitutional and European law. However, it is always required that the basic proceedings have at least begun or have even been exhausted so that the facts (the 'facts of the case') have already been established at that point. Thus, there is little to be found concerning the question of the emergence of legal facts. Therefore, let us take a closer look at the three types of proceedings in which facts are established. In civil proceedings, one citizen sues another. This includes, for example, disputes between landlord and tenant or employer and employee. In criminal and administrative proceedings, the state sues the citizen. In this case we are confronted with fraud, murder, and theft, or overly large chicken coops and swimming pools.

In civil proceedings, the principle of production or negotiation applies. According to this, what the parties present to the judge by consensus is considered a fact. What is fact is therefore determined by the parties. If the disputing persons A and B both state that the traffic lights were green when B drove his car through them, then it is a fact for the judge. The fact that the traffic light may have been red is of no interest. What is presented by the disputing parties is considered to be true. In Roman law, this was elegantly summed up with *da mihi factum, dabo tibi ius* ('give me the facts, I'll give you the law').

This framework includes two important points: First, the parties determine what is fact. And secondly, the facts are borne by the consensus of the parties or, if they disagree, determined by the judge on request. At first glance, this might be disturbing to non-lawyers: Why is it of no importance in trials what actually happened? Why can't the judge question eyewitnesses or look at the data from a surveillance camera to determine whether the traffic light was actually green? This is because the main focus of civil proceedings is that – roughly speaking – the involved parties walk out of the courtroom pacified. The public's interest in a fair decision based on facts that are as objective as possible is not of priority here. The so-called 'formal truth,' which results from the consensually presented facts, is sufficient for this type of process.

Once the fact-finding is completed (*da mihi factum*), it comes to the heart of the legal work – the subsumption. In subsumption, 'the facts are brought under the norm' or, to put it more pathetically, the factual is interwoven with the normative. We will return to this procedure later. As soon as this has been done, the judge pronounces the law (*dabo tibi ius*) in the form of a judgement or a decision. This is based on the following steps of procedure:

1) Determination of the facts ('Sachverhalt').
2) Legal assessment/subsumption
3) Delivery of the judgement or order

At the same time, there are administrative and criminal proceedings to be executed. In this case the state is involved, which investigates 'ex officio' what really happened. In contrast to civil proceedings, it is not the principle of negotiation but the principle of investigation that applies here. The facts are not negotiated but investigated. In this kind of search for facts, a distinction must be made between different procedural stages, especially in criminal proceedings:

1) Preliminary investigation – Is there an initial suspicion? (suspect)
2) Preliminary proceedings – Is there sufficient suspicion? (accused)
3) Main proceedings – Is the suspect guilty? (defendant/accused)

In the first two procedural stages, the facts are determined by the public prosecutor (e.g., by searching for and questioning witnesses) while in the main proceedings they are decided by the judge (by questioning the same witness again). For the judgement it is of relevance what facts the judge was able to establish. This is the stage for which the procedural rules of fact-finding were established. Once the facts are established in the main proceedings, i.e., the so-called 'facts of the case' are determined, they are legally assessed by the judge – as in civil proceedings. In a last step, the judgement will be pronounced.

## 3. Rules of Fact-*Finding*

Based on the distinctions discussed above, the different procedures used by the court to determine the facts on which its judgement is established can be outlined in more detail. In all areas of law, the separation between facts and law can already be found in the judgement, since the facts are always decided first, followed by a legal evaluation.

### 3.1 Facts in Civil Proceedings

Determining the facts of a case in civil law is one of the most difficult tasks, especially for aspiring judges and lawyers. The basic principle is easily comprehensible: As already explained, civil proceedings are about the legal dispute of two (or more) legal subjects of civil law, i.e., citizens who are of equal rank before the law. Since the latter bring the matter before the court to resolve their legal dispute, the main principle is that the parties determine the procedure and the subject matter of the proceedings. It follows that the parties determine the beginning – by filing a lawsuit – and the end – by judgement, settlement, or discharge – of the legal dispute. Central to the present discussion is that the parties determine the factual basis of the legal dispute at the same time. This results from the so-called 'principle of contribution' ('Beibringungsgrundsatz') according to which the court may only base its legal assessment on those facts that have been submitted by the parties. Two basic constellations must be distinguished: First, the parties can present facts in agreement. In this case, the court has no possibility to review the facts. However, in the second case, there are usually factual differences concerning the decisive points of the dispute, so that a taking of evidence is necessary. This determines which alternative of the facts presented by the parties is correct.

This two-tiered approach results in the distinction of who must present a certain fact (so-called 'burden of presentation') and who must prove it (so-called 'burden of proof').

### 3.1.1 The Presentation

Based on the alternative facts presented by both sides, it is in a first step the court's task to determine which points are in dispute. Insofar as the court is presented with a concordant set of facts, it is bound by these and is, so to speak, 'blind' to everything that is not directly presented by the parties. If the buyer of an item – e.g., a toaster – wants to return it because of a defect, he must also claim that it is defective. In the case of the toaster, this would be the fact that it does not heat up sufficiently. Whether the court must examine how the toaster heats up depends on the reaction of the seller: If the seller refuses to take back the toaster – and of course also to refund the purchase price – by claiming that the low temperature is a special energy-saving function, then the seller must also claim that the toaster is not defective. As a consequence, the low temperature is a fact that the court can no longer examine. In order to be open to judicial review, the seller is required to dispute the temperature that the toaster reaches.

At this point, it must be emphasized that as long as a fact is undisputed, it does not matter whether or not it is actually true or at least true to the knowledge of the court. In principle, the parties of civil proceedings have a duty to tell the truth.[1] However, this only concerns the circumstances that are in dispute between the parties, i.e., it does not embrace undisputed cir-

---

1  § 138 para. 1 ZPO.

cumstances.² Therefore, it is also possible that even if the court knows that a certain fact described by the parties is not true, it may be 'forced' by them to accept their view. If the parties agree that there was one meter of snow on the day in question in August, this is to be accepted by the court as true, even if it is false according to its own knowledge. The court's own expertise is only relevant when it comes to assessing the alternative facts that can be considered.

Furthermore, everything – and here the burden of proof plays a decisive role – that is asserted by one party and not contested by the other in a sufficiently substantiated manner is assumed to be true.³ If it is said that an item is defective – e.g., that a pool is leaking – the seller must claim that this is not true. In our example, that means that the pool is leak-proof. Thus, what one party claims but the other does not dispute can become part of the facts of the case.

It is important to note that under certain circumstances more stringent requirements are to be placed on such a denial. It may be sufficient for one party to claim that a fact of the other party is not true.⁴ Normally, the other party does not have to give reasons why this is the case and how it could have happened otherwise. However, under certain circumstances, such a proof may be required: If it is rather difficult for one side of a dispute to make a factual allegation, while the opposite side can do so easily, this advantaged side cannot limit itself to denying it.⁵ If the subject matter of the dispute touches, for example, the internal production process, it is not possible for the individual purchaser to overlook it as a whole. Therefore, the manufacturer cannot limit himself to denying that a mistake has been made during the quality control. He must rather describe the circumstances that prove that the necessary care was taken. Only if he substantiates this, the objection is relevant, so that the fact is disputed.

---

2  Stadler ZPO 2022: § 138 para. 2. The citations here and in the following comply with the rules of a quotation system used in German Law. In the case of comments to paragraphs the respective commentators are not individually indicated in the bibliography, while the respective books of commentaries are listed under the names of their editors/authors in alphabetical order.

3  Results from § 138 para. 3 ZPO.

4  Laumen 2016: 3$^{rd}$ chap., para. 12.

5  Federal Constitutional Court, Decision 06.10.1999, Az. 1 BvR 2110/93, Rn. 40, NJW 2000: 1483.

## 3.1.2 Proof

Once it has been determined which facts are undisputed and which are disputed, the next level is to determine the facts for the judgement. This is done through procedures of taking and assessing evidence.

### 3.1.2.1 Strict Evidence Procedure

In principle, there is the so-called 'strict evidence procedure' for this. There are written rules on which evidence is admissible and in which procedure it has to be collected.[6] In civil law, the *numerus clausus*[7] of evidence applies with the testimony of witnesses, the expert appraisal, the visual inspection, the deed and – as subsidiary evidence – the hearing of the parties.[8]

The most common means of evidence is the witness. The witness is supposed to tell the court about his or her own perceptions in the past. At the same time, the witness is the most uncertain means of evidence, since both the human sensory apparatus and the human memory are not geared to testifying in a court case.[9] This is most obvious in road traffic. Without aids, it is impossible to determine what specific speed a vehicle is traveling at, or how large a certain distance is. For the court, therefore, error is much more likely than lying to prevent a testimony that is not consistent with the actual course of events.[10]

The expert appraisal is supposed to inform the court about valid principles of expertise, the state of the art and to assess a situation accordingly. A visual inspection is deployed when it comes to examining the condition of a certain object. Finally, the deed concerns the content of a specific document.

### 3.1.2.2 Free Assessment of Evidence

The fundamental standard is the free assessment of evidence by the court.[11] This concerns a subjective standard of the court when it considers the proof of a fact to be proven: "The judge may and must, however, be content in actually doubtful cases with a degree of certainty that is useful for practical life and

---

6   Laumen 2016: 2$^{nd}$ chap., para. 24.
7   Bacher ZPO 2022: § 284 para. 11.
8   §§ 371 ZPO.
9   Häcker 2021: para. 13.
10  Ibid.: para. 14.
11  § 286 ZPO.

that silences doubts without excluding them completely."[12] It is important that a differentiation according to the individual case is made, whereby the possibilities of proof are also to be considered. For example, the statement that a document has been sent is not sufficient as a proof that it has been sent off. Although in Germany around 99.995% of all letters are sent correctly, a simple proof is possible by using a registered letter. In contrast, the probability of a paternity test of 99.95% is sufficient, as a further proof is simply not possible.[13]

Certain rules of evidence may contain an exception to the free assessment of evidence, e.g., in the case of a document. In this case the court must accept the content of the document as accurate, unless the opposing party succeeds in proving that the document itself has been falsified.

This results in two constellations that are to be examined for fact-finding:

#### 3.1.2.2.1 The Proof of a Certain Fact Is Provided

If a party succeeds in convincing the court of an alleged fact with the evidence offered, the court will base its legal assessment on this.

#### 3.1.2.2.2 Proof Cannot Be Provided

The situation becomes more difficult, however, if a party does not succeed in proving a certain fact, the so-called 'non-liquet situation.' In this case, the so-called 'burden of proof' must be applied: According to this, it is asked who has to provide the evidence for a disputed fact.[14] These regulations are very differentiated in detail and depend on the respective substantive law. In principle, however, the person who has to prove a fact and thus bears the burden of proof is the one who benefits from it. If, for example, in proceedings for compensation for pain and suffering, it is argued that the injured party suffered a long-term restriction of mobility as a result of the injury, the injured party must prove this by submitting medical reports. If he or she fails to do so, the court cannot use the long-term consequences as a basis for assessing

---

12 "Der Richter darf und muss sich aber in tatsächlich zweifelhaften Fällen mit einem für das praktische Leben brauchbaren Grad von Gewissheit begnügen, der den Zweifeln Schweigen gebietet, ohne sie völlig auszuschließen." "Anastasia" Federal Constitutional Court, Judgement 17.02.1970, Az. III ZR 139/67, NJW 1970: 946.
13 Federal Constitutional Court, Judgement 14.03.1990, Az. XII ZR 56/89 FamRZ 1990: 615–616.
14 Laumen 2016: 9$^{th}$ chap. para. 2.

the damages for pain and suffering. The burden of proof thus ultimately determines as a legal rule which factual basis has to be considered if an actual clarification of a circumstance is not possible. It is important to note that the party not burdened with proof does not have to prove the opposite: if the burdened party fails with its submission, the submission of the opposing party applies.

## 3.2 Facts in Criminal Proceedings

While civil proceedings are subjugated to the will of the parties, criminal proceedings deal with the situation that the citizen faces the state. This implies a relationship of superiority and subordination. Due to this relationship, the so-called 'official investigation principle' ('Amtsermittlungsgrundsatz') or inquisition principle applies here, i.e., the court has to determine the actual facts independently of the submissions of the persons concerned.[15]

The basis of the entire procedure is the rule-of-law principle that doubts are always to the benefit of the accused, 'in dubio pro reo.' Therefore, the accused himself does not have to prove his innocence; rather, it is necessary that the facts he is charged with are fully proven. It does not have to be established that the accused is innocent. The latter does not have to prove his innocence either. The only decisive factor is whether a conviction is likely on the basis of the evidence available.[16] A special constellation of this principle is the so-called 'choice determination.' This occurs when a decision between two factual constellations cannot be made without a doubt, the alternatives are further comparable in terms of legal ethics, and at least one alternative is realized in any case.[17] If a car that has been proven to be stolen is discovered in the possession of a defendant, there is either the possibility that he stole it himself or that he bought it from the thief. In the first case he would be guilty of theft, in the second case of accepting stolen property. If one were to strictly apply 'in dubio pro reo,' one would conclude that both offenses are not existent, since they are mutually exclusive, and none can be proven beyond reasonable doubt. In order to avoid such an unsatisfactory result, a conviction according to the milder offense – in this case receiving stolen goods – is

---

15 § 155 para. 2 StPO, Schmitt StPO 2020: § 155 para. 2.
16 Schmitt StPO 2020: § 170 para. 1.
17 Fischer StGB 2021: § 1 para. 33.

possible. Theft and purchasing stolen goods have a comparable unlawful content, since both are directed against the property of others, so that a decision between the two does not seem necessary.

The investigations are not conducted by the court itself; rather, it is the responsibility of the prosecutor to gather both incriminating and exculpating facts for the accused and to bring them to court. Therefore, the criminal proceedings are divided into the following sections:

### 3.2.1 Preliminary Investigation

The standard here is the initial suspicion, i.e., the possibility of a prosecutable offense exists according to criminalistic experience. There are no restrictions concerning the possible factual basis. The initial suspicion can thus arise from a multitude of circumstances. For example, in the case of a car driver who is found to be under the influence of tetrahydrocannabinol (THC), regular consumption can be concluded from the presence of tetrahydrocannabinol-carboxylic-acid which is why the initial suspicion of illicit possession or even trafficking can be deduced

### 3.2.2 Investigation

If such an initial suspicion is assumed, the preliminary proceedings are to be opened. Here, the prosecutor examines whether a conviction of a criminal offense is probable – the so-called 'sufficient suspicion' – and exists.[18] Since the standard is the probability of conviction, the prosecutor must forecast the court's decision. Therefore, it is necessary to ask not only about the facts of the case but whether a conviction is possible according to the evidence of the criminal proceedings.[19] Thus, a strict standard is set for the factual basis, already taking into consideration the principle of doubt.

In criminal proceedings, the confession of the accused, the testimony of witnesses, the expert opinion, objects of inspection as well as documents count as evidence. The collection of this evidence is also specifically regulated. While in civil proceedings it is basically irrelevant how a party obtains evidence, in criminal proceedings only facts that the state has obtained in a legally regulated procedure can be recognized as evidence.[20] Thus, a judicial

---

18 § 170 StPO; Schmitt StPO 2020: § 170 para. 1.
19 Higher Regional Court (OLG) Karlsruhe, Decision 16.12.2002, Az. 1 Ws 85/02, Rn. 20, juris.
20 Decision 16.06.2015, Az. 2 BvR 2718/10 and also BVerfGE 20, 162 (223).

order is required for the interception of an accused's telecommunications, which also requires an offense of considerable importance regulated with the help of an exhaustive list. If questioning of witnesses during a court hearing is not possible, the accused must at least have the possibility of an adversarial questioning through his or her lawyer. If these requirements are not met, it does not automatically follow that evidence cannot be used. Rather, the public's interest in criminal prosecution must be weighed against the accused's interest in complying with the rules of criminal procedure.[21] A result of this can be that a certain piece of evidence cannot be introduced into the proceedings, although it would prove the guilt of the accused beyond doubt.

When it comes to evidence, the confession, or the admission of the accused, is central, as this is the starting point for determining the facts of the case. However, a confession must always be verified and cannot simply be assumed to be true.

Witness statements are the most frequent but also the most difficult evidence in criminal proceedings. Witness testimony also poses the problem that witnesses can refuse to testify in later proceedings. If this is the case for justified reasons, especially when it comes to close family members, statements made beforehand may no longer be used in the court proceedings.[22] Also, the former interrogators can then no longer be questioned about the statement as 'hearsay witnesses.' This often leads to dismissals, especially in domestic violence proceedings, because the injured parties subsequently refuse to testify, while objective proof is not possible without their testimony.

Less important are deeds and visual inspection. Experts play a role especially in medical matters.

If, at the end of the investigation, the prosecutor concludes that a conviction is likely because of the admissible evidence, a public prosecution must be filed. In doing so, the prosecutor names the evidence gathered from which the accused facts arise and thus creates the basis for the judicial investigation of the same.

### 3.2.3 Criminal Trial
Subsequently, the court itself examines whether the basis of the case file offers sufficient suspicion of the offense.

---

21  Federal Constitutional Court, Decision 13.05.2015, Az. 2 BvR 616/13, HRRS 2015 Nr. 824 Rn. 41.
22  Schmitt StPO 2020: § 252 para. 12.

If this is the case, the hearing takes place. Here, the aforementioned standard is further tightened: The basis of the judgement is only the evidence of the aforementioned categories and that which has been introduced into the main hearing (principle of orality or 'Mündlichkeitsgrundsatz'). Even if a witness has already testified in the preliminary proceedings, he or she must now make this testimony again so that it can find its way into the judgement. Likewise, the procedure for taking evidence is precisely regulated.

The appraisal of the evidence is ultimately the task of the court. Here, too, there is a free assessment of the evidence.[23] Regulations according to which a certain piece of evidence has an absolute evidentiary value are missing. In principle, the above-mentioned standards also exist here, wherefore the court must only reasonably exclude possible doubts. The court's free assessment of the evidence can only be subsequently reviewed to determine whether it is contradictory, unclear or incomplete, or whether it violates the laws of reasoning or established principles of experience ('Erfahrungssätze').[24] Thus, the assessment of evidence in the so-called "pistachio ice cream case[25] was criticized by the Federal Supreme Court: After several members of a well-situated family from Stuttgart had already died under not entirely clear circumstances, the youngest daughter ultimately died of food poisoning after eating pistachio ice cream with her aunt, who had married into the family. A post-mortem examination later revealed arsenic poisoning. Due to the chronological sequence, it was clear that the arsenic had been administered to the deceased two hours before the first symptoms. Although the parents could thus also be considered as perpetrators, the previous court convicted the aunt on the basis of several pieces of circumstantial evidence: She had been present at all other unexplained deaths of the family, furthermore, she had removed food supplies after the death from the house and had finally attracted attention with inappropriate behavior at the funeral. The Federal Supreme Court allowed the appeal against this, as the assessment of the evidence against the aunt was only based on circumstantial evidence which was interpreted negatively to her disadvantage. The necessary conviction of the commission of the offense could not be drawn from this. The murder was not solved by the courts.

As a result, it should be noted that due to the strict regulation of the gathering of evidence in criminal proceedings and despite the principle of offi-

---

23   § 261 StPO.
24   Fischer StGB 2021: § 261 para. 39.
25   Federal Court of Justice (BGH), Judgement 31.07.1996, Az. 1 StR 247/96, HRRS database.

cial investigation, the result can often deviate from the actual circumstances, since there either remains a point of contention or certain evidence cannot be gathered according to the prescribed procedure.

## 4. Finding, Constructing, and Manufacturing Legal Facts

The basis of a correct (in the highest claim: just) judgement is the truth of the facts. We argue that the facts in a trial are ultimately always legal facts, facts of law, which make only a limited claim to truth. A claim to objective truth – assuming that it exists and can be determined from unlimited evidence and resources – cannot be made for several reasons:

The law itself limits the determination of facts for a variety of reasons. One such reason is, for example, the rule of law in the case of the provocation of a crime which is contrary to the rule of law: A person who has no intention of committing a crime is persuaded to do so by an undercover investigator. So even if the rule of law could access evidence, sometimes it forbids itself to do so. Often it might be restricted to look for evidence at all: intelligence can sometimes be withheld if state or military secrets are involved. Even if evidence, as already described, was obtained with other means of proofs than those permitted in the respective type of proceedings, it will not be used. As explained in the previous section, there are prohibitions of evidence (prohibitions of facts of evidence, prohibitions of means of evidence, prohibitions of methods of evidence and relative prohibitions of evidence) which limit the investigation of facts.

The assessment of the (usable) evidence is also still subject to the court, i.e., the respective judge: due to the principle of free assessment of evidence, the judge still has a great deal of leeway in evaluating the evidence and ultimately recognizing a legal fact.

However, a restriction does not only result from the restriction of the means and the leeway of the judges but also in the possible scope of the means by which facts can be established. Whereas in criminal proceedings the official investigation principle applies, and the state mainly takes the investigation of the facts into its own hands (although the defense can still present facts), in civil proceedings it is left to the litigants through the principle of production ('Beibringungsgrundsatz'). The big difference is not necessarily a result of the circumstance that the parties are private: This could be supported by the fact that litigants are usually not legally pre-educated when experiencing the legally relevant life event (for example, an accident) and the subsequent reporting of it (usually to the police). Those who do not know which circumstances are legally relevant also pay less attention to them. If one's own perception is trained by prior legal knowledge, for example through police training or a law degree, there is a higher probability of more consciously perceiving the decisive circumstances.[26] In the trial, however, not only the private parties but also the public prosecution must rely on (mostly) legally untrained witnesses. The real difference lies in the different resources of the state and the private sector and thus in the possible extended possibilities of hiring expert opinions et cetera. However, no matter who investigates, resources are always limited. A trial may not take an infinite amount of time, nor do the public prosecutor's office or the parties to the trial have an infinite amount of money at their disposal.

The overall result is that the scope of what could potentially be recognized as fact in a trial depends very much on the parties, the prosecution, and the judge. In addition, there is limited evidence as well as limited resources of time and money. Therefore, the question of objective truth is not forming the basis of the court's decision. However, according to the generally accepted view, this would be the basis for a correct judgement. How can one speak of correctness if the facts of the case cannot claim to be objectively true?

At first glance, 'truth' seems to imply that there are things that exist independently of our imagination and that there is only one complete and correct description of how the world is (so called ontological realism).[27] It is difficult to prove this assumption with philosophical arguments. Without going into further detail on individual concepts of truth and their application in factfinding, the focus here should rather be on the fact that even with a concept that does not have such high requirements, truth cannot be met in a legal context because of the limitations discussed above. Even if one does assume unlimited resources, reliable witnesses, etc.: the scientific and philosophical determination of truth is entirely distinct from the legal determination of facts.[28] In science, there is a free choice of methods. The only limitation of science is one of logical necessity: the method must be scientifically proven. In the legal process, methods do not only rely on scientific interests but mostly on the constitutional principle of the rule of law. Therefore, one can rather

---

26  In favor of this position: Upmeier 2010: 72.
27  Definition from Putnam 1981.
28  Upmeier 2010: 147.

state (metaphysically-realistically) that there are different degrees of approximation to 'the' truth. This idea is also supported by the concept of 'finding the verdict,' to which the court retires before pronouncing the verdict. But just as the judgement is not 'found,' a finding of facts does not take place in the determination of the facts. The verdict does not reveal itself to the judge. This romantic notion, along with the elevated sitting position of the judge, the illocutionary force of the judgement, the required elevation of the persons in the courtroom, underscores an almost theological authoritativeness. If one had to formulate this process in constructivist terms, one would say that truth is constructed. However, this assertion is too simple in its brevity. Even if what is determined legally is always subjectively colored and sometimes also wrong, it is not completely arbitrary. To call the determination of facts a *finding* or simply a *construction* would be wrong. Since the term 'manufacture' no longer refers to traditional but to modern craft work in which highly specialized workers from different disciplines work together on a final product and the court precisely uses such highly specialized methods to determine the facts of a case by being very careful in its construction, we may speak of *manufacturing legal facts*.

The judgement is limited in the scope of its claim, despite the coercion it imposes: It is only absolute as far as the established facts are concerned. These facts can – with good reason – only be determined by limited means. In a further step, another limitation is added to the subsumptions made so far: in certain cases – so-called 'hard cases' – one cannot necessarily assume a single correct decision.[29] However, this is what judges convey in the language of their judgements: Every judgement contains the only correct normative assessment of the only correct set of facts. The fact that these limitations of the claim are not linguistically conveyed to laypersons is an existing challenge.

## Bibliography

Baumgartel, Gottfried/Laumen, Hans-Willi/Prütting, Hanns (2016): *Handbuch der Beweislast*, Köln.
Bender, Rolf/Häcker, Robert/Schwarz, Volker (2021): *Tatsachenfeststellungen vor Gericht*, München.

---

29  In favor of this position: Dworkin 1977; convincingly arguing against this position: Siedenburg 2016.

Dworkin, Ronald (1977): "Can Rights be Controversial?", in: id. (ed.): *Taking Rights Seriously*, Cambridge/Mass., 279–290.

Fischer, Thomas (2021): *Strafgesetzbuch. Mit Nebengesetzen*, München.

Hau, Wolfgang/Poseck, Roman (2022): *BeckOnlineKommentar Zivilprozessordnung*, München.

Meyer-Goßner, Lutz/Schmitt, Bertram (2020): *Strafprozessordnung mit GVG Nebengesetzen*, München.

Putnam, Hilary (1981): *Reason, Truth and History*, Cambridge.

Siedenburg, Philipp (2016): *Die kommunikative Kraft der richterlichen Begründung. Zur Argumentationsfigur der einzig richtigen Entscheidung*, Baden-Baden.

Upmeier, Arne (2010): *Fakten im Recht. Eine Untersuchung zur Tatsachenfeststellung im Rechtsprozess*, Baden-Baden.

# LITERATURE AND ARTS

# Towards a Poetics of Fact
## Subjugated Knowledges, Historiographic Metafiction, and the 'Terrible Truth' behind Words in Early Nineteenth-Century American Literature

Stefan L. Brandt (University of Graz)

## 1. Introduction: Towards a Poetics of Fact

In his well-known Gothic short story "The Legend of Sleepy Hollow" (1819),[1] American writer Washington Irving relates the following fantastic, yet allegedly historical account: A headless horseman, the restless ghost of a Hessian trooper killed by a cannonball during the Revolution, terrorizes a Dutch settlement in the New York area, haunting the town's superstitious inhabitants with his bloodthirsty appearances. Set in 1790, just one year after the U.S. became a republic, the events narrated in the tale – albeit clearly fanciful in nature – are portrayed as evidenced by fact. In a characteristic passage, Irving cites – through the voice of his narrator – "the most authentic historians" (273) who have collected and collated the "floating facts" (ibid.) surrounding the Headless Horseman. While subtly challenging the reliability of these reports (by means of conjuring up an unsettling image of volatility and flux), the reference to *floating facts* is also supported – and, on the level of narrative transmission, authenticated – by the seemingly 'factual' composition of *The Sketch Book of Geoffrey Crayon, Gent* (the volume that "Sleepy Hollow" is part of).[2] In many ways, Irving's story is symptomatic of the hegemonic imagi-

---

1 Irving 1993 [1819]: 272–297.
2 The 34 essays and short stories of Irving's *Sketch Book* are organized in a mock-documentary fashion, with the fictional Dutch historian Diedrich Knickerbocker appearing as the actual author. In the sketches, the line between fact and fiction is constantly blurred. "So vividly and naturally are these scenes of humor depicted," Irving's narra-

nation in late-Enlightenment America that meandered smoothly between the established templates of fabulous, truthful, and satirical historiographies, all of these employing the notion of *floating facts* as a key pattern.[3]

This essay deals with the phenomenon of *floating facts* in early nineteenth-century U.S. literature.[4] My basic premise is that the paradigms of factuality and fictionality became contested in post-revolutionary America, with increasingly blurred boundaries between fact and fiction. With Romanticism becoming the dominant literary movement after the Revolution, "distinctions of genre, fact and fiction, literary and subliterary had to be reconstructed."[5] What followed – at least in the genre of historical fiction that used elements of both facticity and narrative embellishment – was, in Cathy Davidson's words, "an intentional blurring of the division between fiction and fact and an invitation to the reader to enjoy that same blurring."[6] If we conceive of post-revolutionary American literature as a dynamic field of cultural interaction, in which the texts involved readers in the playful acts of fictional fact-making, we come to the following questions: How were facts circulated and negotiated in

---

tor utters in one section, "that they become mingled up in the mind with the facts and personages of real life." (Ibid.: 92)

3   According to Hayden White, three versions of historiography dominated in eighteenth-century cultural practice: fabulous (historical tales that included fictional elements), true (factually accurate representations), and satirical (accounts designed as critiques of the dominant historical discourse). (Cf. White 2014: 49–53)

4   American writing in the late eighteenth century was obsessed with 'truthfulness' as an ethical ideal. Two of the most widely received novels of the early period of U.S. literature, William Hill Brown's *The Power of Sympathy: or, The Triumph of Nature. Founded in Truth* (1789) and Susanna Rowson's *Charlotte Temple. A Tale of Truth* (1791), focus on 'truth' as a key paradigm, even though from a distinctly sentimental perspective. 'Truth,' in these novels, carries a notion of moral rectitude rather than an appeal to candidness. With the emergence of a more independent strain of thought in the 1820s (accompanied by the arrival of transcendentalism and the empowerment of the self), new modes of representing truth as an individualized concept became desired forms of cultural identity-fashioning.

5   Kelly 1990: 158.

6   Davidson 1986: 143. Analyzing, among others, Brown's *The Power of Sympathy* (1789), Rowson's *Charlotte Temple* (1789), and Hannah Webster Foster's *The Coquette* (1797), Davidson demonstrates that the confusion of the boundaries between fact and fiction was an important parameter in post-revolutionary writing, which conveyed to readers that the sentimentalized events they were reading about were "founded on fact," as Foster already claims in the title page of her novel. (Cf. ibid.: 83–109, 140–150)

literary texts during this time? Which counter-hegemonic forms of fact-formation became viable in literary practice? To elucidate these questions, I will propose the concept of a *poetics of fact* as a hermeneutic tool. Hereby I define a counter-normative mode of representation in literary texts that encompasses and hails what Foucault has described as "subjugated knowledges."[7] It is the goal of this essay to isolate an aesthetics of what I term *poetic factuality* in early nineteenth-century American writing. One could assume that – with the arrival of Enlightenment thinking – a fully-fledged sense of rationalism had developed in the new nation around 1800. My analysis, however, contends that a *hybrid* version of factual and fictional representation was more compatible with the emergent needs of readers in the nascent republic that could only be satisfied by a combination of fact-based tales and Romanticist narrativizations.[8] Far from intimating a clearcut distinction between history and fiction in texts of the time, I want to emphasize what has been called "the problematic relationship of fact, fiction, and literariness in Romantic culture."[9] My focus here lies on Catharine Maria Sedgwick's influential novel *Hope Leslie*, first published in two volumes in 1827, and how it reconstructs the history of native people in colonial America in a poetic fashion. Employing the technique of historiographic metafiction, *Hope Leslie* – arguably one of the most unusual texts ever published in America – calls attention to the subjective reality *behind* the official version of American history, especially concerning the atrocities committed against natives.

The concept of a *poetics of fact* is not limited to the nineteenth century but can be viewed as a diachronic parameter that helps us understand the constant struggle in Western culture between fact and fiction, history and rumor, truth and gossip. Consider the following citation from a science-fiction classic written more than a century later, namely Ursula K. Le Guin's *The Left Hand of Darkness* (1969):

---

7    Foucault 1980: 82.
8    In Davidson's words, many post-revolutionary novels suggested, at least partly, "a kind of covenant between the reader and the text" by mentioning, in the frontmatter to the books, truth and fact as reference points. (Ibid. 1986: 96) Likewise, Kelly, in his reading of Walter Scott's popular historical novel *Waverley* (1814), points out that "[t]he combining of fact and fiction delighted most readers and critics [...]." (Kelly 1990: 172) Similar to the British writer Scott, who related the history of Scotland in a fictional manner, American writers such as Sedgwick inspired readers to explore the in-between territory of historiography and fiction.
9    Ibid.: 166.

> I'll make my report as if I told a story, for I was taught as a child on my homeworld that Truth is a matter of the imagination. The *soundest fact* may fail or prevail in the style of its telling: like that singular *organic jewel* of our seas, which grows brighter as one woman wears it and, worn by another, dulls and goes to dust. Facts are no more solid, coherent, round, and real than pearls are. But both are sensitive.[10]

In the passage, the first-person narrator Genly Ai, a male Terran explorer, ponders about his mission to go to the planet Gethen to negotiate a collaboration of humanoid worlds. By choosing this quote from Le Guin's 1960s sci-fi novel as a reference point for my essay on literature of the 1820s, I want to draw attention to the *diachronic* dimension of the fact/fiction conjunction. Truth, we learn in *The Left Hand of Darkness*, is no more than a cultural construct, designed to tell stories and create a sense of communal identity.[11] The 'facts' taken for granted in a given culture are likened in Le Guin's novel to the beads of a necklace worn by a woman. This reference evokes the established image of native women in colonial America greeting the white explorers, yet representing their own versions of history and culture. It is no coincidence that the English ethnographer and translator Thomas Harriot uses a similar image (see figure 1) in his "Brief and True Report of the New Found Land of Virginia" (1590) when describing native women: "They wear a chain about their necks of pearls or beads of copper, which they much esteem [...]."[12]

Harriot's graphic depiction of indigenous people as *factual*, yet at once also *fictionalized* creatures allows him to interconnect what he calls "the greatness of the facts" (5) to the natives' (mostly unknown) "traditions and stories." (Ibid.) These passages from Harriot's early treatise illustrate how closely interwoven factuality and imagination have traditionally been in the dominant Western imagination since its colonial beginnings. The interpretational sovereignty regarding the 'truthfulness' of *established* facts on the one hand and the abject nature of *unacknowledged* facts on the other is linked to what, in

---

10   Le Guin 2010 [1969]: 1, emphasis added.
11   Le Guin's emphasis on a *floating* connection between fact and fiction is underpinned by the book's transgression of oppositional corporeal and spatial spheres. Not only are the Gethenians marked as androgynous creatures that know no clear gender boundaries, the novel also bridges the gap between the terrestrial and the extraterrestrial as well as that between present and future.
12   Harriot 1590: 12.
13   Picture taken from ibid.: 13.

*Figure 1: A native woman's pearl necklace as a symbol of the conjunction between fact and fiction.*[13]

a Foucauldian sense, could be called the power/knowledge dynamics.[14] Facts and truth cannot be claimed to encapsulate some atemporal essence or purity. Rather, in Hayden White's words, history itself must be considered

> a construction of those who already enjoy membership and indeed privileged positions in already formed communities. No appeal to "the facts" alone can touch this construction, because these same constituencies control what will count as the appropriate kind of science for determining, not

---

14  Foucault's coinage of power/knowledge suggests that our conception of the world is deeply conjoined with questions of hierarchy and privilege. "Each society has its régime of truth, its 'general politics' of truth: that is, the types of discourse which it accepts and makes function as true [...]." (Foucault 1980: 131)

only "what are the facts" but also and most important "what can count as a fact."[15]

Living in an era in which words can quickly assume the force of a firestorm through social-media platforms such as Facebook and Twitter, we are well aware of the extraordinary power that language has over our imagination. In a way, we are what we 'hear.' Or, in the Derridean sense: *"There is nothing outside of the text."*[16] Our understanding of the world is fundamentally shaped by the dominion of words. And the written or spoken word, endlessly reiterated in chains of autopoietic systems of reduplication, is able to substitute our sense of the 'factual' and effectively replace first-hand experience.[17]

A *poetics of fact* – a retelling of seemingly 'factual' events in a way that acknowledges the subjective quality of all representation – can embolden us to expose the *personal* dimension of history and recognize the constructedness of official versions of reality. The idea of a *poetics of fact* is akin to what Jacques Rancière has called "poetics of knowledge,"[18] whereby he defines "a study of the set of literary procedures by which a discourse escapes literature, gives itself the status of a science, and signifies this status." (Ibid.) Following Rancière's approach, I propose the idea of a *poetics of fact* as a literary strategy in Romanticism that challenges the paradigm of factuality and melds it with an alternative model of poetic articulation. Davidson postulates in *Revolution and the Word* that the "usual prescriptions for fiction and history"[19] were not seldomly reversed in the literary imagination of the early nineteenth century. Analyzing James Fenimore Cooper's euphemistic 1822 response to Royall Tyler's historical novel *The Algerine Captive* (1797), Davidson

---

15   White 1994: ix–x.
16   Derrida 1997: 158, emphasis in the original. Due to the difficulties of translating this sentence accurately, Spivak adds both the original quote and an alternative in square brackets: "[there is no outside-text; *il n'y a pas de hors-texte*]." (Ibid., emphasis in the original)
17   In his iconoclastic polemic *Kindly Inquisitors*, Jonathan Rauch uses the term "knowledge industry" to describe a social system that autopoietically produces its own facts and truths, following the mission "to tell us how things 'really' are." (Rauch 2013: 38) The result of such biased knowledge production is not a sober and truly objective version of reality but, as Hans Rosling et al. have postulated, an "overdramatic worldview" that shows a blatant lack of what the authors call "factfulness." (Rosling 2019: 16)
18   Rancière 1994: 8.
19   Davidson 1986: 200.

summarizes Cooper's viewpoint as follows: "History is a fiction and the novelist is the true historian." (Ibid.) To conceive of literary texts as harboring a *poetics of fact* also means to challenge the opposition between fact and fiction and intimate that 'fact' itself is an essentialist category that should be rethought.[20] In the following, I will showcase how such a poetics of fact can operate in literary works to interrogate what Foucault terms "the order of knowledge."[21] Catharine Maria Sedgwick's novel *Hope Leslie* shall serve as a key example to illustrate how 'knowledge' can be inventively re-interpreted in literature and equipped with a sense of poetics.

## 2. Subjugated Knowledges, Aural Aesthetics, and the Politics of Denunciation

Designed as a historical romance, *Hope Leslie* bestows a powerful voice to two groups that were widely misrepresented in antebellum literature – women and Native Americans. Sedgwick's book shows how in early American culture – that is, the Puritan Era – a *semblance* of veracity often replaced truth.[22] It demonstrates how defamation and social exclusion became the basis for communal knowledge. At the same time, *Hope Leslie* also teaches us how a *poetics of fact* can be instrumental in overcoming rumor and hearsay. Set in seventeenth-century New England, the novel revolves around the twin figures of Hope Leslie (the English immigrant William Fletcher's affable stepdaughter) and Magawisca (a Pequot chief's passionate daughter adopted by the Fletcher

---

20   The term 'knowledge' has been widely applied to systems of thought and belief in general. Foucault's coinage of power/knowledge, for example, suggests that our conception of the world is linked to the microstructures of empowerment and hierarchization. In postmodernist theory, 'knowledge' is often used in the plural form, thus hinting at the complexities and oftentimes subjective appearance of 'knowing.' Donna Haraway, for example, speaks of "situated knowledges," thus indicating that knowledge is always subject to change, dependent on its cultural and temporal context. (Cf. Haraway 1991: 111)

21   Foucault 1980: 128.

22   In a private letter (written as a response to a reader), Sedgwick articulates her "filial reverence" for the Puritans, simultaneously underlining that "their bigotry, their superstition, and above all their intolerance, were too apparent on the pages of history to be forgotten." (Sedgwick, quoted in Nelson 1992: 193)

family). Hope and Magawisca are caught in a whirlwind of increasing tensions and armed conflicts between the white settlers and the natives in the Massachusetts Bay Colony. *Hope Leslie* distances itself decisively from the Puritans' "self-righteous historiography,"[23] which seems burdened with misrepresentations and a lack of authentic voices from women and natives. Truth, the book suggests, can hardly be found in the authorized historiographies presented by Puritan annalists but rather in forgotten counter-histories.

The character of the native Magawisca is a key figure in this rejection of conventional historicism. Magawisca's first appearance in the second chapter already marks her as a non-conformist character, "clothed in her Indian garb"[24] and "having shewn a loathing of the English dress." (22) In the novel's preface, Sedgwick clarifies that there can naturally be no authoritative model for those portions of historical practice that remain unwritten: "The writer is aware that it may be thought that the character of Magawisca has no prototype among the aborigines of this country." (4)

Portrayed as a subaltern figure who gradually emancipates herself from the yoke of hegemonic ascriptions, Magawisca is an example of what Foucault has described as "subjugated knowledges."[25] By this term, Foucault defines "something which in a sense is altogether different, namely, a whole set of knowledges that have been disqualified as inadequate [...]: naïve knowledges, located low down on the hierarchy, beneath the required level of cognition or scientificity." (Ibid.) "[L]isten to me," thus Magawisca addresses both the readers and the Puritan characters in one of the novel's key scenes: "[W]hen the hour of vengeance comes, if it should come, remember it was provoked."[26] Through the voice of Magawisca, the passage juxtaposes the common stereotype of the irrational Indian with a new narrative pattern that, despite being marked as different, evokes reason, empathy and understanding.

The credibility of the Magawisca character is further enhanced by her counter-figure in the novel, the sinister Jennet, a busybody in the village who personifies malevolent talk as opposed to facts. Jennet is the archetypal Puritan fanatic who raises testimony against socially ostracized individuals such as Nelema, an old native woman who helps both Magawisca and Hope Leslie. Jennet's disparaging characterization of Nelema as "the old heathen witch"

---

23  Pelegri 2009: 136.
24  Sedgwick 1998 [1827]: 22.
25  Foucault 1980: 82.
26  Sedgwick 1998 [1827]: 48.

(107) and "that mother-witch" (69) is presented as symptomatic of Puritan hypocrisy. As Jennet denounces natives as "offspring of a race that are the children and heirs of the evil one," (39) the novel reminds us that her "tongue far outruns [her] discretion." (Ibid.) Jennet is associated with the harmful practice of eavesdropping that produces half-truths and lies rather than an accurate representation. At one point, she feels "tempted beyond what she was able to hear, drew nigh to the door with a cat's tread, and applied her ear to the aperture." (312) The novel here explicitly mentions the "interesting relation" between "speakers and listener." (Ibid.)

*Hope Leslie* interrogates the accuracy of 'historical truth' by employing a compositional technique I describe as *aural aesthetics*. Instead of showing the reality of New England Puritans in the form of visual images, the book takes recourse to the motif of the 'ear,' a key metaphorical device in discourses of denunciation and defamation. Using the typical narrative techniques of sentimental fiction (focus on individual agency and imagination), Sedgwick draws the readers' attention to the harmfulness of "fables" (106) and "gossips." (112) Through its aural aesthetics, *Hope Leslie* debunks denunciation as a tool of Foucauldian power/knowledge in the Puritan era. Life in Colonial America can be seen as a textbook lesson about the dangerous effects of denunciation. The trial against Ann Hutchinson and her ensuing banishment from the Massachusetts Bay Colony in 1637 stands as an example of defamation as social control. After Hutchinson was banned, women were – by law – no longer allowed to speak in churches. Puritan society went along with these practices out of fear of persecution. As Sedgwick's novel showcases, there are always alternatives to conformist behavior. The book's ambiguous title alludes to the main character, the rebellious Hope Leslie, but also functions as a pun to the word 'hope*lessly*,' alluding to situations in which we feel trapped, but hope is still a reference point.

This sense of hope that shimmers through in *Hope Leslie* is connected to the body's ability to adapt to its environment, especially when it comes to organs linked to the senses. Sedgwick's novel suggests that all forms of gossip and denunciation rely on the ear as an organ of reception. Following this narrative trajectory, the book proposes a rediscovery of the 'ear' as a metaphor for communicative exchange. We have to listen *differently*, the novel tells us, in order to reach a point of true insight and understanding. *Hope Leslie* is a stunning and courageous text that debunks the insidious nature of denunciatory practices which in many ways have built the fundament for modern-day America.[27] Gossip – as a trivial, community-based form of denunciation – is negotiated in the novel as a malicious counter-discourse to science.[28] As Rachel Brownstein notes, "[g]ossip is a way of turning life into story."[29] In this sense, it resembles fiction. While gossip cannot be classified as literature in the classic sense, it encapsulates elements of the narrative. And, of course, not all forms of gossip are pure denunciation. There is what one scholar calls "serious gossip,"[30] a form of intimate verbal exchange between two or more people that is meant to "reflect" about the speakers and "reflect" their knowledge of one another."[31] Yet, there is also gossip as "distilled malice."[32] This form of gossip denunciation aims at "circulating truths and half-truths and falsehoods," (ibid.) playing with reputations, and attempting to purify the community through social exclusion. In the logic of denunciation, such accusations speak on their own, even though their substance may long have crumbled. The English philosopher Francis Bacon noted more than 400 years ago that rumors contain an eerie power that can hardly be invalidated once released into the world: "Slander boldly, something always sticks."[33]

Denunciatory practices can be an effective tool of social control. Most importantly, denunciation can become an apparatus of cultural formation, by manifesting a divide between the 'self' and the 'other.'[34] Denunciation culture may manifest itself in drastic events such as the Salem Witchcraft Trials of 1692/93 and the McCarthy Era of the late 1940s and early 50s. But it also

---

27 Another influential text from the early nineteenth century dealing with the detrimental effects of denunciation is Washington Irving's 1807 short story "The Little Man in Black." Similar to Irving's "Sleepy Hollow" in its equivocal narrative structure, "The Little Man in Black" relates the story of an innocent small-town pariah whose existence as a "poor outcast" is shaped by "the gossips of the neighborhood" that make any objective evaluation from his fellow citizens impossible. (Cf. Irving 2011 [1807]: 6, 1)

28 Following Block and Madden, I am using the term 'science' not in the sense of the word that is attributed to it today, but "in the more general ways it was understood in Sedgwick's day." (Block/Madden 2003: 23)

29 Brownstein 1982: 7.

30 Spacks 1986: 5.

31 Ibid.

32 Ibid.: 4.

33 Bacon 1597: 392. This translation is provided in Bacon's text itself. The original Latin phrase appears thirty pages earlier: "Audacter calumniare, semper aliquid haeret." (Ibid.: 362)

34 Cf. Butler 1997: 129.

presents itself in the seemingly trivial practices of denigration and non-fact-based accusation in everyday life. *"Everyone knows you can't disprove a rumor,"*[35] the ill-fated protagonist Hannah in Jay Asher's *Th1rteen R3asons Why* (2007) informs us. When another character tells Hannah that she *"knows the rumors,"* (65) Hannah replies: *"You can't know rumors. [...] You can hear rumors [...], but you can't know them."* (65–66) Discourses of denunciation are deeply interwoven with acts of storytelling. Denunciatory practices usually pick up an already existing narrative and extrapolate on it in order to augment its credibility. This brings us to three fundamental questions: Why are such stories told in the first place? Why do we listen? And what can we do when we become the subject of unjustified denunciation?

As an answer to the third question, namely, what we can do about the spreading of falsehoods, *Hope Leslie* proposes a revision of existing narratives through a *poetics of fact*. This revision needs to counter the schemes and stratagems of denunciation that operate on a fine level. Semi-fictional characters in the novel, such as the powerful governor John Winthrop, communicate to the public a devious kind of truth that unfolds its true force in the people's imagination. They do so by using innuendo and suggestion as tools of manipulation. This rhetoric in the receptive mind evokes "much more than [meets] the ear,"[36] to cite Sedgwick's novel. The author's reinterpretation of the phrase "more than meets the eye" is indicative of the *Hope Leslie*'s aural aesthetics that connects the Puritan discourses of witch-hunting and missionizing not only to the "abusive ceremonies" (207) of sermon culture but also to the judgmental aspects of eavesdropping and defamation, especially bigotry and chauvinism. (Cf. 312)

The written or spoken word, endlessly reiterated in chains of autopoietic systems of reduplication, is able to substitute our sense of the *'factual'* and effectively replace it by hearsay. Derrida describes this process of de-factualization as follows: "At the origin there is a rumour, an 'it is said,' an 'it is said that he is supposed to have said.' The origin of a rumour is always unknown. Indeed, this is how a rumour is identified."[37] Derrida's description of rumor as a source of non-factual meaning-making may remind us of the prototypical Trumpist mantra of subliminal denunciation: "A lot of people

---

35   Asher 2017 [2007]: 30, emphasis in the original. The title of Asher's book is stylized as "Th1rteen R3asons Why" to highlight the number 13.
36   Sedgwick 1998 [1827]: 156.
37   Derrida 1994: 176.

are saying ..."[38] This type of slander is capable of obscuring the more complicated realities of what the philosopher Edmund Husserl has called "life-world" [*Lebenswelt*].[39] What people *say* and what they *hear* often conceals whatever realities lie behind the gossip – power games, social control, and survival instinct. The following section deals with how *Hope Leslie*, operating as historiographic metafiction, salvages fragments of a subjugated 'life-world' and thus enables access to what the novel discloses as the 'terrible truth' behind words.

## 3. Historiographic Metafiction and the 'Terrible Truth' behind Words

In his philosophical study *The Names of History: On the Poetics of Knowledge*, Rancière provides a vivid example of how 'facts' are often rendered indistinguishable from acts of imagination. "[T]here are facts," he observes, "that do not belong to the discursive order but require a discursive act, none other than interpretation."[40] Many subjective and individual 'facts' are disguised from the public view and have to be excavated by means of literary revisionism. "[B]etween the facts and the interpretation," Rancière maintains, "there is an obstacle to overcome, a thick cloud of words to dissipate."[41]

Sedgwick's *Hope Leslie* manages to penetrate this 'thick cloud of words' in order to reveal what is described as the 'terrible truth' *behind* words. As stated in the novel's preface, the author's goal was "to illustrate not the history, but the character of the times."[42] In a procedure that would be called 'constructionist,' had the novel been published in our day, *Hope Leslie* creates an *alternative history*[43] with "delineations [in which] we are confined not to the actual, but to the possible."[44]

---

38   Johnson 2016: n.p.
39   Husserl 1970 [1936] : 103–189. Cf. Käufer/Chemero 2015 : 39.
40   Rancière 1994 : 32.
41   Ibid.
42   Sedgwick 1998 [1827]: 3.
43   I borrow this phrase from Jeffrey Insko's essay on *Hope Leslie*'s revision of conventional historicism. (Insko 2004: 179) Discussing "the novel's many historical and temporal entanglements," Insko concludes that "*Hope Leslie* provides an alternative conception of what history is." (Ibid.: 180)
44   Sedgwick 1998 [1827]: 4.

Intentionally blurring the lines between "our histories" (3) – that is, the white, hegemonic view of the nation's past – and various hidden versions of history, *Hope Leslie* functions as "historiographic metafiction."[45] By this, Hutcheon defines a type of popular text that is "intensely self-reflexive" and "paradoxically also lay[s] claim to historical events and personages." (5) In historiographic metafiction, the lines between fact and fiction appear obscured. "[R]ather than asserting the unique possibilities of fiction as compared to history proper," one scholar observes, "the preface [to *Hope Leslie*] actually calls attention to their *affinities*."[46] As a result, readers of Sedgwick's novel face the challenge of uniting the actual historical events and personae (the Pequot War, John Winthrop, and so on) with their imagined – and often mythologized – literary versions. *Hope Leslie* suggests, in Amy Dunham Strand's words, that "both history and fiction are forms of representation with ongoing rhetorical and political effects."[47] In the book's preface, an invitation is directed towards readers to become actively involved in the process of historical meaning-making: "These volumes are so far from being intended as a substitute for genuine history, that the ambition of the writer would be fully gratified if, by this work, any of our young countrymen should be stimulated to investigate the early history of their native land."[48]

In its rejection of claims of writing 'genuine history,' *Hope Leslie* demonstrates a self-conscious, almost postmodernist approach.[49] The novel subtly delegates the responsibility for a truthful comprehension of history to an implied reader stylized as an "enlightened and accurate observer of human nature."[50] Following Strand's argument, the novel here not only "reconstruct[s] the past by 'putting the chisel' into new hands," but also employs "reverberating rhetorical effects, simultaneously constructing and impacting the present,

---

45 Hutcheon 2000: 105–123.
46 Insko 2004: 186, emphasis added.
47 Strand 2009: 19.
48 Sedgwick 1998 [1827]: 4.
49 On the novel's use of self-conscious imagery – especially its "complex preoccupation with language" and the inclusion of "conflicting levels of signification," see Ford 1997: 81–92. Cf. Pelegri 2009: 140.
50 Sedgwick 1998 [1827]: 4. Sedgwick's reference to the 'enlightened reader' recalls the famous phrase in the "Declaration of Independence": "[L]et Facts be submitted to a candid world." (Jefferson et al. 2008 [1776]: 54, emphasis in the original; cf. Ferguson 1994: 127)

[...] to re-make history, but also, perhaps, to make history happen."[51] Similarly, Insko characterizes the set of appellative narrativizations in *Hope Leslie* as "anachronistic imaginings"[52] that disrupt a traditional conception of history. The novel's tightrope act between historicization and fictionalization allows its author to demand a new, alternative mode of history-making[53] that subverts the conventional boundary between *myth* and *science*.

Notably, science is portrayed in *Hope Leslie* not as a monolithic block of rationalist truisms but rather as a set of "scientific truths – about medicine, race, or gender" that "individuals may accept or reject."[54] While dealing with many scientific insights (for example, regarding progress and human rights), Sedgwick's novel also suggests that individuals may well "come to discover new ones."[55] In the context of nineteenth-century literature, science cannot be limited to 'natural science' (as our contemporary mindset would suggest); on the contrary, science was perceived, according to *OED*'s definition, as "a connected body of demonstrated truths [...] which includes *trustworthy methods for the discovery of new truth* within its own domain."[56] In his study of denunciatory speech, Jonathan Rauch invites us to interrogate the conventional distinction between 'subjective' myth (as relying on imagination) and 'objective' science (as sticking to "good old hard facts"[57]):

> The difference between a scientific society and a mythmaking group is not that one relies on imagination while the other does not; it is that the skeptical and empirical rules set up a tension which makes imagination its own watchman.[58]

In a similar fashion, *Hope Leslie* encourages its readers to look skeptically at the facts, events and personae they know from history books. By overtly deviating from the official version of historiography, the novel invites us to challenge the

---

51 Strand 2009: 20.
52 Insko 2004: 179.
53 Hutcheon points out that historiographic metafiction often uses the "conventions of historiography" (e.g., the use of paratextual devices) to "both inscribe and undermine the authority and objectivity of historical sources and explanations." (Hutcheon 2000: 123)
54 Block/Madden 2003: 22.
55 Ibid.
56 Quoted in ibid.: 23, emphasis added by the authors.
57 Rauch 2013: 69.
58 Ibid.

'facts' as we know them, thus elevating imagination itself to a kind of "watchman,"[59] to borrow Rauch's phrase. While questioning the claim to absolute truth often attributed to science, *Hope Leslie* also sets apart science from gossip and denunciation. In the opening sections of the first chapter, the book clearly speaks out against "vain speculation and idle inquiries"[60] that may lead to an infinite process in which one is forever "inquiring and inquiring, and never coming to the truth." (6) The character of the native woman Magawisca is presented as the novel's narrative linchpin, who, by virtue of her heroic resistance to the repressive culture of Puritanism, stands above the evils of denunciation: "I am your prisoner," she tells the British rulers, "and ye may slay me, but I deny your right to judge me." (302) The hierarchy between the colonists and Magawisca, *Hope Leslie* indicates, is grounded in superficial judgment. This judgment, naturally linked to the ear as a receptive organ, is conveyed through hearsay but is not substantiated by what actually happened in colonial history, especially during the Pequot War of the 1630s.

The relation between Magawisca and Hope Leslie is equally signified through the contact of mouth and ear. But this time, the transfer of thoughts is marked as ingenuous and deep, for example, when Magawisca, in the eighth chapter of the second volume, "lower[s] her voice for Hope's ear only." (282) A similar scene of a truthful exchange of words occurs in the following chapter when Hope's half-brother Everell "whisper[s] words into Magawisca's ear." (310) Not only does the novel conjure up a situation of intimacy and "kindness," (ibid.) it also lets us share the reactions of Magawisca who *rises* as Everell whispers in her ear. The intimate exchange of thoughts – as opposed to the spread of hearsay – is staged as an act of true understanding and a deeper visceral knowledge. Magawisca also appeals to her father, the deluded Pequot chief Mononotto, to listen not to the sounds of destruction engendered by his blind hatred, but to what she calls the "song [...] of happiness." (87) Magawisca's emotional speech is garbed with a sense of aural aesthetics, expressed through the interplay between ear and mouth: "Nay, father, listen not to the sad strain; it is but the spirit of the tree mourning over its decay; rather *turn thine ear* to the glad song of this bright stream, image of the good." (Ibid.)

*Hope Leslie* does not fundamentally reject the power of the ear as a receptive organ, but it urges us to rely upon real stories, told by real people, and not

---

59 Ibid.
60 Sedgwick 1998 [1827]: 5–6.

upon hearsay. In one of the novel's key scenes, Magawisca is equipped with an authoritative voice that allows her to give a dramatic recitation of "the last acts in the tragedy of her people." (48) Her performance, the novel suggests, is a "new version of an old story" (55) that replaces the stereotyped version of native identity in the readers' imagination. As such, it stands in drastic contrast to the "pernicious lore" (6) of Puritanism, in which natives are often "represented as 'surly dogs.'" (3)

Notably, Sedgwick's novel conveys this *new version of an old story* through the focalizer of a white character, Everell Fletcher, who has already heard all circumstances about the Pequot tribe and their allegedly causal role in the war of 1636 to 1638. Or so he thinks. However, as the novel reminds us, the character had only "heard them in the language of the enemies and conquerors of the Pequods [sic]; and from Magawisca's lips they took a new form and hue." (55) When Everell listens to the native woman telling *her* version of the gruesome battles between settlers and natives, it seems to him that her narration "was putting the chisel into the hands of truth, and giving it to whom it belonged." (Ibid.)

What *Hope Leslie* here effectively accomplishes is a *poetics of fact*. It capitalizes on the real suffering of native American people and invites us to sympathize with this subjugated voice. In doing so, the book urges us to rely not on second-hand knowledge of exchanged words but rather on our own perception. The "terrible truth" (10) of real life-experiences, the novel suggests, is not only invisible to the fleeting eye, it is also inaudible to an ear that only listens superficially.

My analysis of *Hope Leslie* has demonstrated that a *poetics of fact* can be an effective literary strategy to engage in an interpersonal dialogue on historical events and personages. In contrast to mere gossip knowledge, historiographic metafiction combines an interest in the personal with the desire to stay true to the life-world, the *Lebenswelt* of actual people.[61]

The literary strategy of a *poetics of fact* is thus not so dissimilar from the method of *epochē* – sometimes described as the *bracketing* of natural phenom-

---

61  For Husserl, actual experience is the crucial factor that fills the 'life-world' with its essential component – namely life. "To live is always to line-in-certainty-of-the-world. Waking life is being awake to the world, being constantly and directly 'conscious' of the world and of oneself as living *in* the world, actually experiencing [*erleben*] and actually effecting the ontic certainty of the world." (Husserl 1970 [1936]: 142–143, emphasis in the original)

ena – employed by transcendental phenomenology.[62] "In carrying out this epochē," Husserl explains, "we [...] continue to stand on the ground of the world; it is now reduced to the life-world which is valid for us prescientifically; [...] we may take the sciences into consideration only as historical facts, taking no position of our own on their truth."[63] Magawisca's recital of her people's hidden history in Hope Leslie is a good example of how this "life-world" can be revealed in literature as the "realm of original self-evidences."[64] While the official Puritan historiography – that legitimized sphere of "secure facts" that seems "undisturbed by any noticeable disagreement"[65] – is exposed as a non-feasible "theoretical-logical substruction,"[66] Magawisca's own story points to the field of "the subjective" which is "distinguished in all respects precisely by its being actually *experienceable*."[67]

By inspiring an "ontology of the life-world"[68] – in other words by invoking and reanimating a set of untold stories of colonized people in the Americas – Hope Leslie gives voice to an abject discourse that is not part of the history books and thus commonly banned from the discursive order. In its consequential "historical relativism,"[69] the novel makes us aware that the difference between official historiography and narrative fiction is always skin-deep. The search for the underlying 'truth' of a native American 'life-world' [*Lebenswelt*] that permeates Magawisca's narration leads us *beyond* the barriers of hearsay and rumors into what New Historicist Stephen Greenblatt has termed a "poetics of culture,"[70] namely the study of the collective production of cultural practices. To recover and reanimate the "poetics of everyday behavior in America"[71] means, for Sedgwick, to endow indigenous people, whose lives have long been subjugated by hegemonic practice, with an unequivocal and empowered voice.

62 Cf. Käufer/Chemero 2015: 34–35.
63 Husserl 1970 [1936]: 147, emphasis in the original.
64 Ibid.: 127.
65 Ibid.: 138.
66 Ibid.: 127.
67 Ibid., emphasis added.
68 Ibid.: 173.
69 Cf. Gould 1994: 641–662.
70 Greenblatt 1990: 1.
71 Ibid.: 8. Greenblatt borrows this phrase from literary scholar and historian Juri Lotman.

## 4. Conclusion

To conclude, Sedgwick's novel *Hope Leslie* teaches us that there is, in fact, an alternative to simply accepting and replicating denunciatory practices. We "*can't know rumors*,"[72] to cite once again from Jay Asher's novel, but we can try to understand how they work. The characters of Hope Leslie and Magawisca are powerful literary examples of counter-discourses that tell a "new version of an old story"[73] and replace the superficial truth of hearsay by the "terrible truth" (10) of the life-worlds of actual people.

In this sense, the novel encourages us to search for the *subjugated knowledges* behind the talk, to listen to a *poetics of fact* that surpasses the foul talk of defamation. This kind of truth, symbolized by Magawisca's retelling of her people's story, may be shocking at first. Yet, it renders a deeper sense of historical practice that manifests itself not in rumor or hearsay but on a visceral and poetic level. This *poetics of fact* is ultimately more satisfying to the reader, since it endows us with a deeper understanding of reality, a type of understanding that is founded not in the circulation of rumors but in actual, firsthand practice.

## Bibliography

Asher, Jay (2017) [2007]: *Th1rteen R3asons Why*, London.
Bacon, Francis (1597): "The Essays: 'Colours of Good and Evil' and 'Advancement of Learning'", New York, in: https://archive.org/stream/essayscolou rsofgoobacouoft/essayscoloursofgoobacouoft_djvu.txt (17.04.2022).
Block, Shelley R./Madden, Etta M. (2003): "Science in Catharine Maria Sedgwick's *Hope Leslie*", in: *Legacy* 20/1/2, 22–37.
Brown, William Hill (2009) [1789]: *The Power of Sympathy: or, The Triumph of Nature. Founded in Truth*, Ithaca, NY.
Brownstein, Rachel M. (1982): *Becoming a Heroine: Reading About Women in Novels*, New York.
Butler, Judith (1997): *Excitable Speech: A Politics of the Performative*, New York/London.

---

72   Asher 2017 [2007]: 65.
73   Sedgwick 1998 [1827]: 55.

Davidson, Cathy N. (1986): *Revolution and the Word. The Rise of the Novel in America*, New York/Oxford.

Derrida, Jacques (2020) [1994]: *The Politics of Friendship*, trans. George Collins, London/New York.

— (1997) [1967]: *Of Grammatology*, trans. Gayatri Chakravorty Spivak, Baltimore/London.

Ferguson, Robert A. (1994): *The American Enlightenment, 1750-1820*, Cambridge, MA/London.

Ford, Douglas (1997): "Inscribing the 'Impartial Observer' in Sedgwick's *Hope Leslie*", in: *Legacy* 14/2, 81–92.

Foster, Hannah Webster (1855) [1797]: *The Coquette; or, The History of Eliza Wharton. Founded on Fact*, Boston.

Foucault, Michel (1980): *Power/Knowledge. Selected Interviews & Other Writings*, ed. Colin Gordon, trans. Colin Gordon et al., New York.

Gould, Philip (1994): "Catharine Sedgwick's 'Recital' of the Pequot War", in: *American Literature* 66/4, 641–662.

Greenblatt, Stephen (1989): "Towards a Poetics of Culture", in: Veeser, H. Aram (ed.): *The New Historicism*, New York/London.

Haraway, Donna J. (1991): *Simians, Cyborgs, and Women: The Reinvention of Nature*, New York.

Harriot, Thomas (1590): "A Brief and True Report of the New Found Land of Virginia. Excerpts", London, in: nationalhumanitiescenter.org/pds/amerbegin/exploration/text4/Harriot_Brief_and_True_Report_1590.pdf (15.04.2022).

Husserl, Edmund (1970) [1936]: *The Crisis of European Sciences and Transcendental Phenomenology*, ed. David Carr, Evanston.

Hutcheon, Linda (2000) [1988]: *A Poetics of Postmodernism. History, Theory, Fiction*, New York/London.

Insko, Jeffrey (2004): "Anachronistic Imaginings: *Hope Leslie*'s Challenge to Historicism", in: *American Literary History* 16/2, 179–207.

Irving, Washington (2011) [1807]: "The Little Man in Black", in: Boddy, Kasia (ed.): *The New Penguin Book of American Short Stories*, London et al., 1–8.

— (1993) [1819]: *The Sketch Book of Geoffrey Crayon, Gent.*, London et al.

Jefferson, Thomas et al. (2008) [1776]: "The Declaration of Independence", in: *The Declaration of Independence & The Constitution of the United States*, New York, 53–58.

Johnson, Jenna (2016): "'A lot of people are saying ...': How Trump spreads conspiracies and innuendo", in: *The Washington Post*, https://www.washin

gtonpost.com/politics/a-lot-of-people-are-saying-how-trump-spreads-c onspiracies-and-innuendo/2016/06/13/b21e59de-317e-11e6-8ff7-7b6c1998b 7a0_story.html (21.04.2022).

Käufer, Stephan/Chemero, Anthony (2015): *Phenomenology. An Introduction*, Cambridge, UK/Malden, MA.

Kelly, Gary (1990): "The Limits of Genre and the Institution of Literature. Romanticism between Fact and Fiction", in: Johnston, Kenneth R. et al. (eds.): *Romantic Revolutions. Criticism and Theory*, Bloomington/Indianapolis.

Le Guin, Ursula K. (2010) [1969]: *The Left Hand of Darkness*, New York.

Nelson, Dana (1992): "Sympathy as Strategy in Sedgwick's *Hope Leslie*", in: Samuels, Shirley (ed.): *The Culture of Sentiment: Race, Gender, and Sentimentality in 19$^{th}$-Century America*, New York/Oxford, 191–202.

Pelegri, Teresa Requena (2009): "Bringing Out Censored Stories and Reassessing the Past in Catharine Maria Sedgwick's *Hope Leslie*", in: *Coolabah* 3, 136–142.

Rancière, Jacques (1994): *The Names of History: On the Poetics of Knowledge*, trans. Hassan Melehy, Minneapolis/London.

Rauch, Jonathan (2013) [1993]: *Kindly Inquisitors. Expanded edition*, Chicago/London.

Rosling, Hans/Rosling, Ola/Rosling Rönnlund, Anna (2019): *Factfulness. Ten Reasons We're Wrong about the World – and Why Things Are Better Than You Think*, London.

Rowson, Susanna (1814) [1791]: *Charlotte Temple. A Tale of Truth*, New York.

Scott, Walter (2011) [1814]: *Waverley*, originally published as *Waverley; or, 'Tis Sixty Years Since*, ed. P.D. Garside, with an introduction by Ian Duncan, New York et al.

Sedgwick, Catharine Maria (1998) [1827]: *Hope Leslie; or, Early Times in the Massachusetts*, ed. with an introduction and notes by Carolyn L. Karcher, New York et al.

Spacks, Patricia Meyer (1986): *Gossip*, Chicago/London.

Strand, Amy Dunham (2009): *Language, Gender, and Citizenship in American Literature. 1769-1919*, New York.

Tyler, Royall (2002) [1797]: *The Algerine Captive, or, The Life and Adventures of Doctor Updike Underhill*, New York.

White, Hayden (2014) [1973]: *Metahistory. The Historical Imagination in Nineteenth-Century Europe*, Baltimore.

— (1994): "Foreword", in: Rancière, *The Names of History*, vii–xx.

# 'Writing Facts' and 19th-Century English Realist Fiction
## Theoretical Reflections and the Complexity of the Relationship in Charles Dickens' *Hard Times,* and George Eliots *Adam Bede*

Werner Wolf (University of Graz)

## 1. Introduction: Fact-Writing and Fiction – a Relationship with a Variegated History[1]

'Fiction,' by its very name, is commonly understood as the opposite of fact. Thus, a literary genre which uses, at least in English, this term as its denomination appears to be an unfitting choice for a volume sporting the topic "writing facts." Indeed, strictly speaking, fiction seems to have nothing to do with facts. Yet, literary history belies this impression. In 'fact,' the role of 'writing facts' is anything but immaterial to the development of fiction in general, and the novel in particular, with which I will be concerned in the following. Rather, the novel's relationship with facts has a variegated and interesting history. This is true both with respect to the more or less factive objects of novels, and the ways and effects of novelistic storytelling which oscillate between seemingly objective, factual[2] narration and the laying bare of fictionality or, rather, fictiveness. From the 'editor's' claim that his text is "a just history of facts," as made in the "Preface" to Daniel Defoe's *Robinson Crusoe,*[3] to a postmodernist narrator's metafictional disclaimer, "I wander the island, inventing it"

---

1    My thanks are due – as so often – to Cecilia Servatius and Jutta Klobasek-Ladler for their expert help with the manuscript.
2    For the use of 'factive/fact' vs. 'fictive/fiction' in an ontological and 'factual(ity)' vs. 'fictional(ity)' in a reception-oriented sense, see below.
3    Defoe 1719/1965: 25.

(the first sentence in Robert Coover's short story "The Magic Poker"),[4] dealing with facts has obviously changed in a drastic way. After the 'rise of the novel' as we know it, epitomized by *Robinson Crusoe*, 19$^{th}$-century realism appears to be a continuation, if not an intensification, of the preceding proto-realism, especially when it comes to often critical (hetero-)references to individual geographical, sociological, historical, etc., facts of contemporary reality and/or making the reader believe in the facticity of the represented world.

In view of this privileged place of the 19$^{th}$-century novel in the history of the relationship between fact and fiction, I will, in the following, focus on English 19$^{th}$-century realist fiction by way of two mid-century examples which appear to me to be of particular relevance: Charles Dickens's *Hard Times* (1854), and George Eliot's *Adam Bede* (1859). From a superficial point of view, the relationship between 19$^{th}$-century realism and positivistic fact-orientation appears to be un-problematic. At closer inspection, however, this relationship turns out to be more complex, as will be shown with respect to the two novels mentioned. *Hard Times* implies a strong criticism of a one-sided contemporary belief in positivistic facts as the only phenomena one ought to care or know about, a belief drastically represented by the fact-ideology as practiced in the school of Mr. M'Choakumchild. However, when it comes to the reception attitude presupposed by the novel, the seeming factuality of the represented world (within the reception contract of illusionist storytelling) is never really challenged. Something similar can be said about *Adam Bede*, albeit with the difference that the criticism of a belief in objective facts is here not transmitted through the reprehensible activities and attitudes of problematic characters but rather through an authorial narrator who, at times, betrays a remarkable, if limited, skepticism towards objective storytelling.

My remarks will be structured as follows. First, I will briefly deal with the concept of 'fact' and with related terminology and concepts such as truth, reality, and aesthetic illusion as a 'reality effect' of sorts occurring in the process of reception. In the preliminary theoretical reflections on the fact/fiction opposition and the use of facts in novels, I will also characterize the proto-typical relationship of 19$^{th}$-century realist fiction with these concepts. In the ensuing two chapters, the two novels and their complex relationships to facts, factuality, and the immersive illusionist reading-effect will be discussed, before placing, in conclusion, the position of these novels in a wider historical context between romanticism, modernism and post-modernism.

---

4  Coover 1969/1970: 20.

## 2. 'Fact(s)': Concept, Terminology, Related Concepts, and the Prototypical Relationship of Realist Fiction to These Concepts

What is a 'fact'? In the present contribution, while this question cannot be answered in detail in a philosophical sense, it can be addressed with respect to the common-sense use of the term, which is also the sense relevant to literary studies. Generally, according to the *New Oxford Dictionary of English*, a fact is "a thing that is indisputably the case."[5] More precisely, and as mentioned in the call for papers of the conference on which the present publication is based, one may describe 'fact' in accordance with today's usage as a verifiable phenomenon of reality believed to exist independently of the observing subject and thus objectively true. The belief in such facts and such a reality is what I term 'epistemological realism.' Fact, in this context, has an obvious relationship to the notions of 'objectivity,' 'truth,' and 'reality' (which I will also refrain from further discussing here). It should be noted, however, that in today's use of the term the etymological origin of *factum* is obscured: *factum* as something made or created (especially by God – the "Nicean Creed" refers to this meaning twice in a positive and once – concerning Christ – in a negative sense).[6]

For literary and media studies, a further antonymic concept is of obvious importance, namely 'fiction,' which in English has the somewhat unfortunate double meaning as a literary genre (as used in the title of the present contribution) and as an ontological or reception-centered category (related to construction, simulation, invention, delusion or lie and opposed to truth and reality). The complex literary relationship between fact and fiction has been systematized in a thought-provoking way by Andreas Kablitz (2008): he distinguishes between an ontological or referential and a reception-centered facet of the opposition, which results in two pairs of opposition (see Figure 1). With somewhat clumsy English translations, the ontological facet is the opposition between **facticity** and **fictiveness** (or factive vs. fictive), while the

---

5   *New Oxford Dictionary of English* 1999: 656–657; note the interesting implied reference to a community within which something is 'indisputable'!
6   "Credo in unum Deum [...] **fact**orem caeli et terrae [...] et in [...] Iesum Christum [...] genitum, non **factum** [...] consubstantialem Patri; per quem omnia **facta** sunt [...]"; from another, more (post)modern, point of view, used by deconstructivists and the like, the constructivist nature of so-called facts is highlighted, and this may also serve to gesture to the obscured etymology in which fact and fiction become merged.

reception-centered opposition may be called **factuality** vs. **fictionality** (or factual vs. fictional). The advantage of the differentiation is the possibility of distinguishing between what is the case in a given text (the first pair of terms) and how and in which cognitive frame a given text is received (the second pair of terms). Novels, for instance, are generally read in the cognitive frame of fictionality, while autobiography is received, as a rule, in the frame of factuality. However, both genres can contain factive as well as fictive elements: a novel may refer to real historical persons but characterize them with fictive features, while an autobiography may combine facticity with fictive (untrue) self-stylizations or errors. One may say it is the predominance of either facticity or fictiveness in a genre and/or convention which makes it eligible for the respective frames through which it is received (with literary deviations being possible in fictional biographies parading as factual ones, for instance).

*Figure 1: Aspects of the fact/fiction opposition in literature (and other arts/media) after Kablitz 2008*

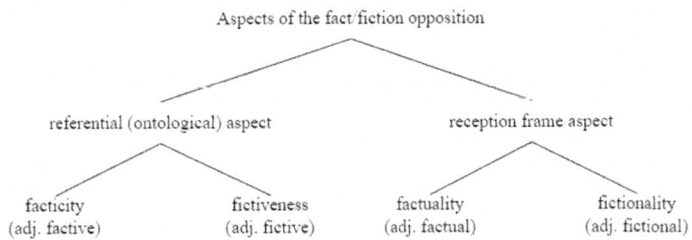

A further differentiation is helpful for our context, namely one with respect to where facts, their discussion, or the impression of factuality are created or occur: within a literary text and its represented world or in the relation between this text-world and the recipient (see figure 2).

As for the latter, '**extracompositional**' facets of facts and related concepts, they concern two aspects: a) an impression a text and the world represented in it creates in the recipient, and b) the referential, or, as I term it, heteroreferential relation[7] between text (world) and the world of reality or facts.

---

7    The term serves to distinguish between hetero-reference and self- as well as metareference. (Cf. Wolf 2009: 16–25).

In the former, '**intracompositional**' case, facts or the concept of 'fact' can occur in two forms: facts can either be thematized (in the mode of '**telling**') or be observed (and believed) as parts of the represented world (in the mode of '**showing**'). The **thematization of facts** may refer to mentions of truthful phenomena by characters or the narrator as opposed, for instance, to lies; in rare cases, it may also include quasi 'philosophical' discussions of the existence and perception of facts and related concepts and problems. The **showing of facts** refers to the world building of literary texts which create their own realities by positing the existence of their elements. Here, again, an opposition exists between fictional facts and mere dreams, illusions, simulations, etc., in short, elements of the represented world that are supposed to be taken seriously as fictional facts and those that are not.[8] The 'facts' a novel creates or refers to can – and in fact often do – coalesce in the recipient's mind into a more or less coherent representation of a world in which one has the impression of being immersed – in short, they are the buildings blocks of 'aesthetic illusion.'[9]

This reader-related immersion, or in Roland Barthes's term 'effect of reality,'[10] can be differentiated according to its nature or 'level.' On a first level, we encounter the general impression created by immersive or illusionist works of an 'as-if-reality.' As I have discussed elsewhere, the creation of **aesthetic illusion** can in principle occur in both texts that are read in the framework of factuality and in texts that are received under the auspices of fictionality.[11] Likewise, both fictive and factive representations can exist within either frame, and the respective objects can trigger an impression of being immersed in the respective worlds regardless of their ontological or referential status. When these worlds are narrative worlds (as in fiction) and not, for instance, descriptive worlds (as in much poetry) the impression of a quasi-reality is enhanced. The reason for this is that aesthetic illusion is essentially coupled with experientiality. As experience is arguably more intense when related to dynamic objects in time, the immersive part of aesthetic illusion (as opposed to the quantum of distance and media-awareness which keeps it from becoming a delusion) is intensified by the essentially dynamic nature of narrativity.

---

8   In narratology, parts of these 'deleted' or non-'factual' facts have been discussed under the terms 'disnarrated elements' (cf. Prince 1996: 98) and "shadow stories" (Abbott 2015).
9   Cf. Wolf 2013.
10  Cf. Barthes 1968.
11  Cf. Wolf 2013.

As opposed to this first and general level of the impression of a quasi-reality which, owing to the common reception contract of a 'suspension of disbelief,' we tend to provisionally accept as if it were fact, there is a second level implied by some works: This is the additional impression that one is not confronted with **a** reality or with fictional facts but with **our** reality as we know it or with reality *tout court* and thus with actually, or seemingly, ascertainable facts of contemporary or historical reality. In literature, this impression is termed '**referential illusion**.' One should, however, note that referential illusion is not co-extensive with aesthetic illusion but a special case of it.[12]

*Figure 2: Aspects of 'fact' relevant to fiction*

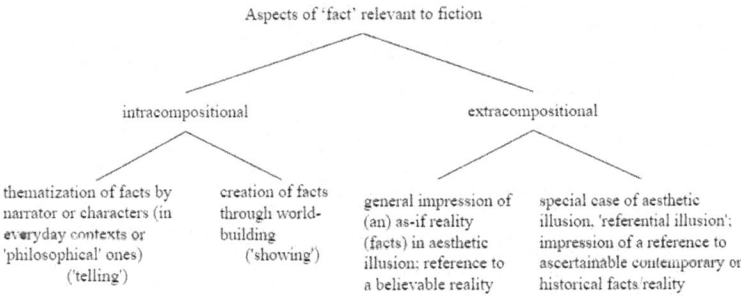

To sum up: aesthetic illusion (as well as its breaking) can occur both within the frame of factual and fictional reception; it always creates the effect of an experienceable reality and thus of 'facts,' that is, being immersed in **a reality**; in some rare cases, the additional impression is elicited of being immersed in **reality *tout court***.

It should be noted that literary hetero-reference comprises references to **general** facts of life as well as **specific** references to contemporary or historical reality. 'Reference' can in both cases imply positive reference but also problematization or, in extreme cases, for instance in postmodern deconstruction, denial.[13]

---

12   Cf. ibid. 2008.
13   It should be noted, though, that even the most radically anti-referential (or anti-mimetic) texts cannot dispense with using references to the world of our experience and knowledge (hence to what Iser called the 'repertoire,' cf. Iser 1975: 299).

What is now the prototypical position of 19<sup>th</sup>-century realist fiction in relation to these aspects, uses, and impressions of 'fact'? Generally, one can align this kind of novel with what was termed 'epistemological realism' above. This can already be seen in the intracompositional dealing with facts: in realist fiction, the represented world, as a rule, is a system of probable, believable (fictional) facts, and the phenomena of this world are observable and (ultimately) explicable rationally or, at least in an inner-worldly way, without recourse to transcendental or supernatural agencies. This can, for instance, be seen in the frequent use of physiognomic descriptions of characters' faces and bodies, since such descriptions are based on a belief in transparency, that is, in the belief (or, we tend to say today, myth) that empirically observable surface facts reveal underlying character dispositions and histories.[14] Moreover, the fact-orientation of realism can be observed in the emphasis placed on the ultimate revelation of truth and facts wherever they are temporarily obscured by characters and the novel's action. This emphasis is also responsible for the frequent 'disillusionment' of characters as a topos of realist story telling. The underlying positivistic belief in the unproblematic existence of facts and the possibility of accessing and representing them correctly also renders the problematization of facts as such through characters of the narrator relatively rare in realism.

As for the extracompositional aspect of dealing with facts and concomitant reception effects, 19<sup>th</sup>-century realist novels are, according to widespread opinion,[15] based on the belief in an objective, subject-independent reality to whose facts they refer, often in a concrete and specific way, and about which they try to create a consensus between implied author and reader.[16] This optimistic, positivist epistemology is supported by a pervading illusionism and thus by the novels triggering the impression, in the readers, of being immersed in a quasi-reality. While this general illusionism is also true of Gothic fiction or, for instance, H.G. Wells' science fiction, realist novels, in addition, frequently elicit the impression that the readers are confronted with contemporary reality as they know it from experience of history. Realist fiction thus often reaches the second level of illusionism, namely referential illusion. Symptoms of the fact that realist writing tends towards this direction include the use of well-known settings with real place-

---

14   Cf. Wolf 2002a, Wolf 2002b.
15   Cf. Ermath 1983: 77.
16   Cf. Fluck 1992: 27, 35.

names, the choice of temporal settings that are contemporary or quasi contemporary, and the representation of characters from all classes and milieus observable in Victorian society. In harmony with the middle-class orientation of this society and the predominantly middle-class readership, both the dominant reservoir of characters and most of the implied norms tend to show clear middle-class preferences. All of this creates the impression that the represented world is an extension of the (middle-class) readers' world.

This is, perhaps, best illustrated by the frequent use of the formula "one of those" as, for instance, in the initial characterization of Marty South in Thomas Hardy's novel *The Woodlanders*: "She was one of those people who, if they have to work harder than their neighbours, prefer to keep the necessity a secret as far as possible [...]."[17] "One of those," here and elsewhere, is an appeal to the reader to link the observation following this formula to their own world-knowledge and thus both an appeal to see, and a confirmation of, the close relationship between the novel's world and their own world. This strategy of realist storytelling to reference experiential reality may even be so intense that the frame of fictionality, in which realist fiction, like all fiction, is read, may temporarily be obscured in favor of the opposing framework of factuality. As announced above, the complex relationship between (seeming) fact writing and 19th-century fiction will be illustrated in the following by two examples.

## 3. Charles Dickens' *Hard Times*: The Implied Criticism of Facts in a Novel Based on Critical References to Contemporary Facts of Life

"Now, what I want is, Facts. Teach these boys and girls nothing but Facts. Facts alone are wanted in life. Plant nothing else, and root out everything else. You can only form the minds of reasoning animals upon Facts: nothing else will ever be of service to them."[18] These are the instructions of a major character, Mr. Gradgrind, which he gives to the schoolmaster M'Choakumchild in the opening of Dickens' *Hard Times*. This *medias-in-res* beginning is emblematic of

---

17  Hardy 1999 [1887]: 16.
18  Dickens 1854/1969: 47. References to *Hard Times* (Penguin edition) in the following in the abbreviated form: "*HT*: page number". In the case of subsequent quotations only with page numbers in brackets.

the relevance of this novel to our topic 'writing facts.' Indeed, I do not know of any other 19th-century novel in which facts and a fact-centered worldview are so pervadingly thematized and its effects so graphically shown, more precisely, in which such a worldview is so devastatingly criticized.

The details of this criticism in this frequently discussed novel are too well known[19] to require further belaboring, so that I can restrict myself here to a few 'facts': The fact-ideology at issue in the novel is represented by a number of negative characters, some of them with telling names denoting facets of their negativity: the schoolmaster M'Choakumchild; the industrialist Gradgrind; the "banker, merchant, manufacturer" and alleged self-made man Bounderby; and, moreover, the dandy and promoter of statistics Harthouse. Their fact-centered ideology is based on a materialist empiricism, positivism, and utilitarianism, in which only reason (cf. *HT*: 62), measurable and classifiable facts, and their general calculability in statistics and economics count. This ideology is linked to a view of man in which self-interest, or rather selfishness (Harthouse's belief "everyman is selfish in everything he does") (205), and generalities rather than individuality (131–132) are emphasized. The effects of this ideology are critically shown in several fields.

The first fact-related issue the reader is confronted with right from the above-quoted opening scene onwards is education, epitomized by M'Choakumchild's model school and the education of Mr Gradgrind's children Tom and Louisa and his foster-daughter Sissy, an education in which "it hailed facts all day long." (95) The importance of this area, in particular in a moral respect, is underlined by the titles of the novel's three parts which suggest a natural causality between "Sowing" (Book 1), "Reaping" (Book 2) and "Garnering" (Book 3). The consequences of an education exclusively based on 'facts,' which suppresses fancy or imagination, and neglects morality speak for themselves: Sissy is unhappy, and so is Louisa, who is encouraged, especially by her egoist brother, to enter a merely rational marriage (from which she tries to escape in an all but adulterous affair with Harthouse). Yet it is Tom who, besides the model-pupil Bitzer (see III.8), is the most glaring illustration of what can be 'reaped' and 'garnered' from the 'seeds' of an erroneously fact-centered education and a neglect of morality in particular (which is also present in Harthouse's moral indifference and relativity): Tom becomes a gambler and a criminal: he steals a considerable sum of money, for which he directs suspicion on the innocent worker Stephen Blackpool,

---

19   Cf. Simpson 1997, notably 1–11.

who then, in his flight from criminal persecution, has an accident and dies. Tom himself is ultimately forced to flee Britain, repents too late, and dies on his return journey.

Another area where the pernicious effects of the fact-ideology loom large is the industrial world in the manufacturing city of "Coketown", described by Dickens in the well-known chapter entitled "The Keynote:" "COKETOWN [...] was a triumph of fact; it had no greater taint of fancy in it than Mrs Gradgrind herself." (*HT*: 65) The novel represents at large the poor labor conditions of the working class, the "unnatural" (ibid.) life they are forced to lead, and its consequences: poverty, rebellion (in the chartists), alcoholism (in Stephen's wife), and endless suffering. It is made clear that all of this is connected with the view that only material facts, in this case, the calculable financial profit of the masters, count.

A third area, in part linked with the industrial theme, is aesthetics. The exclusive reign of useful, utilitarian facts is most graphically illustrated in the terrible architecture which this mindset produces. This refers to Gradgrind's Stone Lodge, to Bounderby's home, and, above all, to Coketown at large. It is a town full of "severely workful" and monotonously repetitive buildings (ibid.), where "[a]ll the public inscriptions were painted alike, in severe characters of black and white," and where "[t]he jail might have been the infirmary, the infirmary might have been the jail, the town-hall might have been either or both [...] Fact, fact, fact, everywhere in the material aspect of the town." (66)

All in all, the criticism of the fact-ideology implied in *Hard Times* rests on its following deficiencies:[20] It is wrongly holistic owing to its claim to embrace the totality of reality. It is reductionist in disregarding or neglecting essential human dimensions: moral and religious feelings, general emotions, human motivations, imagination/fancy, and individuality.[21] And it is generally accused of forming an inadequate approach to human nature and reality at large. Its negative effects impact vast areas of reality: education, ethics, religion, arts/literature, economics and society at large, and last but not least, epistemology.

In the face of such an intracompositional indictment of 'facts' – can one say that *Hard Times* is really a realist novel, for which, as was said above, the

---

20   As partly detailed by Nussbaum 2001 [1991].
21   There are numerous references to human nature and its incalculability, starting with p. 48.

validity of facts must be postulated? Do facts here only play a role as the cornerstones of a pernicious ideology which the novel strives to dismantle in favor of ethics and the imagination? No, facts do play a major and positive role both on the intra- and extracompositional level, that is, both with respect to the relation between the novel and contemporary reality and the way and effects of the world building within the novel.

As for the extracompositional reception effect created by *Hard Times*, it is in line with all realist fiction in its eliciting aesthetic illusion, even to the extent of creating a referential reality effect. As opposed to, notably postmodernist fiction, the reader is at no point meant to doubt the reality of the fictional facts.

In addition, the impression is frequently elicited that the novel deals with specific aspects of contemporary reality and thus at times adds 'referential illusion' to the general aesthetic illusion it elicits. This impression of referential illusion is corroborated by the history of the novel's gestation: *Hard Times* first appeared in serialized form in Dickens's weekly journal *Household Words* in 1854 and, as Simpson convincingly argues in a chapter entitled "The Interdependency of the 'Great Magazine of Facts' and 'Hard Times'",[22] manifests a common concern with contemporary England and a remarkable "correspondence between the journalism and the fiction."[23] The fact-orientation of the novel has also been acknowledged by its generic classification as an 'industrial novel' or 'Condition of England novel.'[24] These designations, which have traditionally been used for a special sub-genre of 19th-century realist fiction dealing with the problems of the Industrial Revolution, imply a clear critical hetero-reference to the poor living conditions in industrial towns and 'chartism' and 'chartists,' the forerunners of modern trade unions, as a reaction to what was referred to as the "Condition of England Question" (Dickens is known to have visited the Midland industrial town of Preston in order to study this problem,[25] which is why Preston is generally considered to be the model on which Coketown was created). Yet, the novel's gestures at contemporary facts of life go further: they also include the well-known references to the "Manchester Lancasterian School"[26] and the importance given in con-

---

22   Simpson 1997: 4.
23   Ibid.
24   Cf. Lodge 2001 [1981]: 400.
25   Cf. Maack 1991: 138.
26   Cf. Craig 1969: 22–23.

temporary politics to statistics as published in the so-called blue books. (cf. *HT*: 96, 131 and note 26, 327–328) And, last but not least, the main critical object of the novel, namely the fact-ideology, shows clear references to contemporary utilitarianism, materialism, and positivism. While *Hard Times* as literature presupposes, of course, the reception frame of fictionality, these details gesture towards an occasional readability with the frame of factuality in mind.

Admittedly, the in part highly satirical representation of the above-mentioned facts, which, as in all satires, goes along with their distortion,[27] relativizes the realist 'fact-writing' nature of *Hard Times*, and so does Dickens' general tendency towards sensationalism, caricature, and occasional sentimentalism (for instance, observable in the scene of Stephen's death after having fallen into what aptly is called "Hell Shaft"). *Hard Times*, with its sentimentalism and socially critical and satirical exaggerations, is thus hardly an example of novelistic fact writing in the strictest sense. Indeed, where was there ever a school as one-sided as M'Choakumchild's (and directed by a teacher of such a tell-tale name!), and where was there ever an industrial city with *such* monotonous architecture and life as Coketown, and where can or could one really encounter a fact-propagating character such as Mr. Gradgrind, whose outer, regular appearance – to which we will come back later – is so much in harmony with his attitudes and inner convictions?

Yet, satire also implies clearly readable hetero-referentiality to its objects in real life, for otherwise it would not work. This realist hetero-referentiality of the novel and its relevance to contemporary reality is underlined by the subtitle of the one-volume edition, *For These Times*, and its own fact-orientation is thematized in one of the rare direct metafictional self-characterizations of the book by the narrator, who calls it "the present faithful guidebook." (*HT*: 54). This metaphor aligns *Hard Times* with a non-fictional genre bound to facts as typical of realist fiction.

The novel's implied fact-orientation not only shows in the intracompositional detailed world building as typical of realism but also in the emphasis on disillusionment, which is responsible for the novel's tendency to reveal obscured fictional facts and the truth in the course of the plot: this applies to the debunking of Bounderby's myth of the self-made man by his mother which

---

27   Satire works, according to a concise formula by Preisendanz (1976: 413), on the basis of the principle of "transparent distortion" ("transparente Entstellung").

shows that he had a very comfortable childhood and upbringing,[28] and especially to Gradgrind, who over several steps is made to see his error in giving his children a wrong education.[29]

Thus one can say that, on the one hand, facts do play a (positive) role in *Hard Times*, and its affiliation with realism is to a large extent justified (except for the caricatures and theatrical sentimentalism/sensationalism typical of Dickens in general).[30] On the other hand, the novel is not only fact-oriented itself but, as detailed above, is also an indictment of relentless fact-orientation. Yet, what are we to make of this ambivalence? What is, after all, the real view on facts in the worldview implied in *Hard Times*? This is an epistemological question and in harmony with what Warning, drawing on a formula by Umberto Eco,[31] considers one of the major functions of literature, namely to form epistemological allegories.[32] Doris Feldmann (1986), in an illuminating article, endeavors to highlight what she considers a certain skepticism towards objective facts which she sees at work in *Hard Times*. To substantiate this claim, she quotes some elements in which characters are given clearly subjective perspectives but neglects the fact that the narrator is ultimately reliable and an agency able to highlight erroneous views as such (for instance, Bounderby's conviction that "dissatisfied" workers invariably are "fit for anything," a "fiction" as the narrator says and as Stephen's history shows [*HT*: 211]). While it is true that the epistemologically sharpened gaze of the narrator recognizes the subjective element in the perception of others,[33] his own perceptions and statements of fictional facts are hierarchically superior and never relativized so that, in sum, no epistemological skepticism can be derived from the novel. This is in part acknowledged by Feldmann herself, who states that the novel ultimately does not contain "a radical epistemological skepticism." (cf. *HT*: 227) Consequently, one can state that while facts as part

---

28  Cf. Humphreys' (2008: 395) felicitous formulation: "Bounderby, one of the hard fact man, is really the great fiction-maker in the novel [...]." Appearances can lead to deceptions and illusions, but eventually – and this is important for the epistemology underlying realism – the facts of reality are allowed to surface.
29  One fictional fact, however, remains obscure, namely the reason for Sissy's father to abandon her (cf. 308: "never will be known," as Sleary says).
30  For a certain ambivalence in the relationship between *Hard Times* and realism, see Kearns 1992.
31  Cf. Eco 1967 [1962]: 151–159.
32  Cf. Warning 1990: 357.
33  Cf. Feldmann 1986: 206.

of the fact-ideology illustrated in *Hard Times* are subject to a critical perspective, this criticism does not aim at facts *per se* but at their exaggerated and absolute position in an ideology and in the one-sided, wrong use made of them in the practice of life. All of this testifies to the reality and in part importance of facts, but also to their relativity.

The implied positive norms point to this relativity and in particular to the poverty of the fact-ideology represented in the novel by emphasizing additional or alternative accesses to facts and an ultimate reality: In this context, we encounter traditional values, such as "the wisdom of the heart" (246), love (as propagated by Sleary),[34] "fanciful imagination" (92), epitomized by the circus world and, by implication,[35] also literature and, thus, Dickens's own literary product(s). This latter aspect is best perceptible in the fanciful similes and metaphors which the narrator uses in describing the monotonous reality of Coketown in the afore-mentioned chapter "The Keynote" (in itself an imaginative musical metaphor).[36] Most important, though, for the relativity of facts is the novel's endorsement of a view of man that allows for areas inscrutable to reason but that can nevertheless be experienced by the heart. This includes the "unfathomable mystery" presented by even the "meanest" of individual human beings (*HT*: 108), human morality (as the narrator reflects: "not all the calculations of the National Debt can tell me the capacity for good or evil, for love or hatred [...] in any single moment of the soul," ibid.). And this also includes religion, that is, Christianity (I here differ from Feldmann[37]); although Victorian realism is generally characterized by a tendential secularization which brackets off metaphysical explanations and frames of references in favor of secular ones.[38] And yet, at times, realist novels show curious 'lapses' into remnants of an old episteme in which the supernatural and religion played a greater role in this respect. In *Hard Times* such traces may, for instance, be seen in the narrator's – and no doubt also the implied author's – belief in the superior dignity of "the work of GOD" as opposed to "the work of man." (*HT*: 108)

---

34  "[...] there ith a love in the world, not all Thelf-interetht after all" (*HT*: 308); the novel shows that love is not restricted to humans but extends to animals such as Merrylegth, "Sissy's father's dog" (*HT*: 307).
35  Cf. Feldmann 1986: 204 and note 22.
36  Cf. also "like the painted face of a savage," "Serpents of smoke," "like the head of an elephant." (*HT*: 65)
37  Feldmann 1986: 210–211.
38  Cf. Wolf 1998: 438–442.

As a result, *Hard Times* does not invalidate a belief in the objective existence of facts (Feldmann's emphasis on subjectivity implied in the novel therefore appears to be exaggerated). Yet the realm of facts is both enlarged and restricted: On the one hand, it is enlarged, since certain elements of human nature are also represented as facts although not as calculable ones, in particular psychological needs such as the yearning for fanciful entertainment, for which the circus world caters. It is restricted, on the other hand, since there are areas of mystery which are part of reality but cannot be ascertained as facts in a positivistic way. As the narrator says: "Supposing we were to reserve our arithmetic for material objects, and to govern these awful unknown quantities [of human nature] by other means!" (108) Reason as an epistemological means thus does have a place in *Hard Times*, but not one of absolute power,[39] for it must be coupled with the wisdom of the heart, with imagination and "other means" which, no doubt, include literature itself with its fanciful imagery as displayed in *Hard Times*. In sum, there is a complex relationship between *Hard Times* and facts, an ambivalence which, however, does not destroy the basis of a largely unshaken belief in an objective reality 'outside' fiction. It includes both facts and inscrutable mysteries, and both may be accessed, at least to some extent, through fictional literature such as *Hard Times*.

## 4. George Eliot's *Adam Bede*: Narratorial Uneasiness with the Representation of Objective Facts. A Novel Based on and Criticizing Historical Facts

George Eliot (Marianne Evans), in her novels, appears – at least at first sight – to testify to an attitude towards facts and their role in (social) reality that is less ambivalent, relativizing, and critical than the one observable in Dickens's *Hard Times*. The subtitle of Eliot's best-known novel *Middlemarch* (1871/72), *A Study of Provincial Life*, aligns her with the endeavor of French realists and naturalists in particular to close the gap between fiction and science by giving fiction a scientific, and that is fact-oriented, touch.[40] While, as is well known, Balzac chose biology as the model of accounting for the diversity of character

---

39   Cf. Nussbaum 2001 [1991]: 437.
40   For the close relationship between George Eliot and 19th-century science, see Shuttleworth 1984.

in *La Comédie humaine*,⁴¹ Zola tended towards various branches of science and scholarship, including sociology and historiography,⁴² and based his fiction on extended research of individual milieus as a preparation to the writing of the individual parts of his novel cycle *Les Rougon-Macquart: Histoire naturelle et sociale d'une famille sous le Second Empire*. In a similar way, Eliot's use of the term 'study' for *Middlemarch* suggests a fact-oriented representation of contemporary provincial life in England and, more strongly than with Dickens, implies an affinity with the reception frame 'factuality' into the general literary frame of fictionality.

In *Adam Bede*, the novel in focus here, this fact-orientation is emphatically and famously propagated and combined with a poetological program of realism in what can be called a *locus classicus* of English realist aesthetics: the metafictional chapter 17, entitled "In Which the Story Pauses a Little."⁴³ The terms the narrator uses here are, besides "fact" (*AB*: 221) as the object of his⁴⁴ mimetic representation, "truth" (222) and "truthfulness" (223) as the attitude to achieve his realist ideal. This ideal consists in "giv[ing] an exact likeness" of reality, including humble everyday reality as epitomized in Dutch $17^{th}$-century genre painting, of which the narrator includes two ekphrastic descriptions. (Ibid.) All of this is destined to contribute to an ethical function Eliot's realism is meant to fulfill (and which she already pursued in her first novel, *The Sad Fortunes of the Reverend Amos Barton* [1857]), namely to elicit sympathy even with humble, morally mediocre, and fallible characters – which is why one may label her particular kind of realism 'sympathetic realism.'⁴⁵

The chapter in question is triggered by a problematic non-reaction of the parish priest of Broxton, Rector Irwine, to the selfish courting of the beautiful Hetty by a young squire and heir to an aristocratic estate, Arthur Donnithorne. In fact, Arthur is about to start an amorous relationship with Hetty in spite of the fact that the class difference between the two of them makes

---

41  Cf. Kablitz 1989.
42  Cf. Warning 1990.
43  Eliot 1985 [1895]: 221–230. References to *Adam Bede* (Penguin edition) in the following in the abbreviated form: "*AB*: page number". In the case of subsequent quotations only with page numbers in brackets.
44  In harmony with the common practice of attributing the author's sex to the narrator, and since 'George Eliot' is a male pseudonym, the narrator will here be referred to with the masculine form.
45  For the importance of an ethics of empathetic 'sympathy' in Eliot's works, see Nünning 2015.

marriage highly unlikely (a 'fact of life' which Hetty does not consider properly. (Cf. *AB*: 196) What is more likely is that Hetty becomes pregnant and is then abandoned by Arthur, which is what does happen. But, before it comes to this, Arthur wants to make a clean breast of his feelings and moral scruples. Yet the rector, being dependent on Arthur's father, is too delicate or pusillanimous to speak his mind. And so, the chance of reforming the potential 'rake' Arthur is lost – with catastrophic consequences for Hetty in the following story (she will abandon her baby, be sentenced to death, and ultimately be transported to the colonies). This over-cautious conduct of the priest in a decisive moment is criticized by a fictitious lady reader, who complains about the unedifying portrayal of the rector and would have preferred that the narrator "had made him give Arthur some truly spiritual advice" and, if necessary, "improve[d] the facts." (221) To this, the narrator opposes his feeling of being "obliged to creep servilely after nature and fact," a fact-orientation which he then develops into a programmatic aesthetics of a "faithful representation of commonplace things" and behavior rather than of rare "prophets," "heroes," and "sublimely beautiful women" (224), "picturesque lazzaroni or romantic criminals." (225) Thus, the narrator clearly espouses a realist and anti-romantic, and in any case anti-conventional, aesthetics based on the conviction: "It is so very rarely that facts hit that nice medium required by our own enlightened opinions and refined taste," (221) Rather than an infraction of conventions, the narrator "dread[s] nothing […] but falsity," even if "[f]alsehood is so easy, truth so difficult." (222) Yet in spite of this difficulty, his aim is a representation of common, average reality "as if I were in the witness-box, narrating my experience on oath." (221)

The novel – with some exceptions – follows this fact- and truth-based aesthetics. As in *Hard Times*, the fictional world shows its fact-orientation through detailed world building that contains a plethora of real-life (hetero-)references. These include, for instance, references to the work life of carpenters (the profession of the eponymous central character), to religious life at the end of the turn of the 18/19th century (the tensions between Methodism and the Church of England in particular) and to contemporary social problems (the utter dependence of tenant farmers on their landlords, abusive attitudes of young aristocratic heirs to village beauties). And, like Dickens in *Hard Times*, the implied attitude towards, among other things, the problematic social facts is clearly critical.

Yet, unlike Dickens's novel, in *Adam Bede* there is less satirical distortion and more serious, quasi objective representation of country life around 1800.

As has been pointed out,[46] the novel can be read as a fulfilment of Eliot's own plea for a book "studying the natural history of our social classes, especially of the small shopkeepers, artisans and peasantry" which she made in her essay (published in 1856 in the *Westminster Review*) on Wilhelm Heinrich von Riehl's sociological study on "the German peasantry,"[47] an essay which Cunningham qualifies as "a programme of sociological research into the life of ordinary England." (Ibid.) The parallels between Eliot's wording "natural history" and Zola's later novel cycle, which also sports 'natural history' in its subtitle, are striking and gesture towards a common quasi scientific, fact-oriented concern in realist and naturalist novel writing. Incidentally, this orientation was also perceived by Eliot's first readers, albeit in a negative light, as the criticism of the alleged incompatibility between the "brutal facts" represented in the novel with "a work of Art" in a contemporary review shows.[48]

Where, however, yet another parallel with *Hard Times* appears is in the extracompositional effect created by both novels: they both elicit a strong belief in the quasi factuality of the represented storyworlds and thus keep the reader immersed in them through a powerful aesthetic illusion that is sometimes even expanded to referential illusion. This powerful impression is strengthened in *Adam Bede* by a number of devices: They include graphic descriptions of (here often idyllic rural) settings and of the main characters but also – quasi covertly – by the appeal to a world (knowledge) shared by both narrator and reader through the frequent use of the phrase "one of those." (See, e.g., *AB*: 67, 293, 225) In addition, the term "fact" appears a number of times in the novel, although intracompositional thematization of the concept 'fact' is less frequent than in Dickens's novel (where, as we have seen, it is linked to an ideology thematized in the storyworld). When the term 'fact' appears in Eliot's text, it does so without the negative connotations it has in *Hard Times*. Moreover, its occurrence is not limited to a quasi grammatical expletive of the conjunction 'that', as in the phrase 'the fact that,' but "fact" – besides its telltale use in the aforementioned programmatic chapter 17 – frequently refers to givens of the fictional world (e.g., 178, 181, 221, 268, 323) and thus emphasizes not only the belief in its assumed factuality which all illusionist representations require but more specifically the firm spatial and historical setting of the storyworld in a recognizable English reality.

---

46  Cf. Cunningham 1996: x–xi.
47  Ibid.: x.
48  Quoted from ibid.: xxiii.

So far, one may have received the impression that *Adam Bede*, much more than *Hard Times*, is in harmony with the contemporary veneration of objective positivistic facts and strives to represent them in novel form. Yet this impression is misleading. For the narrator – and one may with confidence claim the implied author as well – is quite conscious of the problems, if not impossibility, of objective representation: this consciousness derives from the awareness that the subjectivity of perception is inescapable and that experience and representations stemming from it are therefore also tinged by subjectivity. Interestingly, the narrator enters this relativization and his uneasiness with exact and objective fact writing into the very program of realism discussed above, when he says: "I aspire to give no more than a faithful account of men and things as they have mirrored themselves in my mind. The mirror is doubtless defective; the outlines will sometimes be disturbed; the reflection faint or confused; [...]." (221) To speak of such a "defectiveness" of the literary mimetic "mirror," which is the narrator's (and implied author's) mind, is a clear acknowledgment that absolute truth is cognitively and epistemologically impossible and that therefore "there is reason to dread" the very opposite of what the program of realism strives for, namely "falsity." (222)[49]

Eliot's skepticism towards the accessibility of objective facts can be illustrated with one particularly tell-tale detail, namely the handling of physiognomic descriptions. As I have detailed elsewhere,[50] such descriptions are a privileged site when it comes to ascertaining the position of the worldview implied in a text concerning the epistemological question of the readability of the world and its perceivable facts. The reason for this is the literary convention that descriptions are rarely 'innocent': they do not simply make the reader 'see' something in an imaginative perceptual sense, they are also frequently enriched with implicit connotations, explicit evaluations, and other elements of meaning which make the reader 'see' the described character or object in the cognitive sense of 'understanding'. In this context, 'transparent' physiognomic descriptions are depictions of bodies and faces in which

---

49  In *Middlemarch*, at the beginning of chapter 27 (p. 296), the authorial narrator uses a well-known simile (the "concentric circles" produced by a light shining on a scratched surface) for the same purpose of laying bare the subjectivity of the perception of reality and facts, the "flattering illusion of a concentric arrangement," that is, of some seemingly objective fact, while it is in reality the subjective "candle" of a subjective consciousness which produces the impression depending on its point of view. (Cf. Nünning 2015: 124; Postlethwaite 2001: 115)

50  Wolf 2002b.

the perceivable surface, the fact of the bodily signifier, is – often explicitly – linked to, and gives access to the hidden character beneath this surface as its 'signified.' Frequently, the meaning of bodily details is made explicit in the narratorial discourse, and where such semiotically 'transparent' descriptions precede the actions of the described character – as is often the case, descriptions being a convention of character exposition not only in realism – the subsequent behavior is in line with the meaning and expectation elicited by these descriptions. On the level of the implied worldview, this can then be read (by way of the afore-mentioned 'epistemological allegorization' operating in literature) as an indication of a positive, unproblematically optimistic attitude towards the readability of the world and its facts. In contrast to this, 'opaque' physiognomic descriptions do not yield results with respect to the readability of the respective character on the basis of an allegedly transparent semiotic relationship between what can be observed as a bodily fact on the surface and a deeper essence and, per extension, the represented world may remain partially 'opaque' and inexplicable as well. Such descriptions may thus betray some degree of epistemological skepticism as part of the implied worldview.

In *Hard Times*, descriptions, physiognomic and otherwise, tend to be epistemologically transparent. For instance, the representative of the condemned fact-ideology, Thomas Gradgrind, after having his say on the necessity of teaching facts only at school, is introduced on the first page, to give just one of the many details, as showing "bald head […] all covered with knobs […] as if the head had scarcely warehouse-room for the hard facts stored inside." (*HT*: 47) Needless to say, the character is then shown to behave exactly in the way this description makes us expect.[51]

Eliot, in *Adam Bede*, also introduces such elements of transparency in some of her physiognomic descriptions, notably at the beginning when it comes to outlining the appearance of the eponymous hero: His strong body is said to betray racial origins by pointing to his being a "Saxon," while "the dark eyes that shone from under strongly marked, prominent, and mobile eyebrows indicated a mixture of Celtic blood" and that his "face" showed "no other beauty than such as belongs to an expression of good-humored honest intelligence,"

---

51  Cf. also Wolf 2002b: 396–398. Interestingly, the same transparency extends, in *Hard Times*, to the description of the main setting, industrial Coketown, the (highly satirical and rhetorical) portrait of which is metafictionally announced in the chapter title "The Keynote" (ch. I.5).

(*AB*: 50) a narratorial qualification to which the character, in his behavior and actions then is shown to conform. Yet, this is not the whole story. Consider the description of Hetty's beauty in the context of her being an object of male desire:

> The dear young, round, soft, flexible thing! Her heart must be just as soft, her temper just as free from angles, her character just as pliant, [...] Every man under such circumstances is conscious of being a great physiognomist. Nature, he knows, has a language of her own, which she uses with strict veracity, and he considers himself an adept in the language. Nature has written out his bride's character for him in those exquisite lines of cheek and lip, in those eyelids delicate as petals, in those long lashes curled like the stamen of a flower, in the dark liquid depths of those wonderful eyes. (197–198)

However, as opposed to the higher authority of the 'descriptor' of the passage quoted from *Hard Times*, this description is rendered from a limited, subjective and biased point of view (here the view of a lover): "It was very much in this way that our friend Adam Bede thought about Hetty; only he put his thoughts into different words." (198) And while the satirical bias in Dickens's description of Gradgrind turns out to be justified and thus approaching objectivity, the subjectivity of Adam's gaze is treacherous, for Hetty, with her self-delusions, coquetry and hard-hearted neglect of her own abandoned baby, is anything other than an ideal woman. Appropriately, the narrator relativizes Adam's all too positive physiognomic impression by stating:

> Nature has her *language*, and she is not unveracious, but we do not know all her intricacies of her *syntax* just yet, and in a hasty *reading* we may happen to extract the very opposite of the real *meaning* [...] One begins to suspect at length that there is no direct correlation beween [sic] eyelashes and morals or else, that the eyelashes express the disposition of the fair one's grandmother, which is on the whole is less important to us. (198–199, my emphasis)

This is a clear warning against physiognomic naivety – interestingly expressed in linguistic, almost semiotic terms (in italics). If the 'syntax' of natures 'fact-writing' is not clear for us to read, what we consider as facts becomes problematic.

However, such a departure from an optimistic fact-reading is, in Eliot's fiction, as yet not coupled with a diffidence towards fact-writing, as the opening metafictional paragraph by the narrator indicates:

> With a single drop of ink for a mirror, the Egyptian sorcerer undertakes to reveal to any chance comer far-reaching visions of the past. This is what I undertake to do for you, reader. With this drop of ink at the end of my pen I will show you the roomy workshop of Mr Jonathan Burge, carpenter, and builder in the village of Hayslope, as it appeared on the eighteenth of June, in the year of our Lord 1799. (49)

While the simile of the "sorcerer['s] [...] visions" might be read as an indication of fictionality, the opposite is true here – the use of the mirror, the mimetic metaphor par excellence which we encounter here again, testifies to this: what is 'conjured up' in the narrator's mirror is not (as one might think) fantasy but a world anchored as solidly in fact as the date and the name of the village are meant to indicate.

The only drawback with respect to this typically realist claim is an episode in which the implied author deviates from a major rule of realism, namely, never to include supernatural elements: In a memorable scene, Adam works late at night, appropriately on a coffin, a task which he has taken over from his dipsomaniac and sloppy father, who has once again not come home in time. While doing so, Adam twice hears a strange knocking at his door which he opens and twice finds no-one before the house. This incident makes Adam "shudder" and reminds him of the "willow wand" as a "sign when some-one was dying." While this could be discounted as a subjective "superstition" of Adam's, fostered by the "blood of the peasant in him" and the stories "told him" by his "mother," there is one detail in the story which belies this: Adam's dog Gyp appears to be startled repeatedly by this knocking as well, each time giving a loud "howl." (93–94) The narrator does everything to dispel 'unrealist' surmises the reader may get from the episode, but the subsequent story appears to endorse the supernatural, for shortly afterward we learn that Adam's father has in fact died, drowned in a stream, while Adam heard the knocking. This is a coincidence (?) which is never really explained, so that one is almost nudged towards a supernatural assumption. Making readers accept something supernatural, be it ever so insignificant for the plot as a whole, is a puzzling departure from the, as we have seen, almost scientific fact-orientation of this realist novel, all the more so as the author is known to have been an atheist for a long period in her life.[52]

---

52 To some extent, this 'puzzle' may be explained as a residue of an older episteme in a novel which, in its 'rage for explanation,' harnesses a striking plurality of methods and

What does all of this amount to with respect to Eliot's 'fact writing' in *Adam Bede*? On the one hand, one must state the following: The aesthetics on which the novel is explicitly based endorse a positive attitude to 'fact writing': the novel is a prime example of fact-friendly realism by an author who emphasized "patient watching of external facts" as a scientific way of accessing truth.[53] As could be observed with respect to *Hard Times* (and perhaps even more so, since *Adam Bede* never caricaturizes), Eliot's way of writing elicits a powerful immersion in a represented world that can be experienced as if it were a world of real facts – the introductory metaphor "sorcerer" has an indicative value in this respect, too, gesturing towards the 'magic' of aesthetic illusion.[54] Moreover, *Adam Bede* is firmly based on historical and social facts, which (again as with *Hard Times*) at times elicits elements of referential illusion and gestures towards a readability in the frame of factuality. In addition, as I have detailed elsewhere,[55] the novel not only posits the facts of the represented world but strives to explain them to the reader as much as possible. This applies in particular to the characters' actions and motivations, so that clear cause and effect relationships appear again and again (this is even done more systematically than in *Hard Times*).

On the other hand, the novel contains some elements that run counter to an easy endorsement of objective facts: besides the strange inclusion of the possibly supernatural (which is absent in *Hard Times*), there is above all a marked diffidence towards physiognomic readings which we did not find in Dickens. Of course, from a modern perspective,[56] physiognomics – in particular as a characterological reading of physiognomies – is a pseudo-science and not affiliated with facts. Yet, this was not seen as such by all in the nineteenth century. Hence, an emphasis on subjective misreadings not only of physiognomies but generally, as chapter 17 of *Adam Bede* eloquently indicates, is a noteworthy relativization of the belief in objective facts. While *Adam Bede* is certainly not based on a downright epistemological skepticism which would deny the existence or accessibility of facts altogether, the novel is informed by

---

ideas in order to account for the fictional facts while the implied author is aware of the limitations of all explanations. (Cf. Wolf 1998)
53   From Eliot's essay "The Influence of Rationalism", quoted from Postlethwaite 2001: 108.
54   For the "air of reality" of *Adam Bede*, see also Gill 1980: 26.
55   Cf. Wolf 1998.
56   Which is not so 'modern' after all, since Lichtenberg, in the 18th century, was already skeptical about the physiognomic teachings of Johann Kaspar Lavater, the most important contemporary representative of this pseudo-science.

a remarkable ambivalence that is noteworthy in the history of literary 'fact-writing' and concomitant epistemological stances.[57]

## 5. Conclusion: *Hard Times* and *Adam Bede* – Ambivalence towards Fact-Writing and Different Historical Affiliations

On the basis of general theoretical reflections on the complexity of the relationship between fact and fiction we have seen that both *Hard Times* and *Adam Bede* as realist novels show a strong concern with facts and fact-writing, albeit in different ways. What they share is a realism-typical focus on contemporary (or recent) historical reality, and on the lower classes in particular, and the eliciting of a powerful aesthetic illusion, that is, a belief in the verisimilitude of the represented worlds and, at times, even a referential illusion in the facticity of the representation of aspects of reality. In their intracompositional showing and thematization facts, the latter being particularly outstanding in *Hard Times*, as well as in their extracompositional immersive effects on the reader, they thus can be considered remarkable examples of $19^{th}$-century literary attempts at fact-writing. While the constituents of, and happenings in, the represented worlds are clearly fictive and presuppose a reading under the auspices of fictionality, the realism in the representation and its at times historically specific and thus 'factive' hetero-referentiality invite the readers to occasionally adopt a reception frame of factuality which permits them to consider parts of the novels as sources of socio-historical information.

However, as we have seen, the attitude towards facts is ambivalent in both novels, although from different motivations and with different historical affiliations. In Dickens's novel, in spite of the importance which fact-writing has, a hostility towards facts as absolutes in contemporary fact venerating ideologies in education, economy, and society at large is clearly marked. Moreover, as typical of Dickens, the satirical and social-critical function of the novel at times leads to a distortion of the strict credibility of fictional facts such as the exaggeratedly monotonous aspect of Coketown or some character-caricatures such as Mr. Gradgrind's portrait. In *Adam Bede* criticism is also conveyed but

---

57   For the ambivalence underlying Eliot's thoughts (an awareness of the subjectivist difficulties in the perception and processing of facts and the simultaneous maintenance of the "goal of impartiality" and hence of objectivity), see Anger 2001: quotation on p. 92.

without the distortion of satire, as the novel strives to elicit sympathy even with fallible characters rather than harsh criticism.

Another difference between the two novels lies in the historical affiliation of the implied positions that create tensions with an unmitigated trust in objective facts. In *Hard Times*, crude fact-veneration and the reliance on economic reason is opposed to a celebration of the imagination which points back to romanticism. One might even see relationships between the implied norms of this novel and Wordsworth's sonnet "The world is too much with us" and its indictment of "getting and spending."[58] In *Adam Bede*, while a certain Wordsworthian nostalgia with respect to rural life cannot be overlooked,[59] distance towards an overly optimistic perspective on objective facts comes from an epistemological awareness of subjectivity as a relativizing factor of all reality perception – which arguably also applies to fact-writing. In this, *Adam Bede* does not point back to romanticism but rather forward to modernism. A remarkable proto-modernist element gesturing towards modernism's focus on subjectivity is to be found in the ambivalent attitude towards the readability of physiognomies. This ambivalence includes a 'reliable' portrait, such as the one given of the eponymous hero but also an incipient skepticism towards too much trust in 'physiognomics.' It is a skepticism which Virginia Woolf will later radicalize in storytelling that showcases the subjectivity and constructivism of perception, as is the case in her 'anti-physiognomical' short story "An Unwritten Novel" (1921/1991).[60] All of this is, however, at best a proto-modernist awareness of subjectivity in dealing with facts, since the aesthetic and epistemological basis of *Adam Bede* remains rooted in the notion of facts existing independently of subjectivist distortions[61] and of truth as the ideal of literary representation, and this truth includes the representation of social milieus and external details, toward which Woolf was highly critical.[62]

---

58  Cf. also Lodge 1969 [1966]: 99, who sees a relationship between *Hard Times* and Shelley's "criticism of the 'accumulation of facts'" in the latter's "Defence of Poetry".
59  Cf. Gill 1980: 29: "George Eliot's vision of rural life is [...] essentially Wordsworthian."
60  In this story, a focalizer who is apparently quite confident about her ability to read faces, observes a female fellow traveler in a railway compartment and, on the basis of her physiognomy and facial expression (pathognomy), constructs a whole 'novel' about her, which, however, turns out to be false – which is why the imaginary 'novel' remains 'unwritten.' (Cf. Wolf 2002b: 412–416)
61  Cf. Anger 2001.
62  Cf. her parodic criticism of Arnold Bennett's 'Edwardian' (i.e., late Victorian realist writing style) in her essay "Mr. Bennet and Mrs. Brown" (Woolf 1928 [1924]).

All in all, both novels, for all their affiliation with realist fact-writing, also testify to the complexities of, and tensions in, the relationship between fact and fiction. They also show that even realism, which from a postmodernist perspective was a period of almost naïve veneration of positivistic facts and fact-writing, was not so naive after all. And these novels perhaps also show something else: With an eye to the romantic affiliation of *Hard Times* and the proto-modernist attitudes discernible in *Adam Bede*, one may be led to suspect that the oppositions literary historians have created from various perspectives in their fact-writing, oppositions between the mentalities and epistemologies allegedly underlying epochs and trends such as romanticism, realism, modernism, and postmodernism are – at least to some extent – facts in the etymological sense: *facta*, constructions. They are indispensable and useful for orientation but must again and again be subject to scrutiny – in order to approach the elusive ideal which Eliot's narrator so eloquently propagated in chapter 17 of *Adam Bede*, namely Truth.

## Bibliography

Abbott, H. Porter (2015): "How Do We Read What Isn't There To Be Read? Shadow Stories and Permanent Gaps", in: Zunshine, Lisa (ed.): *The Oxford Handbook of Cognitive Literary Studies*, Oxford, 104–119.
Anger, Suzy (2001): "George Eliot and Philosophy", in: Levine (ed.), *The Cambridge Companion to George Eliot*, 76–97.
Barthes, Roland (1968): "L'Effet de réel", in: *Communications* 11, 84–89.
Coover, Robert (1970) [1969]: "The Magic Poker", in: id.: *Pricksongs and Descants*, New York, 20–45.
Craig, David (1969): "Introduction", in: Dickens, *Hard Times*, 11–36.
Cunningham, Valentine (1996): "Introduction", in: id. (ed.): Eliot, George: *Adam Bede*, Oxford, vii–xl.
Defoe, Daniel (1965) [1719]: *Robinson Crusoe*, Harmondsworth.
Dickens, Charles (1969) [1854]: *Hard Times*, Harmondsworth.
Eco, Umberto (1967) [1962]: *Opera aperta: Forma e indeterminazione nelle poetiche contemporanee*, Milan.
Eliot, George (1985) [1859]: *Adam Bede*, Harmondsworth.
— (1965) [1871]: *Middlemarch*, Harmondsworth.
Ermath, Elizabeth Deeds (1983): *Realism and Consensus in the English Novel*, Princeton, NJ.

Feldmann, Doris (1986): "Erkenntnis und Sprache in Charles Dickens' 'Hard Times'", in: *Literatur in Wissenschaft und Unterricht* 19, 195–214.

Fluck, Winfried (1992): *Inszenierte Wirklichkeit: Der amerikanische Realismus. 1865-1900*, München.

Gill, Stephen (1980): "Introduction", in: Eliot, George: *Adam Bede*, 11–39.

Hardy, Thomas (1999) [1887]: *The Woodlanders*, Harmondsworth.

Humphreys, Anne (2008): "Hard Times", in: Paroissien, David (ed.): *A Companion to Charles Dickens*, Malden, MA, 390–400.

Iser, Wolfgang (1975): "Die Wirklichkeit der Fiktion. Elemente eines funktionsgeschichtlichen Textmodells der Literatur", in: Warning, Rainer (ed.): *Rezeptionsästhetik: Theorie und Praxis*, München, 277–324.

Kablitz, Andreas (2008): "Literatur, Fiktion und Erzählung – nebst einem Nachruf auf den Erzähler", in: Rajewsky, Irina O./Schneider, Ulrike (eds.): *Im Zeichen der Fiktion. Aspekte fiktionaler Rede aus historischer und systematischer Sicht*, Stuttgart, 13–44.

— (1989): "Erklärungsanspruch und Erklärungsdefizit im 'Avant-propos' von Balzacs 'Comédie humaine'", in: *Zeitschrift für französische Sprache und Literatur* 99, 261–286.

Kearns, Katherine (1992): "A Tropology of Realism in 'Hard Times'", in: *English Literary History* 59, 857–881.

Levine, George (ed.): *The Cambridge Companion to George Eliot*, Cambridge.

Lodge, David (2001) [1981]: "How Successful Is 'Hard Times'?", in: Dickens, Charles: *Hard Times*, New York, NY, 400–409.

— (1969) [1966]: "The Rhetoric of 'Hard Times'", in: Gray, Paul Edward (ed.): *Twentieth Century Interpretations of "Hard Times": A Collection of Critical Essays*, Englewood Cliffs, NJ, 86–105.

Maack, Annegret (1991): *Charles Dickens. Epoche – Werk – Wirkung*. Arbeitsbücher zur Literaturgeschichte, München.

Nünning, Ansgar (2015): "'The Extension of our Sympathies': George Eliot's Aesthetic Theory and Narrative Technique as a Key to the Affective, Cognitive, and Social Value of Literature", in: Meretoja, Hanna et al. (eds.): *Values of Literature*, Leiden/Boston, MA, 117–136.

Nussbaum, Martha C. (2001) [1991]: "The Literary Imagination in Public Life", in: Dickens, Charles: *Hard Times*, New York, NY, 429–439.

Pearsall, Judy (ed.) (1999): *New Oxford Dictionary of English*, Oxford.

Postlethwaite, Diana (2001): "George Eliot and Science", in: Levine (ed.), *The Cambridge Companion to George Eliot*, 98–118.

Preisendanz, Wolfgang (1976): "Zur Korrelation zwischen Satirischem und Komischem", in: id./Warning, Rainer (eds.): *Das Komische*, München, 411–413.

Prince, Gerald (1996): "Remarks on Narrativity", in: Wahlin, Claes (ed.): *Perspectives on Narratology: Papers from the Stockholm Symposium on Narratology*, Frankfurt am Main et al., 95–106.

Shuttleworth, Sally (1984): *George Eliot and Nineteenth-Century Science: The Make-Believe of a Beginning*, Cambridge et. al.

Simpson, Margaret (1997): *The Companion to 'Hard Times'*, Mountfield.

Warning, Rainer (1990): "Kompensatorische Bilder einer 'wilden Ontologie'. Zolas 'Les Rougon Macquart'", in: *Poetica* 22/3–4, 355–383.

Wolf, Werner (2013): "Aesthetic Illusion", in: Bernhart, Walter/Mahler, Andreas/id. (eds.): *Immersion and Distance: Aesthetic Illusion in Literature and Other Media*, Amsterdam, 1–63.

— (2009): "Metareference across Media: The Concept, its Transmedial Potentials and Problems, Main Forms and Functions", in: id. (ed.) in collaboration with Katharina Bantleon and Jeff Thoss: *Metareference across Media: Theory and Case Studies – Dedicated to Walter Bernhart on the Occasion of his Retirement*, Amsterdam/New York, NY, 1–85.

— (2008): "Is Aesthetic Illusion 'illusion référentielle'? 'Immersion' and Its Relationship to Fictionality and Factuality", in: *Journal of Literary Theory* 2/1, 99–126, 171–173.

— (2002a): "Gesichter in der Erzählkunst: Zur Wahrnehmung von Physiognomien und Metawahrnehmung von Physiognomiebeschreibungen aus theoretischer und historischer Sicht am Beispiel englischsprachiger Texte des 19. und 20. Jahrhunderts", in: *Sprachkunst* 33, 301–325.

— (2002b): "'Speaking faces'? – Zur epistemologischen Lesbarkeit von Physiognomie-Beschreibungen im englischen Erzählen des Modernismus", in: *Poetica* 34, 389–426.

— (1998): "'I must go back a little to explain [her] motives [...]' – Erklärung und Erklärbarkeit menschlichen Verhaltens, Handelns und Wesens in englischen Romanen des Realismus: 'Hard Times' und 'Adam Bede'", in: *Germanisch-Romanische Monatsschrift* 48, 435–479.

Woolf, Virginia (1991) [1921]: "An Unwritten Novel", in: id.: *A Haunted House and Other Stories*, London, 14–27.

— (1924/1928): "Mr. Bennet and Mrs. Brown", in: id. *Collected Essays*, vol. 1, London, 319–337.

# A 'Real' Novel?
## Narrating Facts in *El hombre que amaba a los perros*

*Iyari Martínez Márquez (Universidade Católica Portuguesa)*

A couple of weeks ago, I moved to Giessen in Germany. New city, new language, new name for almost everything; new all. This experience, as a whole, is not only mine. Many people find themselves in such a situation every day. However, what is special to me is how much relief I felt when I saw a Woolworth store in the mall near my new home. I was born in a small city in Mexico, where Woolworth did not exist. I lived there for almost 30 years until I moved to Madrid to study. The last Woolworth store in Spain closed in 1980. This was 34 years before I arrived in Spain's capital. There is certainly not a single Woolworth in Lisbon, where I moved afterward. But now there was one. So, how come I felt calmer when I saw the big red letters on the billboard? Letters that I had never seen in real life until that moment?

In 1975 Judith Kerr published *The Other Way Round*, the second book of her *Out of the Hitler Time* trilogy, in which the main character Anna and her family experience the most intense German air raids on London. At some point in the novel, Anna goes to a Woolworth store to buy something, because it was the cheapest store around. This memory stayed with me for years. I must have read the novel when I was 15 years old, and the recollection came back the moment I saw those big red letters. "This is a cheap store," I thought, "it is the same store where Anna used to shop." Why did I know that for a fact? Because a mixture of reality and memory, straight from a narrative work, had just saved my day.

This is, of course, a very private story, and it involves only a minimum number of facts. Or what could be considered to be facts. Or, even better, a double layer of 'factual' events. On the one hand, I undoubtedly moved to a different town in a different country, and I definitely (and awkwardly) did not speak the local language. At the same time, the Woolworth store is there, at the Neustädter mall. On the other hand, Kerr's book exists. You can easily get a copy and read it. Furthermore, in the book, Anna, in fact, goes to a store that exists in her world. A small but important detail here is that such a store 'also' exists in our world. But not only the store. It is a fact that her context too refers to a real event in history, namely London being bombed by Nazi Germany's forces during WW2, while her story as a Jewish refugee resembles countless similar stories from that period. Like many other things and events that exist in both worlds, hers and ours.

A couple of questions comes up here: If I am aware that Anna does not exist in my world and that her story is a fictional narrative despite the many correlations with our world, why was I able to relate her Woolworth to my Woolworth? By which means did Kerr's depiction of London meld with my reality of a German city? How does such a process of mixing fiction and fact work? Can this process be applied to narratives in general?

I would like to answer these questions by starting with the last two of them. A good way to do so is to look at a genre that is deeply related to narrative forms: historical novels. This particular genre allows a closer view at the described 'overlapping' process, since it appeals to factual events while also filling up the spaces between them. The long tradition of the genre gives an idea of the importance of reporting such events in a narrative form and the need to relate them to characters, feelings, and actions. Hence, narrative "might be well considered a solution to a problem of general human concern, namely, the problem of how to translate *knowing* into *telling*, the problem of fashioning human experience into a form assimilable to structures of meaning that are generally human rather than culture-specific."[1] Furthermore, "[w]e may not be able fully to comprehend specific thought patterns of another culture, but we have relatively less difficulty *understanding* a story coming from another culture,"[2] or, if I may add, *about* another culture.

Yet another important trait of the historical novel, that adds to make it suitable for the purposes of this study, comes from the process that determinates our reading process: "[i]n order to understand and evaluate a story, we often implicitly decide which genre it represents. In the semiotics of stories, genres are the analogs of species in biology – we apply them for fast and useful categorization."[3] Thereby we expect certain inputs from any given text, according to the category we establish for them. We enter, then, in the realm

---

1   White 1980: 5.
2   Ibid.
3   Brandt 2009: 6.

of 'possible worlds,' and these possible worlds created by literary artifacts are affected by forces that may create the plot and lead the story forward, on a larger or smaller scale. Which forces are they? Following Brandt, these elements are what gives each text a worldly context, what determines the rules of each world, from a middle ground to the 'real' world. Adding magic locally or globally will lead us to the realm of the fantastic while the addition of fatal forces leads us to the grotesque or the absurd. It is not the interest of the present paper to discuss the nomenclature or nature of such divisions and genres but to be aware that distance and proximity from the 'real' world create a set of different scenarios in which stories develop.

Within these possible worlds, we must acknowledge that there are a variety of ways to create and develop them. Some stories can take place in entirely imaginary places and with imaginary characters. Other stories 'reproduce' a certain reality that vaguely reminds us of any city or character through narrative strategies such as never mentioning a name or avoiding details. One can think of Dostoyevsky's cities or Kafka's characters. Some other species of stories, as Brandt would put it, place fictional characters in 'real' contexts, as in the story that served to introduce the present paper. In the case of historical novels, the strategy is to present all these elements in order to create a relation with reality: verifiable characters, places, and events. The blank spaces, or 'the missed scenes,' between events are filled through the authors' imagination, their artistic practice, and the intentions behind their narrative work. In this sense, a historical novel makes use of a strategy that puts the genre in a close position to historical writing, according to Hayden White.[4]

However, it is important to remember that neither of the previous, and inconclusive, possible ways to approach a story play entirely by the rules of our reality. Each of the given examples belongs to a particular space, with a particular set of rules that make sense and work accordingly to the logic that builds up the narrated world. This is especially obvious in the case of a wholly fictive universe, where 'imaginary' or 'non-real' forces such as magic are overall present and dominant. But as these forces shift towards a zero degree of their agency in the stories, following Brandt's idea on genres, the narration starts taking place in (a) 'reality,' or to what can be understood as a 'real world' that seems to mirror our own world, and one might forget that every fiction belongs to a realm of its own. This inclination to relate fiction to

---

4   White 1981, 1980.

our own reality has been called "pseudo-mimesis"[5] by Czech critic Lubomir Doležel. In the case of historical novels, the narrations propose a "transworld identity"[6] within the possible world semantics domain, which

> claims that Tolstoy's fictional Napoleon or Dicken's fictional London are not identical with the historical Napoleon or the geographical London. It insists that fictional individuals are not dependent for their existence and properties on actual prototypes. Still, persons with actual world "prototypes" constitute a distinct semantic class within the set of fictional persons; an ineradicable relationship exists between the historical Napoleon and all fictional Napoleons. However, this relationship extends across world boundaries, fictional persons and their actual prototypes are linked by transworld identity.[7]

It is within this frame that an overlapping of fiction and reality is possible. Ever since they belong to two different dimensions but do, however, maintain a transworldly identity that makes it possible to identify one *in* the other. Furthermore, and continuing with Doležel, it is also important to keep in mind that "[t]he fiction makers practice a radically nonessentialist semantics; they give themselves the freedom to alter even the most typical and well-known properties and life histories of actual (historical) persons when incorporating them in a fictional world."[8] The overlapping becomes clearer by following this train of thought.

In order to illustrate the ideas regarding the superposition of fiction and reality presented so far, I would like to consider Leonardo Padura's essay *La novela que no se escribió: Apostillas a El hombre que amaba a los perros* (2013-2018) which is a reflection on the writing process of his novel *El hombre que amaba a los perros* (2009) and provides an example of the construction of a historical novel that engages with the aforementioned narrative strategies. As for the novel, Padura presents a three-fold narration, in which different perspectives converge around a major historical event: Liev Davidovich Trotsky's assassination by the hand of Ramón Mercader in 1940 in Mexico City. To begin with, we are presented with a thread that narrates Trotsky's life from the moment of his exile from the USSR. We are 'witnesses' of his dislocations between Turkey, France, Germany, Norway and, finally, Mexico. We follow his thoughts on the

---

5   Doležel 1998.
6   Ibid.
7   Ibid.: 16–17.
8   Ibid.: 17.

global political context of the time but also take a look on his daily life and his preoccupations and relations with his family and friends. Secondly, we are faced to Ramón Mercader's story, one that took him from his involvement in the Spanish Civil War to a collaboration with the Stalinist secret police and the execution of one of the most discussed crimes of the 20$^{th}$ century. And, finally, we have a third story line that refers to an entirely fictional Iván Cárdenas and his encounters with Ramón López, Ramón Mercader under a false name, in La Habana. Within this thread, we 'hear' the narration of Ramón Mercader's story.

As for the essay on the process of the novel, Padura presents the personal interests that led him to write down such a text, but he also describes his approach to the writing of the characters. Furthermore, Leonardo Padura gives an insight into his journalistic process that allows him to obtain information and to be as close as possible to 'reality.'

The best way to present my argument is to split it in two parts: A first section will take a look at Padura's construction of his characters and the novel by departing from his own exegesis of the work and by following his opinions on how his artistic work shaped an alternate, possible, world for these characters. In this section, thus, it is my aim to show that Padura is very aware of the limits of his desire to be as 'faithful' to reality as possible, and, also, of the limits of the narrative to build up the tension between the characters. In the second section, I would like to discuss an idea on the process through which these transworld characters integrate into reality via the reader's cognitive process which involves their imagination, but also both their episodic and semantic memory. In other words, I would like to argue for a two-way gaze regarding the relation between our world and the possible world: one that comes from the author's writing and codification process, and another that depends on the decodification (and recodification) that takes place on the reader's end.

## 1.

A first element to which I would like to bring attention in *La novela que no se escribió* is the resonance between Padura's personal take on the drawing of his characters and on the nature of such characters that are based on historical, real, figures. Let us take a look at his first reflection on the different degrees of difficulty when it came to fictionalizing both historical characters in order to create their transworldly mirrors:

> [...] how to deal with the writing of a novel with one character able to fill it with information and another blurred behind a barely known, and hardly real, biography that has been fictionalized and distorted in many of its passages by the subjectivity and the informants' search for limelight, but also by other interests (political, family, sectaries)?[9]

It is a central question when storytellers face the complex task of mixing their own vision, their world making activity, with facts in order to give the reader a deceiving perspective that can confuse them, a *trompe l'oeil* created entirely for the illusion to be part of our reality. In this way, the transworldly nature of the characters, and their context, is a masquerade behind documented events and characters (which do not lose their transworldliness in any case but appear to be real and relatable to their 'real' pairs; a sort of doppelganger between their world and our world).

Padura argues that his approach was different for each character. Due to the amount of information about Liev Davidovich Trotsky's life, his own autobiography and Isaac Deutscher's work particularly, Padura's strategy is to narrate Trotsky's inner life, giving weight to his private thoughts and inner dialogues concerning his context, which are "essential elements of his individuality, so important for the *creation* of the character but barely decisive for the *historical frame* [...]."[10] In this sense, the facts are not only given in contextual form but also in the known events that involved Trotsky in person, his dislocations around the world as exiled, the houses where he lived, the people he talked to, all the elements that surround the character and that cannot be changed to maintain the 'real' mask. Hence, the fiction comes in the form of his inner life. A different situation appears when dealing with Mercader's character:

---

9   Padura 2019b: 130. "¿Cómo lidiar en la escritura de una novela con un personaje capaz de atiborrar con la información y con otro difuminado tras una biografía real a duras penas conocida y en muchos de sus pasajes bastante ficcionada o distorsionada por la subjetividad y hasta la búsqueda de protagonismo de los informantes y por los más diversos intereses (políticos, familiares, sectarios)?" All translations from this book are my own.

10  Ibid.: 131. "[...] los componentes esenciales de su individualidad, tan importantes en la *creación* misma del personaje pero apenas decisivos para el *cuadro histórico*, [...]." My emphasis.

Ramón Mercader, on his side, is an absolutely literary construction, elaborated from a few reliable bibliographical references and many contextual elements that should or could influence him: the epoch's conflicts during his lifetime. In this way, the bibliographical elements are inserted in real events such as the establishment of the Second Republic in Spain and the Civil War (1936-1939), in which Mercader took part, his becoming a Soviet secret agent and the political and ideological environment of the time [...], which allowed me to sketch a character from what *actually* happened in his life and, over all, *what could have happened accordingly to that historical context.*[11]

It becomes clear that Leonardo Padura is aware of the transworldly nature of the characters in his novel and of the *possible world* they inhabit and in which the events 'could have happened.' Ever since his writing strategies are in line with the idea that

[p]ossible worlds semantics makes us aware that the material coming from the actual world has to undergo a substantial transformation at the world boundary [...] actual-world (historical) individuals are able to enter a fictional world only if they become possible counterparts, shaped in any way the fiction maker chooses.[12]

At this point one can come back to Hayden White's idea of narration as problem solver which touches the question of knowing and telling. I would like to consider this in connection with the analysis of Leonardo Padura's reflections on his own work. What is the problem that is being solved by this story? What exactly is coded here? The answer to this question relies on the third narrative thread: Iván Cárdenas. The character's importance can be seen in two ways; first, as a sort of 'key master' that opens and closes the doors in the narration,

---

11  Padura 2019b: 131–132. "Ramón Mercader, por su lado, es una construcción absolutamente novelesca, elaborada a partir de unos pocos referentes biográficos creíbles y de muchos elementos contextuales que debieron o pudieron influirlo: los conflictos de la época que le tocó vivir. De este modo, los datos biográficos son insertados en acontecimientos reales como el establecimiento de la Segunda República en España y la Guerra Civil (1936-1939) en la cual Mercader participó, su conversión en agente secreto soviético y el ambiente político e ideológico del momento [...], con lo cual pude ir moldeando un personaje a partir de lo que realmente ocurrió en su vida y, sobre todo, *de lo que pudo haber ocurrido de acuerdo a ese contexto histórico.*"

12  Doležel 1998: 21.

allowing us to approach Mercader's story. However, Cárdenas' role goes beyond a purely literary consideration, he is a representation of an entire Cuban generation, deprived of means to access the events outside the island, and, furthermore, outside the official pro-Soviet perspective of the world: "Iván is a fictional entity, built with elements from many different lives, real or possible, known by first or second hand, since I decided to make him into a synthesis of many experiences lived by a specific Cuban generation, to the generation to which I belong."[13] Padura encodes the answer to the problem of knowing and telling as such: The novel links isolated dots of information and events of the 20$^{th}$ century to which a whole generation only gained access through narrative and fictional means. Beyond the documented facts, Padura reaches back to the people that met Ramón Mercader during his time in Cuba, like doctors and family members. Thus, the possibility to fill in the blanks is a result of this form of writing facts. Hence, the last words in Padura's essay:

> [...] through emails, phone calls, face-to-face comments, and, also, letters received through postal service, dozens of Cuban readers expressed, in their own words, the same reaction to the book: they thanked me for writing the novel, because, by reading it, they have learned many stories that they did not know, and even they have learned many things from their own and personal history.[14]

Leonardo Padura codifies these elements, and it becomes the readers' task to decodify and recodify them by their own means and through their own cultural frame. This involves a series of knowledge that functions as a 'tool kit' to perform the task of making sense out of the text.[15] Thus, it is necessary to understand that a part of the responsibility concerning the overlap between

---

13  Padura 2019a: 59. "Iván es un ente de ficción, construido con elementos de muchas vidas, reales o posibles, conocidas de primera o de segunda mano, pues me propuse convertirlo en una síntesis de diversas experiencias vividas por una generación específica de cubanos, la generación a la cual pertenezco."

14  Ibid.: 172–173. "Porque a través de correos electrónicos, llamadas telefónicas, comentarios cara a cara e, incluso, cartas recibidas por el correo ordinario, decenas de lectores cubanos me expresaron, con sus palabras, la misma reacción a la lectura del libro: me agradecían que hubiera escrito la novel pues, leyéndola, habían aprendido de muchas historias que no conocían e incluso, habían aprendido muchas cosas de su propia y personal historia."

15  Cf. Bruner 1991.

facts and fiction relies on the reader's own strategies and abilities to approach a fictional narrative.

## 2.

If on the author's side the overlapping between fiction and reality forms part of a strategy, a well-crafted *trompe l'oeil*, in order to cross the line between actual/empirical/historical and possible worlds, the reader's side is no less interesting in terms of the decodifying strategies that need to be followed in order to understand the world created by the writer. How do the readers enter such a world? Where does this process take place? Is it in the reader's imagination? Is it a matter of purely understanding of the text? The language? Are there different ways to understand a certain narrative by different readers? How does this de(re)codification process affect the reader's reality? How do fictional facts overlap with real facts? Lubomír Doležel offers an answer to all these questions:

> Readers access fictional worlds in reception, by reading and processing literary texts. The text-processing activities involve many different skills and depend on many variables, such as the type of reader, the style and purpose of his or her reading, and so on. But possible-worlds semantics insists that the world is constructed by its author and the reader's role is to reconstruct it. [...] Having reconstructed the fictional world as a mental image, the reader can ponder it and make it a part of his experience, just as he experientially appropriates the actual world. The appropriation, which ranges from enjoyment through knowledge acquisition to following it as a script, integrates fictional worlds into the reader's reality.[16]

Some of Doležel's points need to be further explored in order to clarify the process that permits the reader to 'appropriate' the author's proposed world. For this purpose, I would like to argue that a way to understand such processes can be found in the cognitive theories' approach to literature, particularly by simulation theory.

*Simulation*, as a cognitive process, takes place within the mirroring activity that is performed by our brain when a mental image is projected, either by imagining an activity we need to perform, the act of reading, or any other

---

16  Doležel 1998: 21.

mental process that involves our imagination. In this sense, we *picture* ourselves making coffee, for instance, taking into account all the elements that will sourround such activity. Furthermore, we can also imagine any possible obstacle to our goal. This is a very simplistic example, since simulation is also used to prepare ourselves for interactions with other persons, calculating possible outcomes, and predicting the other's feelings towards our actions.[17] In this sense, we can distinguish between goal-oriented simulations and interpersonal simulations: "When we simulate objects, we tend to follow prototypes. When we simulate actions, we often follow scripts – at least if the actions are limited and routine enough to be covered by scripts."[18]

In this way, the reader enters a mental *simulation* of the writer's world in which he or she adopts a proper point of view, provided by the writer in the form of the narrator, and by putting oneself into the story. This creates the possibility for the reader to not only *experience* the fictional world but also to create experience from it. Turning whatever event takes place in the story into a personal event to be used to project future outcomes is what we do with our real-world experiences. This passage between worlds is discussed by Gallese and Wojciehowski:

> It appears therefore that the border between real and fictional worlds is much more blurred than one would expect. This finding opens interesting scenarios for a neurocognitive approach to art, in general, and to narrative, in particular. As the Italian philosopher Alfonso Iacono recently proposed, entering into the fictional world of art implies the inhabiting of an intermediate world whose fictional character is naturalized, henceforth it acquires a natural character, in spite of its artificial nature.[19]

Furthermore, according to Turner,[20] human beings have the ability to blend with their imagination. In this way, we can position ourselves into the other's perspective in order to understand their acts, to feel empathy but also to try to figure out their perspective on things, events, and beings. Such a blend is necessary to make the events and characters in the narrative fiction plausible for the readers since it will turn them into 'real' entities, capable of feelings, will, and able to perform actions. This process, then, blurs the line between fiction

---

17  Cf. Hogan 2013.
18  Ibid.: 11.
19  Gallese/Wojciehowski 2011, in: https://escholarship.org/uc/item/3jg726c2 (21.05.2022).
20  Cf. Turner 2007: 90–115.

and reality even more, since the readers have the ability to blend themselves with characters and places in their imagination, which adds to the inherent relation between transworldly elements and their real models, creating the intermediate world, as proposed by Alfonso Iacono: "One enters the picture through the frame forgetting about having entered. This process, which takes place while being in an emotional state and which can be ritualized (actually it is necessary for rituals), is at the origin of the process of naturalization [...]."[21] As such, we have a series of steps that lead to an overlapping between fiction and reality: the readers project a simulation of the fictional world, once 'inside' this world, the reader blends with the characters obtaining in this way an experience that can be extrapolated to the reader's reality. One can now see the impossibility of separating an experience obtained in a transworldly space from its real model. An experience that seems to be applicable to an actual situation. Building up a narrative that allows the reader to project into 'reality' knowledge taken from fiction. Storing this as memories that fill blanks in the reader's view of the world.

However, other elements are necessary to make fictional facts blend with real facts, namely, our previous knowledge about the world. In this sense, we know that building simulations is related to our memory, whether it be "episodic memory" [EM] or a larger and more general "semantic memory" [SM].[22] In this sense, we rely on our past experiences to predict future outcomes, Hogan, exemplifies this by picturing a coffeehouse: if we talk about a known coffeehouse, we will call on our memories of it to simulate it, and any specificity will come from these episodic memories we have of this specific site. However, when we talk about coffeehouses in general, we might also use this episodic memory but only for comparison and to set a series of characteristics shared by what should be called a 'coffeehouse.' Hogan states:

> Thus we may distinguish two levels of simulation – general and particular. These are associated with distinct, although interrelated means of simulation – semantic and episodic memory. Of course, semantic and episodic elements are not fully segregated. In any complex simulation, real or literary, we make use of both. Perhaps even more important, both are integrated with emotional memory. Emotional memories are implicit memories that revive the relevant emotions when they are activated (see LeDoux Emotional). Thus

---

21   Iacono 2010 (quoted in Gallese and Wojciehowski 2011 and translated by the authors).
22   Cf. Hogan 2013. My abbreviations.

an emotional memory of a frightening event will, when stirred, give rise to fear.[23]

Therefore, it is necessary to differentiate between the process involved in the *representation* of unknown spaces and the *recreation* of those spaces that we are familiar with; this is particularly important in the case of a text such as *El hombre que amaba a los perros* that works with transworldly characters and spaces that can be 'lived' and 'verified' with their actual counterparts.

By following the aforementioned difference and Doležel's emphasis on the type of reader, I would like to distinguish two possible readers to illustrate this point: one who *represents* the text entirely (RR1); this means that he/she possesses no information regarding the characters or the spaces which is why they rely on the description of the narrator and on his/her semantic memory. In the case of *El hombre que amaba a los perros*, this is a reader that does not know about the historical person Trotsky, nor about his fatal end. Since for this reader the entire story is a fictional work, he/she would have no problem to separate any information from the real world and to accommodate the gained experience into the proper semantic memory. A second type of reader (RR2) who is familiar with the character's factual history can rely on his/her episodic memory in order to understand the textual information and the adjacent subtexts within it. These readers will bring the experience gained through the text to the real world and apply it to their knowledge about it. Here, the frame to enter and exit the transworldly space and characters is not strictly defined, as the episodic memory will be affected by the information coming from the text. Adding thoughts to the historical figure of Trotsky or filling the blanks in Ramón Mercader's life is part of a strategy that mediates the space between knowing and telling in the sense that Hayden White[24] has proposed. It is a narrative way to construct a story around facts and to anchor fiction to a plausible, yet fictional world.

As one can easily see, the questions coming with the processes of reception and the focus on the role of readers provide notable and significant insights into the processes through which writing (fictional) facts affect the real world and vice-versa. An insight that shows the impact of literature and fiction on our knowledge of the world and the way we learn about it.

---

23   Ibid.: 12.
24   Cf. White 1980.

## Bibliography

Brandt, Per Aage (2009): "Forces and Spaces – Maupassant, Borges, Hemingway. Toward a Semio-Cognitive Narratology", in: *SSRN*, https://papers.ssrn.com/sol3/papers.cfm?abstract_id=1595803 (21.05.2022).

Doležel, Lubomí (1998): *Heterocosmica: Fiction and Possible Worlds*, Baltimore.

Gallese, Vittorio/Wojciejowski, Hannah (2011): "How Stories Make Us Feel: Toward an Embodied Narratology", in: *California Italian Studies* 2/1, https://escholarship.org/uc/item/3jg726c2 (21.05.2022).

Hogan, Patrick Colm (2013): *How Author's Minds Make Stories*, Cambridge.

Kerr, Judith (1987): *En la batalla de Inglaterra*, Madrid.

Padura, Leonardo (2019): *Agua por todas partes*, Barcelona.

— (2019a): "La generación que soñó con el futuro", in: id., *Agua por todas partes*, 57–73.

— (2019b): "La novela que no se escribió: Apostillas a 'El hombre que amaba a los perros'", in: id., *Agua por todas partes*, 127–173.

Turner, Mark (2004): "The Way We Imagine", in: *Journal of Consciousness Studies* II/5–6, 90–115.

White, Hayden (1980): "The Value of Narrativity in the Representation of Reality", in: *Critical Inquiry* 7/1, 5–27.

# Rewriting Gender?
## (De)constructions of Masculinities between Scientific Discourse and Literary Practice

Riccardo Schöfberger (University of Graz)

## 1. Introduction

Facts were put on the table and promptly challenged when feminist journalist Alice Schwarzer and anti-feminist essayist Esther Vilar met for a TV debate on WDR in February 1975.[1] An exchange of views over the topical issue of whether women in West Germany were actually oppressed by men or vice versa had failed due to the vehement rejection of the opposing arguments and had shown the incompatibility of their respective standpoints right from the start. Subsequently, reference was made to scientific data, in order to seek a fact-based way out of the dilemma. Schwarzer and Vilar tried to let the facts speak for themselves,[2] but it turned out that these facts – as common scientific denominators – allowed for opposing interpretations. Both opponents relied on the same surveys, such as the recently published *Die Wirklichkeit der Hausfrau* (*The Reality of Being a Housewife*) by sociologist Helge Pross. However, Vilar interpreted Pross's finding that housewives – in despite of objective disadvantages – were subjectively satisfied with their lives[3] as a mere validation of her thesis[4] that women led de facto a better life than men, while Schwarzer proposed to question the private notion of 'life satisfaction' politically.[5] This

---

1 Cf. Schwarzer/Vilar 1975.
2 Cf.: "Now let's be very concrete, let's leave the metaphysical level, let's talk in facts and figures." (Ibid.: 10:36–10:41) All translations by R.S.. Page numbers in the running text always refer to the original texts.
3 Cf. Pross 1975: 169–200.
4 Cf. Vilar 1973 [1971]: 117–128.
5 Cf. Schwarzer 1975: 214–219.

deconstructive approach would also soon characterize Schwarzer's book *Der 'kleine Unterschied' und seine große Folgen* (*The 'Little Difference' and Its Big Consequences*), in which she tried – in analogy to numerous writers of the time – to rewrite the facts in women's lives.

During the same September days in 1975 when Schwarzer's main text was first available in West German bookstores, a similar debate was sparked in Italy. *Effe*, Italy's first and most widespread feminist magazine, published an article that due to its critique of the leading media's portrayal of feminisms can also be read as a renegotiation of previously valid notions about gender relations. In her opinion piece "Il femminismo secondo 'Il Corriere della Sera'" ("Feminism According to 'Il Corriere della Sera'"),[6] essayist Carmela Paloschi deconstructed a few clauses from the column "Non è femminista la donna bandito" ("The Woman Bandit Is Not a Feminist"),[7] recently published in the newspaper *Corriere della Sera* by Gabriella Parca – a feminist journalist herself, who had become known in the 1960s for the earliest science-oriented surveys of the behavior of Italian women and men.[8] In the Italy of the 1970s, marked by terrorisms and the abortion debate, Parca had now tried to show with figures and data that no factual link between emerging feminisms and terrorisms could be proven.[9] Paloschi was by no means concerned with refuting this thesis, but she did want to make the premises visible that had moved Parca to her query in the first place. Thus, the 'old' feminist assumption that 'new' feminisms posed a threat to men could hide a new fact – that more and more feminists were not aiming at a war against men but rather at a collaborative rewriting of gender and, thus, at "the invention of a world without power."[10]

The abovementioned debates are emblematic of the processes of validating, challenging, and negotiating traditionally accepted gender notions and

---

6    Cf. Paloschi 1975: 9.
7    Cf. Parca 1975: 5.
8    Cf. Parca 1965 and 1959. Parca's surveys are quite comparable to those later published by Pross (cf. in addition to the aforementioned study on housewives, the one on men, which appeared three years later). With regard to the science-orientation, see especially the subtitle of Parca 1965: "A rigorous investigation carried out throughout Italy using scientific criteria".
9    Cf. "The figure of the female bandit therefore has nothing to do with the emancipation of women [...]. [...] it is certainly not by shooting, that we can delude ourselves that we have achieved gender equality." (Parca 1975)
10   Paloschi 1975, 9.

the legitimacy of feminisms in the early 1970s. Declaring something as fact or fact-based served to either affirm or undermine traditional or innovative gender conceptions. In these processes, facts – that is, notions concerning gender considered to be universally true and stable, but paradoxically used selectively and for incompatible arguments – gained a powerful and challenging role. At that time, a (de)construction of gender-related facts promoted the scientification and circulation of feminist discourses, as well as several legislative changes and introductions.[11] But it also posed a male dilemma that oscillated between an uncertainty in light of the deconstruction of traditional masculinity and the need for a pro-feminist collaboration.[12] Consequently, writings positioned towards feminisms commonly dealt with gender-related facts, in order to propagate, discuss or counteract the "normative power of 'facts'"[13] in a phase of journalistic, scientific, and literary boom. To better understand these processes, I will examine two literary and two science-oriented texts published between 1973 and 1975 in German-speaking countries as well as in Italy: *Montauk* by Max Frisch and *Caro Michele* by Natalia Ginzburg, as well as *Der Untergang des Mannes* by Volker E. Pilgrim and *Maschio per obbligo* by Carla Ravaioli. By comparing these texts, I would like to stress that the powerful and challenging role of gender-related facts becomes understandable by looking at the interrelations between scientific discourse and literary practice. Accordingly, an analysis of the textual interrelations can be particularly suitable to illuminate the affirming, refuting, or subversive functions of facts. If the early 1970s are regarded as a first peak of the intensifying debate on gender issues after 1968,[14] this trend can also be seen as a consequence of manifold relations between European and US-American feminist discourses. By participating in these discursive relations, the selected texts show fundamentally different ways of dealing with the same gender dilemmas. In this respect, the comparison of texts from different cultural areas is meant to emphasize the diversity inherent to processes of validation and representation of facts. Since it is precisely at this time that masculinity increasingly came

---

11  Cf. Kahlert 2003: 87, and Bock 1988: 54. Cf., e.g., the introduction of the divorce law in Italy in 1970, the introduction of the right to abortion in the German Democratic Republic in 1972 and in Austria in 1975, and the reform of family law in Italy in 1975 and in the Federal Republic of Germany in 1976.
12  Cf. Krammer 2018: 135–136, Bellassai 2011: 126–137, and Schneider 1974: 113–116.
13  Daniel 2001: 18.
14  Cf. Bojar 2022: 28–38.

into the focus of feminist renegotiations as a construct in need of explanation and change, in this paper I will shed light on the (de)construction of masculinity-related facts and propose this as a complementary perspective to grasp the rewriting of gender in the early 1970s. Specifically, I will show that the two science-oriented texts, i.e. Ravaioli's and Pilgrim's, aim at affirming the feminist (de)construction of masculinity and supplementing it with new perspectives, while the two literary texts, i.e. Ginzburg's and Frisch's reflect and problematize an uncertainty that accompanies such groundbreaking processes.

## 2. Natalia Ginzburg and Carla Ravaioli: Rewriting the Facts of Male Dis-/Reorientation

> Il mondo ora è pieno di questi ragazzi, che girano senza scopo da un posto all'altro. Non si riesce a capire come invecchieranno. Sembra che non debbano invecchiare mai. Sembra che debbano restare sempre così, senza casa, senza famiglie, senza orari di lavoro, senza niente.[15]

At the beginning of her 1973 essay "La condizione femminile" ("The Female Condition"), the Italian writer Natalia Ginzburg wrote that she did not love feminism, although she shared all of its practical demands.[16] What she rejected was essentially the deconstructive approach advocated by Schwarzer and Paloschi – especially since she believed to recognize in feminism an "attitude of the mind" (182) that challenged stable notions of gender. In this regard, she spoke of "a vision of the world that, in the end, does not reflect reality" (183) and attributed it to a tendency towards abstraction that would produce a loss of facts. This abstraction would supposedly replace the true/false

---

15  "The world is now full of these young people, wandering aimlessly from one place to another. There is no telling how they will grow old. It seems like they should never grow old. It seems like they should always stay this way, with no home, no families, no work schedule, no nothing." (Ginzburg 1973: 71–72)

16  Cf.: "I don't love feminism. I do, however, share everything the women's movements demand. I share all or almost all of their practical demands." (Ginzburg 1974: 182–183)

dichotomy with moral claims,[17] and thus produce unstable, unsettling, and incorrect gender conceptions. Moreover, by favoring women, this feminist tendency would disregard the "fatto, noto e indiscutibile" ("noted and indisputable fact") (182) that there are no qualitative but only mutual differences between men and women[18] – a fact becoming more glaring than ever in the early 1970s, as she pointed out. Nonetheless, it is noteworthy that Ginzburg's position concerning gender differences was rather ambivalent, since she had already criticized 'female' writing in previous decades: She deemed it too abstract and emotional, whereas she wanted to approach 'male' writing, which she believed to be more sober and fact-based, as she stated in a 1963 interview with essayist Oriana Fallaci.[19] This ambivalence can also be observed in light of her 1949 essay "Il mio mestiere" ("My Craft"), in which Ginzburg wrote that she has been terrorized by the idea of being recognized as a female writer,[20] while in 1963 she claimed that a woman should write 'like a woman' but again strive for the abovementioned 'masculine' qualities.[21]

This is arguably the reason why a similarly plain writing style still characterizes *Caro Michele* (*Dear Michele*) In this epistolary novel, published in 1973, Ginzburg deals with the issue of a radical loss of facts in an era of feminist and terrorist uncertainty. Here, the time after 1968 appears to be shaped by the difficulty of assigning clear meanings to increasingly isolated, contradictory, and fragmentary facts. Indeed, the fictional facts regarding the central figure of Michele can be summarized quickly: At the age of 21, he leaves his dying father, his lonely mother and a pregnant girlfriend in Rome and moves to England – a few months later he is killed during a student protest in Belgium. However, the letters that relatives and friends write to and about him feature perspectives that are incompatible with one another and therefore

---

17  Cf.: "In feminism, at the center are not [...] the false and the true, but [...] revenge, vindication, humiliation and pride." (Ibid.: 184)
18  Cf.: "Feminism assumes that women [...] are better than men. [...] Qualitatively, they are equal. The difference between man and woman is the same as the difference between the sun and the moon, or between day and night." (Ibid.)
19  Cf.: "To write like a man means to write with the detachment, the coldness of a man. Something women are rarely capable of." (Fallaci 2015 [1963]: 321)
20  Cf.: "I terribly wanted to write like a man back then, I was terrified that somebody could tell I was a woman from the things I wrote." (Ginzburg 1962: 80)
21  Cf.: "A woman must write like a woman but with the qualities of a man." (Fallaci 2015 [1963]: 321)

do not allow a definitive interpretation of these few facts. It remains uncertain, for instance, whether Michele fled from entanglements with family or with terrorism, whether he is really the father of the child, and why he is finally stabbed in Bruges.[22] In *Caro Michele*, the possibility of knowing, saying or thinking anything with absolute certainty is largely prevented. The resulting discomfort is stressed by Ginzburg, showing the need for facts as more urgent than ever for the post-1968 era. As a prime example, it was also hitherto necessarily the case that "to know if one is the child of another [man], there are no safe systems" (167) – nevertheless, that the scientific proof of paternity is considered indispensable for family cohesion appears as a novel phenomenon here. Michele's obscure destiny appears in the novel not as an individual example but rather as representative of an entire generation that is devoid of home, family, and memory, wandering the world "aimlessly from one place to another" (71), eventually dying for abstract ideals.[23] This conflict between the facts of life and the pursuit of fictional ideals particularly affects young men. In contrast to the more practical and active female figures, all young men are unsuccessful artists or writers and are depicted as being out of touch with reality, as well as weak in decision-making, and sexually indecisive.[24] The failed painter Michele, described in the letters alternately as homosexual and as "ambidextrous," (107) i.e. bisexual, is neither able nor willing to fulfill his parents' expectations of him as the "only male child." (7) He lacks the pragmatism of his sisters and cares as little for his potential offspring as he does for his terminally ill father. When his father eventually dies, Michele explains neither his absence at the funeral nor his renunciation of the inheritance. Therefore, the apparently fact-based masculinity is replaced by an "absence of man"[25] and a gender-related void, the filling of which Ginzburg will reflect in later essays and novels.[26] In this context, Michele's indifference towards a ruinous tower left to him by his father, which neither the sisters nor other characters want to preserve, appears as symbolic[27] in view of a renunciation of supposedly stable orientations to masculinity: "[…] you never

---

22   Cf.: "[…] these are all hypotheses. In truth we don't know anything and all we will be able to know will be other hypotheses." (Ginzburg 1973: 174)
23   Cf.: "Above all I thought that young people were dying, that young people were risking death […] for political or pseudo-political reasons." (Ginzburg 1999: 144)
24   Cf. Bazzocchi 2018: 105.
25   Therein, Ginzburg will recognize a motif central to *Caro Michele*. (Cf. 1999: 144)
26   Cf. Minetti 2018: 118.
27   Cf. Niefanger 2021: 663–664.

think about the tower. Viola and Elio wanted to buy it from you, but they went to see it and were disappointed [...]. And then this tower looks like it will fall down if you just touch it." (120–121) These male figures' discomfort with the behavioral patterns expected from them in family and romantic relationships should be considered in light of Ginzburg's above-mentioned essayistic diagnosis about the occurrence of an unsettling loss of facts in the early 1970s. In *Caro Michele*, masculinity is depicted as a normatively transmitted, albeit now blurred relationship between sociocultural meanings and anatomical conditions. Ginzburg's representation aims at illustrating and emphasizing a new cultural discomfort.[28] As she will clarify in a 1990 interview, she attributed this unease to the productive correlations between feminist demands, changing gender roles, and a pervasive cultural, social, and political upheaval in the 1970s:

> Ma, io credo che negli anni settanta ho sentito che circolava un disagio, e mi sembrava che derivasse da quest[a] [rottura culturale]. [...] c'è anche qualcosa nel femminismo che non mi piace, voglio dirlo. Io certo che sono femminista [...] però il femminismo ha creato un qualcosa di competitivo che non mi sembra giusto [...]. E questo fa sì che le donne, oggi, sentano molto la solitudine, e gli uomini non sanno che ruolo avere, e le donne sanno che ruolo avere, però sentono la mancanza degli uomini. [...] E penso che se ho raccontato qualcosa, forse, nei miei romanzi, ho cercato di raccontare questo: la solitudine delle donne e la fragilità degli uomini.[29]

With this statement, Ginzburg points out a dilemma that is apparent in both her examined texts: Although feminisms would have reinforced the orientation of women, the former asymmetry of roles that had to be fought against has now been reversed to the detriment of disoriented men. Indeed, it is especially in regard to masculinity that the relationship between facts and established interpretations appears to be undermined by her texts. By doing so,

---

28  Cf. Solte-Gresser 2014: 73–74.
29  "But I think in the seventies I felt that there was a discomfort circulating, and it seemed to me to derive from that [cultural rupture]. [...] I want to say that there is also something in feminism that I don't like. Of course, I am a feminist [...] but feminism has created something competitive that doesn't seem right to me [...]. And this makes women, today, feel a lot of loneliness, and men do not know what role to assume, and women know what role to assume, but they miss men. [...] And I think that if I have told something, perhaps, in my novels, I have tried to recount this: the loneliness of women and the fragility of men." (Ginzburg 1999: 184–185)

Ginzburg takes a dismissive stance towards the feminist deconstruction of facts. Nevertheless – as she would also partly acknowledge in the following years[30] – she employs a merely provisional knowledge of coeval feminist theories for her writing. It was neither true that all feminist positions advocated a superiority of women, nor that they renounced a fact-based rewriting of gender conceptions.

For it was precisely male disorientation, which Ginzburg depicted as a downside of feminisms and as the painful consequence of a loss of facts, that was considered by feminist essayist Carla Ravaioli to be a symptom of a desired reorientation of men and an indisputable fact. As she argued, the phenomenon was inspired by feminist demands, but in the first place it could point out already existing dilemmas of masculinity. She wrote that in the early 1970s, more and more men began to question the role assigned to them on the basis of biological characteristics: "Symptoms that this may happen, or rather that it is happening with increasing frequency, are not lacking. [...] today young men especially do not seem to agree so much anymore: being a king does not seduce them anymore."[31] She authenticated this shift as a fact through sociological references and she used it as a starting premise for her science-oriented text *Maschio per obbligo* (*Male Out of Obligation*) in which she argued that most positions within the women's movement still disregarded the fact that a normative commitment to traditional gender roles was no longer satisfactory for many men either. Therefore, challenging the relationship between gender and role would be necessary for men: "[...] the battle for the liberation of the male from the fictitious role to which he has been condemned is just another face of the liberation of the woman." (back cover) Ravaioli proposed – perhaps for the first time in Italy – a scientific perspective on masculinity, to foster a rewriting of facts and a pro-feminist rejection of the sex-role concept. What is remarkable about her text is that the traditional relationship between anatomical conditions and sociocultural meanings is viewed as a fiction, resulting in a 'destiny' that must be refuted: "[...] the male role is a prefabricated destiny no less than the female one."

---

30  In 1990, Ginzburg said in an interview that her critique of 'female' writing as inherently 'sticky' had been based on past beliefs; in the same interview, she also conceded that equality between men and women had, in fact, still not been achieved entirely and everywhere. Nevertheless, she emphasized her conviction that feminisms could only endorse a partial, namely a 'female' view of the world. (Cf. ibid.: 29–30, 185–187)

31  Ravaioli 1973: 10.

(9) While Ginzburg deplores the undermining of this relationship as unsettling, Ravaioli sees in male discomfort a discomfort with masculinity itself. By deconstructing the deterministic relationship between biological sex and sociocultural gender, she seems to reinforce an emerging feminist thesis that developed at the same time in other cultural areas too and still appears discursively effective today.[32] Since she believes that the reference to biological knowledge is hiding the danger of an allegedly 'natural' legitimation of traditional masculinity (cf. 21–22), she finds it more effective to deconstruct cultural knowledge and the genesis of gender-related facts and attributions taking place within it. By pointing out the constructiveness of gender, she attempted to open up a conceptual space for the development of new ideas about masculinity: "For women as for men, it is a matter [...] of beginning to modify culture by modifying themselves [...]." (73) Ravaioli argues that male uncertainty was based on the difficulty of living up to the myths and ideals of patriarchal masculinity, and proceeds to validate this through the textual examination of an extensive corpus of advertising material, literary texts, and schoolbooks.

---

32   Cf., e.g., Repo 2016: 84, and Schwarzer 1975: 190–194.

## 3. Max Frisch and Volker E. Pilgrim: Rewriting the Facts of Male Lives

> Über Liebe, als Beziehung zwischen den Geschlechtern, gebe es nicht Neues mehr zu berichten, das habe die Literatur dargestellt in allen Varianten ein für allemal, das sei für die Literatur, sofern sie diesen Namen verdient, kein Thema mehr – solche Verlautbarungen sind zu lesen; sie verkennen, daß das Verhältnis zwischen den Geschlechtern sich ändert, daß andere Liebesgeschichten stattfinden werden.[33]

The necessity for a reassignment of gender-related facts can concurrently be found in texts by Max Frisch. The Swiss writer firstly positions himself towards feminisms in *Tagebuch (Journal)*, in which he evokes – under the heading "WOMEN'S LIBERATION"[34] – the symbolic image of a facts-demanding woman and a snoring man, who had discussed the naturalness or construction of the differences between women and men without being able to find a common and fact-based way out of the dilemma. Frisch later also steers towards the same topic in his autofictional story *Montauk* (1975). "He is resolutely in favor of it, [...] nothing is more urgent in our society,"[35] he has himself say – under the analogous heading "WOMAN'S LIBERATION" – to his young lover Lynn during an American weekend recounted in *Montauk*. Here, the two days form the starting point for an examination of the "Tatbestände" ("facts of the case") (122) regarding his destructive love relationships, first and foremost the one with Austrian writer Ingeborg Bachmann. It is exactly Bachmann whom he quotes at the beginning of the story to explain the truth claims of his ex-

---

33   "There is nothing new to report about love as a gender relationship, literature has presented that in all its variants once and for all, it is no longer a topic for literature, if it deserves this name – such statements can be read; they fail to recognize that gender relationships are changing, that other love stories will take place." (Frisch 1975: 89)
34   Frisch 1972: 373. English original.
35   Frisch 1975: 89. The following heading is English original.

amination: "TRUTH IS REASONABLE TO HUMAN BEINGS." (24)[36] On the same page, Frisch attributes the fact that this claim is to be accompanied by a rewriting of his masculinity to the influence of Philip Roth's recently published novel *My Life as a Man* (1974), which also deals with a destructive love relationship: "Why would I shy away from the German title: Mein Leben als Mann? I want to know what I, writing under the compulsion of art, learn about my life as a man." (24)

This project, which Frisch wants to realize "without inventing anything" (82) and using an objectifying third-person narrative – from which he expects, as he writes in *Tagebuch*,[37] greater knowledge of the truth – takes the form of a confessional writing. The resulting search for facts and meaning aims at resolving the dilemma of whether he should feel guilty for his destructive vice "MALE CHAUVINISM" (94, English in the original) or whether the misery in his love relationships could be explained by an intrinsic misunderstanding between men and women.[38] However, the attempt to assign to the facts of his life new meanings that would also be valid from a feminist standpoint fails because of his belief that cross-gender writing is still impossible in a language that does not implicitly reproduce the existing gender power relations. As initially assumed by the abovementioned snoring man in *Tagebuch*, and later suggested by Frisch as a plausible response to the dilemma of whether gender relations are biologically fixed or culturally constructed, the women's movement itself had so far failed because "women do not have their own grammar for their way of thinking but are dependent on male language"[39] and on "categories of male thinking." (371) Probably for this reason he wrote to Bachmann in the 1950s that "We need the representation of man by woman, the self-representation of woman." (90) In light of this necessity, Frisch's disorientation towards feminist demands could be attributable to the paradoxical fact that *Montauk* contains a representation of women by a man, and the self-representation of a man. For if a male writer inevitably reproduces male supremacy and domination by writing his 'life as a man,' a pro-feminist collaboration of men through writing can only seem futile.

---

36  Cf. also Bachmann 1959: 2:39–2:42.
37  Cf.: "For the purpose of confessional literature (maximum uprightness towards yourself), the third-person form is more appropriate." (Frisch 1972: 310)
38  Cf. John-Wenndorf 2014: 403.
39  Frisch 1972: 148.

While the belief in an inherently different genesis of facts and meanings in men and women is reminiscent of Ginzburg's ambivalent aspiration for 'male' writing, in Frisch's writing this seems to be accompanied by a tendentially essentialist understanding of gendered writing. On the one hand, Ginzburg's separation of 'female' and 'male' writing still considers the possibility for female writers to approach a writing that traditionally seemed reserved for men – a possibility which recalls the Woolfian ideal of an incandescent-creative "androgynous mind."[40] On the other hand, in Frisch's texts it is precisely this blending of gender categories that seems unthinkable and impossible. As a result, he claims that he can only write about women "my invention, my draft on their nature" (118) and that, in his love relationships, he "always live[s] in ignorance of the situation." (139) Eventually, this finding leads him to invite a deconstructive reading of his own text: "THIS IS AN HONEST BOOK, READER/ AND WHAT DOES IT HIDE AND WHY?" (197) A recounted talk with an American student, who does not ask the usual questions of secondary literature but questions whether the central figure of Frisch's novel *Stiller* really wants his wife to be redeemed or rather wishes to be her redeemer can be considered emblematic of this. (Cf. 18) Since a deconstruction of gender-related facts is occurring in this passage, Frisch's writing can only give a partial answer to this question – as to his initial question of guilt – because, according to him, he can provide merely a 'male' answer, and not one that is valid regardless of gender.

A similar representation of a man thinking "[...] all in opposites and contradictions, not in associations and unions,"[41] and almost unknowingly wielding destructive power, can also be found in one of the earliest German-language texts proposing a science-oriented perspective on masculinity: *Der Untergang des Mannes (The Downfall of Man)*. Starting with the motto "The man is socially and sexually an idiot" (10), writer and activist Volker E. Pilgrim positioned himself – concurrently with Ravaioli – towards the feminist thesis that there is no deterministic relationship between sex and gender while attempting to validate this as a fact through an often paltry – but symptomatic of earliest men's studies – examination of psychoanalytic and ethnological texts. He argued that feminist scholars have proven Freud's dictum "Anatomy is destiny"[42] to be fiction "wrapped in a scientific construction." (152) Both in

---

40 Woolf 1993 [1929]: 52.
41 Pilgrim 1973: 193–194.
42 Freud 2000 [1924]: 249.

Pilgrim's and Ravaioli's texts, the importance of Freud's thesis is striking. Being both restrictive and suggestive, its function is remarkably homogeneous: positioning the writer in the ongoing debate about the fixed or fluid quality of gender roles and relations. Thus, in texts such as Vilar's *Der dressierte Mann* (*The Manipulated Man*) and Wilhelm Bittorf's "Der anatomische Imperativ" ("The Anatomical Imperative"),[43] the deterministic relation between anatomy and destiny is revisited as a kind of pre-scientific fact and seen as foreshadowing affirmation of traditional female roles. Conversely, in both selected texts, Freud's thesis is questioned as an outdated factual relic and taken as an occasion for a re-writing of gender-related facts. Hence, for Pilgrim and for Ravaioli, it became an indisputable fact that neither anatomy determined destiny, nor that nature determined man. Nevertheless, men would continue to destroy nature, women, and themselves.

What is remarkable about *Der Untergang des Mannes* is that in view of a male reorientation, that Pilgrim considered indispensable, he proposed to question the factual relationships of men with women, whereas in Frisch's text a similar approach turned out to be inadequate to answer the question of male guilt. Particularly in light of a pro-feminist collaboration between men and women, Pilgrim suggested that the hitherto tacitly legitimized male domination must now be scrutinized and questioned substantially: "In order to learn fundamental things about the woman, it is not yet possible to ask what *she* wants. Instead, the man must be examined: what does *he* want from the woman, how does *he* relate to her?" (70, original emphases) In such a framework, a rejection of the belief in an incompatibly 'male' or 'female' genesis of facts and meanings seems to come gradually into focus, since both gendered perspectives are first understood as culturally different, but they can then become compatible with each other. On the one hand, the mood of upheaval or even decline prevailing in Pilgrim's text may recall Ginzburg's depiction of feminisms as both the consequence and the source of an unsettling paradigm shift in the early 1970s. On the other hand, in this case we find an attempt not merely to deplore a loss of facts and the rejection of traditional notions of gender but to write new facts in order to motivate cross-gender acknowledgment of feminist discourses.

---

43  Bittorf 1975.

## 4. Conclusions

The texts I have selected have one thing in common: they address a destabilizing dilemma concerning the meaningfulness of gender relations and roles – a dilemma that became topical in the early 1970s.[44] Within feminist discourses, this perspective corresponded to the deconstruction of a deterministic relationship between anatomical conditions and sociocultural meanings, as well as to the construction of new gender conceptions. All the authors I have examined saw the necessity to position themselves towards this paradigm shift and an arising male dilemma through writing. However, the processes of validating, challenging, and negotiating facts taking place in these texts differ fundamentally. In her epistolary novel, Natalia Ginzburg shows that an unambiguous interpretation of plain facts has become problematic in the post-1968 era and diagnoses a disorienting loss of facts that has afflicted masculinity. In his autofictional story, Max Frisch sees irreconcilable gender differences in the genesis of facts and meanings. This is the reason why he is finally denied a rewriting of the facts of his "LIFE AS A MAN" (152, English in the original) and of his relationships with women in a meaning that would also be valid from a cross-gender perspective. In contrast, it is precisely the deconstructive undermining of normative and essentialist gender differences that motivates both Carla Ravaioli and Volker E. Pilgrim to outline a male reorientation through a (de)constructive rewriting of sociocultural facts and meanings. Both science-oriented texts attempt to confirm and alter the gender status quo by advancing a collaborative rewriting of gender-related facts and thus enabling innovative perspectives. Conversely, an altering or rejecting depiction of gender discomfort accompanying these processes and the aesthetic problematization of these perspectives are reserved for the literary texts. Since all the selected texts – like both introductory debates – concern the same gender dilemmas but deliver fundamentally different ways to acknowledge them, the presented comparison highlights the fact that the processes of (de)construction and representation of gender-related facts are diverse, contradictory, and controversial.

---

44  Cf., e.g., Rigoletto 2014: 139, and Kosta 2001: 224.

## Bibliography

Bachmann, Ingeborg (1959): "Aus der Rede Ingeborg Bachmanns zur Verleihung des Hörspielpreises der Kriegsblinden vom 17. März 1959 in Bonn", in: https://www.mediathek.at/portaltreffer/atom/1571A721-0A5-00013-00 000CD4-15711836/pool/BWEB/ (03.01.2022).

Bazzocchi, Marco Antonio (2018): "L'estinzione della specie maschile. Caro Michele di Natalia Ginzburg", in: Spinelli (ed.), *Mascolinità nella letteratura italiana contemporanea*, 105–116.

Bellassai, Sandro (2011): *L'invenzione della virilità. Politica e immaginario maschile nell'Italia contemporanea*, Rome.

Bittorf, Wilhelm (1975): "Der anatomische Imperativ", in: *Der Spiegel* (30.06.1975), 42–43.

Bock, Ulla (1988): *Androgynie und Feminismus. Frauenbewegung zwischen Institution und Utopie*, Weinheim/Basel.

Bojar, Karen (2022): *Feminist Organizing Across the Generations*, London.

Daniel, Ute (2001): *Kompendium Kulturgeschichte. Theorie, Praxis, Schlüsselwörter*, Frankfurt am Main.

Fallaci, Oriana (2015) [1963]: *Gli antipatici*, Milan.

Freud, Sigmund (2000) [1924]: "Der Untergang des Ödipuskomplexes", in: id.: *Studienausgabe. Band 5: Sexualleben*, Frankfurt am Main, 243–251.

Frisch, Max (1975): *Montauk. Eine Erzählung*, Frankfurt am Main.

— (1972): *Tagebuch 1966-1971*, Frankfurt am Main.

Ginzburg, Natalia (1999): *È difficile parlare di sé. Conversazione a più voci condotta da Marino Sinibaldi*, ed. Cesare Garboli/Lisa Ginzburg, 1999.

— (1974): "La condizione femminile", in: id.: *Vita immaginaria*, Milan, 182–190.

— (1973): *Caro Michele. Romanzo*, Milan.

— (1962): "Il mio mestiere", in: id.: *Le piccole virtù*, Turin, 71–88.

John-Wenndorf, Carolin (2014): *Der öffentliche Autor. Über die Selbstinszenierung von Schriftstellern*, Bielefeld.

Kahlert, Heike (2003): "Weibliche Autorität in der Wissenschaft. Dekonstruktion der herrschenden Denktradition", in: Niekant, Renate/Schuhmann, Uta (eds.): *Feministische ErkenntnisProzesse. Zwischen Wissenschaftstheorie und politischer Praxis*, Opladen, 81–103.

Kosta, Barbara (2001): "Väterliteratur, Masculinity, History", in: Jerome, Roy (ed.): *Conceptions of Postwar German Masculinity*, Albany, NY, 219–242.

Krammer, Stefan (2018): *Fiktionen des Männlichen. Männlichkeitsforschung in der Literaturwissenschaft*, Vienna.

Minetti, Beatrice (2018): "Il vuoto del maschio. Stereotipi e anti-stereotipi della maschilità nei romanzi di Natalia Ginzburg", in: Spinelli (ed.), *Mascolinità nella letteratura italiana contemporanea*, 117–127.

Niefanger, Dirk (2021): "Turm/Leuchtturm", in: Butzler, Günter/Jacob, Joachim (eds.): *Metzler Lexikon literarischer Symbole*, Stuttgart, 663–664.

Paloschi, Carmela (1975): "Il femminismo secondo 'Il Corriere della Sera'", in: *Effe* 8 (09.1975), 9.

Parca, Gabriella (1975): "Non è femminista la donna-bandito", in: *Corriere della Sera* (12.08.1975), 5.

— (1965): *I sultani. Mentalità e comportamento del maschio italiano*, Milan.

— (1959): *Le italiane si confessano*, Florence.

Pilgrim, Volker E. (1973): *Der Untergang des Mannes*, München.

Pross, Helge (1978): *Die Männer. Eine repräsentative Untersuchung über die Selbstbilder von Männern und ihre Bilder von der Frau*, Reinbek bei Hamburg.

— (1975): *Die Wirklichkeit der Hausfrau. Die erste repräsentative Untersuchung über nichterwerbstätige Hausfrauen: Wie leben sie? Wie denken sie? Wie sehen sie sich selbst?*, Reinbek bei Hamburg.

Ravaioli, Carla (1973): *Maschio per obbligo. Oltre il femminismo verso l'abolizione dei ruoli istituzionali*, Milan.

Repo, Jemima (2016): *The Biopolitics of Gender*, New York.

Rigoletto, Sergio (2014): *Masculinity and Italian Cinema. Sexual Politics, Social Conflict and Male Crisis in the 1970s*, Edinburgh.

Schneider, Peter (1974): "Die Sache mit der 'Männlichkeit'. Gibt es eine Emanzipation der Männer?", in: *Kursbuch* 35, 103–132.

Schwarzer, Alice (1975): *Der 'kleine Unterschied' und seine großen Folgen. Frauen über sich – Beginn einer Befreiung*, Frankfurt am Main.

Schwarzer, Alice/Vilar, Esther (1975): "TV Duell: Esther Vilar vs Alice Schwarzer (February 06.1975), in: https://www.youtube.com/watch?v=-NufFVuXN84 (20.12.2021).

Solte-Gresser, Christiane (2014): "Literaturwissenschaftliche Masculinity Studies am Beispiel der Erzähltexte von Natalia Ginzburg", in: Fellner, Astrid M./Conrad, Anne/Moos, Jennifer J* (eds.): *Gender überall? Beiträge zur interdisziplinären Geschlechterforschung*, St. Ingbert, 65–94.

Spinelli, Manuela (ed.) (2018): *Mascolinità nella letteratura italiana contemporanea*, Paris.

Vilar, Esther (1973) [1971]: *Der dressierte Mann*, München.

Woolf, Virginia (1993) [1929]: *A Room of One's Own and Three Guineas*, London.

# The Loss of Biodiversity in the Anthropocene and Its Representations in Literature and the Arts (Late 20th and Early 21st Century)

*Annette Simonis (University of Giessen)*

## 1. Introduction

Nowadays an increasing ecological awareness is not only present in public and political discourse but can also be traced in European literature since the beginning of the 21st century. The rising interest in ecological topics has inspired a number of novels and best-selling books in the course of the last two decades. On the first image, I have arranged a selection of recent book covers illustrating the sudden emergence of ecology in contemporary literature (see figure 1). This is just a random collection of recently published titles, including fictional works and literary essays without any claim to completeness.

Among the favored topics of the last few years is the ongoing extinction of natural species due to climate change and the destruction of natural environment – a precarious development and phenomenon which scientists also call the loss of biodiversity.[1]

Writing about these issues in fictional works evidently transcends the entertaining qualities of narratives usually expected when talking about popular fiction and other iconic aesthetic works. What exactly characterizes this new wave of narratives and aesthetic essays aiming at distributing knowledge or intensifying our awareness of the risks at stake if our natural environment and its seemingly abundant resources steadily diminish and disappear?

The topics of ecological concerns such as climate change, species extinction, and loss of natural habitats have inspired many writers and artists

---

1 See the illuminating multidisciplinary collection of articles in *Loss of Biodiversity*, ed. Sharon L. Spray/Karen Leah McGlothlin 2003.

*Figure 1 showcases the surge in topical literature focusing on ecological problems like climate change and species extinction.*

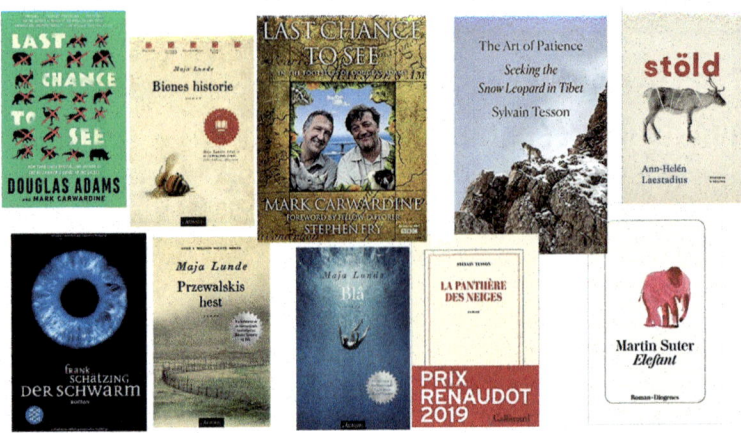

around the globe. Their works provide concise examples of a very productive and sometimes complex process of oscillation between fiction and fact.

Before I will discuss some of the most striking examples to illustrate this idea in more detail, it seems useful to briefly dwell on the notion of factuality and fictionality respectively. This raises the question in which sense the difference between the two concepts and their mutual interaction does apply to my material and my observations.

## 2. Factuality and Fictionality in Literary Texts and the Arts

When speaking about the fictional and factual aspects of literature and the arts in this article, I will resort to some implicit presuppositions and concepts which I would like to explain in the following part of my essay. We all have a common-sense notion of what is meant when talking about factuality or facts. This pre-scholarly, common idea is roughly summarized in the following definition in the *Collins Dictionary*: "Something that is factual is concerned with facts or contains facts, rather than giving theories or personal interpretations. Synonyms are: true, objective, authentic."[2] At first sight, this explanation sounds quite simple and straightforward. The current scholarly and philosophical definitions, however, are mostly much more subtle and far more comprehensive. As it turns out, the task of defining what exactly constitutes the 'mere facts' proves to be quite challenging when considered from a more philosophical perspective. The same holds true when approaching the problem from a narratological point of view. In their introduction to the recently published *Handbook of Factual Narrative* Monika Fludernik and Marie-Laure Ryan offer a diligent and complex definition including a considerable amount of critical reflection:

> Another issue raised by the notion of factuality concerns the rigidity of the distinction between true and false information. In classical logic, true and false are regarded as binary categories that do not admit of degrees. But while a factual text is meant to elicit belief in the receiver, this belief can be either weak or strong. Depending on the genre, audiences will grant factual texts various degrees of credibility, and they will be more or less tolerant of unverified or unverifiable information. In oral narrative of personal experience, for instance, audiences accept exaggerations, embellishments, and free reconstruction of dialogue, regarding the story as true in its broad outline.[3]

Fludernik's and Marie-Laure Ryan's approach seems very plausible and differentiated in many respects, although some questions still remain open to further discussion: What exactly are the deductions from their findings with regard to the relationship between factuality and fictionality within narratives, especially with reference to fictional texts? If the concepts of fact and fiction can no longer be considered a binary opposition, as Fludernik and Ryan rightly assume, what, then, are the further implications of this insight?

As we have seen, the terms factuality and fictionality are not mutually exclusive. They are not directly opposed to each other, either. In which way, then, are we to conceive of their mutual relationship? Fludernik and Ryan suggest a gradation, a range of various degrees of credibility. What precisely does this mean with reference to literary texts or works of art? At first sight, one might conclude that the more fictional and aesthetic elements a text or

---

2  See the straightforward entry "factual" in the online edition of the *Collins Dictionary*: https://www.collinsdictionary.com/dictionary/english/factual (27.04.2020).
3  Fludernik/Ryan 2020b: 11.

an aesthetic representation includes, the less authentic it is. This conclusion, however, does not sound quite convincing. As we will see below, the examples from my sample point in quite a different direction.

In fact, I would like to argue that it is often quite misleading to assume that factuality and fictionality in a given text are inversely proportional, i.e. that the credibility of the facts would be diminished by the fictional framework. Employing aesthetic or poetic elements does not necessarily diminish the factual aspects of the representation, the attribution of authenticity. On the contrary, our awareness of the means of construction may even enhance the effect of authenticity, the impact of a narrative or a sequence of images.

Evidently, fictional and aesthetic elements in literary texts and other media prove to be more than a mere framework that could be isolated from its factual content. They are part of the aesthetic expression, which is in turn intricately interwoven with the factual core or meaning. The process of reception is often much more subtle than the simple choice between true or false, authentic or fictitious. Our disposition to believe in the authenticity of a given text depends on genre conventions and expectations as well as the cultural and historical context shared by the author and his or her readers.

In this sense, fictional works can be far more compelling and more poignant than reports and analyses. Their powerful appeal to our imagination, which is in turn rooted in a collective or cultural imaginary shaped by multiple artistic, literary and aesthetic traditions, exerts a considerable impact on our perspectives, our cognitive and emotional response. In so far, there can be no doubt that fictional texts substantially contribute to our cultural knowledge in general and to our individual knowledge in particular. Knowledge or insight can be considered as being based on a more or less convincing interpretation of facts,[4] be it empirical observations or scientific experiments, whereas the 'bare facts' themselves are largely inaccessible to the human mind.[5]

Binary oppositions like the one between fact and fiction, or truth and invention, are theoretical constructions, whereas in reality the boundaries are fuzzy and fluid.[6]

---

[4] Cf. for instance Danto 1984.
[5] Cf. the interesting study on Nietzsche by Gori 2019: 62.
[6] As Ryan has shown, narrativity itself is also characterized by a certain degree of fuzziness. (Cf. Ryan 2007)

In the following, the interrelatedness and various interactions between factual and fictional aspects can be explored in more detail with reference to the continuous loss of biodiversity which undoubtedly constitutes an urgent problem and a considerable social and political issue. In order to illustrate the impact of the issues and problems implied, let me quote from an extract from the European Commission's 2030 *Biodiversity Strategy Paper*:

> Plant and animal species are disappearing at an ever faster rate due to human activity. What are the causes and why does biodiversity matter? Biodiversity, or the variety of all living things on our planet, has been declining at an alarming rate in recent years, mainly due to human activities, such as land use changes, pollution and climate change.[7]

The European Commission presented the new 2030 Biodiversity Strategy in May 2020, "following calls from the Parliament in January 2020 to address the main drivers of biodiversity loss and set legally binding targets."[8]

In how far and in which respect does this topic constitute a larger concern that is not only negotiated by politicians and sociologists but has also attracted much attention in recent cultural studies? In her seminal study *Imagining Extinction: The Cultural Meanings of Endangered Species* Ursula K. Heise points out aptly:

> We are currently facing the sixth mass extinction of species in the history of life on Earth, biologists claim – the first one caused by humans. Activists, filmmakers, writers, and artists are seeking to bring the crisis to the public's attention through stories and images that use the strategies of elegy, tragedy, epic, and even comedy. *Imagining Extinction* is the first book to examine the cultural frameworks shaping these narratives and images.[9]

This conception of cultural imaginings, as proposed by Heise, is indeed very illuminating and entails further questions relevant for a detailed investigation.

> How, when, and why do we invest culturally, emotionally, and economically in the fate of threatened species? What stories do we tell, and which ones do we not tell, about them? What do the images that we use to represent

---

[7]  https://www.europarl.europa.eu/news/en/headlines/society/20200109STO69929/biodiversity-loss-what-is-causing-it-and-why-is-it-a-concern (27.04.2022).
[8]  Ibid.
[9]  Heise 2016: Cover text.

them reveal, and what do they hide? What kind of awareness, emotion, and action are such stories and images meant to generate? What broader cultural values and social conflicts are they associated with?[10]

In her book, Heise draws attention to the circumstance that there is a large number of tales and documentaries on the mass extinction of species that participate in certain literary and aesthetic genres and thus employ typical literary devices and narrative strategies which can best be analyzed by literary historians. It is noteworthy that her focus is on stories and images – both constituting powerful means of aesthetic expression.

In the following second part of my article, I would like to take a closer look at some of the recent fictional texts on the extinction of species, the ongoing anthropocene and the human animal relationships involved. My examples have moreover in common that the visual experience is prominent, either on a level of figural language, including metaphors and imagery, or by the use of intermedial compositions of texts and images.

## 3. Forms of Storytelling Oscillating between Factual Documentation and Fictional Narrative

My first example is drawn from the iconic novel by the Norwegian best-selling author Maja Lunde, *The History of Bees* (*Bienen Historie*), which was first published in 2015. The time frame of the narrative is quite sophisticated and multidimensional, but the first part is clearly revealed as a dystopian outlook on the year 2024, because it starts by mentioning the name of the female narrator and by offering a precise specification of time and place: TAO, District 242, Shirong, Sichuan, 2098. The beginning of the first chapter presents a detailed depiction of the Chinese woman at work, performing her daily labor in a large field of fruit trees:

> Like oversize birds, we balanced on our respective branches, each of us with a plastic container in one hand and a feather brush in the other. I climbed upwards, very slowly, as carefully as I could. I was not cut out for this, wasn't like many of the other women on the crew, my movements were often too heavy-handed. I lacked the subtle motor skills and precision required. This

---

10   Ibid.: 165.

wasn't what I was made for, but all the same I had to be here, every single day, twelve hours a day.[11]

The powerful image of the human being moving as an oversized bird among the branches of a tree, in order to perform the task of pollination usually attributed to animal agents like bees and other insects, functions as an interesting metaphor for the anthropocene. The impact of the opening passage largely relies on the immediate visual presence of the somewhat grotesque and enigmatic bird-like figures clumsily moving on the branches and accentuates the precarious efforts taken by human beings in order to substitute animals and compensate for their loss. The readers are thus stimulated to visualize the scene and search for answers as to what has necessitated such actions. When first reading this passage, I regarded the image and the action described as a poetical invention typical of dystopian novels. As the discussion by readers and critics in social media and reviews reveals, many readers believed the idea of people climbing into trees in order to pollinate the blossoms to be purely fictional. This misleading conclusion is apparently inspired by the genre framework of the dystopian novel, stimulating the readers' expectation of a society controlled by a totalitarian regime and dealing with future inventions and cultural techniques yet unknown. Hand pollination, however, has become a common practice in the province of Sichuan in China after the bees became extinct in the region, as a prize-winning documentary *More than honey* (2012) has reported in detail. This documentary by Swiss director Markus Imhoof has been rightly praised for its revealing insights and diligent scientific research and has become known as "most successful documentary of the year."[12]

In an interview, Imhoof explained his motives and the methods of his investigation: "It was just a view I chose – of what would happen if we didn't have any bees. I travelled to four farms in China where they were doing hand pollination. I chose one employing mainly women."[13] Imhoof's documentary film thus provided detailed information about the global situation of endangered honeybees and, to a certain degree, made the vanishing of the bees accessible to cultural knowledge.

---

11  Lunde 2017 (Kindle edition, no page numbers).
12  https://www.austrianfilms.com/news/en/more_than_honey_wins_lola_for_best_docu mentary (27.04.2022).
13  Interview with Markus Imhoof 2012.

The film has indeed been very successful, yet three years later Maja Lunde's novel almost immediately became an international bestseller and reached an even wider international audience. Lunde's book has attracted even more attention than the film and, especially in Germany, stimulated diverse activities and initiatives to save the bees as well as a veritable flood of novels and narratives dealing with the topic. Apparently, popular fictions like Lunde's novel are more liable to alert the readers' awareness and trigger their emotional and personal response than other discourses and sources of information.

As a second example, I would like to briefly touch upon another popular novel, entitled *Elefant*, by Swiss author and screen writer Martin Suter. In Suter's novel, significantly, the title figure is an animal agent, a pink miniature sized elephant which turns out to be the product of genetic manipulation, a so-called glowing animal well-known to specialists in this field of scientific research. Usually, glowing animals serve as indispensable instruments in the investigation of diseases like aids and cancer and the production of possible remedies: In 2011, researchers from the U.S. and Japan used the green protein to help them monitor the activity of a gene they had inserted into cats which helps them resist the feline form of Aids. Cats are one of the few animal species that are normally susceptible to such viruses and scientists say that the experiment is designed to help better understand Aids in both cats and humans.

These scientific data and facts have been presented to a larger public in diverse journal articles since their discovery around 2008. Let me quote an instructive passage from an article recently published in an internet journal:

> Pigs that glow from inside out and glow-in-the-dark cats and dogs may sound, and look, pretty ridiculous, but scientists are increasingly using genetically modified animals in an effort to help them understand diseases that affect humans. One way they are doing this is by inserting fluorescent proteins, generally a green protein found in the Aequorea Victoria jellyfish, into animals, making them glow. The fluorescent proteins help scientists to monitor the performance of genes that they have altered. The pioneers of this method were even awarded the 2008 Nobel prize in chemistry for their efforts.[14]

---

14   Bloomfield 2013, in: https://www.mic.com/articles/40527/7-genetically-modified-animals-that-now-glow-in-the-dark-thanks-to-science (27.04.2022).

In the case of the glowing elephant in the novel, however, the motives of his origin were commercial and illegal. But this information is not revealed to the reader and the human protagonists of the novel from the very beginning. The first encounter of the elephant in the book, therefore, sounds like a passage from a fantasy novel and, consistently, it resorts to the typical genre characteristics of "hesitation,"[15] as described by French critic Tzvetan Todorov in his famous introduction to fantastic literature. From the point of view of the human protagonist, a homeless person called Schoch who found the animal in his retreat, the appearance of the pink elephant constitutes a marvel and a mystery which he cannot easily explain, oscillating between thinking he is still drunk after a hangover or having indeed encountered a supernatural being. The opening passage is subtly recalling these literary components of fantasy with Schoch acting as an unreliable witness:

> It couldn't be withdrawal syndrome as he'd had plenty to drink. Schoch tried to focus on the object. A child's toy, a tiny elephant as pink as a marzipan piglet, but more intense in colour. And glowing like a pink firefly, right at the back of the hollow, where the ceiling of the cave met the sandy ground. [...] He closed his eyes and tried to get something like sleep. But then he had a 'merry-go-round', which was what he called those states of inebriation when everything started spinning the moment he crawled into his sleeping bag. In all these years he'd never managed to put his finger on what caused drunkenness to become a merry-go-round. [...] everything was still spinning. Maybe it was something to do with the weather. [...] He'd never found out whether it was better to keep his eyes open or closed either.[16]

Significantly, the protagonist hesitates and seems to doubt the existence of the small pink elephant, while confronted with the enigmatic animal. He observes it more closely, yet he still cannot make up his mind about the nature of the phenomenon.

> Schoch opened them. The toy elephant was still there, but it appeared to be a little further to the right. He closed his eyes again. For a moment the little elephant spun beneath his eyelids, leaving a streak of pink. He immediately wrenched his eyes open. There it was, flapping its ears and lifting its trunk into an S-shape. Schoch turned over onto the other side and tried to stop

---

15 Todorov 1975: 25.
16 Suter 2018.

the spinning. He fell asleep. Schoch crept out of his sleeping bag and tried to breathe deeply to calm the pounding of his heart. What he could see wasn't a hallucination. You couldn't touch hallucinations. But what was it? A miracle? A sign? Something mystical?[17]

While Schoch is still wondering and hesitating, the narrative exactly corresponds to the genre conventions of fantastic literature. According to Tzvetan Todorov, the protagonists of fantastic tales and the readers find themselves in a situation of uncertainty about the nature of the phenomena encountered or described. Thus, they experience a characteristic process of oscillation between confirming the observations and doubt, a hesitation that can be perpetuated till the end of the narrative. In this respect, Martin Suter's novel toys with the genre expectations of fantasy and speculative fiction without ultimately confirming them. Again, scientific phenomena and factual aspects are disguised as fictitious and while we primarily consider them as typical elements originating in the vivid imagination of an ingenious novel writer, they are gradually revealed as realistic elements – whose real-life counterparts are forming part of our contemporary reality. The text establishes an interesting relationship between the scientific discourse on glowing animals and the prototypical genre expectations of fantastic literature as described by Todorov. On the whole, the retardation of insights into the factual phenomena seems to enhance the impact of the knowledge rather than to diminish its effect, because it comes to most of the readers as a sudden revelation.

## 4. Representations of the Loss of Biodiversity in Contemporary Artist Books

As we have seen above, rhetorical and metaphorical techniques serve a double function in the narratives focusing on biodiversity loss. On the one hand, they underscore the aesthetic quality of the text and intensify the reading experience. On the other, they also trigger a cognitive process in the readers that ultimately leads to insights into the scientific aspects of the phenomena in question. When popular novels negotiate issues originating from scientific research, they contribute to the dissemination of expert knowledge and

---

17   Ibid.

stimulate their readers to participate in the discussion of the possible consequences and implications.

Apart from the novel, there is another very successful and more subtle literary genre which presents and illuminates the extinction of species in the age of the anthropocene, namely the 'bestiary'[18] in the form of the artist book. In this literary genre, texts are accompanied by images, paintings or photographs, which greatly enhances their impact on the reader. The intermedial framework provides a very powerful means of commemorating and retracing the extinction of species caused directly or indirectly by the agency of human beings in the anthropocene.

Fascinating examples of the mutual interaction and interplay of facts and aesthetic elements can be found in the work of Errol Fuller, a British writer, artist and animal painter, who has published a whole series of artist books dedicated to the subject matter of endangered animals. These artist books combine zoological texts and personal observations with outstanding drawings and paintings. The book design is expensive and also artistically designed.

Fuller's recent book *Lost animals* surprisingly dispenses with colorful illustrations. Instead, it is based on a collection of black and white photographs from the early twentieth century. The author elaborately explains his motivation and the reasons for this choice of rather inconspicuous images:

> When friends or acquaintances thumbed through the book a peculiar and unexpected thing became very noticeable. They were attracted by the high quality of the paintings, of course, but they were truly riveted by the photos. They would pause over them and just gaze, sometimes even raising the book towards their eyes in the vain hope that this action would allow them to see more – more than there really was to see! Almost always the same question cropped up. "Is this real or have you just faked it?" All this was despite the fact that most of these images were, inevitably, poor in quality (for many were taken in difficult circumstances in the early days of photography), and showed little detail.[19]

He further elaborates this idea with reference to the special aura encapsulated within ancient photographs, poignantly enhancing the sense of irretrievable loss:

---

18   Cf. Simonis 2017a.
19   Fuller 2014: 8.

> It seems that a photograph of something lost or gone has a power all of its own, even though it may be tantalisingly inadequate. But despite all of the handicaps, these photos are evocative and moving records of creatures that are gone. They are close enough to touch – almost, but not quite![20]

The passage quoted above also explains why Fuller refused to digitally remaster the pictures. The aesthetic design and selection of media, i.e. in this case the choice of old photographs, are crucial and interwoven with the central functions of cultural memory, the slow and incomplete process of reconstruction by memory:

> A photograph of an animal long-gone evokes a feeling of loss more than a painting ever can. Often tinted sepia or black and white, these images were mainly taken in zoos or wildlife parks, and in a handful of cases featured the last known individual of the species.[21]

The book includes rare black and white photographs of various extinct mammals and birds like Tasmanian wolves, ivory-billed woodpeckers, and the quagga which looks like a hybrid of horse and zebra. (See figure 2 and 3)

Another book about endangered or mostly extinct animals, which is to a certain extent comparable to Fuller's collection, has been published by the author Luc Semal and the photographer Yannick Fourié. The work is entitled *Le Bestiaire disparu. Histoire de la dernière grande extinction*, assuming the role of providing a chronicle of recent species extinction. The considerable size and expensive design of the volume indicate that the genre, again, is the artist book. Each double page offers a complex intermedial composition which consists of a small miniature picture, i.e., a painting of the animal species in question, followed by a larger text on the left page while the page on the right contains a full-size photograph of a museum exhibit, a stuffed animal, also called taxidermy. Notably, the background color of the photos is frosted black throughout the book.

The photographic images were taken by Yannick Fourié in the Dutch museum *Naturalis* in Leiden. Apart from the expected naturalist descriptions of the species, their scientific Latin name, their appearance, distributions, natural habitats, etc., the texts often include small narratives, mostly anecdotes about the fate of individual animals. They tell memorable stories with comic

---

20   Ibid.
21   Ibid.

*Figure 2: Tasmanian wolf (Thylacinus cynocephalus) Image of a juvenile male thylacine at Hobart Zoo taken by B Sheppard in 1928. Sadly, the animal died the day after it was photographed.*

or tragic elements often illustrating the human animal relation before the species became finally extinct. These fictional elements are characteristic of Semal's bestiary. At the same time, the photographs enhance the impression of constituting a well-designed work of art beyond mere embellishments. They are aesthetic objects, employing subtle techniques to attain special effects. The overall impression conveyed by the dark background color is that of melancholy and mourning.[22] The photographs thus testify the irreversible loss of species (involving numerous individual deaths), the loss of biodiversity, and, at the same time, they appeal to the readers' imagination and initiate a process of collective mourning or cultural commemoration.

One critic has noted that the lighting of Fourié's photographs is sparse and selective, sometimes leaving part of the animals' face in the dark as is the

---

22   Cf. Simonis 2017b.

*Figure 3: A quagga mare at the London Zoo in 1870; this is said to be the only specimen photographed alive. Contributed by Harvard University, Museum of Comparative Zoology, to the Online Biodiversity Library: https://www.biodiversitylibrary.org/page/28201475/#page/209/mode/1up*

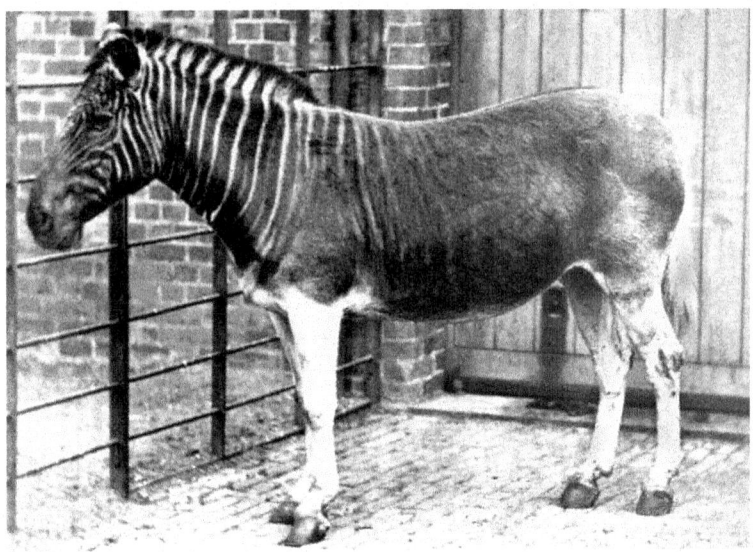

case in the picture of the Java tiger.[23] The critic considered this as a technical deficiency, not noticing the aesthetic aim of the strategy. The shadowy part of the pictures and the highlighting of selective parts of the animal body are intentional because they contribute to the dominant impression of fragmentation, defiguration and decomposition. Since the species presented in Semal's bestiary cannot be revived, there seems to be a cultural need of commemorative work, a kind of collective grief work ('Trauerarbeit'). When examining the anecdotes more closely, this crucial impression is confirmed on the textual side of the volume.

The small narratives often recall a harmonic relationship between the human beings and animals before the contact is disturbed and disrupted by

---

23   Alberti 2014, in: https://www.spektrum.de/rezension/buchkritik-zu-bestiarium/1322037 (20.04.2022).

death or the moment of extinction. It seems that those species which appeared trustful and friendly to humans were on the whole even more prone to extinction.

Here are two examples highlighting this fatal relationship:

There is an anecdote about a laughing owl (Ninox albifacies) from New Zealand who proved a Musical Owl: "He could still be lured from his hiding place in the rocks after dark by the sound of an accordion. The bird would then pass silently over the musician and, finally landing nearby, would listen until the music stopped."[24] (See figure 4)

The anecdote quoted above is embedded in an elaborate account of the species' characteristics, the date and particular circumstances of its first discovery, and the multiple reasons for its extinction. Similar embedded narratives about the interactions of individual animals with human beings can be found throughout the volume. Some of them showcase the deplorable outcome of these interactions and the premature deaths of the animals.

Then, for instance, a highly revealing anecdote about a Falkland Fox from the Falkland Islands can be found:

> Captain John Strong and his crew there discovered a curious canine, half wolf, half fox, the only land mammal on this uninhabited archipelago. The animal was so docile that they tamed one and embarked it as a mascot on their ship, the Welfare. He lived like this for several months with the sailors, until an encounter with the French fleet ended up in a violent cannonade: terrified, the beast jumped overboard and drowned.[25]

In the case of the Falkland Fox the death of the individual animal serves as a metaphor and anticipates the moment of species extinction.

In Semal's bestiary of extinct animals, the structure of the texts as a whole turns out to be quite complex. They provide scientific biological information as well as fictionalized material in the form of snapshots of individual memories which include fictional and subjective aspects. Accompanied by the powerful visual dimension of artistic photographs, the function of the book clearly goes beyond providing factual information, though this might have been the primary intention of its authors. The elaborate structure and design of the

---

24   Semal 2014: 86.
25   Ibid.: 66.

*Figure 4: Male laughing owl mount from the collection of Naturalis Biodiversity Centre, Naturalis Biodiversity Center/Wikimedia Commons*

book seek to involve the readers in a multidimensional cultural process of commemorative work, appealing to their imagination and provoking an emotional as well as an intellectual response.

## Bibliography

Alberti, Jürgen (2014): "Nur noch Erinnerung", in: *Spektrum*, https://www.spektrum.de/rezension/buchkritik-zu-bestiarium/1322037 (20.04.2022).

Bloomfield, Aubrey (2021): "Biodiversity loss: what is causing it and why is it a concern?", in: https://www.europarl.europa.eu/news/en/headlines/society/20200109STO69929/biodiversity-loss-what-is-causing-it-and-why-is-it-a-concern (20.04.2022).

— (2013): "7 Genetically Modified Animals That Now Glow in the Dark Thanks to Science!", in: *Mic*, https://www.mic.com/articles/40527/7-genetically-modified-animals-that-now-glow-in-the-dark-thanks-to-science (20.04.2022).

"factual", in: *Collins Dictionary*, https://www.collinsdictionary.com/de/worterbuch/englisch/factual (20.04.2022).

Danto, Arthur C. (1985): *Narration and Knowledge: Including the Integral Text of Analytical Philosophy of History*, New York.

Fludernik, Monika/Ryan, Marie-Laure (eds.) (2020): "Introduction", in: *Narrative Factuality: A Handbook*, Berlin/Boston.

Fuller, Errol (2014/2021): *Lost Animals: Extinction and the Photographic Record*, London.

Gori, Pietro (2019): *Nietzsche's Pragmatism: A Study on Perspectival Thought*, Berlin/Boston.

Heise, Ursula K. (2016): *Imagining Extinction: The Cultural Meanings of Endangered Species*, Chicago/London.

— (2010): *Nach der Natur. Das Artensterben und die moderne Kultur*, Frankfurt am Main.

Imhoof, Markus (2012): "The bee whisperer was very busy. Interview with Mark Imhoof", in: *Exberliner*, https://www.exberliner.com/film/the-bee-whisperer-was-very-busy/ (20.04.2022).

— (2012): *More than honey*. Documentary.

Lunde, Maja (2017): *The History of Bees*, New York.

— (2015): *Bienes Historie*, Oslo.

Ryan, Marie-Laure (2007): "Toward a Definition of Narrative", in: *The Cambridge Companion to Narrative*, ed. David Herman, Cambridge, 22–35.

Semal, Luc/Fourié, Yannick (2013): *Le Bestiaire disparu. Histoire de la dernière grande extinction*, Toulouse. (German edition: Bern 2014).

Simonis, Annette (2019): "Intermediality in Twentieth Century Animal Poetry: Guillaume Apollinaire – Ted Hughes – Durs Grünbein", in: *Taking Stock –*

*Twenty-Five Years of Comparative Literary Research*, ed. Achim Hölter/Norbert Bachleitner, Leiden, 372–396.

— (2017a): *Das Kaleidoskop der Tiere. Zur Wiederkehr des Bestiariums in Moderne und Gegenwart*, Bielefeld.

— (2017b): "Le Bestiaire disparu/Das verschwundene Bestiarium. Zeugnisse kultureller Erinnerung an die Tierwelt als Ausdruck kollektiver Verlusterfahrung", in: *Comparatio* 9/1, 61–82.

Spray, Sharon L./Karen Leah McGlothlin (eds.) (2003): *Loss of Biodiversity*, Lanham/New York.

Suter, Martin (2018): *Elefant*, translated by Jamie Bulloch, New York.

— (2017): *Elefant*. Zürich.

Todorov, Tzvetan (1975): *The Fantastic: A Structural Approach to a Literary Genre*, translated by Richard Howard, Ithaca/New York. (French Original: *Introduction à la littérature fantastique*, Paris 1970).

# "One + One is one two. Two is one two"
# (De-)Construction of Facts and Documentarism in Hanne Darboven's *Schreibzeit* (1975-1999)

*Monika Voithofer (University of Vienna)*

## 1. Spatialization of Time

Numbers are one of the most elementary construction kits of our world. Among many other things, we also measure time in numbers. Events – whether subjective experiences or historical landmarks – are fixed to certain days, months, and years. Be it the day of one's birth, the day of death of important persons, the Ides of March or September 11, we all associate certain factual events with certain calendar days. And it is precisely such numbers that form the artistic frame of reference of the German conceptual artist Hanne Darboven (1941-2009). "One + One is one two. Two is one two. That is my original thesis for all the laws that mathematically run through my work. I write mathematical literature and mathematical music," is how Hanne Darboven described her aesthetic approach.[1] She saw herself less as an artist than as a constructivist: "I build something up by disturbing something (destruction – structure – construction). A system became necessary."[2]

In this respect, Darboven developed a very specific system for her artistic treatment of ciphers: They are added, combined and varied, written out in numbers or as words, visualized as lines or cubes and transferred into musical notation and thus her artworks oscillate between a kind of artistic arith-

---

1   As cited in: Kleine 2016: 53. Note: English translations of the quotes, unless otherwise indicated, are by the author of this paper, who takes full responsibility for any errors. Original quote: "Eins + Eins ist eins zwei. Zwei ist eins zwei. Das ist meine Urthese für alle Gesetze, die bei mir mathematisch durchlaufen. Ich schreibe mathematische Literatur und mathematische Musik."
2   Darboven 1999: 62.

metic and geometry in her frame of reference.[3] In so-called daily calculations ("Tagesrechnungen"), she adds up year and day data, resulting in cross totals ("Quersummen"), construction- or K-values ("Konstruktions- oder K-Werte"). Darboven always follows the same scheme she developed: the day and month of the Gregorian calendar are each treated as a unit and added to the last two digits of the calendar year, which are treated as separate, to determine the construction value. Her birthday, as an example, 29 April 1941, results in the construction value 38 in the calculation $29 + 4 + 4 + 1$ while her date of death on 9 March 2009 would correspond to the calculation $9 + 3 + 0 + 9 = 21K$. These ascertained values are the foundation of her works and are represented geometrically, written out in words, transferred into letters of the alphabet or into musical notes.[4]

The moment of temporality gains a completely new dimension and meaning in this processual artistic procedure with calendar data: calendar data as, on the one hand, objective indications of the natural, cyclical course of time and, on the other hand, as an expression of the subjective experience of time, of one's own experiences and events in the sense of an individual and also collective culture of memory. As such 21 June 1905 (21+6+0+5=32K), to which Darboven repeatedly refers (among many other data as, for example, the day of death of Ulrike Meinhof, Mao Zedong or John Lennon) in her major work *Schreibzeit*, which will be dealt with in more detail later in this text, is not just the factual birthday of Jean-Paul Sartre. As a main representative of existentialism, his philosophy provides also significant impulses for the artistic work of Hanne Darboven. "My work is a recording in the sense of existence, it is working through," hence another characteristic quote from the artist about her artistic approach.[5]

By presenting individual sheets with the diverse representations of the daily calculations – which in Darboven's respective works often count several thousand – framed and hung on the walls of exhibition venues, the works gain an additional specific aesthetic quality of spatialization and visualization of the category of time. In their installation-like, yet processual character, the works create a relationship between the individual sheets that is no longer

---

3    Cf. Bippus 1999: 18–19.
4    On specific compositional techniques in Darboven's œuvre cf. Voithofer 2021.
5    Darboven, in: https://www.hanne-darboven.org/kuenstlerin/lebenslauf/ (26.05.2022). Original quote: "Meine Arbeit ist ein Aufzeichnen im Sinne von Dasein, es ist Durcharbeitung."

Figure 1: Hanne Darboven, "Schreibzeit" (1975-1999)

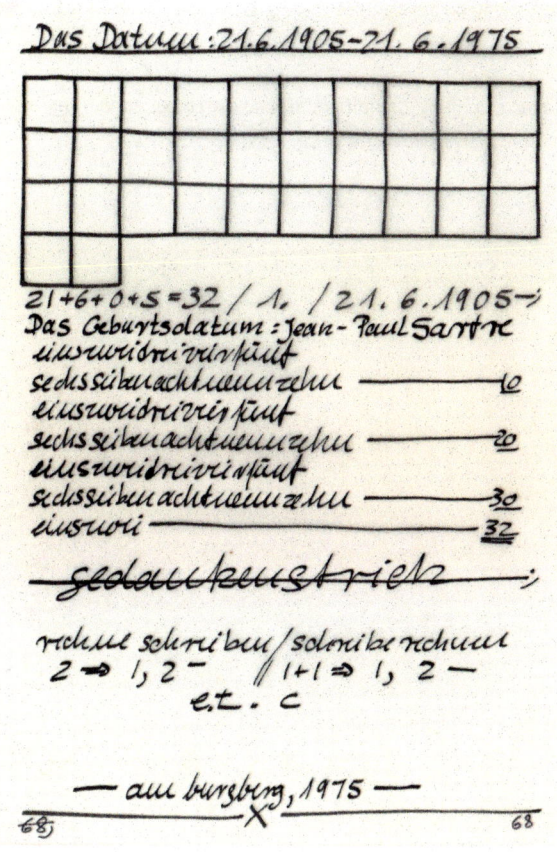

(c) Hanne Darboven Stiftung, Hamburg

merely horizontal but equally vertical, no longer merely unidimensional but equally anachronistical and intermedial and can be conceived as a total work of art.[6]

Working with numbers is something highly artificial. Ciphers are never mere objects that stand alone but always refer to something – a quantity, size

---

6   Cf. Bippus 1999: 20–21.

or, in this case, time. "It's not pure number and has other meanings. If I were making it up, I couldn't possibly write all that. It has to be totally simple to be *real* writing," says Darboven about her artistic approach to numbers.[7]

*Figure 2: Hanne Darboven, Exhibition "Hanne Darboven: Aufklärung – Zeitgeschichten. Eine Retrospektive", Munich, Haus der Kunst 2015*

(c) Hanne Darboven Stiftung, Hamburg

## 2. Writing Frenzy

Alongside arithmetic procedures, writing is the fundamental process in Darboven's œuvre. "Writing, not describing," is her artistic credo in this context.[8] From 1971 onwards, Darboven integrates a wide variety of text types into her work. In the extensive, lengthy, torturous process of transcribing texts – primarily in the German language –, such as the first five cantos from Homer's *Odyssey*, the epilogue from Bertolt Brecht's *Kriegsfibel*, excerpts from poems by

---

7   As cited in: Lippard 1976: 190.
8   As cited in: ibid.: 187. Original quote: "Schreiben, nicht beschreiben."

Kraus, Hölderlin, Brecht, Schwitters, Charles Baudelaire's *Les Fleurs du Mal* or Rückert's "Die Schöpfung ist zur Ruh' gegangen, o wach' in mir" and entries from the Brockhaus-Encyclopedia (such as "proletariat" ["Proletariat"] or the page "cauliflower to flower vases" ("Blumenkohl bis Blumenvasen"), it is the depiction of the internalization and incorporation of these very testimonies of time that is expressed in Darboven's works. The daily calculations ("Tagesrechnungen") are joined by the daily writing ("Tagesschrift") which in the form of uniformly meandering waves – art historian Elke Bippus speaks of "u-bows" ("u-Bögen")[9] as an adaptation of ditto marks used to mark word repetition – recreates in a mantra-like gesture the act of writing itself, the "writing without words."[10] Indeed, her daily writing with its undulating loops also reveals vibrant, rhythmic aspects. In reductionist, insistent repetition – a technique very similar to the procedures of minimal music – a spatial expansion of the perceptual dimension takes place.

Hanne Darboven's opus magnum is appropriately titled *Schreibzeit* (*Writing Time*). The majority of the work was written between 1975 and 1981, and it consists of a monumental volume of almost 4,000 pages, sorted into twenty numbered DIN-A4 and DIN-A3 binders which Darboven herself did not want to be understood as a work of art but as a "political-cultural-historical book" addressed to "everyone."[11] The lengthy process of creating *Schreibzeit* took over 20 years, during which Darboven assembled an extremely diverse wealth of material of text types spanning the end of the 18th century to the second half of the 20th century. Having provided the work with an index, one can consult it to find that its index of names lists about 1,100 entries.[12]

In its early parts, Darboven devotes herself to transcribing parts of *Die Wörter*, a German version of Jean-Paul Sartre's autobiographical book *Les Mots* (*The Words*); an interview with Sartre in the German news magazine *Der Spiegel* published in June 1975 on the occasion of his 70th birthday under the title "Ich müßte sehr niedergeschlagen sein" ("I should be very depressed"), in which Sartre comments on the fundamental importance of writing in his life; and the interview "Das ewig Weibliche ist eine Lüge" ("The eternal feminine is a lie") by Alice Schwarzer with Simone de Beauvoir, also published in *Der Spiegel* a year later in April 1976.

---

9   Cf. Bippus 1999: 19–20.
10  Cf. ibid.: 25.
11  Cf. Jussen 2000: 15.
12  Cf. Busche 1999: 146.

*Figure 3: Hanne Darboven, "Schreibzeit" (1975-1999)*

(c) Hanne Darboven Stiftung, Hamburg

The publication and production history of *Schreibzeit* is long and convoluted, in part due to the work's mammoth scope. It is worth providing a brief overview of its construction history, in order to also give a sense of the work as a whole. Darboven produced the largest part of *Schreibzeit*, more than 2,000 pages, in 1976. Two years later, in 1978, she created the self-contained work

*Bismarckzeit*, which she subsequently declared to be part of *Schreibzeit*.[13] In it, the artist engages – over the course of 900 sheets – with the historical Bismarck era. Or more precisely: She deals with the time of the Prussian Prime Minister and later Chancellor of the German Empire Otto von Bismarck in the period from 1850 to 1890 and sets it in dialogue with themes, events and politics of the then present, the year 1978. One can read not only the life data of Otto von Bismarck but also of his political opponent August Bebel – always accompanied by daily calculations on the respective calendar dates. Furthermore, a transcript of excerpts from the biography of Bismarck by Ludwig Reiners (published in 1970) and the cultural-historical account of that era by Rudolf Malsch (*Deutsche Kultur. Eine geistesgeschichtliche Fibel*, 1951) is interpolated into the work.[14] Darboven relates these historical documents in *Bismarckzeit* to then topical testimonies, such as, for example, an essay by Willy Brandt from 1978 printed in the *Sozialdemokratisches Magazin* with the title "Wir müssen wachsam sein" ("We must be vigilant"), in which Brandt refers to the anti-socialist laws passed under Bismarck. Connections are also made to everyday utilitarian objects from Darboven's personal collection of domestic objects, such as quotes from porcelain plates, like "Einer spinnt immer wenn 2 spinnen wird's schlimmer" ("One is always crazy when two are crazy it gets worse").

Moreover, in *Schreibzeit* Darboven also includes photographs of items that symbolize technological progress – from a cradle to a compass, a globe, a telescope, an ophthalmic optics device or a steam engine. While working on *Schreibzeit*, Darboven was also laying the foundations for her extensive collection of three-dimensional objects (such as everyday utilitarian objects, toys, antiques, musical instruments, mannequins, historical postcards, souvenirs, or objects she herself commissioned to be made), which are integrated into many of her installations, providing a further medial dimension to the work.[15]

It is not until the 1990s that Darboven added a prologue and an epilogue to *Schreibzeit* which consist of about 500 photographic reproductions of books. The prologue shows the photographic reproduction of pages from a historical publication on battles during the Seven Years' War entitled *Gespräche im Reiche derer Todten* (*Conversations in the Realm of the Dead*, 1792). The epilogue shows the 1975 financial record book of the "Strandhalle" in Over at the Süderelbe

---

13  Cf. ibid.
14  Honnef 1999: 37.
15  Cf. Kleine 2016: 52–53.

(close to Hanne Darboven's home and place of work, Hamburg-Harburg), in which the kiosk operator Helga Mahlwitz noted the sale of various drinks using tally marks.[16] After the publication of *Schreibzeit* in autumn 1999 by the Max-Planck-Institute for History in Göttingen, the work could be considered complete.

The historian Bernhard Jussen rightly asks how one should deal with *Schreibzeit* from a scholarly perspective as a volume of contemporary historical and art-historical documents which Darboven herself saw not as a work of art but as a "political-cultural-historical book."[17] Although *Schreibzeit* closely adheres to the format of scientific work with its pagination and source references, the work is, as it were, a fragmentation of individual- and world-history with its renunciation of "chronological linearity."[18] Jussen speaks of a "hermetic offer" of historiography in *Schreibzeit*.[19] Darboven is thus a chronicler and scriptwriter of her own deeply subjective experience of the world which she reproduces in her work according to her very own rules, using the detritus of popular history and ephemera, engaging therefore in a conversation with common daily experience through reproductions of weekly magazines or postcards.

## 3. Archival Art – Its Disclosure of Power Structures and Epistemology

In *Schreibzeit* – as in all of her works –, Hanne Darboven interweaves individual and collective memory by incorporating various semantic reference systems from history, politics and art. The essential moment here is the fusion of subjective experiences with historically recorded events. The contents are inextricably merged in their form and related to each other. Darboven refers to the extra-artistic reality of historical facts and critically reflects and comments on this seemingly objective reality. In doing so, she always makes her intervention in the documents clear and thus follows the artist's self-image as a commenting outsider, an engaged contemporary and a chronicler who must take a political stand.

---

16   Cf. Busche 1999: 155.
17   Cf. Jussen 2000: 28–30.
18   Cf. ibid.: 34.
19   Cf. ibid.: 40.

Jussen hence rightly points out that Darboven's approach differs fundamentally from that of historians, as she does not attach importance to completeness and linearity in the representation of history in her works. In this context, however, it can be asked whether it is not precisely through her artistic treatment of historical facts that the problematic nature of a general historiography as such, its fragility and gaps, are revealed. Under what criteria and conditions do historical narratives emerge? What is considered a historically important fact? What becomes the historical canon and by whom? What events, on the other hand, can be carelessly forgotten and why?

Furthermore, it can be questioned whether it is through her curation and reproduction of historical documents that her personal interpretation and socio-cultural imprint opens up new dimensions and perspectives on the representation of history (in the case of *Schreibzeit* to a very specific section of German cultural history). To what extent, then, does Darboven's work offer epistemological implications?

According to art historian Hans Dickel, Darboven's work examines historiography for its meaningfulness, puts it up for discussion and makes the political dimension explicit in the process: "By calling up historical data, facts and narratives and putting them up for disposal, she contributes to the deconstruction of 'history', disenchants it in its apparent meaningfulness. Instead of an overarching creation of meaning, modern artistic means are used to convey a questioning of meaning."[20] In returning to Darboven's statement, quoted at the beginning of this paper, in which she sees herself not as an artist but as a constructivist, it can be noted, that she disturbs a system – the system of historiography – deconstructs its structure, rebuilds it and reassesses it.

Art critic Hal Foster detects an "archival impulse" in contemporary art since the postwar period in currents and artistic movements such as conceptual art, institutional critique, and feminist art – to which Darboven must be related.[21] According to Foster, the archive is the starting point for those art practices that work with historical information. While Foster does not name

---

20  Cf. Dickel 2016: 104. Original quote: "Indem sie historische Daten, Fakten und Erzählungen aufruft, zur Disposition stellt, trägt sie zur Dekonstruktion von 'Geschichte' bei, entzaubert sie in ihrer scheinbaren Sinnhaftigkeit. Anstelle übergreifender Sinnstiftung wird mit modernen künstlerischen Mitteln eher eine Sinnbefragung vermittelt."
21  Cf. Foster 2004: 3.

Darboven amongst the artists he observes to possess such "impulse" (e.g., the Independent Group, Robert Rauschenberg, and Richard Prince), Darboven can decidedly be placed in this movement. Following Foster's definition of an archival art, her works are "recalcitrantly material, fragmentary rather than fungible, and as such they call out for human interpretation, not machinic reprocessing."[22] The selection of the documents is subject to the highly individual decision of the artist, who thereby takes a self-reflexive stance on her own identity, socio-cultural imprint, art tradition and political life. Foster also speaks of an "anomic fragmentation as a condition not only to represent but to work through." In proposing "new orders of affective association," archival art does not only represent but must also be interpreted.[23] Darboven uses documentary approaches, disrupts, and criticizes the traditional order and functioning of cultural memory. She brings questions of authorship and overlooked or failed ideas from art, philosophy, politics, or everyday life back into focus by installing a kind of counter or complementary memory.[24]

Philosopher Jacques Derrida draws attention to the original meaning of the word archive from the Greek *arkheion*:

> [...] initially a house, a domicile, an address, the residence of the superior magistrates, the *archons*, those who commanded. [...] The archons are first of all the document's guardians. They do not only ensure the physical security of what is deposited and of the substrate. They are also accorded the hermeneutic right and competence. They have the power to interpret the archives.[25]

In this respect, it can be stated that in *Schreibzeit* Darboven not only appropriates factual documents and events from history but also critically reveals and questions the process of archiving documents from history itself. That hermeneutic power of interpreting the archives, which was withheld from the archons, Darboven transfers into her work. She takes the right to (re)interpret factual reports, to place them in various non-linear contexts and to place everyday occurrences – the banal – alongside the supposedly important events or historical landmarks on equal terms. Patriarchal power structures

---

22 Ibid.: 5.
23 Ibid.: 21.
24 Cf. ibid.: 21–22.
25 Derrida 1995: 9–10.

of exclusion are thereby exposed. Questions of relevance and the "biographical unworthiness" of certain groups of people can thus be raised.[26] What and who should be included in a canon of history? What is worth preserving in an archive? Who determines what ultimately finds its way into cultural memory?

The selective documents of *Schreibzeit* are on the one hand a mirror of personal imprints, Darboven's role models and reference works. The great ancestors, who are still seen as influencing reference points of her own tradition – whether positively in the sense of providing important impulses or in the negative turning away from them – are hauntologically evoked.

On the other hand, *Schreibzeit* with the many and disparate archival documents gathered within it, can be read as an expression of cultural memory. In the 1920s, cultural studies scholar Aby Warburg worked out his theory of "social memory," to which the concepts of "cultural memory" and "cultural memory spaces" created by the cultural scientists Jan and Aleida Assmann were related and further elaborated. Cultural memory is a collective term for all the knowledge with which a specific group identifies itself in a specific framework; differentiates itself from other groups; and transmits, reproduces and adapts this knowledge. It is composed of "memory figures," significant events in the past, artistic products and "institutionalized communication."[27] In the self-reflexive debate, cultural memory always takes a stand on itself, is criticized and revised. As Jan Assmann notes: "Cultural memory exists in two modes: firstly, in the mode of potentiality as an archive, as a total horizon of accumulated texts, images, patterns of action, and secondly in the mode of actuality, as the stock of objectified meaning updated and perspectivized from a respective present."[28]

Darboven's artistic work with the archive is a "self-reflexive memory work." "For the artists are not concerned with technical memories, but with a 'treasure of suffering' in which they recognize an artistic fund," says Aleida Assmann.[29] *Schreibzeit* oscillates between individual and cultural memory

---

26  Cf. Schweiger 2009: 32.
27  Cf. Assmann 1988: 9–12.
28  Ibid.: 13. Original quote: "Das kulturelle Gedächtnis existiert in zwei Modi: einmal im Modus der Potentialität als Archiv, als Totalhorizont angesammelter Texte, Bilder, Handlungsmuster, und zum zweiten im Modus der Aktualität, als der von einer jeweiligen Gegenwart aus aktualisierte und perspektivierte Bestand an objektiviertem Sinn."
29  Assmann 1999: 22. Original quote: "Denn es geht den Künstlern nicht um technische Speicher, sondern um einen 'Leidschatz', in dem sie einen künstlerischen Fundus erkennen."

and is thus in a certain sense a mirror and affirmation of the current state of art's tradition anchored in cultural memory.

This documentarism, in which original, authentic documents on history find their way into the work, also has the epistemological potential to create knowledge. One learns not only something about the time from which the materials come but also about how archival studies deal with source material per se. Cultural studies scholar Susanne Knaller sees great potential in the strategies of artistic documentarism with regard to epistemological and ontological considerations as well as socio-critical functions. Documentarism brings concepts of reality, forms of time and models of truth up for discussion and is thus also helpful for meta-reflection on various discourses of science.[30]

Hanne Darboven incorporates history through her writing. *Schreibzeit* consists of the sum of its parts and works relentlessly and openly with ambiguities. In it one becomes aware that historiography is not a static end product but is subject to constant dynamic processes of established norms and values of a culture, in which new insights into the past are brought to light. By asserting the right to (re)interpret and (re)evaluate documents from the archives of history, Darboven not only demonstrates with her work the power to create knowledge but also offers facts that transcend aesthetic concerns.

## Bibliography

Assmann, Aleida (1999): *Erinnerungsräume. Formen und Wandlungen des kulturellen Gedächtnisses*, München.

Assmann, Jan (1988): "Kollektives Gedächtnis und kulturelle Identität", in: id./Hölscher, Tonio (eds.): *Kultur und Gedächtnis*, Frankfurt am Main, 9–19.

Bippus, Elke (1999): "Wiederholungen, Reihen und Netze. Zum Verhältnis von Konstruktionszeichnungen und Textarbeiten im Werk von Hanne Darboven", in: Hamburger Kunsthalle (ed.): *Hanne Darboven. Das Frühwerk*, Hamburg, 17–26.

Busche, Ernst A. (1999): "Hanne Darboven – Themen und Struktur der 'Schreibzeit' (1999)", in: Felix (ed.), *Hanne Darboven. Ein Reader*, 146–156.

---

30  Cf. Knaller 2010: 175.

Darboven, Hanne (1999): "Statement to Lucy Lippard", in: Alberro, Alexander/ Stimson, Blake (eds.): *Conceptual Art: A Critical Anthology*, Cambridge et al., 62–63.

— (n.d.): "Meine Arbeit ist ein Aufzeichnen im Sinne von Dasein, es ist Durcharbeitung", in: https://www.hanne-darboven.org/kuenstlerin/lebenslauf/ (25.05.2022).

Derrida, Jacques (1995): "Archive Fever. A Freudian Impression", in: *Diacritics* 25/2, 9–63.

Dickel, Hans (2016): "Deutsch-deutsche Kunstgeschichte am Beispiel von Hanne Darboven und Werner Tübke", in: *Zeitschrift für Kunstgeschichte* 79, 92–114.

Felix, Zdenek (ed.) (1999): *Hanne Darboven. Ein Reader*, Köln.

Foster, Hal (2004): "An Archival Impulse", in: *October* 110, 3–22.

Honnef, Klaus (1999): "Hanne Darboven – Bismarckzeit (1979)", in: Felix (ed.), *Hanne Darboven. Ein Reader*, 29–47.

Jussen, Bernhard (2000): "Geschichte schreiben als Formproblem: Zur Edition der 'Schreibzeit'", in: id., (ed.): *Hanne Darboven – Schreibzeit*, Köln, 12–42.

Kleine, Susanne (2016): "Biographie Hanne Darboven", in: Galerie Jette Rudolph (ed.): *Philip Loersch. Alphabet. Zur Ausstellung mit Hanne Darboven im Poolhaus Blankenese*, Berlin, 52–53.

Knaller, Susanne (2010): "Realismus und Dokumentarismus. Überlegungen zu einer aktuellen Realismustheorie", in: Linck, Dirck et al. (eds.): *Realismus in den Künsten der Gegenwart*, Zürich, 175–189.

Lippard, Lucy R. (1976): "Hanne Darboven. Deep in Numbers", in: id., *From the Center. Feminist Essays on Women's Art*, New York, 185–195.

Max-Planck-Institut für Geschichte (ed.) (1999): *Hanne Darboven. Schreibzeit*, Köln.

Schweiger, Hannes (2009): "Biographieunwürdigkeit", in: Klein, Christian (ed.): *Handbuch Biographie. Methoden, Traditionen, Theorien*, Stuttgart et al., 32–36.

Voithofer, Monika (2021): *"DENKEN, HÖREN, DA CAPO". Konzeptuelle Musik im 20. und 21. Jahrhundert: Eine Studie zu Genealogie, Materialität, Form und Semantik*, Dissertation, University of Graz.

# MEDIA AND WRITING PRACTICE

# An Iterative Poetics of Writing Facts
## Louis de Cahusac's *La Danse Ancienne et Moderne ou Traité Historique de la Danse* (1754)

Rita Rieger (University of Graz)

With *La Danse Ancienne et Moderne ou Traité Historique de la Danse*, published in 1754, the French dance theorist Louis de Cahusac (1709-1759) presents a revised collection and some new drafts of his articles on "Danse", "Ballet", "Geste", "Figurants", "Fêtes", and "Enthousiasm" written between 1751 and 1757 for Denis Diderot's and Jean le Rond d'Alembert's *Encyclopédie*.[1] With the aim of advancing the 'truth' about dance and hoping to be of some 'advantage' for future readers, as mentioned in the "Avant-Propos",[2] the treatise demonstrates the interrelation between 'writing' and 'fact' through the re-writing of ancient dance theories such as Lucian of Samosata's dialogue *On Dance*, the re-writing of own texts and the articulation of current innovations in mid-18th century European theatrical dance practice, characterized as *danse en action*.

As this paper elaborates, the treatise deals not only with the cultural practice of writing as a historical fact but also gives insight into how writing influences the facticity of facts when it comes to presenting coincidences with 'reality,' 'truth' or the results of some 'acts' and 'actions' in historical writings on dance. Scrutinizing the act of writing allows the discerning of specific types of 'writing facts,' which in the case of Louis de Cahusac's treatise rely on philosophical empiricism and sensualism and will be described in this article as a

---

1    Cahusac contributed with more than 120 articles especially on the topics of dance and opera to the encyclopedian project, where his entries are signed with the letter (B). The first edition of the *Traité Historique de la Danse* was published in 1754 in three volumes at La Haye by Jean Neaulme. The quotes in this article refer to the commented new edition published in 2004 by Nathalie Lecomte, Laura Naudeux and Jean-Noël Laurenti at Paris. (Cf. Cahusac 2004)
2    Cf. ibid.: 36–40.

poetics of iteration. Therefore, this contribution in a first part elaborates on the notions of 'fact,' 'writing' and 'iteration' and in a second one deepens the poetical analysis of the treatise with the aim to present three different types of an iterative poetics of writing facts.

## 1. On the Interrelation of Fact, Writing, and Iteration

The general understanding of 'fact' in European 18th century discourses and cultural practices shows an awareness of the difficulties the term implies as Denis Diderot's entry on "Fait" (Fact) in the *Encyclopédie ou dictionnaire raisonné des sciences, des arts et des métiers* demonstrates: To define 'fact' as the 'coming into existence of a potentiality,' which allows obtaining knowledge of facts by experience such as eye witnessing actions, monuments and artefacts or through oral and written tradition, does not prove to be a suitable characterization.[3] But it indicates the intricacy of the relation between 'truth' and 'fact' that can be analyzed from an ontological, epistemological or logical perspective.[4]

With regard to the ontological state of facts, Diderot proposes in the encyclopaedical entry a three-part classification: Facts are first considered as the acts of the divine which are studied by theology. Second, facts mean all phenomena of nature that are the matter of philosophy and third, facts refer to the actions of human beings which are transmitted by history. Each one of these is equally subject to criticism, particularly concerning the certainty of their facticity of which the verification always remains at least partly subjective since it relies on the faculties of man.[5] In relation to Louis de Cahusac's historical and aesthetic treatise, the second and third classes of facts are the most important ones, since the treatise reflects on the natural phenomenon of movement in dance and its history as well as on the related writing traditions.[6] Considering the ephemeral quality of any action, the way of its trans-

---

3   Cf. Diderot 1781: 786.
4   Cf. Fludernik/Ryan 2020a: 3.
5   Cf. Diderot 1781: 786.
6   With these reflections on historical facts Cahusac's treatise connects to recent studies in historiography. With regard to historical facts, Stephan Jaeger points out with reference to Paul Ricoeur's *Time and Narrative*, that facts are not given in documents but the result of a selection by the historian seen as a function regarding a certain problem. (Cf. Ricoeur 1984: 108 quoted in Jaeger 2020: 337)

lation into words and text becomes crucial particularly with regard to its pastness.

From the beginning of the establishment of the modern fact in science and history in 18th century, historiography has discussed methodological criteria for facts to deal with the unreliability of data and to confront the subjectivity, partiality, ideological prejudices or interests of the historian.[7] Already Diderot discusses the question of certainty in relation to facts: he explains that a person has to confront both, the obstacle of being mistaken and of being deceived by others in the process of perceiving a fact. This in turn depends on the specific disposition of the objects and the subjects involved. Because, on the one hand, the more simple and ordinary the fact is and the more gullible the person concerned is, the greater the level of certainty would appear to be. On the other, the more the person concerned is sensible and the more the facts considered show a certain complexity, the less the certainty of the facticity will be. Hence, dealing with facts challenges not only the acquired knowledge, but it also demands a critical dealing with the passions, prejudices and senses, because even if man relies on his experience, the impressions provoked by an object remain subjective, since their quality in two men can hardly be compared.[8] This leads Diderot to the conclusion that in the end all facticity remains bound to a certain belief.[9] In studying the writing of dance history and of contemporary dance practices, such beliefs become observable and with this the factualization of natural phenomena and human actions. Additionally, in Diderot's classification, the writing itself appears as fact in the sense of action, and serves as both the means and the result of factualization at one and the same time. But what do we mean by 'writing' and how can it be studied in historical texts?

Roland Barthes reflects on 'writing' as cultural practice in *Variations sur l'écriture* (1973). Inspired by Barthes, Rüdiger Campe and Martin Stingelin developed in their writing theories the concept of *Schreibszene* ('writing scene') as a methodological tool for text analysis.[10] Writing as scene results from the arrangement and interaction of heterogeneous elements like language, writing instruments, material and media technologies as well as the physical

---

7   Cf. Jaeger 2020: 338.
8   Cf. Diderot 1781: 787.
9   Cf. ibid.
10  Cf. Campe 2012: 269–282; Stingelin 2004: 7–21; Barthes 1994: 1535–1574.

dimension of gestures within the frame of a certain historical situation.[11] For Stingelin, the instability and heterogeneity of this constellation can also be problematized within the text. Hence, he differentiates between the historical *Schreibszene* (writing scene) and its thematization in the text, the *Schreib-Szene* with hyphen, to which this article refers with the 'written writing scene.'[12] For both scenes, the question of the frame, within which the writing process occurs allows the distinguishing of elements, actions, their relation and effects as accompanying or not belonging to the writing scene. Furthermore, the distribution of roles, for instance of writer, reader, or editor and the directing of the scene provide perspectives on how to approach the process of writing in literary studies. Within this variety of elements, this paper concentrates on the handling of language, the gestural dimension and the question of the direction of the writing scene.

In the context of 18th century dance theory, the gestural dimension unavoidably points at the expressive qualities of the non-verbal body that is discussed within dramatic and dance theories under the topic of 'mime,' particularly concerning the relation between gesture and the expression as well as transmission of emotion. Nevertheless, although Roland Barthes already refers to emotions in the act of writing in *Variations sur l'écriture*, the role of emotions in text production still is hardly explored, as Susanne Knaller remarks.[13] But, whereas Barthes focuses on the pleasure or the boredom as effects of the writing act from a mere physiological point of view,[14] Louis de Cahusac problematizes how passions can direct writing scenes in the sense of influencing the facticity of the content to be written about. Thus, in his treatise the relation between writing and fact is coupled with emotion. This trinity appears on two levels: First, as thematization of positive and negative emotions and their impact on writing. And second, when Cahusac's writing becomes visible as iteration due to the performativity of writing historical and aesthetic dance facts.

In cultural studies the term 'iterative' alludes to the concept of performativity, where it is discussed in relation to citation within the context of language philosophy, writing studies and theater studies.[15] 'Iteration' in the

---

11  Cf. Campe 2012: 270.
12  Cf. Stingelin 2004: 15.
13  Cf. Knaller 2017: 20.
14  Cf. Barthes 1994: 1560.
15  Cf. Wirth 2002: 9–60.

sense of 'citability' characterizes cultural practices in their reproducibility and theatricality.¹⁶ Informed by Jacques Derrida's general observation in *Signature Event Context*, writing as cultural practice is necessarily determined by a general iterability "which links repetition to alterity" so that writing can be legible in the absence of the addressee.¹⁷ For Derrida, a written sign is a mark that remains, but that also includes a "force of breaking with its context," since it can be removed from the contextual constellations of its inscription and by citation be re-contextualised under other circumstances.¹⁸ Writing in the sense of the mastery of sign-systems carries with it the general possibility of removal and grafting.¹⁹ Hence, the iterative handling of the sign system and its results constitute a fact of the writing scene. Looking at iteration in Cahusac's treatise on dance, the focus lies methodologically on the variation in repetition and its function for the production of facts that can be seen as an act of quoting, arranging and re-writing existing fragments.

With it, the meta-reflective question *What or who is directing the writing scene?* arises. Whereas the title of Cahusac's work evokes the factuality of the following lines by the generic concept of 'treatise' as well as by its specification as 'historical,' quite at the beginning of the "Avant-Propos" the author reflects on the question of whether the subject to be written about affects the writing mode, in other words, whether the passions transported and evoked by dance modify the mode of writing a historical and aesthetic dance treatise and consequently concern the written transmission of historical facts.

## 2. Fearing the Attraction of the Object: Paratextual Reflections on Writing a Dance Tract

The first paragraph of the "Avant-Propos" to the *Traité Historique de la Danse* enters in medias res, as it addresses the relation of an assumed objective perspective on historical facts of the writer and the affective impact of the study's object on the dance theorist:

---

16  Cf. ibid.: 42.
17  Derrida 1991: 90.
18  Ibid.: 92.
19  Cf. Wirth 2002: 28. See also the analysis of citation modes in Compagnon 1979. For the practice of patch-writing see the article of Doris Pany-Habsa in this volume.

Il est rare qu'on ne se passionne pas pour les genres d'étude que l'on s'est choisi. J'ai craint ce danger en écrivant cet ouvrage, et pour m'en garantir, je me suis rappelé mille fois les prétentions ridicules des différents maîtres du *Bourgeois gentilhomme*. | Je déclare donc, avant d'entrer en matière, que je ne crois point la danse la plus excellente chose qu'on puisse faire, et que je suis persuadé qu'il y a dans le monde des objets d'une plus grande importance que ne le sont même les beaux-arts.[20]

Whereas Cahusac's declaration concerning the little importance of dance in the second paragraph seems to quote a sworn statement and hence alludes to the juridical dimension of the semantic field of 'fact'[21] – which in a treatise on dance aesthetics cannot be taken otherwise than ironically – the written writing scene in the first paragraph refers to the writer's passion for the subject to be dealt with as a possible obstacle in the creation of historical or aesthetic tracts. Moreover, the writer confesses not only his reservation against an emotional disposition in the act of writing that would contradict the presumed ideal of an objective attitude of an enlightened dance theorist but describes the transformation of a certain required passion for dance into fear when it comes to writing about dance.

Starting from these meta-reflexive considerations of his own emotional disposition in writing the treatise, Cahusac generalizes his self-observation that in studying whatever object, one discovers its utilities and the pleasures it might evoke. And with this, he continues, it is difficult to know the studied objects and to write about them without expressing some considerations that they inspire and deserve. The more the insight advances, the stronger the affective relation of the writer to his object of study becomes : "On voudrait alors, pour l'honneur, pour la félicité de son siècle, faire passer rapidement les découvertes qu'on croit avoir faites, ses réflexions, ses vues dans l'âme de

---

20  Cahusac 2004: 35. "It is rare that one is not passionate about the kinds of study one has chosen. I feared this danger while writing this work, and to guarantee it, I remembered a thousand times the ridiculous pretensions of the different masters of the *Bourgeois gentilhomme*. | I therefore declare, before entering into the matter, that I do not believe Dance to be the most excellent thing that can be done, and that I am convinced that there are objects of greater importance in the world than even the fine arts." (All quotes follow the original orthography. If not indicated otherwise, all translations by R.R.)

21  See the diverse entries corresponding to 'Fait, jurisprudence' in the *Encyclopédie*. (Cf. Bocher d'Argis 1781: 787–791)

tous ses contemporains."[22] Concurrent to the enlightened discourse on *sensibilité*, critical thought is coupled with the aim of transmitting the knowledge gained, by addressing both the cognitive and sensual faculties of man. In Cahusac's writing this relation of rational and emotional disposition crystallizes in an aesthetic concept of enthusiasm, which is conceived as the director of vivid writing scenes as explored in his article on "Enthousiasme" for the *Encyclopédie*.[23]

In opposition to the common understanding of enthusiasm as a kind of 'delusion' or 'mania' that masters or even spares the mind, and which illuminates, raises and inspires the imagination so that the enthusiastic writer is able to do and say extraordinary and surprising things, Cahusac defines enthusiasm as "the masterpiece of reason":

> C'est la raison seule cependant qui le [l'enthousiasme] fait naître; il est un feu pur qu'elle allume dans les momens de sa plus grande supériorité. Il fut toujours de toutes ses opérations la plus prompte, la plus animée. Il suppose une multitude infinie de combinaisons précédentes, qui n'ont pu se faire qu'avec elle & par elle. Il est, si on ose le dire, le chef-d'œuvre de la raison.[24]

In Cahusac's treatise on dance, such a state of enthusiasm in the sense of a specific disposition of reason underlies an ideal writing mode of clear communicating the writing of facts. As will be shown in the following, it emerges in his re-writing of dance history as well as in his demonstrations of the existence of the new genre *danse en action*. Furthermore, with its close relation to reason, the mode of 'enthusiastic writing' differs clearly from other passions that evoke more likely moral dimensions as, for instance, envy. With regard to the poetics of the treatise, it also allows to discern a redoubling of writing facts, that surpasses a simple alternation between rational-analytical and affective-emotional writing modes but creates a specific poetics of iteration.

---

22 Cahusac 2004: 35. "One would like then, for the honor, for the felicity of his century, to make pass quickly the discoveries which one believes to have made, his reflections, his views in the soul of all his contemporaries."
23 Cf. Cahusac 1782b.
24 Ibid.: 517. "It is reason alone, however, that gives rise to it [enthusiasm]; it is [enthusiasm] a pure fire that it [reason] kindles in the moments of its greatest superiority. Of all its operations, it was always the most rapid, the most animated. It presupposes an infinite number of previous combinations, which could only have been made with reason & by reason. It is, if one dares to say it, the masterpiece of reason."

## 3. Writing Facts: Cahusac's Poetics of Iteration

As already mentioned, in Louis de Cahusac's dance treatise, writing facts unfold on two sides: first, in finding different ways to present historical facts of dance history and second, in documenting the diversity of writing as a fact. The two sides cannot be separated and depend on mutual influence. In the following examples drawn from the historical part of the treatise, at least three separate types of iterative writing can be discerned which will be described successively as affecting redoubling of arguments, re-writing of traditional facts and transformative self-citation.

### 3.1 Soaking the Pen in Spite: Writing between Reason and Passion

Whereas Louis de Cahusac opens his treatise with a meta-reflective comment on the positive evaluation related to aesthetic enthusiasm, his meditations on the impact of envy in the writing scene figures as a counterpart. The effects of the latter are introduced with an anecdote about two historical writers of libretti or programs for royal ballets, the poet Isaac de Benserade[25] and his ambitious younger competitor Octave de Périgny, to whom the story alludes only with "le P... de P***."[26] The anecdote is centered on a short plot, that drafts the rivalry of the two dance poets and their dependence on the monarch: With his ballet programs the young poet gains the favors of the king and replaces Benserade until things change and the works of the young star earn a total failure that brings Benserade back to the stage. But instead of enjoying his regained fame, the composer Benserade becomes involved in writing public mock epistles, the negative effects of which fall back on him.[27] Having described the situation and acts of the rivals, Cahusac considers the accompanying negative passions in relation to the writing process in general: "Il est des moments de dégoût, des occasions d'impatience, des préférences piquantes, des coups inattendus, des revers douloureux, des injustices outrageantes. L'âme s'affecte, l'esprit s'aigrit, la bile s'allume, le trait échappe, et

---

25   Isaac de Benserade (1612/13-1691) was a French poet of the courts of Louis XIII and Louis XIV. He wrote romantic verses and libretti for royal ballets and was elected to the *French Academy* in 1674.
26   Cahusac 2004: 194. Octave de Périgny (1625-1670) was a French poet, president of the *Chambre des Enquêtes*, reader of the King and tutor of the Grand Dauphin from 1666-1670.
27   Cf. Cahusac 2004: 191–194.

il nous perd." (194)[28] To prevent the 'lines from escaping,' which in this context can be read equivocally as an allusion to the facial expression as well as to the line drawn by the process of writing, Cahusac recommends to his readers a whole catalogue of measures against similar disgraces : "Du flegme, une étude profonde, beaucoup de patience, un grand fond de fermeté, la certitude que les hommes ne sont pas toujours injustes, le secours du temps, et surtout des efforts redoublés pour mieux faire." (194)[29]

Apart from the presentation of this list of counter-measures concerning experiences of aggression and struggle, Cahusac seems to compete himself in the objective to a vivid presentation of his thoughts in the subsequent paragraph. There he repeats the topic but presents it in an even more affecting mode by showing the negative consequences if the previously mentioned advice is ignored. For that, he not only addresses the readers directly but also drafts a horrific writing scene of a passionate writer troubled by anger and vindictive thoughts, who finally perishes with his rival:

> Une cabale puissante suscite contre vous une foule de juges injustes. Vous connaissez l'auteur de votre disgrâce. La colère vous le peint avec des traits qui rendus au grand jour peuvent le couvrir d'un ridicule éternel. Cette cruelle idée vous rit et rien ne vous arrête. Votre plume se trempe dans le fiel. Vous espérez tracer sa honte, et immortaliser votre vengeance. Quelle erreur! le blanc, contre lequel vous tirez à bout-portant est appuyé sur une colonne de marbre. La balle le perce sans doute ; mais la colonne la repousse contre vous : vous tombez l'un et l'autre frappés du même coup, et vous restez à terre, pour y être foulé aux pieds de la multitude, dont vous auriez tôt ou tard fixé l'admiration, et qui vous méprise. (194–195)[30]

---

28 "There are moments of disgust, occasions of impatience, piquant preferences, unexpected blows, painful setbacks, outrageous injustices. The soul is affected, the spirit is filled with bitterness, the bile is ignited, the line escapes, and it loses us."

29 "Phlegm, deep study, a lot of patience, a great deal of firmness, the certainty that men are not always unjust, the help of time, and above all redoubled efforts to do better."

30 "A powerful cabal raises against you a crowd of unjust judges. You know the author of your disgrace. Anger paints him with features which, when brought to light, can cover him with eternal ridicule. This cruel idea laughs at you, and nothing stops you. Your pen is soaked in spite. You hope to draw his shame and immortalize your revenge. What a mistake! The mark, at which you shoot and which you hit at close range, is leaning on a marble column. The bullet undoubtedly pierces it; but the column pushes it back against you: you fall both struck by the same shot, and you remain on the ground, to

With this passionate writing scene, Cahusac elucidates the influence of socially negative evaluated emotions like anger and envy on the writing process, since they take the direction of the writing scene, guide the pen, metaphorically represent the liquid ink which not only allows revenge to materialize but can transform the passions into transmissible facts via their documentation in dance historical writings.

These examples of the impact of envy build a counterpart to the wished influence of enthusiastic writing scenes as mentioned in the "Avant-Propos". Interestingly, in the context of the problematization of passions in the writing process, Cahusac applies a strategy of repetition and comparison, where he first presents the impact of passions in the writing process in an objective and emotionless manner followed by an affective presentation through, for instance, an allegory about a pen soaked in spite. This allows him to illustrate the competition between the ballet poets mentioned in the passage above. This coupling of a more rational and conceptual discourse with a figurative and emotional discourse builds the first type of an iterative poetics of writing facts in *La Danse Ancienne et Moderne ou Traite Historique de la Danse*. A second type can be seen in Cahusac's re-writing of ancient dance philosophical texts.

## 3.2 Re-Writings of Lucian's Dialogue *On Dance*

Like many other French tracts on dance aesthetics in the 18$^{th}$ century, Cahusac's treatise would appear to have been inspired to a considerable extent by Lucian of Samosata's dialogue *On Dance* which was known in France from the translation by Nicolas Perrot d'Ablancourt of 1654.[31] Most probably Cahusac referred to Perrot's translation as the following comparative reading will show. However, the interesting point is not a verbatim citation but the tiny modifications introduced by Cahusac which allow us to reconstruct the changes in dance aesthetics and dance practice between the 17$^{th}$ and 18$^{th}$ century. To stress the authority of the ancient philosopher, Cahusac dedicates to him a whole chapter entitled "Fragment de Lucien". The often-

---

be trampled at the feet of the multitude, whose admiration you would have sooner or later fixed, and which despises you."

31  From the 17$^{th}$ century onwards, French theories on dance particularly refer to the 35$^{th}$ and 36$^{th}$ paragraphs of Lucians dialogue as can be seen for example in Claude-François Ménestrier's *Des Ballets Anciens et Modernes selon les règles du Théâtre* (1682) or also in the third part of Jean-Baptiste Du Bos's *Réflexions critiques sur la poësie et la peinture* (1719/1733).

quoted passage in the context of 18th century dance theory highlights the cultural relevance of the art of dancing by exposing its complexity. In Nicolas Perrot d'Ablancourt's translation of the ancient dialogue the passage reads as follows:

> Mais sur tout il [le pantomime ou danceur de Balet] a besoin de memoire; car il faut que comme Calcas il sache le present, le passé, & l'avenir, & qu'il les ait tousjours prests en son esprit, pour les pouvoir representer dans l'occasion. Mais il doit savoir particulierement expliquer les conceptions de l'Ame, & découvrir ses sentiments par les gestes & le mouvement du corps. [...] Il faut donc qu'il sache tout ce qui s'est passé d'ilustre depuis le Cahos & la naissance du monde jusqu'à la Reine Cleopatre; car cette science embrasse toute cette étenduë.[32]

Most interestingly, from at least the 17th century onwards Lucian's dialogue is no longer received as a piece of literature in dance historiography but as a factual description of ancient dance practices. The written tradition is considered as trustworthy and serves as a fund of dance aesthetics and dance practical principles. But whereas Lucian stresses the many talents of the *dancer* and the ability of gestures to express any mythological or historical story and any passion or inner motion, Cahusac transfers these qualities to the *composer* of dance pieces and thus points to the processes of conceptualizing and writing about dance:

> Il [le compositeur de ballet] a besoin de se faire de bonne heure une excellente mémoire. Tous les temps doivent toujours être présents à son esprit; mais il doit surtout étudier les différentes opérations de l'âme, pour pouvoir les peindre par les mouvements du corps. [...] "Il faut donc qu'il s'instruise de tout ce qui s'est fait de considérable depuis le développement du chaos et la naissance du Monde jusqu'à nos jours."[33]

---

32  Lucien 1664: 441–442. "But, above all, he [the mime or dancer of Ballet] needs a good memory; because, like Calchas, he must know the present, the past and the future, and have them ready in his mind to be able to represent them on the appropriate occasion. But he must know in particular how to explain the conceptions of the soul, and to reveal its feelings by gestures and by the movement of the body. [...] He must thus know all the endless sequence of things that happened from chaos and the primal origin of the world until the time of Queen Cleopatra; since this art extends through all of that time span."

33  Cahusac 2004: 100. "He [the composer of ballet] must begin to form an excellent memory early. All periods must be present in his mind at any time; but above all he must

Comparing the two quotes, Cahusac's style of quotation from Lucian's dialogue seems to be oriented to the *ars memoriae*, which is more committed to the reproduction of the message than to a verbatim citation. This quotation style was common in the context of lectures given to scholars of philosophy or dance, as can also be seen in the citation mode of the dance theorist Claude-François Ménestrier. The sentence in quotation marks in particular points at the link between repetition and alteration, because the historical span of which a dancer or composer should know the most important events is described by Lucian "from the [...] primal origin of the world until the Queen Cleopatra" and by Cahusac this span reaches "until today."[34]

In 17$^{th}$ and 18$^{th}$ century dance theory, the references to Antiquity serve as argument to foster the legitimacy of dance as an autonomous theatrical genre that no longer needs to be embedded in courtly spectacles or operas. The substitution of the *dancer* by the *composer* and the reformulation of the historical span to be remembered in dance composition, however, underlines not only the changed cultural dance practices, since it refers to the presence of the writer, it also reveals the unstable certainty of written facts, which can easily be transformed with a few words.

As such, the re-writing of the ancient text corresponds to a redistribution of qualities from the dancer to the composer of dance pieces which is an attestation of the changed position that ballet masters had assumed in society at the end of the 17$^{th}$ century with their role departing from that of experts in physical, anatomical and musical arts to that of a well-educated initiate, fully informed and literate in the many forms of writings, such as philosophy, history, literature but also aesthetics and dance notation.[35]

To summarize, the second type of Cahusac's iterative writing produces factual information through writing by the alteration of facts extracted from ancient and contemporary dance theories. This variation in citation can also be observed when dealing with copied fragments of his articles written for the *Encyclopédie* although the iteration takes on a different function there.

---

study the different operations of the soul, so that he can paint them with the movements of the body [...] 'It is therefore necessary that he informs himself about all the endless sequence of things that have been done from the development of the chaos and the primal origin of the world until today.'"

34  Cahusac's wording does neither correspond to Perrot d'Ablancourt's translation, nor to Ménestrier's quotation of Lucian, who both mention the Queen Cleopatra as one end of the historical span to describe the faculty of memory of a dancer.

35  Cf. Huschka 2020: 126.

## 3.3 Transformative Self-Citation in Writing the Origins of Dance

Cahusac dedicates the fourth chapter of the first part of his *Historical Treatise on Dance* to the "Origine de la danse, définition qui en a été faite par les philosophes."[36] In it, he re-writes an idea already published in his article on "Danse" in the *Encyclopédie* with the aim of making it appear more vivid. Like his contemporaries he contributes to a myth of the origin of dance that characterizes dance as a natural mode of expression of the inner movements of the soul via gestures, which is described in analogies to the functions of the human voice:

> Le chant si naturel à l'homme, en se développant, a inspiré aux autres hommes qui en ont été frappés, des gestes relatifs aux différens sons dont ce chant étoit composé : le corps alors s'est agité, les bras se sont ouverts ou fermés, les piés ont formé des pas lents ou rapides, les traits du visage ont participé à ces mouvements divers, tout le corps a répondu par des positions, des ébranlemens, des attitudes aux sons dont l'oreille étoit affectée : ainsi le chant qui étoit l'expression d'un sentiment (*Voyez* CHANT) a fait développer une seconde expression qui étoit dans l'homme & qu'on a nommée *danse*.[37]

In this description of the origins of dance, Cahusac defines dance as dependent on music capable of expressing feelings through bodily movements, gestures and facial expression. Dance is thus conceived as a means of passionate and affective expression comparable to the spoken language in song. Concurrent with dance history as exposed by Jacques Bonnet in *Histoire générale de la Danse sacrée et profane* (1724), but also with language philosophy as, e.g., articulated by Condillac in *Sur la grammaire*, which draws back the origins of verbal language and its expressiveness to nonverbal gestures, the facticity of

---

36 "The origin of dance and its definition according to the philosophers." (Cf. Cahusac 2004: 49–51)
37 Cahusac 1782a: 260. "When song, which is so natural to man, developed, it inspired other men who were moved by it some gestures in relation to the different sounds of which the song was composed: the body then became agitated, the arms opened or closed, the feet formed slow or quick steps, the features of the face participated in these various movements, the whole body responded by positions, shaking, attitudes to the sounds of which the ear was affected: thus, the song, which was the expression of a feeling (*See* SONG) made develop a second expression which was in man that we named dance."

past cultural practices is due to the reliability of texts from past and contemporary writers, as Diderot mentioned.[38] At the same time, Cahusac's article on "Danse" in the *Encyclopédie* serves as an example to constitute the facticity of contemporary dance as a cultural practice that reaches back to the origins of mankind, withholding at that moment in the article that there are several differences between the dances of Antiquity and those of Modernity.

For the treatise *La Danse Ancienne et Moderne ou Traité Historique de la Danse* he re-works the passage of the article, from changing single words, to introducing whole new sentences and giving additional examples up to re-structuring the order of the sentences with the aim to render the idea of the origins of dance more intelligible:

> Le corps fut paisible ou s'agita, *les yeux s'enflammèrent ou s'éteignirent; le visage se colora ou pâlit; les bras s'ouvrirent ou se fermèrent, s'élevèrent vers le ciel ou retombèrent vers la terre;* les pieds formèrent des pas lents ou rapides; tout le corps enfin répondit par des positions, des attitudes, des sauts, des ébranlements aux sons dont l'âme peignait ses mouvements. Ainsi le chant, qui est l'expression primitive du sentiment, en a fait développer une seconde qui était dans l'homme, et c'est cette expression qu'on a nommée danse. (emphasizing R.R.)[39]

In the remodeled quotation, Cahusac particularly emphasizes the importance of nonverbal facial expressions in dance. He thus goes so far as to change their position from the fourth to the second in the list of expressive parts mentioned for a dancer. Furthermore, he specifies the facial movements by describing the expressiveness of the eyes, which can be 'sparkling' or 'extinguished' and by indicating the changing colors of the skin from blush to paleness. This modified description in the historical part of the treatise prepares his characterization of *danse en action*, since it underlines the diverse levels of expression in dance and thus the theatrical meaning of dance that is closely

---

38  Cf. Condillac 1970: 354; cf. Diderot 1781: 786–787.
39  Cahusac 2004: 50. "The body was calm or agitated, *the eyes sparkled or extinguished; the face colored or paled; the arms opened or closed, rose to the sky or fell back to the earth;* the feet formed slow or quick steps; the whole body finally responded with positions, attitudes, leaps, shakes to the sounds of which the soul painted its movements. Thus song, which is the primitive expression of feeling, developed a second form which was in man, and this is the expression which was named dance."

related to the expression of inner movement transported by the eyes.[40] In addition, the movement directions of the arms as given in the revised version that also include arm raising and bending, can also be read as an allusion to mid-18th century theatrical dance practice. In the time of Cahusac, theatrical dance was no longer performed in the center of a ballroom and watched from the galleries as in a 17th century spectacle of the *Ballet de Cour* but was performed on a proscenium stage which offered new perspectives to the public and where the vertical direction of movement offered new aesthetic possibilities for the composers.[41]

With regard to the poetics of writing facts in *La Danse Ancienne et Moderne ou Traité Historique de la Danse*, this third type builds a separate class. Although it shares with the second type of iterative writing the modification of written facts to bring into line traditional writings and contemporary experience, the second type refers to the re-writing of works by other authors, whereas the above mentioned third type refers to a polished self-citation.

## 4. Conclusion

'Writing Facts' in Louis de Cahusac's *La Danse Ancienne et Moderne ou Traité Historique de la Danse* unfolds the complexity of factualization concerning natural phenomena and human actions. This is made possible through writing as cultural practice and simultaneously by writing a historically informed treatise on dance. Scrutinizing this relation, iteration – as discussed in cultural studies – is distinguishable as one of the general characteristics not only of cultural practices such as dancing or writing but also as a characteristic element in Louis de Cahusac's poetics of dance history. Whereas the re-writing of the articles he contributed to the *Encyclopédie* for the treatise aim at a clearer communication of the origin of dance preparing the description of the aesthetic innovation of the *danse en action*, the iteration of Lucian's thoughts about

---

40 Whereas iteration allows a description for the writing of the historical part of the treatise, Cahusac's presentation of the aesthetics of *danse en action* mime contemporary experimental and dialectical methods as the titles of the corresponding chapters announce: "V. Préjugés contre la Danse en action", "VI. Preuves de la possibilité de la Danse en action" and "VII. Supériorité et avantages de la Danse en action." "V. Prejudices against the *danse en action*, VI. Proves of the possibility of the *danse en action* and VII. Superiority and advantages of the *danse en action*." (Ibid.: 227–232)

41 Cf. Schoenfeldt 1997: 77–78.

dancers and their re-contextualization under the sign of the composer permits insight into changed dance practices of the 18th century. The attribution of the mentioned qualities to the composer witnesses the importance of historical and aesthetic texts on dance written by composers since they indicate not only the erudition and the becoming an author of ballet masters but also allude to writing as a proper means in their struggle against being ignored in cultural history and the history of arts. Furthermore, the dance theorist reflects on the relations between 'writing' and 'fact' under the condition of emotional states of mind. He permits an enthusiastic state only in the sense of a masterpiece of reason to determine the direction of the writing scene, but rejects other passions like anger and envy. At the same time, Cahusac not only speaks about the enthusiastic writing but also shows it to the reader by referring with it to the guiding discourses in 18th century dance theory like empiricism and sensualism. Directed by an aspiration to reveal the 'truth' about dance and to be of some 'advantage' for future readers as mentioned in the "Avant-Propos", the treatise reveals the mutual influence between writing and facts together with the role of iteration for both.

## Bibliography

Barthes, Roland (1994): "Variations sur l'écriture", in: Marty, Éric (ed.): *Roland Barthes. Œuvres complètes. Tome II. 1966-1973*, Paris, 1535–1574.

Bocher d'Argis, Antoine-Gaspard (1781): "Fait jurisprudence", in: Diderot/d'Alembert (eds.), *Encyclopédie, ou dictionnaire raisonné des sciences, des arts et des métiers, par une société des gens de lettres*. vol. XIII. ESP-FER, 787–791.

Bonnet, Jacques (2018) [1724]: *Histoire générale de la danse sacrée et profane*, ed. Pierre Michon Bourdelot, Paris, in: https://obvil.sorbonne-universite.fr/c orpus/danse/bonnet_histoire-generale-danse_1724_orig (19.04.2022).

Cahusac, Louis de (2004) [1754]: *La Danse Ancienne et Moderne ou Traité Historique de la Danse. Édition présentée, établie et annotée par Nathalie Lecomte, Laura Naudeix, Jean-Noël Laurenti*, Paris.

— (1782a): "Danse", in: Diderot, Denis/D'Alembert, Jean Le Rond (eds.): *Encyclopédie, ou dictionnaire raisonné des sciences, des arts et des métiers, par une société des gens de lettres*. vol. X. CRITH-DINW, Lausanne/Berne, 259–260.

— (1782b): "Enthousiasme", in: Diderot, Denis/D'Alembert, Jean Le Rond (eds.) *Encyclopédie, ou dictionnaire raisonné des sciences, des arts et des métiers, par une société des gens de lettres.* vol. XII. ELC-ESPA, Lausanne/Berne, 517–523.

Campe, Rüdiger (2012): "Die Schreibszene, Schreiben", in: Zanetti, Sandro (ed.): *Schreiben als Kulturtechnik. Grundlagentexte*, Berlin, 269–282.

Compagnon, Antoine (1979): *La seconde main ou le travail de la citation*, Paris.

Condillac, Étienne de (1970): *Œuvres complètes. Tome V. Art de penser et art d'écrire. Réimpression de l'édition de Paris, 1821-1822*, Genève.

Derrida, Jacques (1991): "Signature Event Context", in: Kamuf, Peggy (ed.): *A Derrida Reader. Between the Blinds*, New York, 82–111.

Diderot, Denis (1781): "Fait", in: id./D'Alembert, Jean Le Rond (eds.): *Encyclopédie, ou dictionnaire raisonné des sciences, des arts et des métiers, par une société des gens de lettres.* vol. XIII. ESP-FER, Lausanne/Berne, 786–787.

Du Bos, Jean-Baptiste (1967) [1733]: *Réflexions critiques sur la poësie et sur la peinture. Troisième Partie*, Genf.

Fludernik, Monika/Ryan, Marie-Laure (eds.) (2020): *Narrative Factuality. A Handbook*, Berlin/New York.

— (2020a): "Factual Narrative. An Introduction", in: id. (eds.): *Narrative Factuality. A Handbook*, 1–26.

Huschka, Sabine (2020): *Choreographierte Körper im Theatron. Auftritte und Theoria ästhetischen Wissens*, München.

Jaeger, Stephan (2020): "Factuality in Historiography/Historical Study", in: Fludernik/Ryan (eds.), *Narrative Factuality. A Handbook*, 335–349.

Knaller, Susanne (2017): "Emotions and the Process of Writing", in: Jandl, Ingeborg et al. (eds.): *Writing Emotions. Theoretical Concepts and Selected Case Studies in Literature*, Bielefeld, 17–28.

Lucien, Samosate de (1664): "De la Dance. Dialogue de Craton et de Lycinus", in: id.: *Lucien de la Traduction de N. Perrot Sénieur d'Ablancourt. Première Partie. Nouvelle Edition revue & corrigée*, Paris, 432–453.

Ménestrier, Claude-François (1682): *Des Ballets Anciens et Modernes selon les règles du Théâtre*, Paris.

Schoenfeldt, Susanne (1997): *Choreographie. Tanzkomposition und Tanzbeschreibung: Zur Geschichte des choreographierten Tanzes*, Frankfurt am Main.

Stingelin, Martin (2004): "'Schreiben'. Einleitung", in: id./Giuriato, Davide/Zanetti, Sandro (eds.): *'Mir ekelt vor diesem tintenklecksenden Säkulum'. Schreibszenen im Zeitalter der Manuskripte*, München, 7–21.

Wirth, Uwe (2002): "Der Performanzbegriff im Spannungsfeld von Illokution, Iteration und Indexikalität", in: id. (ed.): *Performanz. Zwischen Sprachphilosophie und Kulturwissenschaften*, Frankfurt am Main, 9–60.

# Snapshot and Wage Table
## The Importance of Facts in the Reports of Hugo von Kupffer (1853-1928) and Max Winter (1870-1937)

*Mario Huber (University of Graz)*

## 1. Introduction

The main concern of this paper is to revisit and reevaluate the beginning of the century-long debate about 'facts' in German journalism, especially in the subgenre report. After the biased news coverage during the First World War, many journalists in the 1920s voiced their opinion on how to steer journalism 'back on track.'[1] 'Facts' ('Tatsachen') and 'objectivity' ('Sachlichkeit') were the central terms in this debate on the virtues and goals of reporting. The theoretical and practical historic significance of this multi-faceted journalistic movement, which was often labeled as contradictory, is widely recognized by the scientific community.[2]

As a supplement to the existing research – which focuses on the accuracy of the depicted reality in those texts – I want to offer a new perspective on the specific purpose of dealing with facts and objectivity in journalistic works. For this, I will recapitulate the debate, based on theoretical texts written by its arguably most important representative, Egon Erwin Kisch (1885-1948). In the following, I want to show how journalistic objectivity can be framed as a strategic tool with ethical implications rather than as a norm of depicting reality. To this end, I will reach back to a paper by Elisabeth Klaus,[3] who has already made this point about current journalistic practices. The proposed

---

1 For a small but relevant selection of theoretical texts and practical examples in the same vein cf. Schütz 1974.
2 A detailed summary of main talking points can be found in Haas 1999: 218–281 and Patka 1997: 91–111.
3 Cf. Klaus 2004.

new perspective will show that some of the observed contradictions in the discussion during the 1920s vanish if we differentiate between the purposes why facts came into play in the first place. From this point of view, the debate about facts is more a mixture of different goals than a cohesive theory about reality. Finally, I want to show that some of the (seemingly) new ideas in the 1920s can at least be traced back to professional demarcations at the turn of the 20th century. At this time, a countermovement to editorial journalism and the feuilleton gained ground and introduced new methods, such as a heavy reliance on eyewitness-accounts, into German journalism. Hugo von Kupffer's (1853-1928) city-based reports about the emerging metropolis Berlin and Max Winter's (1870-1937) social reports about the working-class environment in Austria-Hungary serve as prime examples for the emerging debate about facts.

## 2. The Debate about Facts in the 1920s

The term 'report' ('Reportage') has its roots in French and American journalism and came into use in the German speaking world at the end of the 19th century.[4] Despite its widespread use and its prevalence in the journalistic canon, there is no universally accepted definition available but rather a 'catalog' of historically changeable requirements for its practical use.[5]

Michael Haller distinguishes between two lines of tradition which merged in the report.[6] On the one hand, aspects of the literary travelogue, which focuses on the traveler and his experiences, can be found. Haller argues that many of the characteristics of the ideal report, i.e., documentation, authenticity, credibility, immediacy, and honesty, can be traced back to the ancient tradition of the literary travelogue. On the other hand, the journalistic eyewitness account also takes a prominent place in the report. Rather than focusing on the traveler/the reporter and his/her point of view, the main goal of the eyewitness account is to show events that would also take place without journalists reporting on them, e.g., war or natural disasters. This analytic distinction between subject-focused and object-focused traditions leads to the idea that the journalist has to be 'on site.' If he/she describes foreign countries or

---

4  Cf. Kostenzer 2009: 82.
5  Cf. Haas 1999: 237.
6  Cf. Haller 2020: 19–50.

other cultures or describes events that are closed to the general public, the aim is that the readers should be able to participate in what happened.[7]

By the 1920s, when it was only a few decades old, the report had already become the topic of a lengthy discussion among practitioners. Heavily influenced by American journalists, reports were widely regarded as a new and adequate way of depicting of the ever-changing and complex post-war reality.[8] Despite the agreement about the genre per se, the beginning debate about permissible methods in its use, especially about the importance of facts, showed major fault lines between reporters.

Hannes Haas focuses on this debate in his book *Empirischer Journalismus* and highlights one aspect of the discussion. He shows that the question about the possibilities of the report in the 1920s is heavily intertwined with the photograph (or the 'snapshot') as a metaphor.[9] He parallels the historic development with the rise of the cultural movement of the "New Objectivity" ('Neue Sachlichkeit'). In this multidisciplinary movement, authenticity, precision and objectivity were seen as absolute virtues and questions about the possibility of depicting reality were very popular. Photography promised to be an ideal implementation of this idea – and therefore it was used to offer (aesthetic) 'instructions' for other forms of representation such as the report.[10]

A prime example of picking up on this idea can be found in the theoretical texts of Egon Erwin Kisch.[11] The "reporter on the move" ('rasender Reporter'), who became synonymous with a certain very popular style of journalism, reflected upon the report and drew many comparisons to photography. This also includes the often-cited foreword of his collection of writings "The reporter on the move" from 1925:

---

7  Cf. ibid.: 34–35.
8  Cf. Haas 1999: 233–236.
9  Cf. ibid.: 262–265.
10 Cf. ibid.: 262. Even though the mentioned ideas about photography were compatible with (popular) contemporary concepts of reality and the relations between subjects and objects, it is worth mentioning that even at the time photographers or intellectuals like Siegfried Kracauer (1889-1966) already moved on to a far more critical view in self-reflection of the art form. (Cf. Knaller 2015: 82–87)
11 This can also be found in the following texts: "Nature of the reporter" ("Wesen des Reporters", 1918), "Dogma of the infallibility of the press" ("Dogma der Unfehlbarkeit der Presse", ibid.) and "Reportage as an art form and a form of struggle" ("Reportage als Kunstform und Kampfform", 1935). (Cf. Kisch 1983a [1918], 1983b [1918], and 1983c [1935])

> The time photographs below were not taken all at once. Subject and object were in different moods at different ages when the pictures were taken, position and light were very different each time. Still, there is nothing to retouch as the album is released today.[12]

Even in this short paragraph, many allusions to photography can be found: Kisch talks about "pictures" in an "album," he reflects upon the incidence of light and reassures the reader that there was no post-processing involved. The recourse to these metaphors is linked to Kisch's idea of a reporter with no bias and his absolute dependency on facts:

> The reporter has no bias, has nothing to justify, and has no point of view. He has to be an impartial witness and to give testimony impartially, as reliably as his testimony can be given [...]. Even the bad reporter – the one who exaggerates or is unreliable – does an important job: because he is dependent on the facts, he has to get knowledge of them, by sight, by conversation, by observation, by information. (659)[13]

The quotes from Kisch's foreword show how closely linked – by metaphorical comparisons with photography – the idea of the ideal reporter (or the ideal report) and the value-free handling of facts are. This connection is in itself not very problematic – and if this would have been the only remark upon the theoretical and practical framework of the report, the discussion probably would have ended soon. But there were not only dissenting voices, which we will talk about soon, Kisch himself also complicated the topic.

Based on his past discussions, in his lecture "From the practice of the local reporter" ("Aus der Praxis des Lokalreporters", 1928) Kisch cites three requirements for reporters: objectivity ('Sachlichkeit'), a sense of social responsibility

---

12   Kisch 1978 [1925]: 660. "Die nachstehenden Zeitaufnahmen sind nicht auf einmal gemacht worden. Subjekt und Objekt waren in den verschiedensten Lebensaltern in verschiedensten Stimmungen, als die Bilder entstanden, Stellung und Licht waren höchst ungleich. Trotzdem ist nichts zu retuschieren, da das Album heute vorgelegt wird." All translations by M.H.
13   "Der Reporter hat keine Tendenz, hat nichts zu rechtfertigen und hat keinen Standpunkt. Er hat unbefangen Zeuge zu sein und unbefangen Zeugenschaft zu liefern, so verläßlich, wie sich seine Aussage geben läßt [...]. Selbst der schlechte Reporter – der, der übertreibt oder unverläßlich ist – leistet werktätige Arbeit: denn er ist von den Tatsachen abhängig, er hat sich Kenntnis von ihnen zu verschaffen, durch Augenschein, durch ein Gespräch, durch eine Beobachtung, eine Auskunft."

('soziales Gefühl') and the will to help the oppressed ('Willen, den Unterdrückten zu helfen').[14] Photography and its metaphorical indifference can only be linked to objectivity, and the latter two requirements cover different grounds. As a result of this proposed combination, an aesthetic norm and broad ideas of social effectiveness are now heavily intertwined. The resulting inconsistency has not only been established with reference to Kisch. Helmut Weiß, for example, writes in relation to the photographic metaphor:

> When it comes to reporting, it is important not just to take photographs, but with a specially selected lens. It is important to show reality as a whole by showing partial excerpts from it and especially the reality of social conditions. It is important not only to nail down the visible things and facts, but to uncover the connections, the contradictions, the background. Ultimately, it is about photographing things not in isolation, but in their concrete context [...].[15]

Weiß argues for using a specific lens for every single photograph. Ultimately, it depends on not photographing things by themselves but in their social context. But this expansion into a spatial dimension is not the only counterpoint. In direct reference to Kisch, Leo Lania (1896-1961) argues for a temporal extension:

> Kisch only feels like a servant of the object. He is a master of the report, his eye is keen, his agility as great as the thoroughness with which he goes about his work. And yet it would be wrong to classify Kisch as a reporter. [...] It is not a superficial clinging to fact that distinguishes the reporter from the poet. [...] The reporter is on a fundamentally different level: the object is only important to him to the extent that it is generally important. And so, he positions himself to his objects not as a – superior or submissive – viewer, but as a spy, whether it is a prison, a madhouse, a mine, a factory.

---

14  Cf. Patka 1997: 103.

15  Weiß 1974 [1931]: 12–13. "Es kommt bei der Reportage darauf an, nicht einfach zu fotografieren, sondern mit einer genau zu bestimmenden Linse. Es kommt darauf an, die ganze Wirklichkeit zu zeigen, indem Teilausschnitte aus dieser Wirklichkeit, aus der Realität der gesellschaftlichen Verhältnisse gezeigt werden. Es kommt darauf an, nicht nur die sichtbaren Dinge und Tatsachen festzunageln, sondern die Zusammenhänge, die Widersprüche, die Hintergründe aufzudecken. Es kommt letztlich darauf an, die Dinge nicht als Einzelheiten abzufotografieren, sondern im konkreten Zusammenhang [...]."

He does not describe, he reveals – he doesn't show things as they are, but as they were and what will become of them [...].[16]

This and other critical remarks on Kisch's work (and the photography metaphor) have already been addressed by Michael Geisler. Kisch's idea of "objectivity," which is very closely connected to the aforementioned representation theory, is flawed from a constructivist point of view. Every journalistic text can only be an excerpt from reality which is selected by the reporter who is responsible for bringing the selected facts in a structured form.[17] But facts remain facts, e.g., three different selections of facts by three different reporters in three different structured forms create three different factual narratives – none of them is objective in a strict sense, but all of them are factual and verifiable against reality.

Upon further consideration, there is not only a certain naiveté to Kisch's idea of "objectivity," which can be seen in the above and further by questioning what remains of the "authenticity" of the eyewitness from a constructionist perspective. But it is also in conflict with his other requirements. The most problematic fault line, I would argue, lies between objectivity and the social commitment of the individual. Every conscious acquisition of a social position is a political decision and can therefore no longer be called objective. In order to counteract social injustice, a reevaluation of the situation must take place. Although this reevaluation can have an (objectively substantiated) just society as its goal, it seems inevitable that a strong subjective position has to be inhabitant for a start.

To mention these concerns about the approach of Kisch, who is arguably representative and in the center of the entire movement in the 1920s, shows

---

16   Lania 1926: 5–6. "Kisch fühlt sich nur als Knecht des darzustellenden Objekts. Er handhabt die Reportage meisterhaft, sein Auge ist scharf, seine Beweglichkeit ebenso groß wie die Gründlichkeit, mit der er bei seiner Arbeit zu Werke geht. Und doch wäre es falsch, Kisch unter die Reporter einzureihen. [...] Es ist nicht Äußerlichkeit, das Haften am Faktum, wodurch sich der Reporter vom Dichter unterscheidet. [...] Der Reporter steht auf einer grundsätzlich anderen Ebene: Das Objekt ist ihm nur so weit wichtig, als es – allgemein wichtig ist. Und so nimmt er zum Objekt seiner Darstellung, mag es sich um ein Gefängnis, ein Irrenhaus, ein Bergwerk, eine Fabrik handeln, nicht die Stellung des – überlegenen oder unterwürfigen – Betrachters ein, sondern des Spions – er beschreibt nicht, er enthüllt – er zeigt nicht die Dinge wie sie sind, sondern wie sie waren und was aus ihnen werden wird [...]."
17   Cf. Geisler 1982: 62–74.

that the discussion quickly leads to a dilemma that either way requires dropping one premise. A report can be objective or endowed with social conscience – but not both at once.

I will now try to reframe the discussion by taking up an approach by Elisabeth Klaus. She focuses on different relations between facts and fiction and distinguishes not only "facts and fiction" but also "facts and truth," "facts and knowledge" and "facts and reality."[18] For this paper, her thoughts on the relationship between facts and reality are most important. She picks up on the constructivist approach, which we got to know through Michael Geisler, and takes it further. No simple juxtaposition of facts could ever make sense if that juxtaposition is not consciously designed.[19]

Klaus asks what objectivity signifies (and implies) under these inevitable conditions and distinguishes three norms of objectivity.[20] First, objectivity can be understood as an aesthetic norm of depicting reality. This falls in line with the representation theory Haas has found in Kisch's work and can be associated with the heavy reliance on photographic metaphors, etc. Secondly, Klaus also looks at objectivity as a strategic ritual, which shows, e.g., its dependency on the place of publication. Thirdly, objectivity can be understood as an ethical norm that means credibility and usefulness. This framework offers the opportunity to read Kisch's three requirements in the context of Klaus' second and third interpretation of objectivity in journalism. Thus, if we move away from the idea that facts and objectivity only mean an accurate representation of reality, apparent contradictions might be resolved. In order to show how the presented approaches – i.e., objectivity and the use of facts as a strategic ritual or as an ethical norm – look like in relatively unambiguous forms, I will refer to two historical examples. First, I will investigate Hugo von Kupffer's texts, in which the strategic component becomes apparent. According to this, Max Winter's work should serve to draw attention to the ethical dimensions of objectivity.

---

18   Cf. Klaus 2004.
19   Cf. ibid.: 110–111.
20   Cf. ibid.: 111–113.

## 3. Objectivity as a Strategic Ritual: Hugo von Kupffer

In order to better understand Hugo von Kupffer's innovations in dealing with facts, a brief look at the history of journalism in Germany is necessary. The late 19th century was dominated by editorial journalism. This term describes the institutionalization of journalistic work driven by technical innovations in the age of industrialization. Inventions such as the telegraph or the rotary press led to profound long-term changes in journalism. Not only that topicality and facts became an essential aspect of reporting. This was accompanied by a standardization of methodical and practical approaches, both in the form of 'tailored' texts with specific wording and in the incipient formation of departments, e.g., for politics, economy, or sport.[21] However, what was neglected in this approach were personal statements by the reporting person and, most crucial, the newspaper editors remained in the editorial office and were not on site.

This development was soon felt by many editors to be very restrictive. The feuilleton was perceived as a counter-movement to this and was set against the formal and content-related specifications of the aforementioned journalistic work method. Since the feuilleton was more concerned with ideological, cultural and moral issues, there was no pressure from being up-to-date and personal aspects could find their way into the texts.[22] But in the end, it was this counter-movement to the editorial journalism that led to another counter-movement: the report.[23]

Hugo von Kupffer is one of the most important figures when it comes to how the report was established in German-speaking countries. Von Kupffer, born in 1853, went to New York in the late 1870s and worked as a reporter for the *New York Herald*. He wanted to bring the American work methods to Germany, which basically meant the use of local reporters with focus on human interest stories and quick reports that relied on eyewitnesses.[24] When he became editor-in-chief of the newly founded proto-tabloid *Berliner Lokalanzeiger* (BLA) in 1883 he had the opportunity to put his ideas about modern journalism into practice.[25] Von Kupffer, who describes his own approach as "objective

---

21  Cf. Roß 2004: 82–86.
22  Cf. ibid.: 87–90.
23  Cf. Eberwein 2014: 125.
24  Cf. Mauch 2019: 249–253.
25  Cf. ibid.: 245.

sobriety" ('objektive Nüchternheit'),[26] relied on local reporters, which, as previously mentioned, did not exist in this form in the German-speaking world at that time. The reason for this tactic was to achieve greater reader loyalty. In the rapidly changing city of Berlin he saw a topic that interested readers and which (in theory and practice) subsequently led to a higher circulation and a better position for the newspaper in the advertising market.[27] This reporting, which was based on public taste[28] and deliberately wanted to be non-political, relied on facts to guarantee authentic news.[29] With a focus on current events, he tried to form an emotional bond with the reader. Therefore the "individual fates" of the "Berliner" played the main role in these texts – and not the "nameless masses."[30] The BLA soon gained ground as an everyday resource in the Berlin of the late 19$^{th}$ century and tried to meet the confusion of the emerging metropolis with the authentic description of the local reporter.[31] However, this was accompanied by the greatest possible omission of political topics.[32]

But von Kupffer not only relied on employees, he also wrote many texts himself. A collection of his reports appeared in book form as early as the late 1880s. Under the title *Reporter Forays* (*Reporterstreifzüge*, 1889, extended in subsequent editions), he published texts that had previously appeared in the BLA and were dedicated to everyday life in Berlin. There he combined the aforementioned reduced communication distance (locally and personally), the focus on vividness and an identifiable journalistic narrator, i.e., the local reporter, and a conscious distinction between reports, editorial journalism and feuilleton.

In his short programmatic preface to *Reporter Forays* he clarifies this approach.[33] He does not see his texts as assessable according to literary criteria but rather as documents of cultural and historical value which were not created at a comfortable desk but "drawn from nature" ('nach der Natur gezeichnet'). But von Kupffer not only distinguishes himself from the office journalists, he also does not want to see himself as a feuilletonist. His role models

---

26 Cf. ibid.: 253.
27 Cf. Michael 2016: 53–54.
28 Cf. Wurich 2019: 46–47.
29 Cf. Mauch 2019: 246.
30 Cf. ibid.: 262.
31 Cf. Michael 2016: 66.
32 Cf. ibid.: 64.
33 Cf. von Kupffer 2019b [1889]: 7–9.

are clearly the American reporters, who rely on eyewitness accounts and interviews. In this approach we already encounter the photo metaphor that would be so dominant in the 1920s: "They [his reports] should differ from the countless 'pictures from Berlin' just as an oil painting made with true or imaginary artistry differs from a raw snapshot."[34]

The program formulated in the introduction can be found throughout the book. In keeping with its apolitical orientation, it contains few value judgments and von Kupffer confines himself to observation. He sticks to what he heard and saw, chooses the themes according to the audience's need for information. And this need for information is broad: Von Kupffer writes (among other things) about a solar eclipse, a remand prison, new nightclubs, the census, the municipal disinfection institute, an executioner, misspelled street signs, the water supply or meat inspections. In connection with the latter there is a nice example of how von Kupffer deals with facts in his texts. In "One Night at the Meat Inspection" he reports about the work that can be verified on the basis of the records:

> Such a station diary is instructive. [...] Figures prove! Therefore, I want to give the reader the following figures: On April 4, 1890, the following quantities of meat were checked at inspection station I: 752 cattle, 873 calves, 301 muttons, 658 pigs – Income for the inspection 1131 marks – 52 meat inspectors employed, 16 samplers, 3 stampers, 4 veterinarians. – In the month of December 1890, the journal gives the following overall result: 5688 cattle, 4777 calves, 2272 muttons, 5090 pigs. – Income 9479 marks 90 pfennigs. For the period from April 1, 1890 to January 1, 1891 I found the following result recorded: 50,450 cattle, 29,321 calves, 21,853 muttons, 37,217 pigs. – Income: 72749 Mk. 20 Pf. – This is the result of the activity of a station.[35]

---

34   Ibid.: 7. "Sie [seine Reportagen] sollen sich von den zahllosen 'Bildern aus dem Berliner Leben' ebenso unterscheiden, wie ein mit wahrer oder eingebildeter Künstlerschaft ausgeführtes Ölbild von einer unretouchierten Momentphotographie."

35   Von Kupffer 2019a [1891]: 180–181. "So ein Stations-Tagebuch ist lehrreich. [...] Zahlen beweisen! Daher will ich dem Leser folgende Zahlen geben: Am 4. April 1890 wurden an der Untersuchungsstation I kontrolirt folgende Fleischmengen: 752 Rinder, 873 Kälber, 301 Hammel, 658 Schweine, – Einnahme für die Untersuchung 1131 Mark – beschäftigt 52 Fleischbeschauer, 16 Probenehmer, 3 Stempler, 4 Thierärzte. – Im Monat December 1890 ergiebt das Journal folgendes Gesammt-Resultat: 5688 Rinder, 4777 Kälber, 2272 Hammel, 5090 Schweine. – Einnahme 9479 Mark 90 Pfennige. Für die Zeit vom 1. April 1890 bis 1. Januar 1891 fand ich folgendes Resultat verzeichnet: 50450

A connection between the purely reporting, fact-oriented approach and the conscious differentiation from the feuilleton can be found in a text about bars frequented by criminals:

> Many feuilletonists have already descended into the so-called criminal cellars [...], they got the obligatory goosebumps, afterward threw away their kid gloves and sacrificed a sea of ink to all the beautiful phrases and fantasies about Berlin criminality. Since, as is well known, within the undemanding framework of this work, only what has been heard and seen is to be told simply and truthfully at the source, not 'feuilletonized,' so I really have to apologize for daring to venture on this much-trodden path at all. Well, my apologies: I'm not going to give you a general crook characteristic, I just want to tell you how a currently off-duty and, as he says, 'retired' criminal thinks and speaks.[36]

As a brief interim summary, it can be said about von Kupffer's writings that facts are used as a strategic ritual. The texts are only marginally concerned with constructing an image of reality that is supposed to be 'more real' or 'more authentic,' although references to photography can also be found. The facts are primarily used to distinguish oneself from other media and reporting styles – with the feuilleton as the biggest adversary. With his strong belief in the truthfulness of the (American) report, he only describes what he has heard and seen, without critical opinion. To put it bluntly, one could say the facts only confirm that the reporter was there, nothing more. In comparison to Egon Erwin Kisch's three requirements, von Kupffer's approach fulfills all

---

Rinder, 29321 Kälber, 21853 Hammel, 37217 Schweine. – Einnahme: 72749 Mk. 20 Pf. – Das ist das Ergebnis der Thätigkeit einer Station."

36 Von Kupffer 2019c [1888]: 66–67. "Feuilletonisten sind schon viele in die sogenannten Verbrecherkeller [...] hinabgestiegen, sie haben die obligate Gänsehaut bekommen, ihre Glacé-Handschuhe nachher weggeworfen und ein Meer von Tinte all den schönen Phrasen und Phantasien über das Berliner Verbrechertum geopfert. Da bekanntlich in dem anspruchslosen Rahmen dieser Schrift nicht 'feuilletonisiert', sondern nur schlicht und wahr an der Quelle Gehörtes und Gesehenes erzählt werden soll, so muß ich mich eigentlich entschuldigen, daß ich überhaupt auf diesen vielbetretenen Pfad mich wage. Nun, meine Entschuldigung lautet: ich bringe Ihnen keine allgemeine Gauner-Charakteristik, sondern ich will Ihnen nur erzählen, wie ein augenblicklich außer Dienst befindlicher und, wie er sagt 'vom Geschäft zurückgetretener' Verbrecher denkt und spricht."

of them but has, due to its apolitical orientation, very limited "social responsibility."

With a view to Klaus' third interpretation of objectivity, Max Winter's reports should now be discussed. These are less strategic than concerned with passing on useful information.

## 4. Objectivity as a Tool of Credibility: Max Winter

Max Winter, born in 1870, was one of the most prominent social reporters at the turn of the 20<sup>th</sup> century. Viktor Adler introduced him to the *Arbeiter Zeitung* in 1895, where he worked as a reporter and an editor (and later as editor in chief). Until 1934, when he had to leave Vienna because of his socialist political views and was therefore threatened by the Fatherland Front, he wrote about 1500 reports for the left-wing newspaper.[37] In addition to other political commitments, he also was vice mayor of Vienna for a few years after the First World War.

Winter was a political writer through and through and had little interest in commercial success. His approach to journalistic work can be summed up as "education and exposure" ("Aufklärung und Aufdeckung").[38] Today, he is considered a forerunner of the historiography of everyday life and his great interest in scientific methods is repeatedly emphasized. The sociologist Isidor Singer (1857-1927), who worked on the social conditions in Bohemia, had an important influence on Winter's work.[39] In his texts, Winter uncovers social circumstances, especially in the precarious milieu of the Austro-Hungarian Empire at the turn of the century. At the center of his research is a public that has so far been unrepresented. His focus is on the massive injustices that the workforce had to endure, combining macroscopic analyzes and individual observations with great methodological diversity.[40]

In 1914, he published a three-part series of articles in the newspaper *Chemnizer Volksstimme*, in which he presented his journalistic (and implicit political)

---

37   Cf. Haas 2006: 9.
38   Cf. Haas 1999: 247.
39   Cf. ibid.: 248. Winter even derived his working concept from Singer's habilitation thesis, *Untersuchungen über die Socialen Verhältnisse des Nord-Oestlichen Böhmen. Ein Beitrag zur Methode Social-Statistischer Untersuchungen*, which was published in 1885.
40   Cf. ibid.: 248–250.

program in quite some detail. Under the title "The local editorial office" ("Die Lokalredaktion") he described the procedures and goals of his approach. In his opinion, sufficient space ('ausreichend Raum'), extensive research ('Zeit für ausführliche Recherche') and a certain amount of courage for a conspicuous presentation of the events ('Mut zur auffälligen Aufmachung der Vorkommnisse') are necessary for effective social reporting.[41]

The reporter, who has to be on site, is also decisive for him. "The editorial board is only paper, life is outside,"[42] he writes in one of the mentioned articles and is in line with von Kupffer and many others. But, as previously mentioned, his approach has less strategic (and market-oriented) reasons than that he is concerned with uncovering grievances. He consistently emphasizes how important the reporter's eyewitness account is to him and derives from this the possibilities of the socially transformative effect of his texts. Accordingly, he writes:

> Invade everywhere, be curious yourself in order to be able to satisfy the curiosity of others, see everything with your own eyes and find out what you can't make sense of by asking experts. But never forget the personal interests with which the person questioned is tied to the matter and then assess, evaluate, apply the answer. Never be a know-it-all. First let yourself be taught by what you have seen and heard, observed and read, but then form your own opinion. (Ibid.)[43]

And further:

> Invade everywhere! Into the shelters for the homeless, hospitals, pubs, brandy shops, mines, state forests, factories, workhouses, tuberculosis shelters, police arrests, prisons. invade the mysteries of the lives of the factory and transport workers, the city and state workers, the vagrants and prostitutes; invade the farms and stables of the landowners and the

---

41  Cf. Winter 1914a: 1.
42  Winter 1914b: 1. "Die Redaktion ist nur Papier, das Leben ist draußen."
43  "Ueberall eindringen, selber neugierig sein, um die Neugierde anderer befriedigen zu können, alles mit eigenen Augen schauen und was man sich nicht zusammenreimen kann, durch Fragen bei Kundigen herausbekommen, dabei aber nie vergessen, mit welchen persönlichen Interessen der Befragte an die Sache gekettet ist und danach die Antwort einschätzen, werten, anwenden. Nie etwas besser wissen wollen, erst sich belehren lassen durch das Geschaute und Erfragte, Beobachtete und Nachgelesene, dann aber ein eigenes Urteil bilden."

welfare policies of Krupp and company; invade the emigrant ships and emigrant bureaus; get into people's cars, look into pots, measure and describe the living quarters, reach out and do the work yourself where it is necessary to research the truth. Never visit princes. But look everywhere, if possible unrecognized and unexpectedly, to make sure everything is right. If he does that, the reporter will bring home one sensation after the other, and above all he will be able to show how incapable today's society is of healing the wounds it inflicts itself on the body politic. [...]. As for people themselves, that's what they want to read about. (Ibid.)[44]

This programmatic approach led to very clear political positions. To this end, Winter presented laboriously compiled facts in his texts, often arranged in tables, from which he then drew conclusions. An example for this is the text "Warehouse worker for a day" ("Ein Tag Lagerhausarbeiter") from 1900. After he went undercover and researched exactly how much the individual work brought in wages and discovered inadequacies everywhere, he came to the following conclusion:

> I thought this calculation was useful so that the Christian gentlemen in the town hall, who for three years had left the demands of the warehouse workers untouched, would finally know what those poor devils have to perform for their shabby wages.[45]

---

44  "Ueberall eindringen! In die Obdachlosenasyle, Krankenhäuser, Volkskneipen, Branntweinbuden, Bergwerke, Staatsforste, Fabriken, Armenhäuser, Tuberkulosenheime, Polizeiarreste, Gefängnisse, in die Geheimnisse des Lebens der Fabrik- und Verkehrsarbeiter, der städtischen und Staatsarbeiter, der Landstreicher und Prostituierten; eindringen in die Höfe und Menschenställe der Ostelbier und in die Wohlfahrtspolitik der Krupp und Konsorten; eindringen in die Auswandererschiffe und Auswandererbureaus; den Menschen in die Wagen steigen, in die Töpfe gucken, die Wohnpferche ausmessen und schildern, selbst arbeitend zugreifen, wo es nötig ist, die Wahrheit zu erforschen, nie Prinzenbesuche machen, sondern überall womöglich unerkannt und unvermutet nach dem Rechten sehen, und Sensation um Sensation wird der Berichterstatter heimbringen, und an allen diesen Sensationen wird er vor allem zeigen können, wie unfähig die heutige Gesellschaft ist, die Wunden zu heilen, die sie selbst dem Volkskörper schlägt. [...] Was die Menschen selber angeht, da lesen sie auch."

45  Winter 1988b [1900]: 13. "Ich hielt diese Berechnung für nützlich, damit die christlichen Herren im Rathaus, die schon seit Jahren die Forderungen der Lagerhausarbeiter unerledigt lassen, endlich wissen, was diese armen Teufel für den schäbigen Lohn leisten müssen."

What is particularly interesting about Winter's texts is the formal design. In comparison to von Kupffer, who, as the example above shows, incorporates his observed facts into the running text, Winter presents his in clear tables. In his text "In the realm of the Alpines" ("Im Reich der Alpinen", 1904) he presents the total wages of the workers involved in steel production:

> Die Grundlöhne beim Hochofen betrugen: (The basic wages at the blast furnace were:)

| | |
|---|---|
| Für (for) 2 Schmelzer (smelters) | à 4 Kr. 80 H. = 9 Kr. 60 H. |
| Für 2 erste Helfer (1st helpers) | à 4 Kr.     = 8 Kr. |
| Für 2 zweite Helfer (2nd helpers) | à 3 Kr. 80 H. = 7 Kr. 60 H. |
| Für 2 Gleisputzer (track cleaners) | à 2 Kr. 80 H. = 5 Kr. 60 H. |
| Für 2 Schlackenpasser (slag passers) | à 2 Kr. 60 H. = 5 Kr .20 H . |
| Für 2 Apparatwärter (operators) | à 2 Kr. 60 H. = 5 Kr. 20 H. |
| Für 2 Gasreiniger (gas purifiers) | à 2 Kr. 40 H. = 4 Kr. 80 H. |
| Für 2 Maßmacher (measurers) | à 2 Kr. 60 H. = 5 Kr. 20 H. |
| Für 2 Maschinenwärter (machine attendants) | à 4 Kr.     = 8 Kr. |
| Für 2 Schmierer (greasers) | à 2 Kr. 70 H. = 5 Kr. 40 H. |
| Für 2 Pumpenwärter (pump attendants) | à 2 Kr. 80 H. = 5 Kr. 60 H. |
| Für 2 Kesselwärter (boiler attendants) | à 2 Kr. 70 H. = 5 Kr. 40 H. |
| Für 2 Fördermaschinisten (conveyor operators) | à 3 Kr.     = 6 Kr. |
| Für Gichtvorarbeiter (blast furnace foremen) | à 3 Kr. 80 H. = 7 Kr. 60 H. |
| Für 4 Gichter (blast furnace workers) | à 3 Kr. 60 H. = 14 Kr. 40 H. |

> Es hatten 32 Mann einen Gesamtgrundlohn von 103 Kr. 60 H. (32 men had a total basic wage of 103 Kr. 60 H.)[46]

The superficial similarity between the reports by von Kupffer and Winter disappears on closer inspection. Winter has no interest in a simple depiction, let alone a photographic reproduction of reality. There are also no strategic claims aimed at customer reach and loyalty. His goal is to make a useful contribution – as in this example by making basic salaries visible[47] or, as in the previous example, by pointing out exploitative employment relationships. With regard to Kisch's basic requirements for the appropriate work of the reporter,

---

46  Winter 1988a [1904]: 157.
47  Cf. Riesenfellner 1987: 136.

Winter leans more towards social responsibility than von Kupffer. In his writing, facts are there to take a stand on workers' struggles for fair treatment – the kind of objectivity Winter cares about.

## 5. Summary

The question of the use of facts in journalism is nearly as old as the genre itself. On the contrary to what is often suggested, the possible answers are far from being unambiguous. If you take a step back from long-lived debate about facts in German-language journalism, different intentions can be identified. At first glance, they are obscured by the prevailing debate about the factual quality of the depiction of the texts. But even if all honest reporters stick to facts, not all of them are equally interested in "reality" but use it, so to speak, for further goals.

Both authors presented here are highly interested in facts. A closer look, however, shows that the reasons for this interest are very different. Considering Klaus' breakdown of the different reasons for the use of facts in journalistic work, the differences between von Kupffer's and Winter's intentions become evident. While von Kupffer is interested in the strategic use of facts in his reports to set himself and his newly founded newspaper apart from the rest of the market, Winter's approach focuses on the purposeful use of facts, i.e. their credibility and usefulness in the workers' struggle for fair treatment. Both emphasize the contextual value of facts including their presentation. With such a look at von Kupffer's and Winter's aims not only Kisch's statement on the debate about facts of the 1920s can be viewed in all its different contours. Also, the varied values that flowed into his three conditions for journalistic work and its only apparent contradictions emerge reframed.

## Bibliography

Bleicher, Joan Kristin (ed.) (2004): *Grenzgänger. Formen des New Journalism*, Wiesbaden.

Eberwein, Tobias (2014): *Literarischer Journalismus. Theorie – Traditionen – Gegenwart*, Köln.

Geisler, Michael (1982): *Die literarische Reportage in Deutschland. Möglichkeiten und Grenzen eines operativen Genres*, Königstein/Ts.

Haas, Hannes (2006): "Max Winter (1870-1937). Leben und Werk", in: Winter, Max: *Expeditionen ins dunkelste Wien. Meisterwerke der Sozialreportage*, Wien, 9–13.
— (1999): *Empirischer Journalismus. Verfahren zur Erkundung gesellschaftlicher Wirklichkeit*, Wien/Köln/Weimar.
Haller, Michael (2020): *Die Reportage. Theorie und Praxis des Erzähljournalismus*, Köln.
Kisch, Egon Erwin (1983): *Gesammelte Werke in Einzelausgaben. Band 8: Mein Leben für die Zeitung. 1906-1925. Journalistische Texte 1*, ed. Bodo Uhse/Gisela Kisch, cont. Fritz Hofmann/Josef Poláček, Berlin/Weimar.
— (1983a) [1918]: "Wesen des Reporters", in: id., *Gesammelte Werke in Einzelausgaben. Band 8: Mein Leben für die Zeitung. 1906-1925. Journalistische Texte 1*, 205–208.
— (1983b) [1918]: "Dogma der Unfehlbarkeit der Presse", in: id., *Gesammelte Werke in Einzelausgaben. Band 8: Mein Leben für die Zeitung. 1906-1925. Journalistische Texte 1*, 208–216.
— (1983c) [1935]: "Reportage als Kunstform und Kampfform", in: id.: *Gesammelte Werke in Einzelausgaben. Band 9: Mein Leben für die Zeitung. 1926-1947. Journalistische Texte 2*, ed. Bodo Uhse/Gisela Kisch, cont. Fritz Hofmann/ Josef Poláček, Berlin/Weimar, 397–400.
— (1978) [1925]: "Vorwort zum 'Rasenden Reporter'", in: id.: *Gesammelte Werke in Einzelausgaben. Band 5: Der rasende Reporter, Hetzjagd durch die Zeit, Wagnisse in aller Welt, Kriminalistisches Reisebuch*, ed. Bodo Uhse/Gisela Kisch, Berlin/Weimar, 659–660.
Klaus, Elisabeth (2004): "Jenseits der Grenzen. Die problematische Unterscheidung zwischen Fakt und Fiktion", in: Bleicher, Joan Kristin (ed.): *Grenzgänger. Formen des New Journalism*, Wiesbaden, 100–125.
Knaller, Susanne (2015): *Die Realität der Kunst. Programme und Theorien zu Literatur, Kunst und Fotografie seit 1700*, Paderborn.
Kostenzer, Caterina (2009): *Die literarische Reportage. Über eine hybride Form zwischen Journalismus und Literatur*, Innsbruck/Wien/Bozen.
Kupffer, Hugo von (2019): *Reporterstreifzüge. Die ersten modernen Reportagen aus Berlin*, ed. Fabian Mauch, Düsseldorf.
— (2019a) [1891]: "Eine Nacht bei der Fleischschau", in: id., *Reporterstreifzüge. Die ersten modernen Reportagen aus Berlin*, 175–181.
— (2019b) [1889]: "Vorwort", in: id., *Reporterstreifzüge. Die ersten modernen Reportagen aus Berlin*, 7–9.

— (2019c) [1888]: "Soldaten-Ede", in: id., *Reporterstreifzüge. Die ersten modernen Reportagen aus Berlin*, 66–72.

Lania, Leo (1926): "Reportage als soziale Funktion", in: *Die Literarische Welt* 2, 5–6.

Mauch, Fabian (2019): "'Unretouchierte Momentphotographien'. Hugo von Kupffers 'Reporterstreifzüge' 1886-1892", in: Kupffer, Hugo von: *Reporterstreifzüge. Die ersten modernen Reportagen aus Berlin*, ed. Fabian Mauch, Düsseldorf, 245–264.

Michael, Hendrik (2016): "'Wir Weltstädter!'. Handlungs- und Deutungsmuster eines neuen Journalisten am Fallbeispiel Hugo von Kupffers (1853-1928)", in: *Jahrbuch für Kommunikationsgeschichte* 18, 51–77.

Patka, Marcus G. (1997): *Egon Erwin Kisch. Stationen im Leben eines streitbaren Autors*, Wien.

Riesenfellner, Stefan (1987): *Der Sozialreporter. Max Winter im alten Österreich*, Wien.

Roß, Dieter (2004): "Fakten und/oder Fiktionen. Zur Geschichte der Beziehungen zwischen Journalismus und Literatur in Deutschland", in: Bleicher, Joan Kristin (ed.): *Grenzgänger. Formen des New Journalism*, Wiesbaden, 74–99.

Schütz, Erhard (ed.) (1974): *Reporter und Reportagen. Texte zur Theorie und Praxis der Reportage der zwanziger Jahre. Ein Lesebuch*, Gießen.

Weiß, Helmut (1974) [1931]: "Schärfere Waffen für die Literaturfront – Kurzgeschichte und Reportage", in: Schütz, Erhard (ed.): *Reporter und Reportagen. Texte zur Theorie und Praxis der Reportage der zwanziger Jahre. Ein Lesebuch*, Gießen, 52–58.

Winter, Max (2006): *Expeditionen ins dunkelste Wien. Meisterwerke der Sozialreportage*, ed. Hannes Haas, Wien.

— (1988): *Arbeitswelt um 1900. Texte zur Alltagsgeschichte von Max Winter*, ed. Stefan Riesenfellner, Wien.

— (1988a) [1904]: "Im Reich der Alpinen", in: id., *Arbeitswelt um 1900. Texte zur Alltagsgeschichte von Max Winter*, 151–163.

— (1988b) [1900]: "Ein Tag Lagerhausarbeiter", in: id., *Arbeitswelt um 1900. Texte zur Alltagsgeschichte von Max Winter*, 12–29.

— (1914a): "Die Lokalredaktion I. Was ihr fehlt", in: *Volksstimme* (01.07.1914), 1.

— (1914b): "Die Lokalredaktion II. Das Amt des Berichterstatters", in: *Volksstimme* (02.07.1914), 1.

Wurich, Marc (2019): *Urbanitätserfahrung und Erzählen. Berlin-Romane zwischen 1880 und 1920*, Baden-Baden.

# (Body) Positivity in Social Media
## Mise-en-scène and Performing Digital Facticity

*Elke Höfler (University of Graz)*

## Introduction

In a first step, this article takes up digitality as both a feature and a designation of the 21$^{st}$ century and sets it out as a framework before going into the postulate of singularity as a central moment of self-promotion in social networks, in general, and on Instagram as a social network mainly used by young people, in particular. In doing so, it will be shown which tendencies dominate self-promotions and how they may influence young people. Above all, mental health, and body image (keyword: body positivity) are often negatively influenced by staging a performed digital facticity. The article is intended as a call for a critical approach to and reflection on present-day phenomena and not as a call to abandon social networks. They are part of contemporary society with its culture of digitality and as such their strengths should be leveraged.

## 1. A New 21$^{st}$ Century Culture

Researchers from various disciplines, for example cultural studies (e.g., Stalder), didactics (e.g., Siemens), sociology (e.g., Reckwitz), have used diverse terms to describe the 21$^{st}$ century and its different designations: knowledge society, information society, and network society.[1] In the 21$^{st}$ century, classic roles are blurring and with them divisive structures. Anyone can be an author, reader, and publisher in the Social Web. As a viewer of a post on Instagram, we are readers; if we write a comment or give a 'like,' we interact and go from reader to author. If we write our own post, we are the author,

---

1  Cf. Stalder 2017: 30–34.

if we share it, we are the publisher. Especially these last two roles cannot be clearly separated anymore. This means that the production of information is often increasing exponentially, and information is disseminated quickly within social networks and communities worldwide. The world is opening up or moving closer together, depending on the perspective. Editorial structures, as known from newspapers or magazines, are disappearing or gone. Information is frequently no longer checked for accuracy, relevance, and up-to-datedness before publication. Facts and opinions are mixed, as are facts and falsifications. A new culture is emerging. Those who take a closer look at the 21$^{st}$ century from the perspective of these current social phenomena and constellations identify a "culture of digitality,"[2] which Felix Stalder, a Swiss cultural and media scientist, fixes on several inherent parameters in his book of the same name.

## 1.1 A Culture of Digitality

Culture and cultural notions, according to Stalder, are negotiable and changeable depending on place and time. Culture is not a static phenomenon. It is, instead, "characterized by a juxtaposition, co-existence, and opposition of processes of dissolution and constitution."[3] In coexistence, this means that "self-determination and heteronomy [become] entangled up to a certain point where both poles constitute each other."[4] This raises the question of whether the "aesthetic projections – immateriality, perfection and virtuality – that continue to determine the image of the 'digital'" must, can or should be discarded, as currents towards post-digitality suggest. Stalder states that "the presence of digitality beyond digital media [...] gives the culture of digitality its dominance."[5] As a result, society experiences a "diversification and liquefaction of cultural practices and social roles."[6] Individual realities of life become topics of public interest and social relevance: such as the decision for a certain way of eating (e.g., the increasing importance of clean eating, veganism, and superfoods), a specific body cult (e.g., the everydayness of tattoos and piercings, or numerous fitness initiatives), or the importance of one's own

---

2 Ibid. If not indicated otherwise, all translations are by E.H.
3 Ibid.: 17.
4 Ibid.
5 Ibid.: 19, 20.
6 Cf. ibid.: 48–49.

well-being achievable e.g., through courses teaching yoga or mindfulness, or digital detox. Behavior that was once prevalent in subcultures becomes mainstream. Due to the possibilities of (digital) dissemination via social networks – such as Instagram for example – that are hardly limited in time and place, these behavioral attitudes are no longer a latent but a constitutive feature of social discourse.

According to Stalder, there are three forms of digitality: referentiality, communality and algorithmicity. The latter refers to machine-provided filtering strategies, to cope with the high informational load within the World Wide Web, whereas referentiality could be seen as an inter-approach: users create cultural artefacts that interrelate. These references can be obvious or latent, they can be recognizable to all or only to a specific group. Society is built of different groups and cultures, i.e., according to Stalder, "formations that produce self-referential worlds that modulate different dimensions of existence [...]. Dynamics of network power operate in them, configuring voluntariness and coercion, autonomy, and heteronomy in new ways."[7] People decide whether to participate or not based on rational or emotional considerations. These considerations are reflected in both the choice and the quality of interaction and participation in the culture of digitality. It is therefore incumbent on individuals to "more or less bindingly determine how they relate to themselves, to each other and to the world, and to which frames of reference their actions should be oriented."[8] Emotion and rationale play just as significant a role in decision-making as a latent mentality of comparison.

## 1.2 A Culture of the Attractive

In his works, the German sociologist and cultural scientist Andreas Reckwitz studies the role of emotionality in the modern age.[9] In a monograph of the same name, he describes the contemporary modern society[10] as a "society of singularities" and defines its culture as a *"culture of the authentic,* which is at the same time a *culture of the attractive."*[11] Singularity, authenticity, and attractiveness are three adjectives to qualify the society we nowadays live in.

---

[7] Cf. ibid.: 13.
[8] Stalder 2017: 16–17.
[9] Reckwitz 2019a and b.
[10] It should be noted that this is an analysis of the developed societies.
[11] Reckwitz 2019a: 10.

Reckwitz emphasizes that our society and its actions would follow the *"logic of the particular."*[12] According to the author, attractiveness, authenticity, and singularity are motives that influence our actions and subsequently our interactions. To give an example: Companies, but also educational institutions, have been looking for and pointing out their unique sales argument to promote their products and artefacts and to reach their (future) customers' and students' attention.

People are seeking and cultivating their own talents, "life [is] not simply lived, it is curated."[13] The late-modern subject is constantly performing their supposed and/or staged self, highlighting their unique natural and non-artificial selling points, in front of their audience. "Only when it appears authentic it is attractive."[14] Reckwitz, in his monograph, updates the concept of identity described in the 1960s by Erikson:

> *Identity in the modern sense* means a person's consciousness of being different from other people *(individuality)* as well as remaining essentially the same person, distinguished by certain characteristics, over time *(continuity)* and across different situations *(consistency)*.[15]

Individuality in the late-modern age seems to be synonymous with singularity or the special. Individuals show off their individuality regarding their clothing styles, their dietary habits, or a specific body cult as well as their cultural preferences in the fields of music, art, or literature. To stay authentic, these cultivated and staged individual character traits must show both continuity and consistency. Mistakes and slips are discovered by the audience and socially 'punished.'[16]

This corresponds to Stalder's understanding of the culture of digitality, which makes diversity and otherness visible and is the result of a process that has led to a paradigm shift.[17] This paradigm shift is reflected in a revaluation of classical values. Whereas only a few years ago it was important not to stand out but to be conformist, today other values apply: "experimentation,

---

12  Ibid.: 11. If not indicated otherwise, emphasis is in the original citation.
13  Ibid.: 9.
14  Ibid.
15  Erikson 1966: 107.
16  In this context, social punishment means, for example, not receiving attention through likes and comments or unfollowing.
17  Stalder 2017: 33.

openness to new things, flexibility and change have now been established as positively occupied basic values."[18] For Reckwitz, however, the subject's self-determination[19] is no longer a decision independently taken, rather it is omitted in the "striving for uniqueness and exceptionality which to achieve has admittedly become not only a subjective desire but a paradoxical social expectation."[20] What used to be an individual choice is now a social obligation. What is classified as *singular* and *authentic* is not pre-determined but "*socially fabricated*."[21] The valuation and revaluation mechanisms are subject to their own, culturally determined and temporally fluid logics. They are neither static nor stable and least of all predictable. So, what is classified as *unique* and *singular* today may already belong to the mainstream tomorrow. According to Reckwitz, the individual is constantly under pressure, "the social logic of singularities represents for its participants a reality with considerable, even inexorable consequences."[22] Our society and its logics demand steady adaptations as singularities are "what the social revolves around."[23] The latent paradox between the singular and the social reality disappears at second glance: The valorization of one's particularity takes place through the other's judgement, according to Wolfgang Prinz who assumes the social construction of subjectivity:

> The mind is [...] open in two senses: on the one hand, in that it is created and shaped in and through the mirror of others and therefore designs itself according to the model of others. On the other hand, it is open and extremely receptive to all the knowledge it can acquire about the actions, thoughts, and knowledge of others.[24]

The individual may not define itself as an individual but by how others see it. Identity formation and identity development take place via the diversions of judgement by others. Hence, the identity construction is above all other-directed and not self-determined. One's own value is defined and attributed

---

18  Ibid.
19  Cf. Prinz 2016.
20  Reckwitz 2019a: 9.
21  Ibid.: 13.
22  Ibid.: 14.
23  Ibid.: 13.
24  Prinz 2016: 19.

by others. An acting person measures their actions by the audience's reactions. Only if one's actions are noticed and even imitated by others, i.e., what Stalder[25] calls *referentiality*, value is attributed.[26] Authenticity, attractiveness, and singularity serve as assessment criteria. These observations and reflections lead to processes of comparison and a ductus of the comparative and ultimately the superlative in social interaction.

## 1.3 A Culture of Comparison

If it remains for others to recognize and valorize one's singularity as such, this may lead to a change in behavior. The focus of one's own actions is being directed towards the evaluation by the other, thus, performance is shifted from the private sphere to the public sphere. The individual is a "social product"[27] and performs within a network formed by loose and strong nodes determined by an implicit or explicit challenge and pressure to compete with others. One not only tries to eat health*ier* or be fit*ter* than the other but strives, longing for singularity, to eat the health*iest* and be the fitt*est*. Consequently, everyone stages and fictionalizes their lives. The result is an illusionary *mise-en-scène* and a social paradox: Life is documented in its exceptionality and reduced to the positive moments: "The late modern culture of the subject is in a certain sense a *radically emotionalized culture*,"[28] which defines itself through "the production of positive emotions as the central meaning of life" and has become a *"positive culture of emotions."*[29] The joyful satisfaction of one's own needs and the experience of extraordinary moments become central contents of life. Life is celebrated with playful ease and harmony, whereby this celebration is to be seen in its double contingency. The performance is always based on the audience's (i.e., the others') expectations. It does not necessarily arise out of an intrinsic but rather extrinsic motivation: The yoga session to find one's center or the mindfulness seminar are transformed from a private into a public affair. The dichotomy of private and public blurs in the *mise-en-scène* of one's life

---

25   Stalder 2017.
26   Cf. Prinz 2016: 239.
27   Reckwitz 2019b: 206.
28   Ibid.: 205.
29   Ibid.

and status. We are playing the "status game"[30] and it's our status and others paying attention to our status that define who we are.

Paradoxically, however, the put-on positivity and dominance of (positive) emotionality leads "as unintentionally as systematically and to an increased degree to *negative* emotions."[31] The continuous judgement and comparison with others result in "a phantasm that one's own real life – except perhaps in certain, prominent moments – hardly ever satisfies."[32] Reckwitz names "disappointment and frustration, excessive demands and envy, fear, despair and meaninglessness"[33] as possible reactions to a competitive culture of comparison, which can manifest themselves on two levels: Those reactions "either have a self-destructive effect inwardly and express themselves in the aforementioned psychosomatic clinical pictures or destructively outwardly, for example in the form of aggressive hate speech in the social media or even in acts of hatred such as the rampage."[34] The rationality of acting and thinking is often pushed back behind emotionality which is particularly evident in the self-promotion on social networks as a parallel reality.

## 2. Social Networks: The Main Social Space

Participation in the culture of digitality is determined by using social media and especially social networks, where the softening of the traditional dichotomy of private and public is just becoming clear, "as more and more actors with their own claims to meaning step out of the private-personal space" into the public sphere. Social networks have become their "main social space" of action.[35] Participation in social networks is selective; the selection criteria are fluid and can be adapted to the situation: rational and emotional factors (e.g., to form job-oriented as opposed to friendship-oriented networks) can come into play in decision-making. In some networks, the nodes can be looser or tighter. Social networks enable to exchange information, to establish and/or maintain, and to (re)construct one's identity and communication.[36]

---

30   Storr 2021.
31   Reckwitz 2019b: 205.
32   Ibid.: 205.
33   Ibid.: 206.
34   Ibid.
35   Stalder 2017: 38, 39.
36   Cf. Schmidt 2006.

Ten years ago, Kaplan and Haenlein attempted to classify social media and define "theories in the field of media research (social presence, media richness) and social processes (self-presentation, self-disclosure)" as "the two key elements of social media."[37] They state that the "higher the social presence, the greater the social influence that the communication partners have on each other's behavior."[38] Social presence is constitutive for the form and quality of the communicative relationship level. On the other side of their classification, they put self-representation, since people "in any type of social interaction [...] have the desire to control the impressions other people form of them."[39] The reasons for this controlling behavior vary; the authors cite the desire to be perceived and to convey an image that is in line with one's own personality or one's own desires.[40] In this context, Erving Goffman raises the question of the authenticity of self-promotion: "Sometimes the individual will act in a thoroughly calculating manner, expressing himself in a given way solely in order to give the kind of impression to others that is likely to evoke from them a specific response he is concerned to obtain."[41] When we interact with others, we try to obtain information about them. So, it is necessary that one discloses pieces of private information that form the image staged of oneself and thus also influence the relationship. In other words:

> [T]he conscious or unconscious revelation of personal information (e.g., thoughts, feelings, likes, dislikes) that is consistent with the image one would like to give. Self-disclosure is a critical step in the development of close relationships (e.g., during dating) but can also occur between complete strangers; for example, when speaking about personal problems with the person seated next to you on an airplane.[42]

We try to convey a certain image of self, display our status[43] and therefore use personal information to put ourselves in the right frame.[44] In communication, interacting partners are "interested in his general socio-economic status, his conception of self, his attitude toward them, his competence, his

---

37   Kaplan/Haenlein 2010: 61.
38   Ibid.
39   Ibid.: 62.
40   Cf. Storr 2018.
41   Goffman 1956: 3.
42   Kaplan/Haenlein 2010: 62.
43   Cf. Storr 2021.
44   Cf. ibid. 2018.

trustworthiness, etc."[45] While in the real world we draw a distinction between communication with known and unknown people and people tend to be reluctant to reveal too much information – depending, amongst others, on their character and prior experience – this boundary is blurring in social networks when privacy settings are more public than private.

If these considerations are related to the perfection and virtuality referred to by Stalder[46] as characteristics of the digital, and the striving for attractiveness and authenticity described by Reckwitz[47] in the context of the search for recognition and valuation of one's singularity, a paradoxical situation emerges: Self-representation in social networks

> has already become so self-evident and normal that anyone who is not active in this in-between space - which is about to become the main social space – i.e., who does not have a publicly viewable profile [...] or who does not position themselves as a producer of information and meaning and is so inconspicuous online that a search engine query for a name does not return any results, is now negatively conspicuous (or, much more rarely, gains status precisely through this absence.[48]

When everyone is on social networks and everyone posts the same thing, they don't stand out. The singularity, then, results from the absence or the conscious renunciation of self-presentation in the virtual world.

## 3. Comparative Identity Construction in Social Networks

The extension[49] of the real world to include the virtual element of social media leads to various identities and processes of identity constructions for those who move in both worlds. Divergent and convergent identities develop. "A social establishment is any place surrounded by fixed barriers to perception in which a particular kind of activity regularly takes place."[50] The roles assumed

---

45  Goffman 1956: 1.
46  Stalder 2017: 19.
47  Cf. Reckwitz 2019a.
48  Stalder 2017: 39.
49  Cf. Seel 1998.
50  Goffman 1956: 152.

or played in these social establishments are not necessarily the same, the images constructed are not bound to be congruent: "Within the walls of a social establishment we find a team of performers who co-operate to present to an audience a given definition of the situation."[51] This co-operation works if the establishment's boundaries are seen as stable and the different roles can be delineated from each other. "Performance disruptions [...] have consequences at three levels of abstraction: personality, interaction, and social structure."[52] Consequently, an identity construction must not only consider these three levels, which are climatically interdependent, but must learn to do so in both the real and the virtual world. The presentation of the self can differ, the communicative intentions can be different, the rules that apply in both worlds differ from each other.[53] The decision to construct one's own personality leads to consequences in (social) interactions and subsequently in social structures, which will be considered separately in the following sections.

### 3.1 Fictionalization of One's Own Personality

If one assumes with Goffman a "front" that people understand in interaction as an "expressive equipment of a standard kind intentionally or unwittingly employed by the individual during his performance"[54] in order to impress the audience or to convey a certain, stylized, positivized, or staged image of oneself and of one's life, this image might correspond to one's own personality or – depending on the demands of the social establishment – might express a certain expectation. Consistency and authenticity, then, play a crucial role that can be described with Zapp as a "staging of reality."[55] The striving for credibility does not result in authenticity but, according to Knaller and Müller, "to stage authenticity effects." It is a matter of "creating a certain mixture between privacy and public, between intimacy and distance."[56] Which characteristics of one's personality are to be emphasized in the virtual reality of social networks is chosen – as mentioned above – for emotional or

---

51  Ibid.
52  Ibid.: 156.
53  Cf. boyd 2014.
54  Goffman 1956: 22.
55  Zapp 2006: 316.
56  Knaller/Müller 2006: 7.

rational reasons. This leads to a *mise-en-scène*, i.e., a fictionalization of oneself which can result in stylization or transfiguration. Fiction is not seen in contrast to truth but to reality.[57] This means that the self-promotion in social media must be seen as convergent or divergent to self-presentation in real life. This, though, does not imply that the person portrayed in real life is the true personality, as there is a "vertical multiplication of reality"[58] between reality and social media. The various realities refer to each other and, in their entirety, "make up the complex and self-structured reality of our society."[59] So, the virtual is to be seen as a space of "possible possibilities" that allows for a reconstruction of oneself.[60] The characteristics chosen are "not false real objects, but true virtual objects for which the question of real reality is entirely indifferent."[61] Just as literature can influence the formation of opinions and identity construction of its readers, images of the social networks as a parallel construction of reality also influence real life worlds.

## 3.2 Recognition-Induced Interaction

When Reckwitz describes our culture as a "thoroughly psychologized culture that incessantly animates individuals to self-reflection and self-transformation,"[62] the behavior in social networks is reminiscent of Bakhtin's carnivalesque counter-world and allows a breakout from the real world. Thus, somebody living as an outsider in the real world can achieve the recognition and attention in the virtual world that they lack in the real world. Exploiting technical possibilities or effective self-presentation strategies, the individual flees into social networks as if into a parallel counter-world in which they can present themselves in a different way. Performing digital facticity, they can be what they wish to be. By staging and stylizing the self, however, they create an ideal display for their followers. The latter, as a result, play the status game,[63] enter a competitive game in the culture of comparison, and probably recognize their averageness and inadequacy in the real world because they cannot achieve this ideal.

---

57  Cf. Esposito 1998.
58  Esposito 2007: 68.
59  Ibid.
60  Esposito 1998: 269.
61  Ibid.: 279.
62  Reckwitz 2019b: 204.
63  Cf. Storr 2021.

The recognition of singularity is measured via reactions, i.e., the number of followers and likes one receives for a contribution; accordingly, recognition manifests "in the form of positive, negative or no feedback."[64] What counts is the quantity of reactions and not the quality,[65] lack of reactions equals lack of recognition and social death: "It is a sign that communication has broken down, and if this state persists, it results in the dissolution of one's own communicatively-constituted social existence."[66] Interaction loses its reciprocity, "fascination"[67] as the currency of valuation ceases to exist, self-promotion is not perceived or valued (anymore). This might result in new forms of one-sided interaction and expressions of "a perceived discrepancy between expectation and reality": Stalking as an expression of morbid attention, cyberbullying as a negative play with singularity, and ghosting as a withdrawal of attention may be mentioned as examples.[68]

## 4. Instagram as a Platform for Young People to Express Themselves

### 4.1 The Use of Instagram

The annual Youth Internet Media Study (JIM Study) published by the *Medienpädagogischer Forschungsverbund Südwest* (mpfs) provides information about media use among German young people between the ages of twelve and 19. On average, young people spend 241 minutes online every day.[69] Looking at apps that are mainly used, i.e., on a daily basis or several times a week, a clear picture emerges: WhatsApp is used by 92 percent (93% girls | 91% boys), Instagram (in second place) by 58 percent (63% girls | 54% boys), TikTok (in third place) by 46% of the respondents (52% girls | 39% boys). The older the respondents get, the more important the image-dominated realities on Instagram become. To illustrate the development: 15% of the 12-13-year-olds surveyed use Instagram, and among the 14-15-year-olds the number of users doubles

---

64 Stalder 2017: 137.
65 Cf. Reckwitz 2019b: 226.
66 Cf. ibid.: 139.
67 Cf. ibid.: 218.
68 Cf. ibid.: 221.
69 Cf. mpfs 2021: 32.

to 30%. A further jump occurs among 16-17-year-olds: Here it is 50%, a rate that remains stable among 18-19-year-olds.[70] When we take a closer look at Instagram, its use has changed in the last years. In 2018, young individuals answered that "participating in the everyday life of people from one's personal environment documented by photos and videos" was the main motive.[71] Active, personal posting was not in the foreground in 2018: "Only just over one in ten say they frequently post photos or videos themselves."[72] In 2018, Instagram was used more receptively, e.g., by liking others' posts, and semi-receptively by commenting on others' posts. This has changed in 2019, as young people state that they publish an average of three to five posts per week.[73] On average, in 2019, young people have 299 followers (girls: 319, boys: 278), with the number increasing with age. According to their answers, 40 percent of the respondents have made their account public and thus visible to everyone.[74] The boundaries between privacy and the public sphere are blurred; the content can be consumed and commented on or liked by everyone, not just the accepted followers. In 2021, the respondents state that they contribute actively to Instagram (43%), use it to stay up to date regarding fashion trends for example (35%) and to get to know new people (31%).[75] Given their frequent use, it is not surprising that a large number of young people are regularly confronted with negative content such as hate speech. Thus, 58 percent state that they have been confronted with hate messages in the last month and 47 percent with offensive content.[76]

---

70    WhatsApp is relatively stable at all age levels (77% | 71% | 83% | 81%). (Cf. ibid.: 35) The increase between 14-15-year-olds and 16-17-year-olds should be scrutinized more closely. This lack is probably due to a change in the privacy regulations, which some time ago led to many young people switching to alternative messenger services, for example Signal or Telegram.
71    mpfs 2018: 40.
72    Ibid.
73    Cf. mpfs 2019: 32.
74    Cf. ibid.
75    Cf. mpfs 2021: 40.
76    Cf. ibid.: 62.

## 4.2 Dominance of the Visual

In the parallel reality of social networks, a competitive comparability, and a dominance of the visual[77] come to bear, limiting the ambiguity of the written word by defining the relationship between *signifiant* and *signifié*. Instagrammers construct a positively idealized image of themselves in their posts through mechanisms of fictionalization and *mise-en-scène*. They supposedly correspond to the desire of media consumers "for an unvarnished reality" and enable "comparisons to one's own every day and unvarnished existence."[78] Instagrammers perform digital facticity. The focus is on self-portrayal, self-promotion and conforming to specific socially prescribed or self-created ideals of beauty, as Gerdenitsch shows in an empirical study using a quantitative image content analysis of different Instagrammers.[79] Preferred posted content is self-portraying images that are not a reflection of reality, but stylized realities. The focus is on superficial, visually clearly conveyable, and subsequently also perceptible content: The focus is on the self and one's own experiences stylized and hyped into the (staged and supposed) singularity.

Presenting healthy eating habits,[80] celebrating personal fitness[81] and living out an exclusive clothing style construct the image of a perfect world, which for many followers becomes an unattainable goal. Instagrammers frequently appear relaxed, happy, and enjoying themselves. When followers begin to compare their own lives to the lives of (always happy, beautiful, fit and healthy) influencers, they are constantly introduced to, they often feel inadequate and failed. Consuming the images has negative or toxic effects on their own body perception, as Tiggermann and Zaccardo, Fardouly et al. as well as Jackson and Luchner show.[82] The exaggerated thinness of the self-promoters, for example, carries into a lean cult.[83] The desire to emulate Instagrammers leads to a competition of superlatives instead of comparatives. A tendency particularly problematic within the phase of identity construction that takes place during puberty: it is not about being thinner than one is – one wants to

---

77  Cf. Reckwitz 2019b: 225–226.
78  Zapp 2006: 318.
79  Gerdenitsch 2019.
80  Cf. Sachin/Paul 2018.
81  Cf. Baker/Walsh 2018; Tiggermann/Zaccardo 2018.
82  Tiggermann/Zaccardo 2018; Fardouly et al. 2018; Jackson/Luchner 2018.
83  Cf. Ging/Garvey 2018; Parz 2017.

be the thinnest. The construction of one's own identity takes place following and trying to reach unattainable ideals that reveal their own inadequacy to the young people rather than allowing them to perceive or emphasize their own strengths. The call for one's own body positivity, as first undertaken specifically for children by Meschke and Crenshaw, is thereby only one consequence of the self-portrayal and self-promotion machinery.[84]

## 4.3  The Blurring of Reality and Fiction

To achieve the highest possible recognition and valuation of one's images, hashtags are used as keywords that allow an unfiltered dissemination of contributions. Contributions – depending on the kind of privacy setting – are searchable and viewable for a target group beyond close friends. On the interactional level, images on topics such as #healthy or #fitspiration but also on #anorexia can be found without editorial review and according to complex algorithms. The competitive game is started and filled with images whose context or origin is not and cannot be verified. As contributions in different media show, Instagrammers too often are not only willing to risk their lives for the best photo but also to use posing strategies and image editing strategies or (softening) filters that blur the line between reality and fiction. Performing digital facticity means to play with reality and fiction.[85] Even though the images convey the impression of being snapshots, in many cases they are highly staged representations. As models they build up a high pressure to recreate such contributions (think of Stalder's referentiality), which in a competitive culture of comparison must be better, more beautiful, more coherent, because nowadays one is "never satisfied with the way of life once found but always seeks the challenge of the new."[86] An addictive behavior develops; the adrenaline only works when the comparative is possible. The rational moment takes a back seat to emotionalization. Even if one knows to be putting oneself in a dangerous situation for a photo, for example by making maximum use of the space on a cliff or searching for the best angle, one may accept the risk out of considerations of the desire for singularity. Life is no longer lived in the here and now, the moment is not necessarily enjoyed but documented as best

---

84  Meschke/Crenshaw 2020.
85  Cf. Storr 2018 and Stalder 2017: 141.
86  Reckwitz 2019b: 229.

as possible for posterity – or followers – against the backdrop of a dominantly visual culture and the demand "Pic or it didn't happen."[87]

## 5. Body Positivity, Dropouts, and Whistle-blowers

The fixation on the ego and self-promotion, the continuous comparison with others, the latent double contingency of one's own decisions on how to (inter)act appear at first glance to contradict sociability. There are nevertheless some initiatives that try to soften the pressure to perform, the striving for recognition, the "popularity contest" and the constant competitive thinking.[88] They do live in these parallel realities too but want to uncover their mechanisms and strategies. They reveal:

- The intention to share: Is a contribution shared to motivate others to do the same (e.g., baking banana bread, clean eating, veganism) and make the best of a situation or is it self-promotion for promotion's sake? Does one show one's commitment in a voluntary institution or in initiatives like #FridaysForFuture out of conviction to show solidarity, or for reasons of double contingency, because followers expect such behavior, and one wants to receive additional recognition? These questions cannot be answered without empirical surveys; the question of intention often remains unanswered.
- Instagram is not real: The journalist and model Danae Mercer (https://www.instagram.com/danaemercer), amongst others, promotes self-love and body positivity on Instagram. In her contributions, she shows how different body postures are when you are taking pictures, how important it is to tense the muscles, to choose the right angle and, in the process, she also shows that cellulite is just as normal as small 'spare tires' on the belly. She breaks through the positivity of the perfect world on Instagram by talking openly about her miscarriage and her (mental) health problems. In this way, she tries – above all – to convince women to love their own bodies despite or even because of their uniqueness.
- Cross-media reception: To reach different target groups, the influences that Instagram, the beautiful ideal world, the staging of positivity wield

---

87  Cf. ibid.: 235.
88  Cf. ibid.: 216 and Stalder 2017: 141.

are taken up together with their negative consequences and addressed in different media. Meschke and Creshaw address children with their appeal for a lived body positivity,[89] while articles in popular magazines such as Time Magazine, for example, are aimed at a broad audience and refer to the toxic effects of social media on mental health.[90] Numerous TED Talks[91] have addressed the issue from different perspectives, many of them following Katherine Ormerod's ideas as published in her book *Why Social Media Is Ruining Your Life*.[92] These different multimodal publications often pursue the renunciation of social media as a goal but the critical handling and questioning of these media should play a more important role than radical renunciation (in the sense of Dieter Baacke's media literacy mode).[93] Parents as role models and schools as critical friends are called upon to teach strategies for critical and reflective use.

*Mise-en-scène* and the performing of digital facticity are everyday phenomena in social networks. If they are not critically questioned, the staged images are perceived as factual realities and subconsciously serve as role models and unachievable targets. The consequences of these images and their messages having a negative impact on mental health have now been sufficiently empirically proven. Education and awareness raising is needed to maintain body positivity, a healthy body image and a healthy attitude in general. Even more so for children and young people whose identity and self-image are still in formation.

## 6. Conclusion

The described focus on singularity and its recognition and the striving for attention pursued and sought by today's subjects lead to a loss of self-determination and freedom of action. Against the backdrop of a double contingency, people may act in an externally determined way, constantly comparing themselves with others and perceiving the staged self-promotion of the other as an

---

89 Meschke/Creshaw 2020.
90 Cf. MacMillan 2017.
91 To name three examples Ormerod 2019; Parnell 2017; Thomas 2017.
92 Ormerod 2020.
93 Baacke 1996.

ideal and a common standard. Living out one's own positive, almost perfect world generates a feeling of inadequacy. Users of social networks, especially Instagrammers, are willing to go to great lengths to receive recognition in the form of likes or comments. Identity construction here takes place in a competitive way through comparison. Outward appearances obviously dominate. Especially for those young people who still are in search of their own identity and immersed in a social system based on contest, performance, and competition, this constellation might be stressful, as they are not yet solidified in their personal choices. The goal of education and training would therefore be to set a good example for the young people and to break out of the comparison ductus.

The considerations of this paper focus on Instagram but can also be applied to other visually dominated networks, such as YouTube, TikTok and Snapchat. Further research is needed on the topic of self-promotion and its consequences which can serve as a basis for further education and training, also for parents and teachers. Children are often left alone with social networks.[94] They need the support of critically thinking and acting adults to be aware of the strategies of performed (digital) facticity, staging and self-presentation as such and not to adopt them unreflectively in their actions and everyday life.

## Bibliography

Baacke, Dieter (1996): "Medienkompetenz – Begrifflichkeit und sozialer Wandel", in: Rein, Antje von (ed.): *Medienkompetenz als Schlüsselbegriff*, Bad Heilbrunn, 112–124.

Baker, Stephanie A./Walsh, Michael. J. (2018): "'Good Morning Fitfam': Top Posts, Hashtags and Gender Display on Instagram", in: *New Media & Society* 20/12, 4553–4570.

boyd, danah (2014): *It's Complicated: The Social Lives of Networked Teens*, New Haven/London.

Erikson, Erik H. (1966): *Identität und Lebenszyklus*, Frankfurt am Main.

Esposito, Elena (2007): *Die Fiktion der wahrscheinlichen Realität*, Frankfurt am Main.

---

94 Cf. boyd 2014.

— (1998): "Fiktion und Virtualität", in: Krämer (ed.): *Medien, Computer, Realität. Wirklichkeitsvorstellungen und Neue Medien*, 269–296.

Fardouly, Jasmine/Willburger, Brydie K./Vartanian, Lenny R. (2018): "Instagram Use and Young Women's Body Image Concerns and Self-objectification: Testing Mediational Pathways", in: *New Media & Society* 20/4, 1380–1395.

Gerdenitsch, Janine (2019): *Zwischen Individualität und Konformität: Selbstdarstellung auf Instagram*, MA, Graz.

Ging, Debbie/Garvey, Sarah (2018): "'Written in These Scars Are the Stories I Can't Explain': A Content Analysis of Pro-ana and Thinspiration Image Sharing on Instagram", in: *New Media & Society* 20/3, 1181–1200.

Goffman, Erving (1956): *The Presentation of Self in Everyday Life*, Edinburgh.

Jackson, Christina A./Luchner, Andrew F. (2018): "Self-presentation Mediates the Relationship between Self-criticism and Emotional Response to Instagram Feedback", in: *Personality and Individual Differences* 133, 1–6.

Kaplan, Andreas M./Haenlein, Michael (2010): "Users of the World, Unite! The Challenges and Opportunities of Social Media", in: *Business Horizons* 53, 59–68.

Knaller, Susanne/Müller, Harro (eds.): *Authentizität. Diskussion eines ästhetischen Begriffs*, München.

Knaller, Susanne/Müller, Harro (2006): "Einleitung", in: id. (eds.), *Authentizität. Diskussion eines ästhetischen Begriffs*, 7–16.

Krämer, Sybille (ed.): *Medien, Computer, Realität. Wirklichkeitsvorstellungen und Neue Medien*, Frankfurt am Main.

MacMillan, Amanda (2017): "Why Instagram Is the Worst Social Media for Mental Health", in: *TIME Magazine* 25 May 2017, https://time.com/4793331/instagram-social-media-mental-health/ (15.04.2022).

Medienpädagogischer Forschungsverbund Südwest (mpfs) (2021) (ed.): *JIM-Studie 2021. Jugend, Information, Medien. Basisuntersuchung zum Medienumgang 12- bis 19-Jähriger*, Stuttgart, https://www.mpfs.de/fileadmin/files/Studien/JIM/2021/JIM-Studie_2021_barrierefrei.pdf (15.04.2022).

— (2019) (ed.): *JIM-Studie 2019. Jugend, Information, Medien. Basisuntersuchung zum Medienumgang 12- bis 19-Jähriger*, Stuttgart, https://www.mpfs.de/fileadmin/files/Studien/JIM/2019/JIM_2019.pdf (15.04.2022).

— (2018) (ed.): *JIM-Studie 2018. Jugend, Information, Medien. Basisuntersuchung zum Medienumgang 12- bis 19-Jähriger*, Stuttgart, https://www.mpfs.de/fileadmin/files/Studien/JIM/2018/Studie/JIM2018_Gesamt.pdf (15.04.2022).

Meschke, Ady/Cresnshaw, Katie (2020): *Her Body Can*, Houston.

Muralidhara, Sachin/Paul, Michael J. (2018): "#Healthy Selfies: Exploration of Health Topics on Instagram", in: *JMIR Public Health and Surveillance* 4/2: E10150.
Ormerod, Katherine (2020): *Why Social Media is Ruining Your Life*, London.
— (2019): *Why Social Media Is Ruining Your Life*, TEDxManchester, https://youtu.be/sBeWrNgMVeM (15.04.2022).
Parnell, Bailey (2017): *Is Social Media Hurting Your Mental Health?*, TEDxRyersonU, https://youtu.be/Czg_9C7gwOo (15.04.2022).
Parz, Natalie (2017): *Mediale Inszenierung von Essstörungen. Wie soziale Netzwerke der Mager-Kult bei Mädchen fördern*, MA, Graz.
Prinz, Wolfgang (2016): *Selbst im Spiegel. Die soziale Konstruktion von Subjektivität*, Berlin.
Reckwitz, Andreas (2019a): *Die Gesellschaft der Singularitäten. Zum Strukturwandel der Moderne*, Berlin.
— (2019b): *Das Ende der Illusionen. Politik, Ökonomie und Kultur in der Spätmoderne*, Berlin.
Schmidt, Jan-Hinrik (2006): *Weblogs. Eine kommunikationssoziologische Studie*, Konstanz.
Seel, Martin (1998): "Medien der Realität und Realität der Medien", in: Krämer (ed.), *Medien, Computer, Realität. Wirklichkeitsvorstellungen und Neue Medien*, 244–268.
Stalder, Felix (2017): *Kultur der Digitalität*, Berlin.
Storr, Will (2021): *The Status Game: On Social Position and How We Use it*, London.
— (2018): *Selfie: How the West Became Self-Obsessed*, London.
Thomas, Ryan (2017): *Live in the Moment: Delete Social Media*, TEDxAshburnSalon, https://youtu.be/pOchBnZJdEk (15.04.2022).
Tiggemann, Marika/Zaccardo, Mia (2018): "'Strong Is the New Skinny': A Content Analysis of #fitspiration Images on Instagram", in: *Journal of Health Psychology* 23/8, 1003–1011.
Zapp, Andrea (2006): "Live – A User's Manual. Künstlerische Skizzen zur Ambivalenz von Webcam und Wirklichkeit", in: Knaller/Müller (eds.), *Authentizität. Diskussion eines ästhetischen Begriffs*, 316–330.

# 'Patchwriting' as Unintentional Fact Writing

Doris Pany-Habsa (University of Graz)

When we think of writing facts, we primarily think of writing procedures by means of which we intentionally create facts: By using specific strategies of representation and argumentation, we claim the status of facticity for certain propositions. However, there are forms of unintentional fact writing. Such fact writing can occur when the writer lacks knowledge of the specific text features that serve as fact-generating within a particular communication like academic writing. Ignoring such fact-generating features can then lead to an unintended attribution of facticity to certain assertions.

In the context of academic writing, this effect might become relevant for students who are not yet familiar with the norms and conventions of academic texts. The phenomenon of unintentional fact writing particularly displays when students apply a writing strategy called 'patchwriting' which occurs when sources are paraphrased. It consists in copying from a correctly documented source text and in then making small changes like deleting single words, modifying the syntax or applying synonyms. This strategy is frequently adopted by students who are in the early stages of their study programs. By deploying patchwriting, they try to ensure that they accurately reproduce content from sources that are still difficult for them to understand. Despite the intention of inexperienced students to meet the requirements of academic writing in terms of content accuracy, patchwriting tends to entail a violation of academic conventions at the level of handling facts.

In the everyday practice of academic instruction, however, patchwriting is usually perceived only very vaguely as a violation of a standard that is difficult to pin down as such. This uncertainty of what exactly is wrong with patchwriting favors the trend of bringing it close to or even identifying it with plagiarism. In recent years, this tendency has increased in view of heated public debates about plagiarism in higher education and is clearly at the expense of students who by applying patchwriting attempt to live up to the standards of academic writing. Since universities need to provide propaedeutic spaces where academic writing can be taught and learned, it seems important to clarify that on the one hand patchwriting is the effect of a learning process and on the other hand to analyze the academic standards violated by it as a result.

Thus, in the following, I will explore patchwriting both as a learning phenomenon and as an offense to academic discourse conventions. Regarding patchwriting as a specific stage of the learning process students undergo when acquiring academic writing skills, I will draw on insights from composition studies and linguistic writing development research. Linguistic research on academic language will provide the means to understand why patchwriting is a noncompliance with the way facts are handled in academic writing and can be conceptualized as unintentional fact writing. In a first step, the description of an example from everyday teaching practice in academia allows for an overview of the issues patchwriting raises in the context of higher education. After having elaborated on the concept of patchwriting, it will then be argued why patchwriting can be perceived as unintentional fact writing. After a side-glance at the current tendency to consider patchwriting an offense close or equal to plagiarism, I will turn to the reasons why patchwriting is used and close with some suggestions for further research on patchwriting and some hints to a productive approach to this writing strategy in higher education.

## A Case of Patchwriting

The following example case comes from my professional practice as a writing educationalist and director of the Writing Center of an Austrian University. At the beginning of 2021, the office of our university's Study Director contacted me and asked me to examine an inquiry they had received from faculty. The office is managed by a lawyer and deals with legal issues arising in the context of study and teaching. The inquiry concerned a seminar paper from a bachelor's degree program and was in the form of an email. The email said that a group of students from the BA study program had submitted a collaboratively authored seminar paper that, according to the instructors, consisted to a great extent of what they call "a collage of patchwriting."[1]

The instructors had checked the paper with a plagiarism detection software and could state that "in general, the sources of the original texts have been indicated." Nevertheless, they emphasize that, according to their academic understanding, patchwriting is a form of plagiarism. At the same time, they point out the basic definition of plagiarism from the Austrian legal framework, according to which plagiarism only occurs when sources are used "without appropriate identification and citation of the source."[2] Concluding their email, they finally ask if, even with documented sources, the "collage of patchwriting" in the seminar paper should be judged as plagiarism and should be graded negatively.

What is particularly striking about the view of the instructors is that, on the one hand, they clearly recognize that the seminar paper is not plagiarism in the sense of the law, but, on the other hand, they tend to proceed with the patchwritten seminar paper as if it were actually plagiarism. It therefore seems that the violation they perceive in the paper is so serious that they locate it in the legal sphere and equate it to breaking the law. This raises two main questions: What kind of standard, norm or convention did the students exactly violate by patchwriting their seminar paper? And why did the instructors react so strongly to the students' patchwriting which is, as already mentioned, quite common among inexperienced academic writers? Before turning to these questions, I would like to describe some general considerations accompanying the discussions of the concept of patchwriting.

## The Concept of Patchwriting

The term patchwriting was coined by Rebecca Moore Howard in 1992. It served the author to identify a specific writing strategy students adopt when paraphrasing sources: For Howard, this strategy is present when students take passages or sentences from a source and integrate them into their own text

---

[1] This and the following quotes are from the email that the instructors sent to the office of the Study Director on 3rd February 2021.

[2] Österreichisches Universitätsgesetz 2002, II. Teil Studienrecht, 1. Abschnitt, Allgemeine Bestimmungen, Begriffsbestimmungen § 51. (2) 31; in German: "ohne entsprechende Kenntlichmachung und Zitierung der Quelle."

with minor linguistic changes. They modify, for example, the word or sentence order of the source text, replace individual words with synonyms, delete sentence elements or change syntactic constructions. According to Howard's observations, this way of integrating sources into one's own text is particularly widespread among students in their first semesters.[3]

By coining the term patchwriting, Howard pursued the goal of separating the phenomenon from an understanding of plagiarism that dominated American universities at the beginning of the 1990s. According to this understanding, the paraphrase of a source is to be regarded as plagiarism if it remains linguistically too close to the source text, even if the source is correctly documented and cited.[4] Since patchwriting necessarily involves a linguistic proximity to the source text, it corresponds to this definition of plagiarism – regardless of whether sources are documented or not.

Howard counters this with the argument that a legal and ethical stigmatization of patchwriting as plagiarism thwarts an important learning process and criminalizes a crucial learning stage.[5] In order to initiate a change of perspective, she advocates recognizing the value of patchwriting as a learning phenomenon. In Howard's view, patchwriting must be considered as the effort that inexperienced writers make with their still very limited means to gain access to the academic discourse community of their subject.[6]

A few years later, Howard elaborates on possible reasons for patchwriting and distinguishes three of them: The first reason for patchwriting can consist of a student's inexperience with conventions of academic writing; the second, of a student's unfamiliarity with the words and ideas of a source text; and the third, of a student's intent to deceive.[7] In this last case, however, sources would not be documented and the legal definition of plagiarism would in fact apply. This special case of patchwriting can be neglected, however, because Howard's aim in coining the term was to focus on the learning

---

3   Cf. Howard 1992: 233–236. Howard's exact definition of patchwriting is: "copying from a source text and then deleting some words, altering grammatical structures, or plugging in one-for-one synonym substitutes." (233).

4   It can be found, for example, in the 1991 edition of the *Bedford Handbook for Writers*: "Two different acts are considered plagiarism: (1) borrowing someone's ideas, information, or language without documenting the source and (2) *documenting the source but paraphrasing the source's language too closely*." Hacker 1991: 507, my emphasis.

5   Cf. Howard 1995: 796, 802.

6   Cf. Howard 1992: 233.

7   Cf. Howard 1995: 799–800.

of students instead of a priori presuming intentions to deceive. Howard's intention has shaped the use of the term in composition studies and writing didactics, where patchwriting is mainly used when sources are correctly documented.[8]

## The Offensiveness of Patchwriting

Given all this evidence for the inoffensiveness of patchwriting applied by students in academic learning processes, why did the instructors of the example case react so strongly to the student's paper and why did they perceive it as something as serious as plagiarism? The precondition for this view of patchwriting is the modern conception of science as it developed on the threshold from the 18$^{th}$ to the 19$^{th}$ century. At this time, an older conception of science was eroding: one according to which science is to be understood as the totality of knowledge or as a supratemporally valid system of true statements. This understanding of science was replaced by the concept of science as a continuous search for new and always renewable knowledge. This understanding of science as an interminable search for everchanging knowledge was powerfully shaped by Wilhelm von Humboldt who defined science as "something that has not yet been fully found and can never be fully found."[9] This temporalized concept of science, which defines science as a permanent research process, highlights the provisional character of existing knowledge and the need to continuously revise and expand it. In this sense, producing new knowledge by expanding, questioning, and correcting existing knowledge is at the core of modern scientific practice.

This modern scientific practice is accompanied by a specific kind of communication for which, in recent years, the term 'eristics' has emerged in linguistic research on academic writing. The term goes back to the Greek 'eristiké téchnē' ('art tending to dispute') and was originally used pejoratively to brand empty sophist disputation. Despite this negative connotation, linguists have taken up the term and introduced the concept of 'eristic literacy' to characterize the specificity of academic literacy beyond the manifold discipline-specific writing cultures. The foundations for this were laid in the 1990s by Harald

---

8   Cf. among others Jamison 2016, Li/Casanave 2012, and Pecorari 2003.
9   Humboldt 1964 [1810]: 257, my English translation. In German: "etwas noch nicht ganz Gefundenes und nie ganz Aufzufindendes."

Weinrich and Konrad Ehlich. Weinrich spoke of the "criticism imperative" in science, according to which a critical examination of existing knowledge is a necessary condition for scientific activity and writing.[10] Ehlich pointed out that academic texts do not only have an assertive dimension but also an eristic dimension because they are applied to challenge existing knowledge.[11] Since the 2010s, the establishment and elaboration of the concept of 'eristic literacy' has been largely driven by the linguists Helmuth Feilke and Katrin Lehnen.[12]

Now that the importance of questioning and criticizing in academic writing has been highlighted, one can note that referring to existing knowledge of course not only occurs through argumentation and critique. Rather, we can assume that in science there is always something like a "realm of dispute" and a "realm of reliability" to use a compelling pair of terms from Winfried Thielmann.[13] While the realm of dispute refers to all the research findings whose validity is still being discussed and negotiated by a certain community, the realm of reliability is that part of shared knowledge that is recognized as undisputable and binding. Researchers use to refer to it in an affirmative way. Nevertheless, we should keep the concept of eristic literacy in mind because we can assume that in the paradigm of modern science new knowledge always has to cross the realm of dispute before it reaches the binding realm of reliability. At this point, however, we can state that modern scientific practice always includes an affirmative or critical reference to previous knowledge.

In academic texts, this reference to existing knowledge takes the shape of intertextuality. It is a very specific form of intertextuality that can be described with Thorsten Pohl as "explicitly controlled intertextuality."[14] According to Pohl, this explicitly controlled intertextuality is characterized by the following aspects:

1) The references to other texts have to meet the highest standards of precision.[15] This occurs in the form of precise source citations and an appropriate citation apparatus.

---

10  Cf. Weinrich 1994: 3; in German: "Kritikgebot."
11  Cf. Ehlich 1995: 329.
12  Cf. Steinseifer/Feilke/Lehnen 2019.
13  Thielmann 2013: 51, in German: "Streitzone" and "Verbindlichkeitszone."
14  Pohl 2007: 294; in German: "explizit kontrollierte Intertextualität."
15  Cf. ibid.

2) Authors have to be aware of references to other texts and they have to make them identifiable to readers by marking them meticulously with the appropriate means.[16] At first glance, this second aspect may seem not so distinct from the first one, but by 'marking them with appropriate means,' Pohl asserts that in most cases markers like footnotes or in-text citations have to be accompanied by explicit linguistic introductions of references. One can think here of signal phrases like "According to XY" or "XY states that."
3) An academic text usually 'does' something with the texts it refers to. It relates to them affirmatively or critically, which is to be indicated in both cases.[17] This confirmative or critical intertextual relationship needs to be signaled with linguistic means like "As XY has shown in his/her influential study" or "XY makes no attempt here to differentiate between," etc.

All three of these aspects described by Pohl are fundamental, yet we can note some differences concerning their relevance:

If a text completely lacks citation – aspect (1) –, it usually cannot be considered an academic text. It would then be perceived as an essay or at best as a popular science text. If there is a partial absence of citation, i.e., if some of the intertextual references are marked by citations and others are not, then the category of plagiarism comes into play and the text cannot pass as a proper academic text either.

As for aspects (2) and (3) – the linguistic signaling of intertextuality – the conventions and norms are more diffuse and discipline-specific. Roughly speaking, we can say that in the natural sciences a reference to binding knowledge can, in many cases, occur without signal phrases, and in-text citations can be sufficient. In the cultural sciences and humanities, where it is all about discourses, cultural phenomena and their interpretation, this is different. No matter if the engagement with the source is affirmative or critical, it is in almost all cases necessary to introduce references linguistically.

Thus, in the humanities, we would always tend to expect an explicit linguistic signaling of intertextuality in academic texts. And going back to our example case, this seems to apply to the instructors as well, since the student authors of the seminar paper have complied with aspect (1) and have

---

16   Cf. ibid.
17   Cf. ibid.

indicated their sources in the form of in-text citations and bibliography. In contrast, they did not meet aspects (2) and (3) to a sufficient extent.

The question now is why exactly, in the eyes of an experienced academic, this neglect to include aspects (2) and (3) seems to be such an offense, that the instructors tended to place the paper on a level with plagiarism. Apparently, the instructors initially had only a diffuse perception that there was something wrong with the seminar paper and that it somehow did not meet the standards of academic writing. In a first attempt to determine more precisely what the offense or the failure was, they had first checked the student text with the university's plagiarism-checking software. The plagiarism-check, however, only confirmed that there were similarities with the source texts, but these sources were mostly correctly documented. The instructors had therefore realized that aspect (1) was met and that they could clearly exclude plagiarism. Still, they felt that the students had done something wrong, and they continued investigating the case by browsing citation manuals. There they came across the term 'patchwriting' and considered it appropriate to label the student's error. For them, the offense was so strong that they tended to consider patchwriting equal to plagiarism and were ready to grade the paper negatively. Since they were not sure if such a decision was covered by law, they turned to the lawyer in the office of the university's Study Director.

Obviously, the way the instructors had dealt with the matter is quite comprehensible. For it is certainly not a core task of academics to precisely read up on concepts of writing-didactics. Nor do they need to reflect in detail on academic intertextuality norms. They need to do this even less, since experienced academic writers handle the standards and conventions of academic writing largely as practical know-how, which is not automatically accessible to systematic reflection. Of course, academics too operate with explicit knowledge about the genre rules of academic texts, e.g., with knowledge about citation systems or with certain structuring conventions like the IMRAD structure.[18] However, implicit knowledge makes up the main part.

This is a basic argument for the questions that came up with the case example: Why did the instructors react so strongly to the student's patchwriting and why did they perceive it as something as serious as plagiarism? Since the implicitness of genre knowledge poses a methodological problem, one would probably need empirical research to solve it definitively. What I would like to

---

18  The acronym 'IMRAD' stands for the following structure: Introduction, Material/Methods, Results, and Discussion.

elaborate on here is some hypotheses that would have to be empirically tested later on.

In the attempt to find an explanation for the instructors' reaction, at first, I remembered observations made when reading student papers during my doctoral studies in Romance Literature. Sentences like: "Boccaccio develops his institutional argument most fully in the defense of poetry in the Author's Conclusion of the *Decameron* (cf. Eisner 2013: 21),"[19] used to give me the impression that something was wrong. If the person had written: "As Eisner pointed out, Boccaccio develops [...]," everything would have been sound. With the first version, however, the impression arises that something is reproduced without distance, as if it had not even occurred to the student that this was a statement by Eisner that could also be questioned and not to be taken for granted. It even seems as if the student was simply confusing a philologist's observation on a text by Boccaccio with a fact. At this point the concept of 'fact' becomes important.

## Patchwriting and Fact Writing

Relying on implicit genre knowledge, one can say in a first approximation, that when reading such a sentence in a student paper, the impression arises that facticity is falsely attributed to a simple statement that still has to be discussed and verified. This leads to the assumption that the absence of explicit linguistic signaling of intertextuality can become a marker for facticity in academic texts. Or, to put it another way: Given the eristic grounding of academic communication, the absence of linguistic intertextuality markers leads to the perception that the respective content can be referred to as something factual.

The confusion caused by sentences like the one quoted above seems to result from dissonant experiences that we have when reading them. This experience of dissonance arises because, on the one hand, the in-text citation clearly indicates that someone else's statement is being referenced. And, on the other hand, according to the rules of eristic-based scholarly communication, the in-text citation triggers the expectation that the author will likewise signal her or his perspective on the reference in the form of an introduction to or a comment on it. This expectation is not fulfilled, however, because the author's perspective on the reference is missing.

---

19  Fictional example based on Eisner 2013: 21.

In the reader's perception, then, the disappointed expectation triggered by the missing of the author's perspective makes its absence all the more palpable. What is more, the perception that an author's perspective is missing in turn triggers the impression of facticity. This may seem paradoxical and therefore needs to be analyzed more closely – even more so, since the impression of facticity is due to the implicit genre knowledge of academics. It occurs below the threshold of reflection and is rarely based on a systematic consideration of philosophy of science. What is intuitively perceived as factual in the academic context is the following:

1) Something that has not yet been explained, analyzed, systematized, or interpreted. For example, we could say that the starting point of this paper is the fact that a group of instructors approached the legal department with an inquiry about patchwriting, and the goal of the paper is to analyze and interpret that fact.
2) On the other hand, what appears to be fact in scientific communication is something that is accepted by a research community as shared knowledge and no longer needs to be discussed.

(ad 1) As far as the first of these two conceptions of 'fact' is concerned, we are confronted with an understanding of 'fact' that we are also familiar with from everyday life. In our everyday lives, we perceive phenomena and events as facts, even when they are situated beyond interpretation. For example, we use the phrase 'the fact is' (or more explicit: 'Be that as it may, the fact is') when we want to override possible interpretations of a phenomenon and put them up for debate. According to this everyday understanding of fact, a 'fact' is something that has not yet been processed, something that is beyond interpretation and as well beyond valuation. This everyday understanding of fact corresponds to the epistemological perspective of empiricism and positivism. For empiricist and positivist epistemology/philosophy of science, 'facts' are, as Wilhelm Halbfass and Peter Simons write in their article on "fact," "the unprocessed basic material of cognition, not affected by interpretations and hypotheses."[20] In this meaning, 'fact' is still contained in our intuitive understanding of scientific practice.

(ad 2) The second understanding of 'fact,' which is effective in the practice of academic communication and writing is employed when we attribute fac-

---

20   Halbfass/Simons 1998: 911.

ticity to those elements of knowledge that are considered binding and valid by a research community. In this understanding, a fact is what a research community assumes to be something given in the sense that the research community has given it to itself or – in other words – in the sense that the community has 'made' it (as contained in the Latin root of the word fact, *factum*, 'something that has been made'). And 'having been made' means in this case that a research community has elaborated upon, discussed, examined, questioned, criticized, defended, developed, etc. an element of knowledge until it became consensual. The researchers have thus brought it, with more or less effort, through the realm of dispute into the realm of reliability. As science and technology studies have shown, this is the case even with so-called 'scientific facts,' which are supposedly only 'discovered.'

Thus, before a scientific statement acquires factual or fact-like status in this sense, eristic activity has usually taken place. We could also say more casually: In science, there is a certain amount of argumentation or debate until something is indisputable. Once consensus has been reached, the eristic activity stops. And with the suspension of the eristic activity, we also enjoy a suspension of the necessity to explicitly introduce a scientific statement or to comment on it when writing about it. As Bruno Latour and Steve Woolgar have shown in their analysis of scientific statements in *Laboratory Life. The Construction of Scientific Facts*: The more accepted, consensual, and taken for granted a statement is, the fewer signal phrases are used when reference is made to it.[21]

With that in mind, I can now return to the patchwriting issue in the example case and answer the question of why we can conceive patchwriting as unintentional fact writing: The students' patch-written paper contained references but lacked signal phrases. This lack of signal phrases, within academic communication, acts as a rhetorical agent that triggers the expectation that a statement or a proposition is factual or has fact-like status. As this expectation belongs to the implicit genre knowledge of the academic reader, it acts in an intuitive, non-reflective way. As such, both of the conceptions of fact discussed above are activated in the reader's expectation: (1) the positivist conception of fact as something that has not yet been processed, analyzed or interpreted and (2) the consensual conception of fact as an element of knowledge that in a specific academic community is taken for granted and belongs

---

21  Latour/Woolgar 1986: 75–88. Their observations condense to the insight that a "fact is nothing but a statement with no modality […] and no trace of authorship." (Ibid.: 82).

to its realm of reliability. In the perception of an academic reader, it is neither permissible to present a referenced statement as something unprocessed and uninterpreted nor to simply pass it off as consensual knowledge if it was not sufficiently exposed to or shaped by eristic activity. Therefore, the confusion caused by a patch-written student paper comes from the violation of an implicit convention of academic communication according to which the absence of signal phrases indicates the facticity or fact-like status of a statement. If an intertextual reference is marked by an in-text citation and not framed by a signal phrase, it gives the impression that there is an unwarranted attribution of facticity. We can assume that students make this unwarranted attribution of facticity or fact-like status to statements from sources because they are unfamiliar with the corresponding (implicit) convention of academic communication and we can therefore suppose that the false assignment of facticity or fact-like status, which students make by patchwriting, occurs unintentionally. In this sense, we can understand the patchwriting from our example as non-intentional fact writing.

But before turning to the students' perspective and the unintentional character of their mistake, I would like to refer to a contextual aspect that seems significant to fully understand the example case at issue.

## A Sideglance: Plagiarism Scandals and Sensitivity to Norms

This contextual aspect arises from the circumstances in which the request concerning the patch-written seminar paper was made. The request was submitted at the end of January 2021, a few weeks after an Austrian federal minister had to resign because of accusations of plagiarism. This may be a coincidence, but we cannot deny that the tendency to treat a patch-written seminar paper the same as plagiarism is an extremely strong reaction to a mistake that probably happens frequently in student papers. This strong reaction might have to do with the discomfort that the plagiarism scandals of recent years have caused among academics.

These plagiarism scandals have not only led to the resignation of top-ranking politicians, they have also put pressure on universities: For every time a case of plagiarism is discovered and discussed in public, universities face accusations of failing to adequately monitor and enforce compliance with their quality standards. To protect themselves from this kind of accusation, almost all universities in the German-speaking countries, by now, have anchored commitments to the so-called best practice standards in their charters and mission statements and have implemented the use of instruments such as plagiarism-detection software.

However, it seems that these measures are not enough to eliminate the danger and the anxiety of being condemned by the public. Rather, we can observe a dynamic interplay between public accusation of academia and its self-disciplining process. The sociologist Peter Weingart explains this phenomenon from a systems theory perspective: He states a new kind of coupling of the social subsystem of science and the subsystem of the media where the latter has become a constant observer of the former. This constant observation has urged the subsystem of science to make public its internal rules, which until then had been inexplicit and largely unknown to the public. Once made public in the form of 'Codes of Conduct', these rules not only act as a binding framework within the scientific community, but become also a reference for the public when observing and judging science. Weingart notes that this dynamic interplay potentially sets in motion a spiral that pushes rules and demands, the concerns and anxieties related to academic writing higher and higher.[22]

With regard to our example case, we can assume that this interplay of external control and internal self-regulation of universities not only fosters a tendency to codify internal rules but also increases the sensitivity to implicit academic norms like the handling of facts. This increased sensitivity to norms may have made the instructors of our example feel so uncomfortable with the inappropriate factualization inherent to the students' patchwriting. If we assume that the combination of external control and increased internal self-regulation makes implicit norms palpable, it is likely that these implicit norms concern central aspects of research and academic writing. It seems, then, that we are confronted with the violation of a vital academic norm when assertations that do not yet belong to the realm of reliability and are therefore not yet granted fact-like status are treated as factual. The violation seems to consist in skipping the process of debate and intellectual negotiating at the core of research and academic writing practices.

---

22 Weingart 2005: 141–144.

## Patchwriting as a Learning Phenomenon

Generally speaking, students do not adopt patchwriting with the intention to provoke or to deceive their instructors. They adopt it out of inexperience in academic writing – for academic writing is a most complex skill that students acquire gradually by undergoing a learning process. The problem in the discussed case was a lack of knowledge of genre rules and the inappropriate factualization resulting from it. If we look for explanations of how students learn to master the academic genre, we can rely on the insights of linguistic writing development research. Torsten Steinhoff, for example, assumes that students who learn to write academic texts first start with an inadequate use of academic language that he calls "context inappropriate."[23] They then go through various learning stages and finally develop a "contextual fit" by using a "context appropriate" academic language.[24]

Among the learning stages indicated in Steinhoff's model, we can concentrate on the stage of "imitation" here. Imitation occurs at the basic level and means that students try to imitate the formal linguistic characteristics of academic texts.[25] They rely for instance on heavy use of the passive voice and nominalization, accumulate labored vocabulary and strive for overlong sentences. The result usually is a linguistically overly complex text with a lack of consistency in content. According to Steinhoff, this happens because: "In imitation, form is separated from content, and the focus is on form."[26] Nevertheless, imitation is a powerful learning tool. Students linguistically learn a lot from the imitated academic texts; they gradually begin to use the imitated linguistic means consciously and appropriately till they reach the so-called contextual fit.

If we now try to locate patchwriting in Steinhoff's model, we can say that it is probably the most basic form of imitation. Students who adopt patchwriting do not imitate the academic style in general, but they imitate two most basic elements of academic writing: First, they imitate the convention of marking intertextuality by giving a source and second, they imitate the source itself by rephrasing it word by word. With Thorsten Pohl we can therefore say that patchwriting is a form of "developmentally implicit – and thus

---

23  Steinhoff 2007: 137, in German: "kontextinadäquater Sprachgebrauch."
24  Ibid., in German: "kontextuelle Passung" and "kontextadäquater Sprachgebrauch."
25  Cf. ibid.: 143–145.
26  Ibid.: 144.

[...] uncontrolled – intertextuality."[27] We could even say more precisely that it is a form of mis-controlled intertextuality, because students adopt patchwriting out of an intention to control the fidelity to the source at the content level. When they rephrase a source by changing the source's words one by one, they want to make sure that they do not distort its content; and in doing so they end up by creating the effect of an inappropriate factualization of the referenced statements. However, Pohl could show that this implicit and uncontrolled intertextuality decreases later in the students' learning process in favor of the already quoted explicitly controlled intertextuality that is, as we saw, typical for academic texts.

To conclude this section about the reasons for patchwriting in the learning process of students, we can state that patchwriting is a phenomenon of implicit and mis-controlled intertextuality that occurs in the early stages of academic writing. It can be understood as the most basic form of imitation described by Steinhoff, which is a learning strategy adopted to get into academic writing. The causes of this extreme form of imitation are firstly a lack of discipline-specific subject matter knowledge. For students in the early stages, the contents of the sources are new, unfamiliar, and therefore difficult to understand and rephrase. Secondly, inexperienced writers lack understanding of the aim of scientific communication and its eristic quality and, thirdly, they are not yet capable to evaluate if an assertion belongs to the taken-for-granted or to the disputed area of the discipline and has fact-like status or not.

## Conclusion

I started with an example that had emerged in our everyday Writing Center practice. A group of instructors wanted to know if a patch-written seminar paper authored by a group of BA-level students had to be treated the same as a plagiarized text. To answer this, I basically raised two questions: What specifically have students done wrong when patchwriting? And why did this trigger such a strong reaction among the instructors? My answer to the first question was: Patchwriting is a violation of specific academic intertextuality rules. It goes along with a not further elaborated and thus inappropriate attribution of facticity to the academic statements of others. Since patchwriting

---

27   Pohl 2007: 295.

occurs as an unintended effect of the learning process students undergo when they familiarize themselves with academic writing, I labeled patchwriting as unintentional fact writing. With regard to the instructors' strong reaction, I suggested considering plagiarism scandals as contextual amplifiers that lead to an increased sensitivity to implicit norms of the academic discourse. These norms tend to become palpable especially when they regard core aspects of research and academic writing like dealing with the facticity of assertations.

While I could draw on extensive linguistic writing development research to describe patchwriting as a learning effect and as a violation of academic intertextuality norms, I had to hypothesize when going beyond the textual level and describing the meaning of this violation in terms of pragmatics. The effect of the violation of intertextuality norms is usually received intuitively by readers and seems to arise from an absence of certain rhetorical patterns. According to the conventions of the eristically-grounded academic communication, this absence is a marker for facticity or fact-like status. Although I could draw on science studies, especially on Latour and Woolgar, concerning the assumptions about the connection between rhetorical patterns and the attribution of facticity, more empirical research would be needed here to test the raised hypotheses. An aspect that I have neglected and that needs to be examined in more detail later on concerns the connection between patchwriting and the scientific-theoretical sensitization that students undergo as they advance in their programs of study. For the everyday professional practice of academics, a central conclusion can be drawn from the discussed questions: Patchwriting is the effect of a learning process that should be addressed as such. Rather than locating the phenomenon in the sphere of legal violations, it seems more productive to consider it an attempt of students to gain access to academic discourse and writing. A possible response to patchwriting could therefore be to show students how academic intertextuality works by analyzing discipline-specific examples with them.

## Bibliography

Ehlich, Konrad (1995): "Die Lehre der deutschen Wissenschaftssprache. Sprachliche Strukturen, didaktische Desiderate", in: Kretzenbacher/Weinrich (eds.), *Linguistik der Wissenschaftssprache*, 325–351.

Eisner, Martin (2013): *Boccaccio and the Invention of Italian Literature*, Cambridge.

Hacker, Diana (1991): *The Bedford Handbook for Writers*, Boston/New York.

Halbfass, Wilhelm/Simons, Peter (1998): "Tatsache", in: Ritter, Joachim/ Gründer, Karlfried/Gabriel, Gottfried (eds): *Historisches Wörterbuch der Philosophie*. vol. 10: S-T, Basel, 910–916.

Howard, Rebecca Moore (1995): "Plagiarisms, Authorships, and the Academic Death Penalty", in: *College English*, 57(7), 788–806.

— (1992): "A Plagiarism Pentimento", in: *Journal of Teaching Writing* 11(2), 233–246.

Humboldt, Wilhelm von (1964) [1810]: "Über die innere und äußere Organisation der höheren wissenschaftlichen Anstalten in Berlin", in: id.: *Werke in fünf Bänden*. vol. IV: *Schriften zur Politik und zum Bildungswesen*, Stuttgart, 255–266.

Jamieson, Sandra (2016): "Is It Plagiarism or Patchwriting? Toward a Nuanced Definition", in: Bretag, Tracey (ed.): *Handbook of Academic Integrity*, Singapore, 503–518.

Kretzenbacher, Heinz L./Weinrich, Harald (eds.) (1995): *Linguistik der Wissenschaftssprache*, Berlin/New York.

Latour, Bruno/Woolgar, Steve (1986): *Laboratory Life. The Construction of Scientific Facts*, Princeton, NJ.

Li, Yongyan/Casanave, Christine Pearson (2012): "Two first-year students' strategies for writing from sources: Patchwriting or plagiarism?", in: *Journal of Second Language Writing* 21, 165–180.

Österreichisches Universitätsgesetz 2002, RIS – Universitätsgesetz 2002 – Bundesrecht konsolidiert, Fassung vom 28.07.2022 (bka.gv.at), https://www.ris.bka.gv.at/GeltendeFassung.wxe?Abfrage=Bundesnormen&Gesetzesnummer=20002128 (28.07.2022).

Pecorari, Diane (2003): "Good and Original: Plagiarism and Patchwriting in Academic Second-Language Writing", in: *Journal of Second Language Writing* 12, 317–345.

Pohl, Thorsten (2007): *Studien zur Ontogenese wissenschaftlichen Schreibens*, Tübingen.

Steinhoff, Torsten (2007): *Wissenschaftliche Textkompetenz. Sprachgebrauch und Schreibentwicklung in wissenschaftlichen Texten von Studenten und Experten*, Tübingen.

Steinseifer, Martin/Feilke, Helmuth/Lehnen, Katrin (eds.) (2019): *Eristische Literalität. Wissenschaftlich streiten – wissenschaftlich schreiben*, Heidelberg.

Thielmann, Winfried (2013): "Wissenschaftliches Sprechen und Schreiben an deutschen Universitäten", in: *Wissenschaftliche Textsorten im Germanistikstudium deutsch-italienisch-französisch kontrastiv. Akten der Trilateralen*

*Forschungskonferenz 2007-2008*, ed. Martine Dalmas/Marina Foschi Albert/ Eva Neuland, Loveno di Menaggio.

Weingart, Peter (2005): "Öffentlichkeit der Wissenschaft – Betrug in der Wissenschaft", in: id.: *Die Wissenschaft der Öffentlichkeit. Essays zum Verhältnis von Wissenschaft, Medien und Öffentlichkeit*, Weilerswist, 137–147.

Weinrich, Harald (1995): "Sprache und Wissenschaft", in: Kretzenbacher/id. (eds.): *Linguistik der Wissenschaftssprache*, 3–13.

# Cultural Studies

Gabriele Klein
**Pina Bausch's Dance Theater**
Company, Artistic Practices and Reception

2020, 440 p., pb., col. ill.
29,99 € (DE), 978-3-8376-5055-6
E-Book:
PDF: 29,99 € (DE), ISBN 978-3-8394-5055-0

Markus Gabriel, Christoph Horn, Anna Katsman, Wilhelm Krull, Anna Luisa Lippold, Corine Pelluchon, Ingo Venzke
**Towards a New Enlightenment –
The Case for Future-Oriented Humanities**

October 2022, 80 p., pb.
18,00 € (DE), 978-3-8376-6570-3
E-Book: available as free open access publication
PDF: ISBN 978-3-8394-6570-7
ISBN 978-3-7328-6570-3

Sven Quadflieg, Klaus Neuburg, Simon Nestler (eds.)
**(Dis)Obedience in Digital Societies**
Perspectives on the Power of Algorithms and Data

March 2022, 380 p., pb., ill.
29,00 € (DE), 978-3-8376-5763-0
E-Book: available as free open access publication
PDF: ISBN 978-3-8394-5763-4
ISBN 978-3-7328-5763-0

**All print, e-book and open access versions of the titles in our list
are available in our online shop www.transcript-publishing.com**

# Cultural Studies

Ingrid Hoelzl, Rémi Marie
**Common Image**
Towards a Larger Than Human Communism

2021, 156 p., pb., ill.
29,50 € (DE), 978-3-8376-5939-9
E-Book:
PDF: 26,99 € (DE), ISBN 978-3-8394-5939-3

Anna Maria Loffredo, Rainer Wenrich,
Charlotte Axelsson, Wanja Kröger (eds.)
**Changing Time – Shaping World**
Changemakers in Arts & Education

September 2022, 310 p., pb., col. ill.
45,00 € (DE), 978-3-8376-6135-4
E-Book: available as free open access publication
PDF: ISBN 978-3-8394-6135-8

Olga Moskatova, Anna Polze, Ramón Reichert (eds.)
**Digital Culture & Society (DCS)**
Vol. 7, Issue 2/2021 –
Networked Images in Surveillance Capitalism

August 2022, 336 p., pb., col. ill.
29,99 € (DE), 978-3-8376-5388-5
E-Book:
PDF: 27,99 € (DE), ISBN 978-3-8394-5388-9

**All print, e-book and open access versions of the titles in our list
are available in our online shop www.transcript-publishing.com**